Programming for TV, Radio, and the Internet

Programming for TV, Radio, and the Internet

Strategy, Development, and Evaluation

Philippe Perebinossoff
California State University, Fullerton

Brian Gross
EF Education, Jakarta, Indonesia

Lynne S. Gross
California State University, Fullerton

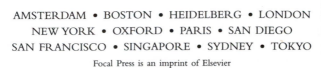

AMSTERDAM • BOSTON • HEIDELBERG • LONDON
NEW YORK • OXFORD • PARIS • SAN DIEGO
SAN FRANCISCO • SINGAPORE • SYDNEY • TOKYO

Focal Press is an imprint of Elsevier

ELSEVIER

Focal Press

Acquisition Editor: Amy Jollymore
Project Manager: Bonnie Falk
Editorial Assistant: Cara Anderson
Marketing Manager: Christine Degon
Cover Design: Dardani Gasc

Focal Press is an imprint of Elsevier
30 Corporate Drive, Suite 400, Burlington, MA 01803, USA
Linacre House, Jordan Hill, Oxford OX2 8DP, UK

Library of Congress Cataloging-in-Publication Data

British Library Cataloguing-in-Publication Data
A catalogue record for this book is available from the British Library.

ISBN-13: 978-0-240-80682-2
ISBN-10: 0-240-80682-4

For information on all Focal Press publications
visit our website at www.books.elsevier.com

08 09 10   10 9 8 7 6 5 4 3

Printed in the United States of America

For

Carol Ames
Donny Sianturi
Paul Gross

&

Ed Vane

Contents

About the Authors

Philippe Perebinossoff

Before joining the faculty of the radio, television, and film department at California State University, Fullerton, where he teaches programming, management, and writing, Philippe Perebinossoff had a 20-year career as a network television programming executive. At ABC, he created guidelines for fact-based programming, evaluated programs for acceptability, and supervised the development of more than 200 telefilms and miniseries. He has also taught at the New School for Social Research; Eastern Kentucky University; State University of New York, Plattsburgh; and University of Southern California.

Brian Gross

Brian Gross is a multimedia artist and educator. He teaches at EF Education in Jakarta, Indonesia; previously, he taught writing, audio production, radio operations, visual journalism, and multimedia design for 5 years at California State University, Fullerton. He has also designed, developed, and gained funding for multimedia arts programs for homeless and at-risk youth in the Los Angeles area. He is a web designer and consultant, and his prose, poetry, musical compositions, videos, art, and theater works have been presented in anthologies, books, galleries, radio stations, and performance spaces throughout the United States and abroad.

Lynne S. Gross

Lynne S. Gross is a professor at California State University, Fullerton, where she teaches radio–television–film theory and production courses, including programming. She has worked as director of programming for Valley Cable TV and as a producer for series shown on commercial, public, and cable television and heard on radio. She is the past president of the Broadcast Education Association and a past governor of the Academy of Television Arts & Sciences. She has written 10 other books dealing with media and many articles for refereed and trade publications.

Preface

In electronic media nothing is forever. New technologies force change. Radio executives discovered the truth of this maxim in the late 1940s when their cozy world was abruptly invaded by an invention called television. Thirty years later, TV was turned upside down by a new use of an old distribution form called cable. Now, the Internet is changing established forms and experimenting with its own possibilities.

But through it all, one thing remains constant: the need for programming content. No matter how state of the art the delivery system is, it does not mean a thing if the consumers are not interested in what is being conveyed. The material must be appealing to audiences, it must be presented in an attractive manner, and it must be equal to the challenges placed against it by all forces that vie for the attention of the public.

The goal of this book is to help you, current and would-be programmers, succeed in a restless, competitive environment by providing practical information about television, radio, and the Internet. Not a theoretical text, this book is designed to give you a close, very personal look at how programming works. It does this by clearly defining key programming concepts in the text and in the glossary (glossary terms are boldfaced the first time they are used) and by including the experiences of programming professionals. Not only will you learn how the process works, but you also will understand how the programming of television, radio, and the Internet affects our daily lives.

We the authors are not clairvoyant, and are no more able to predict what TV, radio, and the Internet will look like in 10 years than anyone else in the business. But a programmer who knows the past and who recognizes that certain guidelines reduce the odds against failure is far more likely to prosper than one who has no touchstones. For that reason, our first chapter deals with the history of programming, outlining the colorful twists and turns that the business has taken over the last 80 years to indicate that current strange and seemingly unprecedented events are not so unusual.

After Chapter 1, the organization of the book follows the process of creating programming and describes the differences and similarities of this process as it relates to various media. Chapters 2 and 3 cover the various ways ideas are generated and the various media delivery systems available for the ideas. It is vital that you know the strengths, weaknesses, eccentricities, and curiosities of each of these media forms lest you design a beach ball for a soccer game. We describe the various marketplaces for which you can construct programming and point out how they differ in terms of creative needs, business arrangements, and distribution.

The development process—how a show gets from an idea to a go-ahead—is described in Chapter 4. As new programmers will discover, the job does not end with the construction of the show. Generally, it also has to be sold. This process has proved difficult for many, but there are techniques that can make dealing with an idea simpler and more effective. One of these techniques involves testing material to see whether it has a chance of enticing an audience and how it can be improved. This process is explained in Chapter 5.

There are no surefire methods of producing a hit product. But there are several creative elements that, if understood and properly incorporated, can provide a better chance of success. Although they do not guarantee a winner, the exclusion of too many of these elements will virtually assure a failure. These ingredients are identified in Chapter 6.

Programmers are not alone when they create program material. With them in spirit and influence, if not in body, are a host of forces that have much to say about the content and placement of programs. In Chapters 7 and 8, we describe the many voices that must be heard before material is seen. These include advertisers, pressure groups, government agencies, in-house departments, and professional critics. They are important influences on programmers and are ignored at great peril.

One of the crucial processes in programming many of the media forms involves the scheduling of shows. Over the years, several strategies have proved successful (and unsuccessful). Programmers must adjust their strategies to changing times and must look vigilantly at the plans and procedures being used by the competition. The vast array of strategies available to programming schedulers is the topic of Chapters 9 and 10.

Regardless how the program material is distributed, there is a need to evaluate its performance. It is not as simple as looking at a Nielsen rating. Many other factors determine the success or failure of a show, and these considerations are reviewed in Chapter 11.

Unfortunately, not every concept works. Cancellations and restructuring are a painful but unavoidable part of the business. When the deed must be done, there is a right way and a wrong way to go about it, as explained in Chapter 12. Sometimes, however, a product can be saved by creative changes, such as sharpening the focus of a sitcom, hiring a new disc jockey, or refreshing a Web site. These possibilities are examined in the same chapter.

No doubt the electronic media business has its fair share of expedient corner-cutters. But we believe programmers behave honorably, for the most part. In Chapter 13, we present a variety of incidents that involve ethical considerations. It is our hope that these examples will alert you to the kinds of ethical decisions programmers face daily and encourage you to consider the norms of ethical behavior when you have to make your own programming decisions.

We believe this panoramic look at how programming's elements are used throughout the industry will provide you with the basic knowledge required by the business. In today's world, a programmer may work for Lifetime's cable TV channel for several years then switch to the commercial network CBS. Someone involved with radio programming may be assigned to oversee the station's Web site. People who understand the processes of programming will have broader knowledge and be more employable than ones who only understand one particular (perhaps soon to be outdated) form of programming.

Throughout the book, we include sidebars that give insight into various issues or principles. TV, radio, and the Internet are involved with entertainment. As such, they tend to attract colorful and unorthodox personalities who help make the business fun, unpredictable, and at times a bit bewildering.

The authorship of this book has changed somewhat from the first edition. Philippe Perebinossoff and Brian Gross are the main authors. Perebinossoff, a professor who has more than 20 years of programming experience at ABC and elsewhere, handled most of the television material. Gross, who has teaching and professional experience in audio and multimedia, wrote the radio and Internet sections. Edwin T. Vane, an original author, is retired, but much of the structure he devised for the book, based on his many years of programming experience at ABC and Group W, survives. Lynne S. Gross, who has cable TV programming experience and has written 10 other books about media, has been a coauthor of both editions.

We give special thanks to the many industry professionals who generously gave of their time to provide students interested in the world of entertainment programming with practical, useful information to enable them to succeed as programmers. Since the previous edition, we have interviewed industry professionals including Susan Baerwald, faculty member at the American Film Institute and former head of miniseries at NBC; Ilene Amy Berg, vice president of current programs at ABC; Beverly Bolotin, executive vice president of client services at ASI; David Brownfield, senior vice president of current programming at CBS; Martin Carlson, vice president of business affairs at Fox; David Castler, president and CEO of ASI; Kevin Cooper, an agent at CAA; Olivia Cohen-Cutler, senior vice president of broadcast standards and practices at ABC; Erica Farber, publisher and CEO of *Radio & Records;* Scott Gimple, creator of "Fillmore"; Robert Green-

wald, producer and director at Robert Greenwald Productions; Doreen Hughes, senior scheduler at ABC; Rick Jones, director of theatrical films at ABC; Kenneth Kaufman, president/COO, PKE; Robert Lee King, a director and writer; Philip Kleinbart, producer and vice president of business affairs at Robert Greenwald Productions; Ron Kobata, a KTLA sales executive; Brian Lowry of *Daily Variety* and *Broadcasting & Cable;* Mitch Metcalf, senior vice president of program planning and scheduling at NBC; Michael O'Hara, a writer and producer; Judd Parkin, a writer and former head of movie and miniseries at ABC; Dan Petrie, Sr., a director; Judith A. Polone, president of movies and miniseries at Lions Gate Entertainment; Eric Poticha, vice president of television at The Henson Company; Randy Robinson, president and executive producer at Randwell Productions; Susan Rovner, vice president of drama development at Warner Bros. Television; Howard Schneider, former vice president of on-air promotions at Fox; Michael Sluchan, director of the development of longform programming at Universal Television; Eric Steinberg, senior vice president of research at CBS; Christy Welker, former head of miniseries at ABC; and Steve White, a producer and former NBC and ABC network executive.

We also gratefully acknowledge other industry professionals we have worked with over the years whose contributions to television, radio, and the Internet provide the text with valuable information and insights. We thank Jon Hughes for the photo of Ira Glass. We also greatly appreciate the suggestions given by the reviewers: Susan Baerwald, American Film Institute; Sylvia M. Chan-Olmsted, University of Florida, Gainesville; Joyce Chen, University of Northern Iowa; Tim Frye, Purdue University; Louisa Ha, Bowling Green

State University; Matt Jackson, Pennsylvania State University; Jong G. Kang, Illinois State University; and Sam Lovato, University of South Colorado. And we are grateful for the support offered by the staff at Focal Press, specifically that of our editor, Amy Jollymore, who was always there with encouragement and thoughtful guidance. We also wish to thank the students at California State University, Fullerton, who read a draft of this text and provided valuable suggestions. A special thanks to Philip S. Mastroianni for his computer knowledge and his work on the index.

Philippe Perebinossoff, Brian Gross, and Lynne S. Gross

1 The History of Programming

In this chapter you will learn about the following:

- Early radio and television programming strategies
- Advertising's relationship to programming through the years
- The golden age of network radio programming and the effect the introduction of television had on radio
- The switch from advertiser-controlled to network-controlled programming
- The legacy of the golden age of television
- Cable and satellite television's effect on programming
- What future programmers need to know about the cyclical nature of programming
- The influence of shorter audience attention spans, interactive content, and new technologies on current programming
- Major trends and developments in programming
- The effect of global markets and government regulations on programming

THE NEED FOR PROGRAMMING

Broadcast media has an insatiable appetite for programming content. With ever more distribution outlets available in the mediums of radio, television, and now the Internet, the demands of the marketplace continue to increase, with no end in sight to the quest for material.

With nearly 14,000 AM and FM radio stations broadcasting across the United States today, most of them 24-hour operations, simple math shows that stations must find a staggering 122,640,000 hours of material to air each year. Most of that material is new or original. Add to that the 100 channels that now broadcast 24 hours a day on two satellite radio services, and you get a sense of the appetite that radio alone has for program material.

In television, the National Broadcasting Company (NBC), which began televised broadcasts April 30, 1939, aired 601 hours of programming in its first year.[1] Forty years later, in 1979, the number of hours NBC was airing per year had risen to 5,000.[2] With the explosion of cable and satellite television services and the subsequent increase in the number of channels available, as well as the adoption of year-round original programming, the need for material continues its dramatic rise.

Now, enter the Internet, with theoretically limitless storage and delivery capacity. With a steadily growing number of consumers possessing broadband Internet connections, a new pipeline and hunger for audio, video,

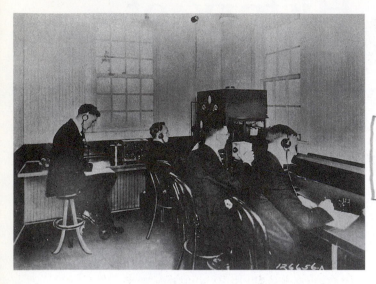

Figure 1.1
KDKA in Pittsburgh launched its radio programming on November 2, 1920, with this broadcast of the Warren Harding–James Cox election results. (Photo courtesy Westinghouse Broadcasting Company.)

and interactive programming is coming online.

All the available outlets clamor for product. Where does all this programming come from, and how does it find its way to an increasingly elusive and fragmented audience?

This chapter provides a brief history of radio, television, and Internet programming. In our quest to demystify programming, we examine early programming strategies and describe some of the major developments and trends that affect programming today. We do not seek to provide a complete history of radio, television, and Internet broadcasting here, but rather to provide examples of some key programming cycles and strategies. Because broadcast media programming is in constant flux, it is important to have a sense of the past to understand the present and anticipate the future.

THE EARLY DAYS OF PROGRAMMING

Early radio did not have programming departments. The novelty of the medium was exciting enough that people would stay glued to their ear-

phones and huge battery-operated sets just to "hear Pittsburgh," that is, hear the call letters and phonograph music coming from station KDKA in Pittsburgh (Figure 1.1), generally regarded as the first radio station.

The early stations were supported primarily by companies that manufactured and sold radio sets, and they programmed whatever free talent wandered into the studio. For most stations, this included a preponderance of would-be operatic sopranos. The goal was to have something on the air to encourage people to buy radios. Eventually, the novelty of radio wore off and performers wanted to be paid, so some economic means of supporting radio had to be found.

American Telephone and Telegraph (AT&T) hit upon an economic idea based on its telephone experience. It established station WEAF as a **toll station.** People would be required to pay a toll to broadcast some message to all radio listeners in the same way that they paid a toll to send a private message from a phone booth. The company built a studio about the size and shape of a phone booth and waited for people to come and pay to send their messages. No one did. After a long struggle, WEAF, in August 1922, finally sold its first message, a 10-minute announcement from a Long Island real estate company that paid $50.

Even after this initial commercial, advertising was not viewed as a primary source of income for broadcasting. Herbert Hoover, who was Secretary of Commerce during the 1920s, said that "ether advertising" was possible, but he quickly dismissed the idea. "It is inconceivable that we should allow so great a possibility for service to be drowned in advertising chatter," he said.[3]

But the production of radio material wasn't going to pay for itself. As

Figure 1.2
KFI, Los Angeles's first radio station, which began broadcasting in 1922, had this rather elaborate studio. Most early studios, although unseen by the listening audience, had elaborate decors that included potted palms, common foliage of the 1920s. (Photo courtesy KFI.)

producers innovated the medium with live music, drama, complicated sound effects, up-to-date news gathering, and even unnecessary elaborate sets (Figure 1.2), the quality of radio programming improved and the expense increased.

Bringing in more income could be accomplished by bringing in more advertising. But as late as 1930, by which time the airwaves were drenched with advertising, the industry was still professing its commercial virginity. Before a Senate committee, Merlin Aylesworth, president of NBC, testified, "I am opposed to direct advertising on the air." When a senator asked him what he meant by direct advertising, he replied, "I mean stating prices."[4] The following year that distinction fell by the wayside as advertising established itself as the means to keep radio growing.

There was a limit, though, to how much advertising the listening public could stomach. Somehow the industry would have to find a way to stretch its resources further.

THE BEGINNING OF NETWORK PROGRAMMING: A NEW LEASE FOR RADIO

The answer the radio industry came up with to maximize its resources was the network. The network system involved producing programs that could be used by a number of stations, thus reducing the cost for each station. Wires could carry the signal of the program produced in New York, networking it to stations in Boston, Philadelphia, Washington, and beyond. The first network to be established was NBC, which in 1926 broadcast its debut program (an orchestra from New York, a singer from Chicago, comedian Will Rogers from Kansas City, and dance bands from other cities) to 22 local stations.

Radio's Golden Age: The Advertising Agency Years

When NBC was formed, it purchased WEAF from AT&T and continued a variation of the toll station concept, wherein **advertising agencies** bought blocks of time for their clients and filled this time with programming and mentions of the sponsor and of its product line. Sometimes the product became part of the story line—the announcer would visit Fibber McGee and Molly and talk about waxing the floor with Johnson's Wax.

The advertisers and their agencies made almost all of the programming decisions, keeping top-level radio network executives informed as needed. The advertisers came up with the concepts, hired the talent, and oversaw the production (Figure 1.3). The networks provided the facilities for distributing the programming around the country. Of course, the advertisers paid the networks for these services.

Under this arrangement, the networks did little programming decision making. As long as the advertiser was happy with the program and its time slot and the material conformed to the network's standards and policies, it was left alone. The networks distributed the programs and collected their money. As a result, many programs aired on radio for years in the same time slot. Jack Benny was on radio from 1932 until the mid-1950s at 7:30 Sunday evening. For much of his reign, he was sponsored by Jell-O. George Burns and Gracie Allen were on from 1933 to 1951, primarily sponsored by Robert Burns cigars. Dramas, comedies, children's programs, soap operas—all were handled by advertising agencies. The only exception was news, which the networks produced and controlled.

The stability of this system led to what is often referred to as the **golden age of radio.** Radio listeners loyal to this exciting new medium tuned in unfailingly to their favorite shows. Writers and performers rose to the challenges of entertaining this rapt audience and, with shows continuing for years, were able to constantly add to and modify the formula of their craft. The golden age of radio also allowed unprecedented events to be staged across the country, uniting individuals in the nation unlike any other media ever had before. The most striking of these events occurred in 1938, when Orson Welles' exceedingly realistic radio adaptation of H. G. Wells's 1898 novel *War of the Worlds* aired. Under Welles' direction, the play

Figure 1.3
The Tommy Dorsey Band was obviously sponsored by cigarettes. Although the home audience couldn't see them, the enlarged cigarette boxes were prominently placed on stage. Because this program was performed before a live audience, the sponsor's product was constantly seen by the studio audience. (Photo courtesy KFI.)

was performed and written so that it would sound like a real news broadcast of an invasion of the Earth by Martians. A short notice that the production was fiction played at the beginning of show, not repeated again until nearly 40 minutes into the show. The broadcast created mass, if not universal, panic. Streets were packed with panicked radio listeners, people hid in cellars and loaded guns, and some even wrapped their heads in wet towels as protection from poisonous Martian gas.

This was the power and reach of the radio networks into people's lives. Because most stations of the day were affiliated with one of the four networks (NBC, CBS, ABC, or the ill-fated Mutual Broadcasting System), stations mostly transmitted network programming with scant locally produced material. The little the individual stations produced on their own was mainly of a public service or phonograph music nature.

THE INTRODUCTION OF TELEVISION AND ITS EFFECT ON RADIO

When television broadcasting started to take off in the late 1940s and early 1950s, television producers adopted the network programming methods used in radio. Once again, advertising agencies provided programs and paid for them in their entirety—such as "Philco Television Playhouse," "Kraft Television Theater," and "Texaco Star Theater." TV adopted not only the programming process of radio but also its stars and advertisers.

Numerous radio programs made the transition to television, where they successfully established themselves—many becoming some of early television's favorite shows. The list of transfers from radio to the medium that featured both sight and sound is a long one (Figure 1.4).

Television's early duplication of radio shows caused radio to take a downturn. Newer and engaging audiences in both sight and sound, television siphoned off radio listeners, giving credence to the fears radio harbored about the threat of television.

While radio was floundering, television was experimenting with its potential. Not content to merely have television become "radio with pictures," early television pioneers, such as Leonard Goldenson, who founded the American Broadcasting Company (ABC) in 1953, sought to make television unique from radio. Goldenson wanted to emphasize television as a visual medium and sought a movie format instead of a radio format. In his autobiography, aptly titled *Beating the Odds,* he describes his plan: "We would put programs on film and show them on the network the same way we showed feature films in theaters."[5] In so doing, he looked to Hollywood for inspiration instead of New York, where radio had been king.

"The Ed Sullivan Show" (1948, 1932)

"The Lone Ranger" (1949, 1933)

"Your Hit Parade" (1950, 1935)

"You Bet Your Life" (1950, 1947)

"The George Burn and Gracie Allen Show" (1950, 1935)

"The Jack Benny Show" (1950, 1932)

"The Guiding Light" (1952, 1937)

"My Friend Irma" (1952, 1947)

"Our Miss Brooks" (1952, 1948)

"Gunsmoke" (1955, 1952)

"The Grand Ole Opry" (1955, 1925)

Figure 1.4

Included here are some programs that transferred from radio to television during the early days of television, illustrating how radio supplied television with some of the new medium's signature programming. The first date indicates when the program appeared on television; the second date shows when it started on radio.

ABC had Goldenson as its visionary in the early days. He was not alone, however, in seeing the potential that television offered. The Columbia Broadcasting System (CBS) had the legendary William Paley whose vision and impeccable taste helped him turn CBS into the "Tiffany" network, a symbol of quality in news and entertainment programming. NBC had the skillful entrepreneur David Sarnoff who saw the future of television in color.

PROGRAMMING CYCLES AND TRENDS

True to his vision, Goldenson contracted with Warner Bros., which produced programming for ABC including, in 1955, "Cheyenne," the first prime-time western. By 1959, there were 28 prime-time westerns on television, illustrating the important tenet that programming tends to move through cycles.

Anticipating the appeal younger viewers offered advertisers, which we describe later in this chapter, Goldenson sought to program shows that would attract a younger audience. He did this because he was convinced that younger viewers would be more open to change, that they would be more willing to turn the dial to ABC than older viewers reluctant to alter their habits. This kind of **counterprogramming** strategy remains a useful weapon in a programmer's arsenal some 50 years later, not just in television but also in radio and on the Internet.

RADIO REDUX: THE SWITCH FROM SHOWS TO FORMATS

Radio needed to fight back to survive the threat of television. According to radio lore, the move to bring radio back to health began when radio group

station owner Todd Storz was in a bar one night in the early 1950s, trying to drown his sorrows about the decreasing income of his radio stations. He noticed that the same musical selections from the jukebox were played over and over. After almost everyone had left, one of the bar waitresses went to the jukebox and, instead of playing something that hadn't been heard all evening, inserted her nickel and played one of the songs that had been heard over and over. This gave Storz the idea for **Top 40** radio, which he and several other station owners used to revitalize radio.

Obviously, Storz's "vision," by itself, did not revive radio. Another important factor was the rise of rock and roll music, which gave radio a new sound and a new audience—teenagers. Thus, recorded music became the primary fare of radio and led to a new structure for radio programming. Importantly, radio became a local rather than a national medium. Characteristics of the local community and the selection of a rigid, daylong **format** became major factors in programming decisions. Advertisers no longer supplied entire programs: they merely bought commercials within news or music programs. Programming decision making rested with the local program managers and station managers, not with advertising agencies as before.

TELEVISION'S GOLDEN AGE OF DRAMA

The **golden age of television** is considered the 1950s, when programs such as "Kraft Theater," "Alcoa Hour," "General Electric Theater," "Philco Television Playhouse," "Playhouse 90," and "The Texaco Star Theater" flourished, seeking to make television the "theater in the home" so many had envisioned.

In keeping with its connection to live theater and because there was no way to record program material in the early days, these shows were almost always performed live. The actors, director, and production team rehearsed for 10 days and then went on the air live, ready to conquer the viewing public.

One of the reasons the golden age figures so prominently in America's cultural history is that it broke in many performers, writers, and directors who went on to significant careers. Actors, for example, include Dustin Hoffman, Robert Redford, James Dean, Jon Voigt, Eva Marie Saint, Marlon Brando, and Paul Newman. Major writers such as Paddy Chayefsky, Rod Serling, Horton Foote, Gore Vidal, and Tad Mosel wrote teleplays during this time, many of them working with legendary television producer Fred Coe, who wanted to use television to bring Broadway to America. Directors such as John Frankenheimer, Sidney Lumet, Sidney Pollack, and Dan Petrie got their start during the golden age.

Drama programming, in particular, was at this time motivated by a desire to make television be all that it could be by bringing new and established talent into people's homes. Media observer Anna Everett notes that during the 1950s, "as the nation's economy grew and the population expanded, television and advertising executives turned to dramatic shows as a programming strategy to elevate the status of television and to attract the growing and increasingly important suburban family audience. 'Golden age' dramas quickly became the ideal marketing vehicle for major U.S. corporations seeking to display their products favorably before a national audience."[6]

Everett saw advertisers using quality dramas to cater to the growing suburban population. As more middle-class Americans purchased television sets, programming appealed to this growing audience. Everett saw Paddy Chayefsky's teleplay "Marty" as the "quintessential" work of the golden age and thought that the title character's quest to be his own man and to "embrace his uncertain future resonated with many of the new suburban viewers" facing similar challenges.[7] Indeed, "Marty" connected with television viewers and went on to further fame as an Academy Award-winning feature, strengthening television's position as a place where quality mattered.

This view of early television's golden age may put too rosy a tint on the programming of the 1950s, ignoring, for example, the control and censorship that advertisers exercised. For example, Alcoa, the sponsor of the "Alcoa Hour," in 1956 did not want a lynching in the teleplay "Tragedy in a Temporary Town" to be set in a trailer park because most mobile homes were made of aluminum, an Alcoa product. Wooden shacks thus had to be substituted for the mobile park.[8] Indeed, not everything on television during this age was of golden quality.

During any age, what resonates with the public, as we have noted, tends to occur in cycles. Many programmers maintain the quality exemplified by TV's golden age, proving the one constant that matters in programming: quality depends upon your point of view. Indeed, some of today's "quality shows," such as "The West Wing," "24," and "Hallmark Hall of Fame," recall television's golden age, delivering prestige and audiences.

But from the viewpoint of advertising, the entity that pays for most media programming, shows with mass appeal, although attracting many consumers, tend to charge the highest rates for advertising time. If an advertiser's product is targeted to a specific group of people, advertising on a quality show with mass appeal, although getting the advertiser's message to its target audience, may also convey that message to countless others. To receive more "bang for the buck," an advertiser might choose to advertise during a lower-quality show, a show that appeals more specifically, even if less ardently than the quality show, to their target audience. For example, in 2003, Turner Broadcasting System (TBS) aired a shark movie, *Red Water,* that received some terrible reviews; one reviewer questioning why TBS called itself a **superstation** if this was the kind of program it offered viewers.[9] The movie, however, scored impressive ratings, beating the competition on ABC, Fox, and the WB. It had action and good production values, and its viewers were not disturbed by the far-fetched plot. *Red Water* is thus the kind of lower-quality, audience-pleasing show that some advertisers might find a better buy.

DIRECTOR DAN PETRIE RECALLS TELEVISION'S GOLDEN AGE

Director Dan Petrie, whose television credits include "Sybil," "Eleanor and Franklin: The White House Years," and the 1985 live television movie, "The Execution of Raymond Graham" and whose feature credits include *Buster and Billie, Lifeguard,* and *Resurrection,* got his start in 1950 in Chicago with "Studs' Place," a drama created by Studs Terkel. He had been teaching at Creighton University in Omaha, Nebraska, where the equipment from WOWTV was housed.

Petrie used this equipment to direct several programs, including a Johnny Carson magic show. After 26 episodes of "Studs' Place," Petrie headed to New York, where he directed many of television's golden age presentations—for example, numerous presentations of "The US Steel Hour," including the original "Bang the Drum Slowly" with a then-unknown Paul Newman in 1957. He also cast James Dean in such programs as "Treasury Men in Action," always looking for the opportunity to cast Dean as a ne'er do well. Seeing her as a star on the rise, he cast Grace Kelly in an episode of "Somerset Maugham Theatre" even after she turned down the $75 top-of-show offer, demanding and getting $125.

Regarding the process involved in live television, Petrie recalled that after several days of rehearsals, the cast and crew would move into the facilities where the show was to be broadcast, known as "going on to fax" ("fax" stands for "facilities"). For an hour program, for example, there would be two days "on fax." There would be a run-through before the dress rehearsal. Some actors would be comfortable going on live after the rehearsal; others would not. Petrie remembers that the silent-screen star Dorothy Gish was so terrified of going on live that when he wished her well, she asked that he pray for her. Another actor froze during the broadcast and was only able to repeat one of his lines, "Call me Bunny," no matter what was said to him, forcing the other actors to improvise with lines such as, "And you'll remember, Bunny, that you were scheduled to go to the hotel to inquire about the whereabouts of your sister who has been missing for years." During rehearsals of a show in which he played a deranged man, Lon Chaney, Jr., picked up the furniture he was supposed to destroy during the broadcast and said, "and then I go like this," stopping short of dropping the furniture. Petrie recalled that during the broadcast, instead of following through and breaking the furniture, he did exactly what he had rehearsed. He picked up the furniture and said "and then I go like this," again putting the furniture down without breaking it.

Recalling the influence of advertisers on programming during the golden age, Petrie remembered when an agency representative came into the control room and saw that one of the technicians was smoking a cigarette that was not the brand sponsoring the show. Petrie was called over and told to have the man get rid of the cigarette or be fired. Petrie understood that if he did not follow through and have the man get rid of the cigarette, he too would be fired, even though what was going on in the control room would never be seen by viewers.

For Petrie, the advertisers' greatest interference in the creative process was the blacklist, a list of performers deemed un-American for alleged Communist ties. All performers had to be "cleared" of any association with Communism before they could be cast, and no one on the list could be cleared. Petrie remembered being called by blacklisted actress Madeleine Sherwood, essentially begging him to cast her in the "Robert Montgomery Presents" production he was directing. Sherwood needed work, but Petrie knew that she could not be cleared. Still, he thought casting her as an extra might slip her under the radar. During a rehearsal, however, the agency representative showed up, zoomed in on Sherwood, and demanded that Petrie "get rid of her." Again, it was understood by Petrie that if he did not get rid of her, he would be fired as well. Petrie is not sure if the sponsor complained or if legendary television golden-age producer Robert Montgomery (father of "Bewitched" television star Elizabeth Montgomery) was offended, but he was fired after his second assignment directing a "Robert Montgomery Presents" because he cast a black actor as the roommate of a white man.

QUIZ SHOWS TAKE CENTER STAGE

The idea of advertisers supplying programming did not work as well in television as it once had in radio. There were several reasons. For one, television programming was much more expensive than radio programming. Advertisers who had easily been able to underwrite the costs of several actors capable of changing voices to play several parts, a sound effects person, a small core of audio technicians, a few writers, and a director found the visual demands for scenery, props, and additional actors and behind-the-scenes personnel more than they could handle financially. As a result, **cosponsorship** sprang up. Two or more companies would share the costs of producing and distributing a television series. Programs would be "brought to you by Colgate toothpaste, Oldsmobile, and Marlboro cigarettes." This form of advertising made it harder for the viewer to identify the program with a specific product than it had been with early radio and some of the single-sponsored presentations of the golden age of television, but it temporarily solved the budget problem.

In addition, strong-minded TV executives were becoming more interested in controlling their own programs. Sylvester L. "Pat" Weaver, while president of NBC from 1953 to 1955, devised what he called the **magazine concept.** Advertisers bought commercial insertions in programs such as "Today" and "Tonight" but had no say about program content. Those decisions were in the hands of the networks.

The trend toward complete network control was accelerated in 1959 when the **quiz show scandals** broke. Quiz programs on which contestants won large amounts of money had become extremely popular. Contestants on "The $64,000 Question" and "Twenty-One" were locked in soundproof booths where they agonized and perspired as they tried to answer very difficult questions. The programs were so popular that Revlon, the company that produced

"The $64,000 Question," found its products had sold out nationwide.

The problem was that some of the more popular contestants on the shows had been coached about the questions they were to answer and about how to act to build suspense and sympathy (see the "Twenty-One" sidebar). This was done in the name of entertainment so that lively, personable contestants could remain on the air and the duller, less likable ones would be defeated.

The television quiz show scandals were dramatized in a 1994 feature film, *Quiz Show*, directed by Robert Redford and starring Ralph Fiennes as Charles Van Doren. The film was based on a section of Richard Goodwin's book, *Remembering America*. Goodwin, who was portrayed by Rob Morrow in the film, spearheaded the grand jury investigation of the quiz shows.

CONTESTANT HERBIE SEMPLE DESCRIBES THE COACHING HE RECEIVED FOR "TWENTY-ONE"

After they picked me, the producer, Dan Enright, took me in hand. He told me that we would go over the questions and answers before each show. He would be my coach. He told me not to worry. I wasn't doing anything wrong. It was just entertainment, show business, and everyone knew that was make-believe. But don't tell anyone, or you'll get into a lot of trouble.

They made sure I always worked with the same man. It was the same with all the other contestants. They thought if something went wrong, if someone complained or said he had been fixed, it would just be one person's word against another's. Nothing could be proved. They didn't realize, or didn't care, that as the show went on, a producer would have to fix several contestants. They thought they were protecting themselves. But even that was make-believe.

My producer didn't just give me the answers, but told me how I should behave. If the questions had four parts, for example, I was to hesitate on part three, pretend to be puzzled, ask if we could return to it after I had given the answer to the fourth part. Jack Barry (the on-air quizmaster) would agree and, after my correct response, would say "Now, Herbie, let's try that third one again." I was supposed to pause, appear as if I was straining, laboring to recall, and then look up toward the camera with the right answer.

It was all done to increase suspense. The contestants were put into an isolation booth, supposedly to prevent coaching from the producers or the audience. Sometimes they shut off the air conditioning in the booth so that I would sweat while pretending to concentrate. We all had a role to play. I was the poor boy from Brooklyn. . . . I was supposed to wear the same old suit every week, and a shirt with a frayed collar. Once I wore a new suit. Producer Dan Enright got mad. "You're not doing your homework, Herbie," he complained.

The contests were usually close. Each question was worth a certain number of points, and the first contestant to reach twenty-one was the winner. The prize money was scaled according to the point spread between you and your opponent. So they wanted to keep the difference small. But as long as you kept winning you stayed on the show. . . .

The whole show was a fraud. Remember how they made a big thing of keeping the questions in a bank vault? Every week a bank official would come on the show and hand Barry a sealed envelope to be opened in front of the audience. Of course, the producer had a copy of those questions in his desk all week. They're the ones who wrote them.[10]

As Goodwin writes, the "exposure of the quiz show fraud took on monstrous proportions."[11] It was seen as a massive betrayal of public trust, America's loss of innocence. Much to Goodwin's displeasure, the networks did not reap most of the blame, claiming they also were deceived and blaming the producers and advertisers.

Goodwin believes the networks knew what was being done. He accuses the networks of cowardice on a grand scale, quoting critic John Crosby who wrote that "the moral squalor of the quiz show mess reaches through the whole industry. Nothing is what it seems in television . . . the feeling of high purpose, of manifest destiny that lit the industry when it was young . . . is long gone."[12] Indeed, the networks fired anyone, guilty or innocent, who was publicly associated with the quiz shows.

THE TELEVISION NETWORKS TAKE OVER PROGRAMMING

For our purposes, the effect of the quiz show scandals cannot be overemphasized. Tabloid headlines proclaimed television's betrayal of the bond between the broadcasters and the public, fueling the furor. As people became increasingly cynical about television, trust needed to be restored. One ready solution was to create **broadcast standards and practices** departments to function as overseers that censored objectionable programming, thus reassuring the public that responsible people were minding the store. More importantly, television changed the way it operated; specifically, advertisers who had controlled television programming during its infancy, including television's golden age, lost their status as the primary programmers at the networks.

Whereas radio networks had already revitalized their programming strategies, ceasing to rely on advertisers and advertising agencies for programming, it was only after the quiz show scandals that television fully embraced a new way of programming. After the scandals, the networks, which were already on their way to controlling programming, really took over. They began selling commercial time in most of their shows rather than allowing advertisers to sponsor them.

This change led to a new philosophy of program decision making. Networks began to consider their programming schedule as an overall entity. Previously, a network generally continued to air a program as long as the advertiser was satisfied with it. But after the quiz show scandals, networks had to take responsibility for the programs they broadcast— and they started to exercise authority over them, using programming to optimize profits from advertising. By the 1960s, the amount of money a network could charge for a commercial depended on its **rating**. Networks, instead of depending on advertisers, depended on the public; the networks wanted shows that produced ratings and thus allowed higher advertising rates. Even if an advertiser wanted to pay the total cost of a program, the network might not want the program because it proved to be a poor lead-in to another program that contained commercials from several advertisers.

This happened in 1963 when the "Voice of Firestone" was canceled. The Firestone Tire Company was the sole sponsor of this half-hour classical music TV program on ABC on Monday nights at 8:30. The audience was small but appreciative, and Firestone wanted to continue sponsoring the program. Unfortunately, the low rating for the show provided a poor lead-in for the show that aired at 9:00 P.M. After Harvey Firestone, the chairman of the

Figure 1.5
Public television's first big hit was "Sesame Street," which reflected the changes to quality brought about by the Public Broadcasting Act of 1967. The children's program was produced by the Children's Television Workshop and began airing in 1969. (Photo courtesy Children's Television Workshop/ Richard Termine.)

company, refused to move the show to Sunday afternoons, ABC cut its losses and canceled the show.

In the 1960s, network programmers started exercising their muscle by controlling what shows would air. Using available research sources, they determined what the public wanted to see: selecting a program such as "Batman," which became the first midseason show in 1965, or a program such as "The Fugitive," which portrayed in a sympathetic manner a man convicted of a crime.

Radio too had started researching its programming decisions—which songs to play for which audiences and how often. More about the development of testing and evaluation strategies is covered in subsequent chapters.

THE DEVELOPMENT OF PUBLIC BROADCASTING

The purest version of network programming began in the 1960s when public broadcasting of radio and television started. By "pure" we mean that the content and shows produced and aired by public broadcasting, at least as it was first envisioned, were determined by the network without concern for the wants of advertisers—because there were no

advertisers. Both public radio and television had been around earlier than the 1960s in a weak form usually called "educational broadcasting." The government had set aside part of the FM band, 88.1 to 91.9, for noncommercial radio services and had reserved specific TV channels in each major market for educational TV. Programming decisions for all educational stations were made locally. Most of the radio stations played classical music and produced talk shows that featured one or two people plus some programs from other local educational stations supplied through an exchange that mailed programs from station to station.

Although there was some excellent programming such as "The Great American Dream Machine," "The NET Playhouse," and "Black Journal," produced by African-Americans, most of the product that aired as educational broadcasting was extremely dull.

Then, in 1967, Congress passed the Public Broadcasting Act, which implemented most of the recommendations made by a blue-ribbon Carnegie Commission set up to develop improvements for educational broadcasting. The Corporation for Public Broadcasting (CPB) was devised to receive funding from the government and apportion it among local public TV stations, the Public Broadcasting Service (PBS) TV network, local public radio stations, and a radio network, National Public Radio (NPR). With this infusion of money from the government, the quality of public broadcasting programming improved significantly (Figure 1.5).

The noncommercial programming structure is different from that of the commercial networks. In television, PBS does not produce any programming itself but rather relies upon its **affiliated "member" stations** to produce shows that it can offer to other stations. Some examples of affiliate-created shows are the popular "Antiques Roadshow," and the critically acclaimed "Frontline," produced by WGBH in Boston, and "Frontier House" and "Charlie Rose," produced by WNET in New York. PBS also acquires programming from foreign countries, such as "Teletubbies" produced by the British Broadcasting Corporation (BBC), and from independent producers, as evidenced in PBS's showing of many independent short films and documentaries.

In public radio, on the other hand, NPR produces much of its own programming—which sets it apart from commercial radio networks that often make programming decisions and do much production at the local level. NPR also acquires limited material from other sources, such as from its member stations. It may acquire shows to make them national, as it did with WBUR in Boston's "Car Talk," or air shows such as "Fresh Air with Terry Gross," produced by WHYY in Philadelphia. NPR's reluctance to air material from public radio stations led several of these stations to form a competing network in 1983, American Public Radio, which, in 1994, after taking a more global stance, changed its name to Public Radio International (PRI). NPR and PRI, however, are not mutually exclusive organizations—many local public radio stations, such as KCRW in Los Angeles, program material from both networks in their daily schedules, such as NPR's "All Things Considered" news program and PRI's "Marketplace" financial show.

Public broadcasting has significantly changed in recent years, causing some observers to question whether the Federal Communications Commission (FCC) qualified too many stations into existence. Because money is tighter and underwriters want to know their money is properly allocated and that their message is coming across. In brief, they cannot ignore ratings and want to know that the shows they are underwriting are delivering an audience. Thus, contrary to the original intent of public broadcasting, ratings have come into play, especially as audiences have become more fragmented and some cable stations have adopted some of public television's fare.

Reluctantly, PBS head Pat Mitchell acknowledged the quest for ratings on public broadcasting and tried to minimize reports of declining ratings for PBS. Underwriters also want their "message of support" to avoid being too discreet. ExxonMobil requested full 30-second spots to continue underwriting "Masterpiece Theatre," and even when this concession was granted, they pulled out, looking for other avenues to explore. ExxonMobil may have chosen to explore other avenues, but 30-second spots, which are increasingly like commercial advertisements, are now more common on public broadcasting. PBS is adamant that its messages are not advertisements, insisting it is careful not to cross the line because its messages do not mention prices, price comparisons, or inducements to buy and do not include jingles or location information. However, Jeffrey Chester of the Center for Digital Democracy said that it is wrong for PBS to insist that its underwriting messages are not advertisements, blaming the FCC for laxity. He says, "but even if it walks and quacks like an ad, the FCC says it's not an ad."[13]

THE FINANCIAL INTEREST AND DOMESTIC SYNDICATION RULE

When advertising agencies were phased out as suppliers of programs, the networks found other means of obtaining program material. They produced a great deal of it themselves and bought from established feature production companies. They also started buying from new independent production companies, such as Mary Tyler Moore's MTM, Norman Lear's Tandem-TAT, and Aaron Spelling Production that had formed specifically to produce programs for television. The networks underwrote most of the cost of production for the right to air the program and to sell commercials within it. In addition, the networks received part of the profit from the sale of the show in the **syndication** or **rerun** markets. With all of these revenue sources, television networks started to look like fat cats getting rich off of the "public" airwaves.

In 1970, the FCC took a hard look at this situation, declaring that the networks had too much power. As a result, the FCC instituted **financial interest and domestic syndication (fin-syn)** rules that barred networks from having a financial interest in programs produced by outside production companies. The networks could no longer receive part of the profits when the programs were sold to stations as syndicated reruns. Rules were also instituted that limited the amount of programming networks could produce themselves.

THE RISE OF INDEPENDENT STATIONS AND SYNDICATORS

A handful of **independent television stations** unaffiliated with one of the major networks—NBC, CBS, or ABC—had existed since early television. Until the 1970s, the programming on independent stations was confined mainly to reruns of network shows. These independent stations seemed to the public to be little more than younger siblings trotting out worn, hand-me-down clothes that the networks had outgrown. The independent stations collected limited revenues from local commercial **spots**

inserted into their network reruns, but many independent stations saw that much more advertising money would be available to them if they could compete with network programs instead of just rerunning them.

With the power of the networks diminished as a result of fin-syn, and with the FCC's simultaneous authorization of more broadcast television stations, the role and presence of independent stations expanded. In 1961, before fin-syn, there were only 28 stations unaffiliated with one of the major networks. In 1979 there were 103, in 1989 there were 339,[14] and in 1994 there were 400.[15]

These independent stations, although still showing network reruns, began to struggle to offer the public something different and to fill the remaining hours of their broadcast day. Initially, independents started running theatrical films broken by commercials. They later branched out to original, **first-run** programs, usually produced by third-party production companies called "syndicators" who sold product to stations as opposed to networks. With so many independent stations on the air, hungry for programming, and with fin-syn laws requiring the networks to purchase programs from third-party syndicators, syndication blossomed into a big and diverse business.

THE EXPLOSION OF CABLE

Meanwhile, a sleeping giant was about to awaken in the middle of the already rapidly changing television landscape. Cable television had been around since the early days of television broadcasting. No one knows exactly how it began, but one story says that it was started by the owner of a little appliance store in central Pennsylvania around 1947. He noticed that he was selling sets only to people who lived on one side of the town. When he investigated, he found that people on the other side could not receive a good signal. So he placed an antenna on top of the hill and ran the signals through a cable down the hill to the homes with poor reception. When someone on the weak side bought a TV set from him, he hooked them to the cable (Figure 1.6).

Cable grew during the early days because the only way communities without TV stations were able to obtain TV programs was to put up an antenna, catch the signals as they traveled through the air, and run a cable, often strung from tree to tree, to individual homes. From the 1940s to the 1970s, cable TV was mainly used to retransmit signals from existing TV stations. Usually these were local stations, but as time passed cable companies imported station signals from distant areas to provide their customers with a wider variety of programming.

Because the cable signals traveled though wire and not through the airwaves, cable systems had more usable channels than broadcasting could accommodate. For example, no local area could air broadcast stations on both channel 5 and channel 6 because the two signals would interfere. But on cable, where the signals were shielded, all the channels (then 2 through 13) could be used. As a result, some of the cable systems provided viewers with inexpensive "local programming" placed on one of the extra unused channels. The most common form of this "programming" was a thermometer and barometer with a camera focused on them to allow local residents to see the temperature and barometric pressure. Not much was needed in the way of program decision making.

Not much was needed in the way of regulation either. Broadcast stations complained to the FCC when some

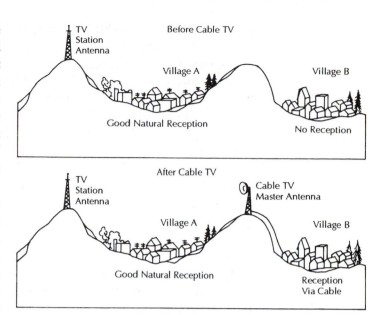

cable systems showed a distant channel playing the same program (e.g., the same "I Love Lucy" episode) as the local station because this practice obviously lessened the audience size for the local station. The FCC responded by establishing a rule called **syndicated exclusivity,** which said that cable systems had to black out the distant station when the programming was the same. But generally the FCC left cable alone to grow on the fringes of the rapidly expanding television universe, and local governments granted numerous cable **franchises.**

But all this changed in the late 1970s when Home Box Office (HBO) began selling a satellite-delivered movie service to local cable systems. Although this was a difficult sell at first, mainly because cable systems did not want to invest in the satellite dish needed to receive the signal, once the idea caught on, the floodgates opened. A variety of cable networks sprung up, offering programming to be placed on the spare channels of the cable systems. So much programming became available that engineers devised ways to show more than 12 channels through the TV set.

Figure 1.6
Early cable TV systems placed an antenna on top of a hill to catch television station signals. Then a wire with the station signals in it, was run down the hill and attached to various homes.

Between 1980 and 2003, the number of households subscribing to cable TV (and its subsequent companion, satellite TV) grew from 22% to 80%. From 1980 to 2001, the advertising dollars spent went from a meager $53 million to a robust $14.5 billion, and the number of programming networks from 1980 to 2003 rose from 8 to 290.[16] Cities that had not needed cable TV because the reception was excellent suddenly found numerous companies pounding on the doors of city hall—all begging for franchises to lay cable in the area and collect their part of the pot of gold at the end of what seemed to be a promising rainbow.

Essentially, cable television services added more independent channels to the already expanding listing of independents. Though some of the new channels, such as ESPN and Cable News Network (CNN), produced most of their own programming, many of the new cable stations clamored for more programming from syndicators, further strengthening the business of syndication.

SYNDICATION IN RADIO

Strong national networks, of the kind that persisted in television, were a thing of the past for radio—it evolved into a local medium. But although there were no laws like fin-syn governing where radio stations obtained their programming, radio stations started to purchase programming from third-party syndicators.

In radio, the line between a network and a syndicator has blurred. Radio stations select material provided by networks, syndicators, and their own local programmers and mesh it into a unified whole with a local feel. In other words, both networks and syndicators serve the same purpose to the programming of local radio stations—they provide content, such as national news reports and other programs that appeal to local audiences in many locations.

NEW NETWORKS WITH TARGETED AND NICHE PROGRAMMING

While networks were losing their definition in radio, new networks were developing in television. The first of these networks, the Fox Broadcasting Company, started operation in 1987. The WB (1990), Universal–Paramount Network (UPN, 1995), and PAX (1998) followed.

When Fox began, it was not officially a network because it did not broadcast more than 15 hours of programming a week (the legal amount needed to be considered a network). It nevertheless provided a large block of programming for many independent stations and cut down on their immediate need for syndicated material.

Standing in the shadow of the three big networks, CBS, NBC, and ABC, these fledgling networks, if they were to survive, had to find a way to wean advertisers from their longstanding relationships with the majors. Instead of trying to compete head to head, these upstarts focused on creating programming that appealed to specific groups of viewers. The initial lineup at Fox, for example, was geared toward urban hipsters. PAX appealed to viewers seeking wholesome family entertainment; UPN to urban audiences seeking comedies with an ethnic vibe; and the WB to teens, teens, and more teens.

On cable television, a similar, though more focused, change occurred as programming executives sought to give their networks a clear identity. If the majors were *broad*casters seeking the widest possible audiences, the cable networks went after the smaller, targeted audience (a technique known as **narrowcasting**). This became known as the search for the "niche" audience—committed viewers who identified with the programming of a particular cable network.

These changes forced the big three to change, too, as you will observe in the next section, where we examine some key broadcasting trends.

THE QUEST FOR A YOUNG DEMOGRAPHIC

Following the arrival of cable and niche programming, mass appeal ceased to be the primary goal of the majors. No longer were they competing simply for a *broad* audience. It was the *right* audience that became the key to success. Many advertisers started to favor certain groups, or **demographics,** of consumers. The coveted demographic quickly became 18 to 49 year olds, ideally 18 to 34. The assumption behind this thinking is that young viewers are freer with their disposable income and that it is important for advertisers to establish brand loyalty early. For example, young people may not be able to afford a new car, but when they can afford one they will purchase the car they are aware of through advertising and they will be loyal to that brand throughout their lives. So goes the thinking, and finding shows that appeal to a young audience has become a programmer's primary mission.

This belief in the power and attractiveness of the young demographic helped Fox when it first aired. The ratings were not stellar, but young people were watching Fox. This became a point of pride, something positive that Fox could say about its slate of shows. Similarly, the WB has received strong advertising dollars for shows such as "Smallville," "Gilmore Girls," "7th

Heaven," and "One Tree Hill." What the WB is proclaiming loudly and consistently is that its shows attract the desirable younger viewers; that the household ratings may not be in the top 10 or the top 20 is secondary, because it is the young demographic that counts, not the household rating.

Ron Kobata, formerly a WB/KTLA sales executive, says that the WB appeals to younger viewers. Younger viewers are what advertisers want, not entire households.

Even syndication, which has traditionally been viewed as a haven for older viewers, wants to lay claim to young viewers. A study by Nielsen Media Research, released in July 2003 by the Syndicated Network Association, says that "About 72% of the audience watching sitcoms in syndication is in the adult 18–49 demographic, compared to 61% of the sitcom audience on cable TV."[17]

This quest for young viewers significantly affected today's programming. If a program tests "old" or is perceived to appeal only to older viewers, chances are it will have a hard time getting on or staying on a schedule. A show such as CBS's "The Guardian," which, according to researchers, was not watched by many under 50, could not remain on the air indefinitely; it was canceled before the start of the 2004–2005 season. The desire for the young demographic influences story selection, language, and most notably pacing. The strategies or types of programming that proved effective with the 18 to 49 demographic are taken into account when developing new programming.

VIEWING PATTERNS AND CHANGING AUDIENCE ATTENTION SPANS

In 1983, a new cable network, Music Television (MTV), caught fire with the

18 to 49 demographic. Some people credit (or discredit) MTV's success in this demographic with subsequent changes in the pacing and cohesion (or incoherence) of television programming. The fledgling network featured back-to-back 3-minute music videos, turning the longstanding television staple of hour or half-hour shows on its ear.

Not only were the "shows" short, but they often sacrificed storylines in favor of spectacle. In some ways, this was the nature of the music video beast. How do you make a story out of a song with a single sentiment, such as Cyndi Lauper's "Girls Just Wanna Have Fun" or the Thompson Twins' "Hold Me Now"? The nonstop spectacle of the music video, many cultural critics have suggested, reduced viewers' attention spans—accustoming them to non-stop action rather than nuanced development.

To be fair, nonstop action was not a new development with MTV or a new concern in television. Programs such as "I Love Lucy" put a high premium on, as Lucille Ball put it, not "losing" the audience by keeping things moving. The criticism that many levy at today's action, though, is that it often relies on simple visual stimulation rather than the dramatic tension that "I Love Lucy" used. In the late 1990s, some shows, especially children's cartoons, became so reliant on quick cuts and flashy graphics that they were linked to causing epileptic seizures in their young viewers.

With so many entertainment choices available on the networks, independents, and cable, programmers believe that they cannot risk losing their targeted audience because a show is not moving quickly enough. Quick action scenes are often substituted for fully developed ones. In television, it is assumed viewers would rather see the action than several expository scenes. Likewise, in radio, talk show hosts go for the controversial, explosive comment, frequently ignoring the background information. Or, in the case of so-called shock jocks, such as Howard Stern, programmers and producers assure that each moment of material is so inflammatory that it needs no introduction or denouement to catch—and hook—a listeners' ear. In 2003, there were more than 1300 talk stations in the country,[18] most of them employing such attention-getting tactics.

Many point to the 1986 debut of Steven Bochco's NBC show "LA Law" as the start of the trend toward short, action-packed scenes in traditional television drama. Programmers think they have to keep it moving to keep the viewer from using the dreaded remote. A show such as Fox's short-lived "30 Seconds to Fame," on which contestants performed for a mere 30 seconds to compete for a $25,000 prize, did indeed keep it moving. In the half-hour show, 24 hopefuls had a half-minute each to make an impression. The creators of this show assumed that viewers could not get bored in 30 seconds.

Shorter attention spans have created a new viewing style called **dropping in,** which takes place when viewers choose to view only a short sequence of a theatrical movie that has aired several times on television. Many viewers are too restless to watch all of a repeat airing of *Pretty Woman,* a favorite drop-in movie, but they are willing to tune in for a favorite scene—for example, when Julia Roberts puts down the salesgirl who had been rude to her.

Producers are challenged by the quest for numerous short scenes. For example, a television movie in the early 1980s might have had 80 scenes in it. Today, that same movie would be likely to have 150 scenes, with no increase in the license fee or in the number of shooting days. How is a producer to make this work? Additional scenes require time and money, and neither is available in the current market. It is not easy to keep adding new scenes, and it requires a lot of inventiveness on the part of the production team to make a tighter, more complicated schedule work. But programmers are ever fearful of losing the audience's attention, and one way to guard against this is to pack more action and less talk or introspection into a scene.

Shorter attention spans coupled with the large number of people who multitask while watching television make programmers think they have to bombard the audience with action to keep them interested. The threats of video games and Internet activity make programming an increasingly difficult task.

THE DECLINE OF LONGFORM PROGRAMMING

The decline of longform programming that started in the early 1990s is another significant change in the broadcasting landscape, one directly connected to viewers' shorter attention spans (Figure 1.7). Viewers find it increasingly difficult to commit to watching a 2-hour block. By the 1990s, programmers might have questioned whether viewers would commit to a miniseries that lasted more than 4 hours, such as "Roots," "The Winds of War," or "Shogun," but now it is considered iffy to expect a viewer to invest even 2 hours in a television movie that is not presold with name recognition much less to commit to a 4 or more hour miniseries spread over several days or weeks (see the miniseries sidebar).

Figure 1.7
The telefilm "Dallas Cowboys Cheerleaders," directed by Bruce Bilson, was the highest rated TV movie of the 1978–1979 season. It aired when longform programming was at its peak. (Photo courtesy Bruce Bilson.)

MINISERIES TAKE CENTER STAGE

Susan Baerwald and Christy Welker were both heads of miniseries at the networks, Baerwald at NBC and Welker at ABC. They were in charge when longform programming functioned as the flagship of the networks. Miniseries tapped the medium's potential and earned large audiences over several nights. Some point to "Rich Man, Poor Man" (1976) as the first major miniseries, but it was "Roots" in 1977 that revolutionized television programming, leading to an impressive list of hits: from "The Winds of War," "Ike," "Shogun," "Holocaust," and "The Thornbirds" to the 30-hour "War and Remembrance" in 1988–1989, the Emmy Award-winning miniseries that killed the form because it cost a then-unprecedented $100 million and did not bring in a large enough audience. Both executives emphasized the importance of presenting a fully developed story as keys to programming success. Fully fleshed stories given adequate time to unfold succeeded on television until the audience looked elsewhere for its entertainment.

If there is a place where contemplative, slower-moving television drama that harkens to the golden age of television persists, it is on public television, although ExxonMobile's withdrawal as named underwriter of "Masterpiece Theater" in 2003 suggests a possible end to an era of leisurely storytelling on public television. PBS's increasing dependence on funding from viewers and corporate underwriters, rather than traditionally nonmarket driven money from the government, puts the future of this bastion of leisurely storytelling in question. With cable television stations such as Bravo, Arts & Entertainment (A&E), Trio, and the History Channel co-opting and, some would say, improving upon PBS's "edutainment" mission, PBS finds itself fighting for audiences like everyone else and adjusting its programming strategies accordingly.

In public radio, however, the pressure to turn to high-octane programming is not as strong. With much lower production costs than television, public radio stations that try to tell the whole story, rather than just the sensational sound bites, can more easily attract a small but loyal audience that will support and keep their efforts solvent through individual contributions. In addition, public radio listeners tend to skew into the middle- to upper-income levels, drawing companies that sell luxury items as underwriters for costs not met by government and individual contributions.

But in commercial radio, the trend toward shorter forms started long before it hit television. Although many **drive time** shows may last several hours, they typically jump quickly from topic to topic, always teasing new topics before frequent commercial breaks.

Interestingly, shorter attention spans seem to coincide with individuals' ability to handle fragmented, nonlinear stories. In her article "Filing the Film Fragments Together," Deborah Hornblow notes that viewers are not put off by fragmented narratives, such as the ones in the feature films *Adaptation* and *The Hours*. She attributes this ability partly to the Internet, television, interactive computer games, and computer use. Television shows such as "The Wire," the departed but still critically acclaimed "Boomtown," and "24" illustrate this type of fragmented, quick-scenes contemporary programming.[19]

SUPERCHARGED PROGRAMMING CHOICES: THE INTERNET

The ultimate in catering to audience attention spans, however, is engendered in the World Wide Web, which started entering the mass culture of the United States in the mid-1990s. With hypertext, links, and ever-present search engines, the audience can wander off as quickly, as often, and as far as they wish.

The key for programmers of web content is to make a website **sticky**—in other words, not necessarily to keep viewers on one page of the site but to give the viewer a diverse buffet of content that will keep them moving from one page to another without clicking to another site. Though modes for advertising on websites, and therefore generating direct revenue, are still developing, advertisements are generally placed as banners along the periphery of each page. This mode of advertising, unlike channel changing with radio and television, makes audience choices to move to other content desirable because it exposes viewers to new advertisements—as long as they stay "stuck" in the domain.

Equally important for web programmers is giving the visitor the impression that content on the site is regularly updated, thus giving them a reason to return. Through experience, web programmers have found that users are not shy about complaining if a site is not updated often enough.

NEW MEDIA RECORDING TECHNOLOGIES

Although less interactive than the Internet, many other new technologies have and are affecting television and radio programming.

Magnetic audio tape was introduced in the late 1940s, but its effect on radio was most noticed on the production side. Shows could now be prerecorded for later broadcast. Bing Crosby was the first to use this technology, recording 26 shows for the 1947–1948 season on a Magnetophon recording device for

delayed broadcast on ABC. Audience members with tape recorders, of course, also had the option to record radio programs and listen to them again, but this capacity did not have a marked effect on radio programming strategies.

Likewise, in 1980 the videocassette recorder (VCR) was introduced into the commercial market, and by the late 1990s it was nearly as common a fixture in consumer's homes as television sets. Programmers first saw the VCR as a danger to their carefully laid programming choices. Members of the public no longer needed to watch programs when the network executives wanted them to; they could tape them and watch at their own convenience, skipping through commercials. But notorious interface challenges with setting up a VCR's record timer dulled the device's promise—and threat. Although many people learned to operate their VCRs, the device's main effect was to draw viewers' attention from broadcast programming. Video rental stores sprung up everywhere, giving audiences more choice about what to watch at home.

The late 1990s and early 2000s saw the introduction of souped-up digital versions of the videotape and VCR. Digital video discs (DVDs) offer higher-quality reproduction of video material than videotape, and set-top hard-disk video-recording devices, such as TIVO, have user interfaces that make recording programs for later viewing much easier than the VCR did. With this new technology, programmers are wringing their hands as they did with the introduction of the VCR. And advertisers worry that the ease with which hard-disk video recorders can skip commercials will force them to reconsider the traditional commercial break advertising strategy—moving toward conspicuous **product placement** and **product integration** in program material.

Cashing in on viewers' short attention spans and the new technologies, both NBC and ABC aired 1- to 3-minute movies in 2003–2004, NBC hoping that inserting 1-minute movies into commercial clusters will keep audiences from switching the dial. Some of 1-minute movies aired in four parts. Television commercials are able to present a full story in 30 seconds, so why should a 1-minute movie not be able to do the same, particularly when viewers have such short attention spans? And why not have 1-minute soap operas, as Soapnet tried in 2003–2004?

By 2002, there were more than 800,000 households with hard-disk video recorders. With many consumers, especially the prized younger demographic, turning to their computers as the hub of media consumption, many manufacturing companies are experimenting with ways to seamlessly pack television, radio, and the Internet into one multimedia box—with one hard-disk onto which viewers can record media from any broadcast medium.

With all of these technological possibilities looming, the art of programming may be affected in innumerable unknowable ways. What used to be niche markets may become big business. For example, there are undoubtedly a large group of people who are horse enthusiasts in the United States. However, the number of horse enthusiasts may not be large enough to make it a sound financial decision for a cable or satellite company to set aside one of their 100 or so channels for a 24-hour horse channel. But with TIVO or other computer-augmented recording systems, a de facto horse channel could be offered to horse enthusiasts without setting aside an actual channel for it. Horse programming could be transmitted as data in the background, over the Internet, or during off hours in the middle of the night to the horse enthusiast's recorder, which would then store it until the viewer is ready to see it.

THE RISE OF CONSUMER-SUPPORTED MEDIA

Although the future of many aspects of programming may be up in the air, it is certain that the viewing audience for traditional advertiser-supported radio and television has been, at least partly, eroded by increasing consumer-supported media offerings.

When television was introduced, the film industry feared for its life as more people stayed home to watch the new theater beamed into their living rooms for "free." Although the audience for films took a hit as a result of television, television no more killed film than film killed live performances. Each medium has its own pull on audiences. Just because audiences may have new choices does not mean that they will abandon the old options.

Still, the number of available consumer-supported media options, such as pay-cable networks, DVDs, and video games, is becoming more attractive to consumers, especially if they have become weary of advertising. In 2002, according to the Communications Industry Forecast by merchant bank Veronis Suhler Stevenson, U.S. consumers spent an average of 3,599 hours with the various forms of media. Time spent with advertiser-supported media, such as traditional radio and television, accounted for 57.8% with consumer-supported media, such as DVD, pay-cable networks, and video games, accounting for the remaining 42.2%. This is a marked change from just 5 years earlier, in 1997, when the distribution was roughly 68% advertiser-supported to 32% consumer-supported media.[20]

THE VIDEO GAME EXPLOSION

Video games, which generate more income per year than theatrical films, allow players to control the action, playing the game when and how they wish, in the process having a direct effect on programming. A video game such as "Grand Theft Auto: Vice City" sold nearly 3 million copies in its first month on the market in 2003, and the gaming industry as a whole had sales of more than $6.5 billion in 2002. There is no evidence that the video game industry has reached its peak (Figure 1.8).

These dollar figures did not go unnoticed by the entertainment industry as video games became an increasingly integral part of people's lives, revealing how the public wants to spend its leisure time. With the VCR, video games, TIVO, and the Internet, it is increasingly clear that the public wants to control its programming choices.

A study released in July 2003 by the Pew Internet & American Life project suggests that the public is capable of exercising this control. The study found that both male and female students who play electronic games are able to do so without neglecting their studies or becoming loners.[21] Television, which began as a family viewing activity, has become the solitary activity, and video gaming with friends has replaced it as the communal viewing activity.

Video game players are used to greater interactivity and to faster action, something programmers are aware of as they seek to retain an audience. Wanting and needing to capture some of the excitement that video games provide, programmers would love to bring groups of viewers to the television set in the same way games attract groups of friends.

To accomplish this, television shows such as TNT's "Witchblade," "Dark Angel," and "Super Mario Brothers"

- Three quarters of Nielsen TV households with a male between 8 and 34 years own a video game system.

- TV viewership among male gamers age 18 to 34 appears to be slightly lower than among males age 18 to 34 in general.

- The average male gamer plays video games about 5 times per week and spends at least 30 minutes doing so each time he sits down to play.

- Nearly as many males 8 to 34 say they prefer playing video games (29%) as say they prefer watching TV (33%). This group also prefers playing sports (48%) and going to the movies (26%) over video games (13%).

- More than one quarter (27%) of active male gamers noticed advertising in the last video game they played, with heavy (31%) and older (35%) gamers being the most likely to recall advertising.

- Heavy gamers are particularly enthusiastic about product integration; more than half (52%) like games to contain real products and most (70%) feel that real products make a game more "genuine."

have attempted to capture the feel of video games by adopting the same visual look and narrative style, much in the way feature films such as *The Matrix* and the video-game-based Lara Croft movies starring Angelina Jolie are structured like video games.

Figure 1.8
Some of the key findings of a 2004 study conducted by Activision and Nielsen.
(Courtesy Nielsen.)

REGULATIONS

After the fin-syn regulations limiting the television network's financial rewards were imposed in 1970, there was, as noted, a proliferation of independent stations and independent producers ready to cash in on the lucrative distribution market. As the number of broadcast choices increased with cable and satellite distribution, an argument surfaced suggesting that strict regulations were no longer needed. The networks lobbied hard that mergers did not hurt program diversity and did not eliminate local coverage. They did not want to be hurt financially, claiming that continued

- In 2002, Warner Bros. Television and in-house studio Turner Television were behind 15 of the 18 pilots ordered by the WB.

- Walt Disney-owned Touchstone Television produced or coproduced all of ABC's comedies and had a piece of at least 21 of 23 pilots.

- NBC Studios produced or had a piece of 17 of the 20 pilots that NBC ordered.

- At Fox, at least 5 of 10 pilots were from parent company News Corp.[22]

Figure 1.9
Ownership of programming.

regulations would destroy them. Conglomerate mergers became the norm for both television and radio as the FCC surveyed the marketplace, agreeing with the networks and deciding that greater **deregulation** was in order.

The result of this deliberation was the Telecommunications Act of 1996, which increased the number of radio stations a single owner could own. In June 2003, the FCC got rid of the **cross-ownership** rules that prevented a broadcaster from owning a newspaper and a television station in the same market and allowed a broadcaster to increase holdings to cover 45% of the country from the 35% that the 1996 Telecommunications Act permitted. Following much debate and controversy, the cap was changed to 39% with further modifications likely. Other chapters will examine the role of the FCC in detail, but it will suffice here to note that the concentration of broadcast ownership has significantly affected programming.

Many people, producers and government representatives alike, believe that consolidation, which results in fewer owners, has a negative effect on programming diversity. They worry that programming will become homogenized as fewer different voices are allowed into the tent. They see fewer risks being taken and argue that hit shows of the past, such as "The Mary Tyler Moore Show" or "Seinfeld," would never have gotten on the air. They also object to the growing number

of programs owned wholly or partly by the networks airing the shows (Figure 1.9).

Others, such as television critic Alessandra Stanley, disagree vehemently that consolidation of ownership destroys programming creativity. She cites "The Wire" on HBO, a gritty police show set in Baltimore created by David Simon. HBO is owned by media conglomerate Time Warner, and for Stanley, "The Wire" is a risk-taking, worthy show that has not suffered by the Time Warner ownership. She believes that television has never been more diverse and that dramas in particular are taking many chances under consolidation.[23]

Consolidation in the ownership of radio stations raises concerns because of radio's local reach. Independent musical artists worry about the centralization of programming and music selection decisions, combined with efforts to maximize profits to keep corporate stockholders happy. Local artists, in the past, counted on local radio stations to help "break" local talent—to either a local or a national audience. Radio corporation executives—such as John Hogan, chief executive of Clear Channel Radio, which owned nearly 10% of all radio stations in the United States in 2003—insist that although ownership may be centralized, programming decisions are left to local programming directors. They admit, however, that their operations are primarily concerned with economics and giving the public what they want—not, as may have been true in the more autonomous past, a passion for exposing the public to inventive or "new" music.[24]

This controversy about the influence of deregulation on programming is not likely to go away soon. Too much money is at stake for both the owners and the independent producers. As independents continue to lose ground to the conglomerates, will creativity and diversity suffer? This heated debate continues on many fronts.

GLOBALIZATION

From the 1970s through the beginning of the 1990s, the active foreign market eased the way for producers and programmers. Significant money could be made through foreign distribution, enabling programmers to relax a bit about budgets as they anticipated that the foreign dollars would provide adequate money to produce a quality production. Likewise, producers were more willing to take on large deficits because they would recoup their investment abroad.

Shows that portrayed Americans in a particular light sold well abroad and made international stars of the cast members. Many times, a performer whose star had faded in the United States remained a significant draw abroad and a major selling point for foreign sales, though of little value to American network executives. Oftentimes, programmers still have to swallow casting such performers in a project simply to keep the foreign potential alive.

Shows such as "Baywatch," which featured beautiful people doing heroic actions; "Beverly Hills, 90210," which revealed American teenagers at their photogenic best; and "Twin Peaks," which revealed a quirkier side of the American way of life performed well abroad. But the foreign market dried up in the last part of the 20th century, hurting both the networks and the producers.

Foreign countries increasingly seek to produce their own programming, but U.S. broadcasters are nevertheless forced to continue to look abroad for revenue, even if the foreign market is not as strong as it was. In addition to producing their own programming and resisting American product, several foreign governments, such as China and France, have imposed severe limits on the number of hours of foreign programming that can be aired, thus hampering the American seller. When foreign broadcasters adapt successful shows that aired in America, they must adjust the formats to suit local customs. For example, Dubai failed to adjust the reality show "Big Brother" to local standards in 2003, and the show was canceled within a month. When this happens, the negative influence of Western culture is blamed, making it even more difficult for American programming to sell abroad.

Germany used to be a major market for Americans, but it no longer buys at the rate it used to. One has only to attend a National Association of Television Program Executives (NATPE) convention, where producers and distributors meet to sell their programs, to realize how difficult it is to make deals abroad. The convention center floors are quiet, and cash registers do not ring. For example, a television movie that would have generated in excess of $1 million in foreign sales several years ago will be lucky to bring in $400,000—and that is little cause for joy. Often, there is no sale, particularly if the program is deemed too soft, as is the case with many movies made for Lifetime, the network for women. Even if there is a sale, it is often the poorer countries that continue to buy American shows at low rates; the richer countries focus on local productions.

Interestingly, the tighter foreign market dovetails with the push toward deregulation. Conglomerates point to the softening of the foreign markets as justification for all the financial assistance they can get.

The global picture is a complex one in terms of both dollars and programming. American theatrical films now make more money abroad than they do at home, and American television sales abroad are shrinking yearly. Complicating the situation is that some countries may not like American politics but they are fond of American entertainment, particularly action-driven product, even if it can be viewed as propaganda for the American way of life. Thus, a broadcaster has to keep the foreign market in mind when making story decisions and casting choices to avoid missing out on what foreign dollars may be available. It is unlikely that a television show that has no foreign sales potential will get on the air, no matter how good it might be.

The rich and dynamic history of broadcasting has been nothing more than a prelude to the changes on the horizon.

The multiplying of channels, the new high-tech delivery systems, and other advances that arrive almost daily will cause constant adjustments in the production and content of programming. As veteran writer Barry Kemp ("Newhart," "Coach," and "Taxi") put it a few years ago, "This expansion of the television landscape has led to a greater competition for viewers than ever before. The result is that we may be finding ourselves in a decade that has the potential to be as creatively exciting as any other in our history."[25]

But these changes will almost surely be modifications of the changing radio and TV universe, whether in the form and styling of programs or the manner in which they are distributed. Therefore, it is essential that you have a solid grasp of the sources that control the flow of television programs, explained in Chapter 2.

EXERCISES

1. Compare a contemporary television show with one from the past. What are the similarities? What are the differences? How does the storytelling style differ? How do the visuals and pacing differ? Is the content "racier"?

2. Listen to radio programs on stations owned by the same company. Describe diversity issues. Are the programs similar?

3. Follow the foreign sales of a particular show to see in which countries the show does particularly well or poorly and attempt to analyze the "why" behind that particular performance.

4. Examine a particular television cycle by looking at shows from the past and the new variations—for example, studying westerns from the 1950s and then examining newer westerns, such as "Deadwood" on HBO. How are they different? How much time elapsed between the two manifestations of the cycle?

5. Do you have brand loyalty to particular products? Which matters more, brand loyalty or price? Are you loyal to a particular television or radio station? Why?

REFERENCES/NOTES

1. Bob Shanks. *The Cool Fire: How to Make It in Television* (New York: Norton, 1976), p. 65.

2. Ken Auletta. *Three Blind Mice* (New York: Random House, 1991), p. 93.

3. Erik Barnouw. *A Tower in Babel* (New York: Oxford University Press, 1966), p. 96.

4. Ibid., p. 238.

5. Leonard H. Goldenson with Marvin J. Wolf. *Beating the Odds* (New York: Charles Scribner's Sons, 1991), p. 104.

6. Anna Everett. "The Golden Age of Television Drama," http://www.museum.tv/archives/etv/index. Accessed July 2, 2003.

7. Ibid.

8. J. Fred MacDonald. *One Nation Under Television* (Chicago: Nelson Hall, 1994), p. 83.

9. Ray Richmond. "Red Water," *The Hollywood Reporter*, August 15–17, 2003, p. 20.

10. Richard Goodwin. *Remembering America* (New York: Harper & Row, 1989), pp. 51–52.

11. Ibid., p. 60.

12. Ibid., pp. 61–62.

13. Pamela McClintock. "Blurred Blurbs: Ad-Free PBS Under Fire for Sponsor Spots," *Daily Variety*, July 10, 2002, p. 13.

14. *1990 INTV Census* (Washington, DC: Association of Independent Television Stations, 1990), p. 18.

15. Sydney W. Head with Christopher H. Sterling and Lemuel B. Schofield. *Broad-casting in America: A Survey of Electronic Media* (Boston: Houghton Mifflin, 1996), p. 67.

16. Sallie Hofmeister. "Sale of Comedy Central Stake Sure is No Laughing Matter," *Los Angeles Times*, April 22, 2003, p. C-8.

17. Kevin Downey. "Syndie Sitcoms, Where the Young Are," http://www.mediahtemagazine.com/news/2003/jul03/jul1414-thurs/news2Thursday.html. Accessed July 21, 2003.

18. Hendrik Hertzberg. "Radio Daze," *The New Yorker*, August 11, 2003, p. 23.

19. Deborah Hornblow. "Fitting the Film Fragment Together," *Los Angeles Times*, February 11, 2003, p. E-5.

20. Veronis Suhler Stevenson. "Communications Industry Forecast," http://www.vss.com/publications/forecast/highlights2002.html. Accessed May 27, 2004.

21. BBC. "Gaming 'Part of Student Life,'" http://news.bbc.co.uk/2/hi/technology/3052482.stm. Accessed July 9, 2003.

22. Joe Schlosser. "Do-It-Yourself Development," *Broadcasting and Cable*, February 11, 2002, p. 12.

23. Alessandra Stanley. "Waterfront Crime, Stripped of Clichés," *The New York Times*, June 2, 2003, pp. B-1, 8.

24. NPR's "Fresh Air" with Terry Gross. http://www.freshair.npr.org. Accessed July 23, 2003.

25. Barry Kemp. "TV an Eroding Medium? Creatively It's Exploding," *Los Angeles Times*, September 9, 1992, p. F-1.

2 Sources of Television Programming

In this chapter you will learn about the following:

- The primary suppliers of television programming content
- The effect of the 1996 Telecommunications Act on the distributors and creators of programming content
- The role of the public, stars, agents, and managers as sources of programming
- What future programmers need to know to succeed as suppliers of programming

Regardless of the electronic media form, the person in charge of programming must figure out how to fill the hours of the day with specific shows, a daunting task. For example, an independent station on the air 20 hours a day, 7 days a week must schedule 7300 hours of programming a year. In 2003, the average home received more than 100 channels. Where does all the programming come from?

The answer is complex. Ideas for programs can originate from just about anywhere. For example, legend has it that one night Mrs. Merv Griffin said to her husband, "Why don't you do a game where the contestants get the answers and have to give you the questions?"

Merv liked the idea, and "Jeopardy" recently celebrated its 40th anniversary.

A big-name independent producer driving to work may hear a radio story about surrogate mothers and think of a heart-tugging idea for a movie-of-the-week. Writers may formulate ideas for a children's program while reading bedtime stories to their children. Early morning disc jockeys have been known to plan skits based on the dreams they had the night before. A soap opera writer has confessed to gaining ideas by going to bars and encouraging people to dump their problems on him. A group of students developed sketches about college dorm life for a public access cable series. You have, no doubt, had several ideas that you felt would make a wonderful TV show, radio program, or website.

BEYOND THE IDEA—INTO THE "DEEP POCKETS"

Simply having a good idea does not a TV series make. Most ideas must be funneled through an organized structure of suppliers. These companies provide the money and the technical and production know-how to make programming a reality. Despite the massive need for product at networks and stations, the

Network	Studio
FOX	20th Century Fox
NBC	Universal
ABC	Disney
CBS	Paramount
The WB	Warner Bros.
UPN	CBS/Paramount

Figure 2.1
Network affiliations with major studios.

number of supply sources is surprisingly limited.

The financial risks of making a program are high. Few companies have the "deep pockets" to suffer significant financial reversals while waiting for the next project to take off and earn money in syndication and subsidiary markets. Buyers tend to rely on suppliers that have delivered successes in the past and have a strong financial basis to survive for more than a season.

A supplier who has not previously **deficit financed** a program, that is, provided the funds that covered the deficit between what the network paid for the program and the cost of production, will generally not be allowed to function as the sole production entity. Such suppliers are traditionally partnered with a company that has previously supplied deficit financing because networks do not cover the full cost of production. In recent years, the deficits have markedly increased, more frequently necessitating those deep pockets.

Programming executives are warned against getting into business with suppliers who lack a substantial track record, both in creating successful shows and in having established a sound financial base. Fledgling executives are frequently challenged by business affairs negotiators: "Why would you want to do business with companies whose finances are so shaky that they can't

come up with $50,000 to close a license fee?" It is thus extremely difficult for newcomers to get in the game.

With the increased number of mergers that have taken place in the world of entertainment since the deregulation in the 1980s, **vertical integration** has become the standard for corporate achievement. With the expanded role of conglomerates, a company can now control both the production of programs and the distribution systems of those programs, making vertical integration extremely attractive to stockholders and division heads alike (Figure 2.1). For example, NBC's strategic alliance with Universal Television in 2003 gave NBC a source of programming that the network could subsequently distribute over the airwaves. NBC, owned by General Electric, had been the last major network that did not have a studio alliance.

Because the networks are parts of companies that now own major studios, the role of "the majors" as sources of programming continues to increase dramatically.

MAJOR PRODUCTION COMPANIES

Large companies such as Universal Studios, Paramount Pictures, Warner Bros., Fox, and Disney have the resources to staff several departments to develop and produce product for commercial and cable television. These majors are the key suppliers of programs for broadcasters. To maintain their dominant positions, many majors strike **umbrella deals** with creative individuals housed at the studio. It is the studio's hope that these deals will lead to the creation of hits, as exemplified by John Wells's deal at Warner Bros., which resulted in "ER," "The West Wing," and "Third Watch," among others.

Broadcast and cable networks, station groups, and stations like to do business with these companies, not only because they have a history of success and access to some of the best producers, writers, performers, and craftspeople but also because they are financially sound and will not have to default on a commitment if unforeseen and expensive hurdles arise. Buyers know that if a program is not coming together well, the majors have the resources to do whatever is necessary to fix it.

Every year, a close tally is kept of the number of pilots and shows a company has received. Bragging rights are at stake; careers hang on these numbers, and a company's financial well-being hangs in the balance.

Warner Bros. Television, under the leadership of Peter Roth and Susan Rovner, achieved impressive results with shows such as "Third Watch." Granted, Warner Bros. has the WB network ready, willing, and able to embrace its development of shows such as "Smallville," and "Everwood" (Figure 2.2), but the success rate of Warner Bros. is nevertheless extremely impressive, a testament to sound programming instincts.

Individuals with an interest in programming as a career might be wise to consider associating with one of the majors early in their careers. Not only will they learn the intricacies of the business but they also will be working with companies that have many offshoots, one or more of which might lead to several different employment opportunities.

Feature films, produced by major companies, are also a source of programming for networks and stations. After a movie has finished its theatrical run, it is released to television. However, networks and stations do not get first crack at it. The distribution is undertaken through a series of **windows**—

Figure 2.2
The series "Everwood" exemplifies the dominance of Warner Bros. as a source of programming. (Globe Photos, Inc.)

the amount of time that transpires as the film is released to different media forms. Often a movie will have a 6-month window between the time it finishes its theatrical run and the time it is available to cable TV **pay-per-view** systems. Then it has another window of a month or two before it is distributed in video stores. Following this is a window that leads to the pay cable services such as HBO and Showtime. Only after all of these stages are films made available to commercial networks. Even further down the pecking order are local TV stations and basic cable networks such as USA Network and Lifetime. The length of time of the various windows differs from film to film. On rare occasions, the order of the releases varies and commercial TV may obtain a movie before it is shown on cable. Sometimes the networks and stations buy the rights to air the films from the major production companies, and sometimes they buy them through syndicators.

A successful, or unsuccessful, showing at the U.S. box office is no clear

Figure 2.3
ABC's perennial ratings workhorse, The Ten Commandments. (Photo © ABC Photography Archives.)

indicator of how a feature film will perform on television. Oftentimes, a film with strong buzz before it opens theatrically will command a high price from the commercial or cable networks only to fail both at the box office and with television viewers. For example, *The Bonfire of the Vanities,* sold to ABC at a high price before opening in theaters, disappointed at the box office, and subsequently performed poorly on the air.

On the other hand, a film that disappoints at the box office can be a surprise hit on television, such as the Julia Roberts/Nick Nolte romantic comedy *I Love Trouble* or *The Shawshank Redemption,* about a prison uprising. Then there is the perennial favorite, *The Ten Commandments* (1956), which defies all analysis, having aired on ABC for more than 30 years around Easter and never failed to generate impressive ratings, proving that new is not always best and that a classic film can bring viewers to the set year after year (Figure 2.3).

Sometimes networks will have too large an inventory of theatrical films, preventing them from acquiring additional films, possibly missing out on a

winner. Also, to show that a network is "in the game," executives may pay a large amount for a "must-have" film, such as *Spiderman,* making it difficult to have money left over to buy a lot of other films for the network. For example, *Spiderman II* sold to Fox and FX for approximately $50 million, a lot of money by any standard. Adding to the complexity of the theatrical acquisition game is the cyclical nature of theatrical films on television. At times, feature films are seen as good fillers for the commercial networks because they tend to perform within a given range; at other times, they are deemed to be "not working." Cable networks such as HBO, Cinemax, The Movie Channel, Starz, or Showtime always want to be able to announce a strong slate of movies, the very movies that everyone wants to see. Direct TV and the other direct broadcast satellite services (DBSs) also play a significant role in the airing of theatrical films, touting their film offerings in competition with the other distribution outlets.

Feature films also have been the basis for many TV series developed by the same major production companies. Before the picture is made, the company will usually negotiate the right to produce a TV version if it seems to lend itself to that medium. Years ago, a small film, *Moonrunners* (1975), written and directed by Gy Waldron, led to the successful series, "The Dukes of Hazard," which Waldron created. Similarly, we cannot forget the granddaddy of them all, "M★A★S★H," or "9 to 5" and "Buffy the Vampire Slayer." Also memorable are a host of television failures such as "Clueless," "Dirty Dancing," and the big 2002–2003 failure of "My Big, Fat Greek Life," based on the surprise hit independent movie, *My Big, Fat Greek Wedding.*

Both the majors and the independents (see the next section) borrow from themselves to develop new shows. Many successful programs contain subsidiary characters who have the potential to carry a new program. Called **spin-offs,** these shows are frequently scheduled immediately following the parent program to maintain continuity with the established audience. "Laverne and Shirley" was spun off from "Happy Days," which also spun off "Mork & Mindy." "A Different World" was spun off from "The Cosby Show," "Frasier" from "Cheers," and "The Ropers" from "Three's Company." (Not all work: stars on one show do not always succeed the next time around. For example, look at the victims of the so-called "Seinfeld" curse, which predicts future failures for the "Seinfeld" cast, such as Michael Richards of "The Michael Richards Show," Jason Alexander of "Bob Patterson," and Julia Louis-Dreyfuss of "Watching Ellie.")

In terms of successful spin-offs, few can rival Dick Wolf's "Law & Order," which spun off "Law & Order: Criminal Intent" and "Law & Order: Special Victims Unit." In 2002–2003, CBS spun off "CSI: Miami" and in 2004–2005, "CSI: New York" from the Jerry Bruckheimer series "CSI: Crime Scene Investigation," a surprise success for CBS, which had expected "The Fugitive," not "CSI," to dominate. "The Fugitive" failed and "CSI" went on to monster-hit status.

INDEPENDENT PRODUCTION COMPANIES

Until deregulation, independent production companies were a prolific source of shows. Known as **indies,** these are usually small companies whose owners frequently function as the chief creative contributors. Indies such as the one formed in 1970 by actress Mary Tyler Moore and her then-husband Grant Tinker made significant contributions to television. Named MTM, its impressive credits include "The Mary Tyler Moore Show," "Hill Street Blues," "St. Elsewhere," "WKRP in Cincinnati," "The Bob Newhart Show," "Lou Grant," "Phyllis," and "Rhoda," the last three being spin-offs of "The Mary Tyler Moore Show."

Notable independents in the 1980s and 1990s include Witt/Thomas/Harris, who created "Soap," "Empty Nest," and "The Golden Girls," and the incredibly successful team of Marcy Carsey and Tom Werner. Former colleagues at ABC, Carsey and Werner's hits include "The Cosby Show," which sold into syndication with an initial offering of more than $500 million; "A Different World"; "Roseanne"; "That '70s Show," which produced superstar Ashton Kutcher; and "That '80s Show" (once again, everything cannot succeed).

Since the deregulation that culminated with the 1996 Telecommunications Act, however, it has become increasingly difficult for indies to survive as prolific suppliers. Because the broadcasters can own the syndication rights, indies often find it difficult to make a go of it financially. Several years ago, Tinker, independent producer and former president of MTM, foresaw the difficulties facing independent producers. "I don't know if the business even exists anymore . . . in a way that I would like to be in it," he said in reference to the already receding network audience, the lower license fees granted to producers, and the rising costs of production. Add mergers, consolidation, and the abolishment of fin-syn (see fin-syn sidebar) and you have the bleak realities that indies face.

THE HISTORY OF FIN-SYN

In the 1960s, the three networks—NBC, ABC, and CBS—funded and produced much of their own programming. They also had a financial interest in programs produced for them by production companies. In other words, the networks would put up some of the money for the productions in exchange for a cut of the profits. Networks also syndicated the programs they produced and some of the ones in which they held a financial interest. They were the ones who sold these programs to local stations (domestic syndication) and to overseas companies (international syndication).

All of this, plus their grasp on 90% of the audience, made the networks powerful. In 1970, the FCC took a hard look at the domination of the networks and decided that the old adage, "power corrupts and absolute power corrupts absolutely," applied. As a result, the FCC instituted the fin-syn rules.

The original 1970 rules stated that networks could only produce and own 3 hours per week of their 22 prime-time hours. In addition, they could not syndicate any of these 3 hours to stations or other buyers in the United States, but they could act as syndicators if they wanted to sell these programs overseas. The rules applied mainly to series. The networks were free to produce, own, and syndicate news, made-for-TV movies, and miniseries.

The result of the fin-syn rules was that the networks had to pull back on production. In general, they did less than the FCC allowed. (In 1987, for example, the only network-owned and -produced prime-time series was ABC's "Moonlighting.") Why bother to set up the structure (and overhead costs) needed to produce and syndicate material when all you had to work with was two or three series? Besides, the domestic syndication market was not that great in 1970 because independent stations had not yet come to the fore. The fin-syn rules were resented by the networks, but they caused only a minor blip in the overstuffed balance sheets.

The players who profited from fin-syn were the Hollywood production companies. The networks had to come to them for almost all of their programming. They received money from the networks, which then had the right to air the programs twice. But once the programs finished their network runs, the production companies, who held the rights, were in a position to capture the profits from the syndication market.

Times changed. Syndication became important; most series, burdened with increasing production costs, lost money until they were sold in syndication. The networks, forbidden from the syndication market, saw their fortunes (and power and audience) plummet. They looked longingly at the profits being made by the indies with whom fin-syn rules forced them to contract for programming.

Along came cable TV. Born in a period of deregulation, the cable companies could own the programs they produced, the networks that distributed those programs, and even the cable systems that delivered the programs to the subscribers. There were no sanctions against cable syndication.

"Why," asked the network executives, "are we saddled with these archaic 1970 rules?" In the early 1980s, the networks began asking this question of the FCC. The FCC set up hearings on the subject. The Hollywood community showed up en masse to protest. Production companies did not want the networks back in the production and syndication business. Led by their flamboyant spokesman, Jack Valenti, then president of the Motion Picture Association of America, the Hollywood producers managed to stall any decision, thus maintaining the status quo. In 1988, the FCC did increase the hours a network could produce per week from 3 to 5, but this bone did little to satisfy the executives' appetites.

Then came Fox in 1987. Fox appeared to be both a network and a production company. 20th Century Fox had been producing movies and television series for many years. When the Fox Broadcasting Company was formed to distribute programs to independent stations, the Fox production company provided some of the programming, as did other production companies such as Columbia Pictures ("Married . . . With Children"). In no way did Fox want to lose out on the money it was making from syndicating its TV series, which included, among others, the highly profitable "M*A*S*H." So Fox Broadcasting Company said it was not a network. According to the FCC rules, a network had to "deliver at least 15 hours of programming a week to at least 25 affiliates in 10 or more states." For several years, Fox kept its program offerings below 15 hours. Then in 1990, Fox decided it would like to program 18.5 hours, so it petitioned the FCC for a waiver from the fin-syn rules. In a spirit of collegiality, it also asked that NBC, CBS, and ABC be given a "waiver." Valenti and company saw through this maneuver and quickly objected. The FCC gave the waiver to Fox but not to the other three.

"Wait a minute," said the networks. "This doesn't seem fair." The FCC, tired of the bickering, told the networks and the Hollywood community to hold meetings on their own and come up with a solution. "If you can't agree," said the commissioners, "we'll get back into the fray and come up with something no one likes." Truer words were never spoken. The two sides stalemated, and, in April 1991, the FCC came up with new rules, which, indeed, no one liked.

Then the 1996 Telecommunications Act abolished fin-syn, making things more difficult for indies, particularly in connection with syndication.

Some independents have succeeded in adapting to the changing climate. Writer and producer Steven Bocho, for one, has been consistently rewarded with hefty development deals based on his ability to generate quality shows such as "NYPD Blue," which provided ABC with one of its highest-rated shows year after year.

Robert Greenwald, a prolific producer of long standing whose credits include the groundbreaking telefilm "The Burning Bed" (1984), about spousal abuse, and "Blonde" (2001), based on Joyce Carol Oates's interpretation of the life of Marilyn Monroe, said that for an indie to survive it must explore creative financial arrangements, such as previously untapped tax credits or filming in different locales (Figure 2.4).

Greenwald notes that the syndication and foreign markets have declined and production costs have risen, yet license fees have not. At one time, a producer might have scoffed at the idea of simply receiving a fee to produce a project, insisting on some type of ownership to cash in on syndication and foreign sales, but that same producer might prefer a fee to ownership in the post–1996 Telecommunications Act climate.

Figure 2.4
Robert Greenwald's production of "The Audrey Hepburn Story" starring Jennifer Love Hewitt was filmed in Montreal. (Globe Photos, Inc.)

Figure 2.5
A photo of the phenomenally successful "CSI," one of Jerry Bruckheimer's television hits. (Globe Photos, Inc.)

One specific adjustment Philip Kleinbart, Greenwald's producing partner, has made is to pay more money to secure the services of a star. He feels that the networks are more interested than ever in star power. Thus, if the network says they will pay no more than, say, $300,000 for a star and the star's representatives want $350,000, Kleinbart may step up to cover the difference. This is not something he would have done previously. In the past, he would have simply "moved on," but that is no longer possible because a backup star may not have the pull to interest investors and the networks in paying for the movie to be made. The whole endeavor and the costs of development up to that point may be lost.

Randy Robinson, whose company, Randwell Productions, produced "Profoundly Normal" (2003) with Kirstie Alley, has survived in a down market by keeping a "tight focus." He does not go after everything hoping that something "will stick." After some 20 years in the business, he also knows the kinds of projects the networks will develop as opposed to the kinds of projects the networks will make and air. Thus, Robinson will not pursue stories he believes will not be produced. He notes that some producers have numerous projects in development, priding themselves on having "30" projects in development, whereas he concentrates on a few projects that he knows have a good chance of being made. This philosophy keeps him focused, enabling him to keep his overhead under control.

Robinson has carved out a niche making movies that are "slightly outside the box." Therefore, he is often called by executives who steer him into key projects. For example, he was once contacted by an executive at CBS who told him he wanted to "gift him into" a project because of his reputation as a niche supplier. Robinson does double duty: he develops and he is on the set every day unlike producers who are either creative producers (development only) or physical producers (involved in production on the set). These factors enable Randwell to survive.

Clearly, Jerry Bruckheimer is one of the most successful independent producers working in television in the early 21st century. When this high-voltage film producer with a knack for intuiting what audiences want turned his attention to television, he and his producing partner, Jonathan Littman, struck television gold. In 2003, his series "CSI" (Figure 2.5) was broadcast in 175 countries, becoming the most-watched television program in the world. As a point of comparison, at its height in the 1960s and early 1970s, "Bonanza" aired in only 70 countries.[1]

According to Rich Bilotti, a media analyst at Morgan Stanley, "CSI" in 2003 supplied more than 24% of CBS's total

Figure 2.6
"From the Earth to the Moon" demonstrated HBO's hold on quality longform programming. (Photo courtesy the Academy of Television Arts & Sciences.)

profit from prime-time programming, about $259 million.[2] When CBS launched the spin-off "CSI: Miami" in 2003, the results were again impressive, making it the most highly rated new show of the season. In addition, Bruckheimer's "Without a Trace" and "Cold Case" both served CBS well, clearly establishing Bruckheimer as the producer of the moment.

In cable, few producers have achieved the success of Tom Hanks and his company. His Emmy wins for both "From the Earth to the Moon" (Figure 2.6) and "Band of Brothers" attest to how high a bar he has established, helping HBO to have a near-lock on high caliber longform programming. The producing team of Robert Greenblatt and David Janollari also had great success on cable with another award-winning HBO program, "Six Feet Under."

When it comes to public television, the indies, as well as the majors, have little involvement. The structure and programming needs of public television are so different from the commercial and cable outlook that production companies do not really fit in.

There are, however, some companies (most of them nonprofit) that supply shows to public broadcasting. One of them, Children's Television Workshop, started in the late 1960s, is in a class by itself. This organization, which has produced such highly acclaimed children's series as "Sesame Street," "Electric Company," and "3-2-1 Contact," is separate from PBS but is so closely tied to it that it could not exist in its present form without the public TV structure.

A newer production company, Ken Burns Enterprises, has supplied public television with some highly rated documentary series, including "The Civil

Figure 2.7
Ken Burns, an independent producer, has supplied PBS with highly regarded series including the groundbreaking "The Civil War." (Photo courtesy Florentine Films.)

channels in particular are receptive to material from the BBC.

It is also interesting to note that the show that launched the prime-time reality game-show craze in 1999, "Who Wants to Be a Millionaire," originated in England. "The Weakest Link," which had a shorter run in prime-time before moving to daytime TV, also originated in England. A particularly successful longer-form reality game show, "American Idol," also was adapted by Fox from a U.K. show. And "Big Brother," which became a summer staple on CBS, was adapted from a show that originally ran successfully in Holland.

It is rare for a show from another country to play unchanged on American commercial television, even if it is in the English language. The sense of pace, the foreign accent of the actors, and the subtle language differences are difficult for American audiences to accept. As always, there are exceptions, such as the bawdy English BBC comedy "Absolutely Fabulous" and the Canadian comedy "The Kids in the Hall," both of which have had successful runs on the Comedy Central cable network in the United States. However, American producers are willing to buy good ideas from foreign creators and "Americanize" them for U.S. viewers.

Turning to public television, for years PBS broadcast so many BBC programs that people quipped that "PBS" really stood for "primarily British shows." This no longer holds true; PBS has sought to "Americanize" itself with more programs from and set in the United States. For example, PBS's "Mystery" has featured more thrillers such as the American Elizabeth George's "The Inspector Lynley Mysteries: A Great Deliverance." And what could be more American than PBS's "Ben Franklin" (2002)?

War," "Baseball," "Mark Twain," and "Jazz," many of which were gathered in PBS's "American Stories" (Figure 2.7). Burns's company, although it is technically independent, has partnered with WETA in Washington, D.C., on five projects.

FOREIGN PRODUCTION SOURCES

American companies are ever alert to the possibility of adapting a foreign success to the tastes of American viewers. Although America is the largest exporter of programs, exporting more shows than it imports, two of the biggest TV hits of the 1970s were modifications of British comedies: "All in the Family" and "Sanford and Son." Many British shows have crossed the Atlantic to America, for example, "Queer as Folk" on Showtime, "Trading Spaces" on the Discovery Channel, and the quickly departed "Coupling" on NBC. Cable

A popular approach in commercial television of recent years has been to develop **coproductions.** In previous decades, this most often meant a foreign company contributed money to an American production in exchange for certain distribution rights overseas. "Not anymore," said David Gerber, the legendary former chairman of MGM/UA Television in charge of worldwide production. "From now on, if we do something together, it's going to have to be a global partnership." By this he means the foreign contributors will participate in story development, casting, and distribution strategy, as well as in the division of profits.

The appeal of a coproduction is that a much larger pool of money is available to the production. A movie of the week that might normally be budgeted at $2 to $2.5 million could go twice that high with foreign investments. These additional funds can give the movie a much larger and richer look and make it more attractive to viewers all over the world. Furthermore, most countries outside the United States have limitations **(quotas)** on the amount of foreign production that can be imported each year. The goal is to protect their actors, producers, directors, and production companies. However, any program partially owned by a company of that country has a much better chance to come in under the quota rules.

There are some drawbacks to coproductions. Not all types of shows are successful overseas. Comedies, in particular, do not travel well. Frequently, the language and situations are too uniquely American to interest or amuse foreign audiences. But as the financial crunch continues to hurt American producers, the search for foreign partners in coproductions will accelerate.

NETWORKS

Sometimes networks are the source of programming for other networks. Gone are the days when a show on one network would not be allowed to have a guest performer from another network.

One network often develops shows for other networks. For example, Fox Studios regularly develops shows for the broadcast competition, as do NBC Productions and HBO Productions.

With the explosion of cable and the trend toward mergers, cross-fertilization of programming sources continues to take place, with the Disney production company providing programs for Disney-owned ABC and the Disney Channel, Fox for FX, and Warner Bros. for the WB. Bravo provides successful shows to NBC (both are owned by General Electric), such as 2003's "Queer Eye for the Straight Guy," which NBC added to its schedule to capitalize on the Bravo show's high cable ratings and national media buzz.

As a result of this cross-pollination, a new form of program sharing, known as **repurposing,** has developed. Repurposing is not the same as rerunning a show on the same outlet or at a much later date in syndication. Nor does it apply to shows that finish their run on one network then "travel" to another network for another run, such as "JAG," which went from NBC to CBS, or "Buffy the Vampire Slayer," which went from the WB to UPN. It is important to note that repurposing takes place during a show's run, not after it. What repurposing does is maximize a show's worth by broadcasting it on a different outlet shortly after its initial airing.

The first show to engage in repurposing was ABC's "Once and Again" in 1999, which aired a couple of days later on the Lifetime cable channel

Figure 2.8
ABC's "Once and Again" starring Sela Ward (pictured) and Billy Campbell was the first show to be repurposed. (Photo courtesy the Academy of Television Arts & Sciences.)

Figure 2.9
Oprah Winfrey's show has been one of the most successful syndicated programs in television history. (Photo courtesy the Academy of Television Arts & Sciences.)

shows may allow them to reach an audience they may not usually attract, an audience that might then be more willing to give a second thought to a network's other programming. The cable networks are also satisfied, not only because network audiences, aware of where the program came from, might seek out the original cable network but also because the rebroadcasting fees received from networks allow the cable companies to improve production values.

The main purpose of broadcast networks is to supply material to broadcast stations and the main purpose of cable networks is to provide material to cable systems. Nevertheless, repurposing is a nice extra for both in a difficult economic climate.

STATIONS

Some stations supply programming to other stations. This is particularly common among group-owned stations, the **owned and operated stations.** Frequently, a station group will try out a program on one of its stations to test its appeal. If it shows promise, it will be extended to the other stations in the group. Finally, if it scores well in these owned markets, it will be offered to other stations around the country. The dating show "Studs" was an example of this gradual "rollout." The program was initially broadcast on Fox's Los Angeles outlet, KTTV. When it enjoyed early success, it was sold to a limited number of stations. By 1992, it was available for sale to all stations.

The industry has also come up with variations on this process. In 1991, Group W and the NBC-owned and operated stations agreed to cooperate on joint development ventures that, if successful, would be distributed nationally by Group W. The incredibly successful "Oprah Winfrey Show" (Figure 2.9)

(Figure 2.8). Similarly, USA Network's "Monk" aired on ABC after its initial showing in 2002. Thus, as demands for programming content increase and money becomes tighter, repurposing allows one channel's programming to become another outlet's offering. The major networks like this arrangement because they do not consider the generally small, niche-like cable ratings to be significant competition and they think that airing successful cable niche

began as a local production of the ABC-owned Chicago station WLS-TV. The station licensed King World to distribute the show nationally, and it now claims a lineup of more than 200 stations.

A unique but growing station-to-station trend involves affiliated stations producing news programs for independents in the same area. For example, WPEC, a CBS affiliate in West Palm Beach, Florida, produced the 10:00 P.M. newscast for independent station WFLX in the same market. WFLX paid WPEC for the program, enabling WPEC to increase its staff by 15 people. The situation is viewed as a win by both stations. WFLX's general manager, Murray Green, said, "If our station started a newscast from scratch, it would take 3 years to get credibility."[3]

A small core of public television stations produces much of what is aired on the other public stations. Leading the way are WGBH in Boston, which produces the popular children's show "Arthur" and "Nova," among others, and WNET in New York, which produces "American Masters" and "Nature," among others. Not everything on PBS is produced by a few stations. For example, 2002's "Ben Franklin" was produced by Twin Cities Public Television. With the financial crunch in public broadcasting, it helps greatly if a station raises a substantial part of the financing before submitting a proposal to PBS for consideration.

BUYERS

It is a truism that buyers are most receptive to their own ideas. Because broadcast buyers are often the owners of a show, it follows that they would look kindly upon their own creations, creations over which they can exercise complete control. Increasingly, programming executives are no longer content to wait for producers to come to them

with ideas. They would rather generate their own ideas and then find the creative team to execute the concept. For example, when Lindy de Koven was head of the longform department at NBC in the late 1990s, all members of her staff were expected to come to meetings with several ideas that could be turned into television movies. Susan Lyne at ABC and Eric Poticha at Fox also saw it as their responsibility to generate the ideas that would end up on the air. Similarly, Michael Sluchan at Universal sees it as his responsibility as a development executive to suggest to other departments how his show should be marketed and publicized.

Independent producers resent this trend among programmers because it minimizes their contribution. They also think that programmers who dictate the ideas are merely protecting their own jobs by taking away the producer's role and giving themselves more to do. Nevertheless, you might consider that individuals who wait for producers to come to them with the good ideas will probably be seen as lazy, lacking the drive and energy to meet the needs of the marketplace.

For producers, the flip side of this is that an idea generated by the network stands a good chance of getting on the air. If you are lucky enough to be "kissed into a project," why should you complain? So what if it was not your idea and you had to stoke the ego of the network executives for their "brilliant insights;" you got the job, right?

The trend toward buyer-generated ideas is not new, although its practice is clearly on the ascent. In his book *Three Blind Mice,* author Ken Auletta states that in the early 1980s Brandon Tartikoff, president of NBC Entertainment, jotted down the phrase "MTV cops" and passed it on to writer Tony Yerkovich and executive producer Michael Mann.

That thought blossomed into "Miami Vice." Another time, Tartikoff visited "an aunt in Miami and came back with the germ for 'The Golden Girls.'" Auletta goes on to quote Tartikoff as saying, "Ten years ago 90 percent of the [program] ideas came from the creative community. Now [1987] it's only 20 percent."[4] Legendary programmer Tartikoff, regarded by many as the programmer's programmer for his repeated successes, clearly saw the future.

The American Music Awards illustrates how the buyer-to-producer process worked and continues to work. In 1973, ABC's 5-year contract to present the Grammy Awards expired. In the judgment of network executives, the rights fees and other requirements for a renewal were too demanding and they elected not to meet the conditions. Instead, they decided to compete with an awards show of their own but with a format more suitable for the viewer and less encumbered by the rituals and political necessities of the National Association of Recording Arts and Sciences, the Grammys' parent organization.

ABC programmers asked Dick Clark to develop a format that would fulfill the goals of the show. Although he had never previously produced a prime-time special, Clark was selected because of his success with "American Bandstand" and his familiarity with the music scene. The American Music Awards pulled in significant ratings for many years.

SYNDICATORS

Syndicators supply a great deal of program material for local commercial stations. Some of this material is produced by the syndicators (first run), some consists of programs that have already run on the commercial networks **(off net),** and the rest is **movie packages.**

First-run syndicated shows must meet the same creative criteria as network programs. The viewers are the same and are not easier on shows simply because the budgets of syndicated shows may be less than those of their network counterparts.

The bellwether forms for Monday-to-Friday syndication have been talk, talk-variety, games, service, and tabloid news. Aside from shows that contain a news element, for example, "Entertainment Tonight," the forms are all capable of multiple productions per day. For example, hour-long talk shows are shot at least on a two-a-day schedule with separate producers responsible for the individual shows. The point is to keep the costs down so that a program can be competitive in the rough-and-tumble syndicated marketplace.

In one season in the mid-1980s, the syndicators went overboard on game shows; in another there was a superabundance of children's cartoon programs. In the early 1990s, talk shows were the rage. And there is the trend for court shows, started by the success of "Judge Judy." In the late 1990s and early 2000s, the syndication market was in a bit of a slump, but it came back strongly in 2002 with the success of "Dr. Phil," coproduced by Oprah Winfrey.

The following first-run syndicated shows generally appear at the top of the household ratings charts. In parentheses is the number of years the show has been on the air as of 2004:

- "Wheel of Fortune" (21 years)
- "Jeopardy" (20 years)
- "The Oprah Winfrey Show" (18 years)
- "Entertainment Tonight" (23 years)
- "Extra" (9 years)
- "Judge Judy" (8 years)
- "Dr. Phil" (2 years)
- "Live with Regis and Kelly" (15 years)
- "Inside Edition" (16 years)
- "Maury" (13 years)

If you intend to enter the syndication field, we encourage you to make your own assessment of the market's needs and stick to your convictions. The competitors are not necessarily smarter or more tapped in; they are just more reactive to the needs of the marketplace.

ADVERTISERS

As you saw in Chapter 1, advertiser-produced programming was the foundation of network programming from the start of radio through the beginnings of television to the early 1960s, when cost considerations made ownership of a single program impractical. Only a few advertisers continued the practice throughout the years, most notably Hallmark Cards, whose "Hallmark Hall of Fame" quality programs have enriched the medium since the early 1950s.

In the hard-pressed broadcasting economy, advertiser-delivered programs are extremely attractive. To the struggling networks, these shows represent time-period sales at full rates. Whenever there is a rumor that a particular advertiser is thinking about fully sponsoring a show, everyone in the business becomes filled with anticipatory excitement.

What has developed as an alternative to advertiser sponsorship in recent years is in-show product placement and product integration (Figure 2.10). This allows the product to be seen in the context of the program without the threat of being zapped or skipped using TIVO during commercials, although USA Network's project "The Last Ride" was heavily criticized as being nothing more than a full-length commercial for Pontiac. Product placement also made it to video games; Electronic Arts, one of the largest video game companies, integrated products from McDonald's and Intel into "The Sims Online Game" to the tune of $2 million.[5] As noted in Chapter 1, con-

Figure 2.10
ESPN's "The Best Damn Sports Show," with Tom Arnold, is generally regarded as one of the most blatant practitioners of product placement. (Globe Photos, Inc.)

sumers are increasingly wary of advertising, and in-show product placement provides advertisers with a real degree of protection.

PHARMACEUTICAL COMPANIES AND PRODUCT PLACEMENT

In 2002, a miniscandal in connection with a different kind of product placement surfaced when it was revealed that stars such as Lauren Bacall, Rob Lowe of "The West Wing" (before he abandoned ship over a pay dispute), and Noah Wylie of "ER" were appearing on television extolling the virtues of a particular drug without disclosing that they were paid consultants for those drugs. Bacall on the "Today" show talked about how the drug Visudyne helped one of her friends who suffered from macular degeneration, an eye disease. Bacall and the show never revealed her financial ties to Novartis, the drugmaker that sells Visudyne.[6] Extolling drugs was deemed unethical once it was out in the open, and broadcasters were quick to announce they would no longer allow this dubious form of product placement to take place.

At the station level and at cable networks, large numbers of programming heads are accepting **infomercials.** These are 30-minute advertisements masquerading as informative shows. They use interviews, demonstrations, and sometimes even dramas to extol the virtues of a particular diet plan, baldness treatment, kitchen gadget, or brand of sunglasses. The advertiser pays the station for the airtime and provides the program.

IN-HOUSE PRODUCTION

Most networks and stations have their own on-staff news personnel who see that the news is produced each day. Reporters hired by the station or network cover specific beats (city hall, Congress, the Middle East) and tape stories about significant events.

The news department also uses information that comes over wire services such as Associated Press and United Press International, tips or camcorder footage from individual citizens, stories in newspapers, and information from various databanks. The news business is rather incestuous in that stations and networks obtain information by listening to each other. CNN, for example, has become a major source of news ideas for other networks and stations.

Often, the news department is autonomous from the programming department. In these cases, the program director has no say over what happens in the news department; the news director makes the decisions. In other organizations, news falls under the aegis of the program director.

The other types of programs most likely to be produced in-house are news-oriented shows such as sports events, documentaries, and public affairs. The news director, the program director, or a committee of network or station managers decides what will and will not be produced. The number of programs, the content of the programs, and the budget for each must be decided in-house.

Live sports events are expensive for networks and local stations because they must pay for the rights to air the games and cover the costs for the people and equipment needed to televise the events. For many years, sports programming was an unqualified moneymaker. Networks and stations bid against each other for the rights in often bitter battles. But the advertising payments became insufficient to cover the costs, and the audience seems to be tiring of the huge amount of sports available on TV. This is why so much sports programming has left the major networks and gone to cable, where audiences can be smaller and costs can be contained. The rising costs of sports have caused a great deal of friction between the networks and their affiliates because the networks have requested that the affiliates cover part of the costs of broadcasting sports.

House-produced documentaries and public affairs shows can also lead to their own brand of problems. For example, after CBS produced and aired "The Uncounted Enemy" in 1982, it found itself engaged in a libel lawsuit against General William Westmoreland. The documentary had accused Westmoreland of purposely deceiving President Lyndon Johnson by estimating that the enemy troop strength in Vietnam was much lower than it really was. Although the case was settled out of court with no clear victor, it demonstrated the difficulties documentaries can cause. Ironically, this is one of the reasons networks prefer to produce their own documentaries rather than buy them from outside sources. At least the networks know the quality of research and the source of the ideas and can defend themselves. If they accept work from outsiders, they are liable but have less knowledge about the process of production.

Documentaries and public affairs programs are broadcast to serve the public interest. Rarely do they recover their costs. Advertisers do not like to sponsor what might be controversial, and audience members often prefer to watch entertainment shows. Public television, not beholden as much to sponsors or underwriters, ventures further than commercial television into documentaries and controversial issues, such as those covered each week by "Frontline" or Bill Moyers' "NOW."

Networks and stations also produce some of their own children's programs. The extent of in-house production is a function of the FCC's mood regarding the content of children's programs. When deregulation is in vogue and programmers are not required to consider the educational content of children's programs, many buy standard animated material from production companies and syndicators. When regulations require that children's programs contain certain educational or social content, the networks and stations often prefer to produce their own so that they can guarantee the needed elements.

A 1990 FCC ruling, the Children's Television Act, made station license renewals partly depend on the quality and frequency of children's programs, changing the relationship between in-house production units and the world of children's television programming. Although this ruling might have been expected to increase the number of children's shows produced in-house, this has not happened.

In the years following the 1990 ruling, children's programming on the commercial networks became increasingly unprofitable, and cable established a stronghold in the genre with such shows as "Lizzie McGuire," "SpongeBob SquarePants," "Rugrats," and "Fairly Odd Parents." Starting in 2002, the commercial networks essentially got out of the children's television business. NBC turned over its block of children's programming to the Discovery network; Fox contracted with the toy manufacturer 4 Kids to handle children's programming; and CBS turned to sister cable company Nickelodeon to provide the children's programming required by the FCC.

Some of the cable networks, however, employ their in-house units on a full-time basis. ESPN and the regional cable networks oversee most of their sportscasts. CNN has charge of the content of its news, and the same is true of The Weather Channel. MTV produces its video-jock programs, but the videos are provided for free by the record companies. C-SPAN produces its own political material. Other networks produce some of their own material. When you see a stand-up comic on any channel, that program has probably been produced in-house. Public affairs and talk shows are also likely to be undertaken by a resident production crew.

Cable systems also use in-house production for local origination shows. A local crew will cover news, much as a local TV station does, and cable system equipment and studios will be used for public affairs programs. In-house production is also used to produce inserts for some of the cable networks. CNN and The Weather Channel, for example, leave time for systems to provide information about local news and weather if they so desire. The same cable system staff that produces local origination produces these inserts.

Public broadcasting stations also produce their own programs, although less than they used to because of declining economics. For example, Los

Angeles's KCET produces the popular series "Life & Times" locally.

MEMBERS OF THE PUBLIC

Shows such as the seemingly perennial "America's Funniest Home Videos," composed of home videos submitted by the viewing audience, make it seem as if members of the public could easily function as programmers. During the height of the reality craze in 2003, some cynics voiced the opinion that anybody could come up with a reality show concept because there were so many on the air and "unbelievably bad."

The reality is that it always has been, and remains today, extremely difficult for an individual to break in. Generally, commercial networks and stations do not accept programming concepts that originate from members of the public. This is not because the talent is not there or the ideas are atrocious but because of legal reasons. Programmers have discovered that the simplest way to avoid litigation for plagiarism is to refuse any submission from an unaccredited source.

Generally, an unacceptable contributor is defined as one who does not have an agent recognized within the industry. When unsolicited program ideas arrive in the mail, network and station employees are instructed to send back the package unopened. If the envelope is not detectable as a program submission and the seal is broken, the company will return the contents with a release form that assigns virtually all the rights to the production company. The terms are so burdensome that the sender is usually never heard from again.

The primary reason commercial and cable networks, as well as production companies, are reluctant to get into business with individuals is that they are afraid of plagiarism—specifically, that the individual submitting an idea will charge that a future show stole their idea without proper compensation. Although networks and production companies take extensive precautions to avoid plagiarism cases, they are troubled with suits year after year. Many are of the nuisance variety and can be quickly disposed of. Others are more serious and require the expensive efforts of a battery of lawyers to refute.

There is one area in cable, however, where members of the public have easier access, that is, cable's **public access** channels where the individual reigns supreme. Of all areas of the electronic media, public access is the most receptive to ideas stemming from the minds of members of the public. Public access is truly a democratized concept. Anyone with an idea who can pull together cast, crew, a little money, and enough time to produce a show may do so. Some people (including any number of college students) have started in public access, learned a great deal, proven themselves, and then moved on to paying jobs in the broadcast or cable worlds.

NEWSPAPERS, MAGAZINES, AND BOOKS

Although programming ideas can come from anywhere, some of the most common sources are newspapers, magazines, and books, which you should be checking constantly.

Many producers scour newspapers religiously, always on the prowl for a story. Sometimes the story can be a small item on the bottom of a page; other times it can be a lead story with explosive headlines. One producer, Joseph Nasser, who had great success in the 1980s and 1990s with true-story television movies, impressed the networks and jealous producers alike with his extensive newspaper database that allowed him to unearth so many adaptable stories. Although asked, Nasser would never reveal the newspapers he included in his database, nor would he reveal how many papers he used or where they were from.

Often, the search for the big story leads to a frantic competition to tie up the rights for a hot article. Getting the rights to the "best" newspaper article can mean the difference between a "yes" or a "no" from the networks. A lot is at stake, and the competition can be fierce.

BROKERING THE PENNSYLVANIA MINERS' STORY

Even in Hollywood, where competition reigns supreme, acquiring the rights to the Pennsylvania miners' story was a race unlike any other. When the story of the trapped miners broke in 2002, it was immediately anointed as the kind of story that had all the makings of a great television movie, as was the case before it when the Amy Fisher sex and murder story broke and after it when the story of the rescue of Jessica Lynch from Iraq caused an avalanche of interest. Some stories instantly capture the imagination of producers and network executives alike, and the miners' story was one of those, clearly a much-needed feel-good story after the horrors of 9/11.

Producers immediately arrived in Somerset County, Pennsylvania, ready to jockey for position and to conquer the miners. One producer got on a plane immediately after hearing about the story. He was on the scene early and was able to meet with the miners. He thought he had the inside track but found himself only one of many after the International Creative Manage-

ment agency became involved. The word from Disney Chairman Michael Eisner came down that this was a story ABC had to have. Large sums of money were offered to the miners, along with a book contract, and a deal was struck. Fully empowered, Quinn Taylor, ABC's vice president of movies, flew to Pennsylvania to hold what was called a "beauty contest," where each of the producing candidates would meet with Taylor and the miners so that the miners could decide who they liked best. Six producers participated in this contest; one quick-thinking producer even stopped at a local store to buy overalls so that the miners would not see him as a slick Hollywood player who wears only Armani.

Only one of the six could win. It was a contest with high stakes: a production order when such orders were harder to come by. The stakes were so high that one of the candidates felt the need to eavesdrop on another player making his pitch to make sure it was a fair competition.

A future programmer who spots a good story might be wise to grab the rights if Hollywood has not sniffed it out yet and if a free or low-cost option is possible. Arming yourself with a story you control gives you a certain amount of clout. You will not be able to produce the story on your own, but you may be able to pair up with a producer or production company with a track record that meets a network's "comfort level."

Many producers have started their careers in this manner. For example, Joannie Marks had the rights to Gloria Steinem's article "A Bunny's Tale," which enabled her to pair up with established producer Stan Margulies to get the movie made for ABC.

Magazine articles are also excellent sources of material. Like everything else in television, magazine popularity is cyclical. There was a time when a *People*

Figure 2.11
Dean Koontz's
Mr. Murder
*starring Stephen
Baldwin is an
example of a best-
selling book well
suited to a
television
adaptation.* (Photo
courtesy Patchett
Kaufman
Entertainment.)

small screen on public and commercial television and on cable. The books of Stephen King, for example, were a big part of ABC's programming strategy for many years. Also, some books are too big for the running time of a theatrical movie, needing the hours that a mini-series can provide (Figure 2.11). Could James Haley's *Roots,* for example, have made television history packed into a 2- or 4-hour time span? Probably not.

Unfortunately, as explained in Chapter 1, viewer attention spans today make the airing of longform program-ming iffy, and book sales to television often suffer. There are exceptions, such as HBO's "Band of Brothers," but it has been a down cycle for books over the last few years. Although Michael O'Hara's adaptation of James Patterson's *First to Die* was a surprise critical and ratings success in 2003, it was cut from 4 to 3 hours because it was feared that audiences would not stick around for 2 nights. Cycles change, however, and some producers think the book business could come back strong because studios are not buying as many books for fea-tures. It would be a mistake for you to ignore the potential of books.

cover article almost guaranteed a "yes" from the network, again instilling a rush to acquire the rights. *Vanity Fair* also had a period in which it was deemed a reli-able source, possibly before it was deter-mined around 2003 that being on the cover of the magazine was a curse, spoil-ing actor Josh Hartnett's meteoric career rise once he became a *Vanity Fair* cover boy.

The *New Yorker* and *Texas Monthly* have also proved to be fertile suppliers of articles that made the transition to the small screen. Interestingly, one of the best television movies, 1983's "Who Will Love My Children," starring Ann Mar-garet and supervised by ABC program-ming executive Ilene Amy Berg, came from an article in the often overlooked, "unsexy" *Reader's Digest.*

Blockbuster books such as *The God-father, The World According to Garp, Seabis-cuit,* and *Memoirs of a Geisha* are usually sold to the movies, but some best-selling books nevertheless have made it to the

MANAGERS, AGENTS, AND STARS

Managers cannot solicit work for their clients as agents can, but because their job is to guide the careers of their clients, they often locate the material that their clients undertake. It often works like this: A manager interests his client in a piece of material. The client becomes committed to the material, and the client's "passion" for the project attracts studio interest. Then the manager, to the consternation of many producers, becomes a "producer" on the project when it is made.

Agents also exercise a great deal of control over programming sources. They represent most books, both big and small, and have deals to represent key magazines and newspapers. Agents will often package properties they represent with their writers, directors, or stars, formulating an attractive combination for the marketplace. In one instance, an agent felt a book his agency controlled would appeal to one of the agency's star clients, a writer-director, and this marriage led to the creation of a successful television program. This kind of mix-and-match technique allows agencies to be powerful originators of programming.

Agents are well connected and can quickly get to rights holders to encourage them to be represented by their companies, again limiting access. It is a double-edged sword for producers: If the person whose story you want is not represented or is represented by hometown lawyers, the negotiations can prove to be difficult because "nobody knows how the system works." If, on the other hand, a major agency gets involved, there is likely going to be a bidding war, the price will go up, and somebody represented by that agency will probably get the rights.

Some stars, such as Roseanne Barr in "Roseanne," have had significant creative input on their shows; other performers have created shows. These entrepreneurial stars survey the marketplace, decide what is needed, and use their clout to push their projects forward. Teen heartthrob Ashton Kutcher created "Punk'd" for MTV, where his friends, such as singer Justin Timberlake, are the butt of televised pranks.

Another way cable and commercial networks have entered business with high-voltage talent is to ask artists about their pet projects. Some of these projects might not be right for the big screen, but they might be just the ticket for the small screen. For example, when producer Kim Rubin learned that Jennifer Love Hewitt had always dreamed of playing Audrey Hepburn, Rubin and Hewitt ran with the idea and "The Audrey Hepburn Story" aired on ABC to strong ratings and favorable reviews. There is also the example of Selma Hayek directing "The Maldonado Miracle" for Showtime in 2003. Many stars create their own companies, sometimes unfavorably and unfairly dismissed as vanity efforts, to make sure that the projects they generate will see the light of day reflecting their particular vision.

In this chapter, we have examined the different sources of television programming. In Chapter 3, we turn our attention to the sources of radio and Internet programming.

EXERCISES

1. Research several television programs, mostly television movies and miniseries, that originated with stories in *The New Yorker, Vanity Fair,* and *Texas Monthly.*

2. Find an article that you think would make a good movie. Explore getting the rights.

3. Locate a program from a foreign country that you think could be successfully adapted for an American audience. What specifically would you have to do to "Americanize" it?

4. Analyze the success or failure of an imported show that has been "Americanized."

5. Analyze the television success or failure of a particular theatrical film. Why did the film work or not work on television?

6. Find a theatrical film that you think could translate nicely to the small screen. Analyze why you think the film could succeed on television.

7. Research an independent production company. How is the company structured? What creative or financial risks does it take, if any?

8. Research the history of a first-run syndicated program.

9. Research the arguments for and against fin-syn.

10. Compare the ratings for a show repurposed from a network to cable and from cable to a network.

REFERENCES/NOTES

1. Bob Shanks. *The Cool Fire* (New York: Norton, 1976), p. 87.

2. Bill Carter. "From Creator of CSI Testament to Himself," *The New York Times,* August 8, 2003, pp. C-1, 4.

3. Murray Green. "More Indies Airing Newscasts Produced by Competitors," *Broadcasting,* September 23, 1991, p. 16.

4. Ken Auletta. *Three Blind Mice* (New York: Random House, 1991), p. 357.

5. Matt Richtel. "Product Placements Go Interactive in Video Games," *The New York Times,* June 25, 2002, pp. C-1, 4.

6. Melody Petersen. "Stars Paid to Tout Cures," *International Herald Tribune,* August 13, 2002, p. 5.

3 Sources of Radio and Internet Programming

In this chapter you will learn about the following:

- The primary suppliers of radio and Internet programming content
- The effect of the 1996 Telecommunications Act on the distributors and creators of programming content
- The role of the public and stars as sources of programming
- What future programmers need to know to succeed as suppliers of programming
- Different radio formats
- Voice tracking
- The influence of payola on radio

Radio and television share a common past in their golden ages of drama programming, but radio's trajectory was forever changed by the advent of television. The coming of the Internet, although perhaps more of a creeping phenomenon than television, already has profoundly changed the way that media consumers view their media meals. The strategies that web programmers employ may make it necessary for programmers of all mediums to adjust their recipes.

SOURCES OF PROGRAMMING FOR RADIO

Radio, after the coming of television, became a medium with a local flavor, mainly focusing on broadcasting music, news, and talk. Radio, although it does not have as high a public profile as television, does have a high presence. In 2002, Arbitron reported that there were more than 13,500 radio stations operating in the United States. With most stations broadcasting 24 hours a day, that means the radio airwaves of the nation consume a staggering 118.3 million hours of programming each year. Even with the addition of the many television stations available through cable and satellite, television cannot possibly match the sheer bulk of radio's programming. This is partly a matter of available bandwidth for broadcasting, but it is even more a matter of economics. Television production requires scripts, lighting, camera operators, makeup, wardrobe, sets, props, directors, grips, catering, actors, studios, editors—the list goes on. Some radio programs, on the other hand, are now produced in a spare bedroom at the on-air personality's home, rigged with a microphone and little else.

Like television, however, many radio programs are produced once to be broadcast many times or, more often, on many stations simultaneously. So, as with television, the sources of radio programming include a system of network- and syndicator-produced materials and local sources of programming.

Syndicator/Network Programming

Although in television, as you saw in Chapter 2, there is a relatively clean delineation between a network and a syndicator, in radio the distinction is murky—especially because of the unprecedented media mergers after the 1996 Telecommunications Act. Major companies such as Clear Channel Communications, Cumulus Media, and Infinity Broadcasting each own radio stations broadcasting a range of formats, from talk to pop to alternative. But these companies do not only provide content to their own stations—they also create syndicated content for other stations.

For example, Metro Networks/Shadow Broadcast Services provides local traffic reports to thousands of radio stations across the country. Metro Networks/Shadow Broadcast Services is a subsidiary of Westwood One, which calls itself a network and comprises eight additional subsidiaries (CNN Max, Source Max, CBS, NBC, Next, WONE, Blaise, and Navigator). Some, such as

Metro Networks/Shadow Broadcast Services, provide syndicated material to stations; others operate stations (which may purchase syndicated material from still other companies). As if that was not complicated enough, Westwood One is a subsidiary of Infinity Broadcasting, bringing still more stations and services into the mix. But it does not end there; Infinity Broadcasting is owned by media giant Viacom, which also owns the CBS and UPN television networks; cable channels such as MTV, Showtime, Nickelodeon, and Black Entertainment Television; and film's Paramount Studios. All of this is subject to change at any moment as media companies spin off subsidiaries and acquire others.

Once you get past the definition of radio networks and syndicators, you are faced with two types of syndicated/network programming that these entities provide to local stations.

Types of Syndication. Some syndicated/network material for radio is produced once to be broadcast many times or on many stations at the same time. Examples of this kind of material are "The Howard Stern Show" (Figure 3.1), Ryan Seacrest's "Weekly Top 40," national and international news broadcasts "at the top of the hour," and nationwide talk shows such as those featuring Rush Limbaugh and Dr. Laura. On public radio, there are also many syndicated/network programs, such as NPR's "Morning Edition" and "All Things Considered" news programs or the lighter fare of "Car Talk" and "This American Life."

Then there is customized syndicated/network material tailored to each station. Scanning through radio stations in a major radio market during rush hour, you might come across the same traffic reporter describing the latest freeway conditions on several stations.

Figure 3.1
Howard Stern's weekday radio program is aired in major markets in the United States. (Globe Photos, Inc.)

The reporter may assume a different tone for each station to match that station's tone.

Voice Tracking. Another type of syndicated/network programming is **voice tracking.** This process is aimed at taking one radio personality and using him or her in many markets but retaining a "local" feel. The deejay's banter may be recorded in two types of segments: general segments and localized segments. The general segments make no reference to local events or information, so they can be played in every market. For the local segments, the deejay will record material specifically targeted to each market in which it will be broadcast. Every station receives the general segments, and each local station gets segments created specifically for the station; it then compiles the show for broadcast from the combination of the two. In some cases, voice talent only records general segments and the local segments are provided by third parties, such as syndicated local traffic, weather, news services, or a combination of these.

With computer programs specifically designed for voice tracking, deejays can often record a 5-hour show in 1 hour or less because the program skips songs and commercial breaks, only playing the beginning and end of material for the deejay's reference. With this sped up production method, a deejay in one city can create original voice-tracked shows for several other markets in the course of an afternoon, earning additional personal income and saving money for the radio company, which would not only have to pay the salary but also the benefits for what may be a less effective deejay with less sophisticated production techniques.

But voice tracking can be a complicated business. In addition, it has not always been successful. The technology for completely automating radio stations using prerecorded talent and computers to cue songs, commercials, and deejay banter has been around for decades but has seen only limited success. Audiences may catch on to the prepackaged quality of the material and do not tend to respond well. Radio, for many people, is not just a content-providing service— they rely on it to keep them company when they commute or do chores around the house. It is hard to feel comforted by the company of radio content that is perceptibly predetermined or preproduced.

The Purpose of Today's Radio Networks/Syndicators

Radio audiences tend to perceive stations as separate entities rather than part of a network brand. Notable exceptions exist, however. In public radio, audiences often associate individual stations with the NPR network even if many programs on the station originate from the local station or PRI. Pacifica Radio, a network of left-leaning radio stations, also has a strong network identity for its small but loyal audience.

In the commercial world, radio network identity faded with the arrival of television but may be making a comeback as part of the aftermath of deregulation, particularly the 1996 Telecommunications Act. The act removed the 40-station cap on nationwide ownership by a single company and allowed companies to own up to 8 stations in a single market, twice the previous limit. Several companies took advantage of the new rules, buying stations across the country.

By far the most ambitious of these companies, owning more than 1200 radio stations in 2003 (around 10% of all radio stations), is Clear Channel. Its biggest rival, Cumulus only owns around 300 stations. With several of its stations, Clear Channel has started to develop a national brand with a federal trademark. Its KISS stations are spread across the country. Although each station includes some locally created programs in its lineup each day, much of the stations' content, especially in smaller markets, is voice-tracked by deejays in other locations. Randy Michaels, former CEO of the company's radio unit, likened their strategy to McDonald's franchise system. "A McDonald's manager may get his arms around the local community, but there are certain elements of the product that are constant," he said. "You may in some parts of the country get chicken, but the Big Mac is the Big Mac."[1]

This new franchise system is in its early stages. For most stations, brand recognition is still not an important issue. What then is the benefit that companies receive in owning multiple stations?

If a network owns, as is often the case, a talk radio, a pop music, and an adult contemporary format station in the same city, there will be little, if any, content produced that could be broadcast on all three stations. There is scarce financial advantage to the network in content development and production because each station must create content appropriate to its own format.

The benefit a network gains by owning many stations is less in terms of sharing production costs and more in terms of sharing administrative costs. Many stations in a network may, for example, operate out of the same building, sharing facilities and management. This shared management arrangement

has aroused considerable controversy in the industry. How, many wonder, can one management team negotiate the peculiarities of both a decidedly non-controversial soft hits station aimed at adult women and the raucous format of an alternative rock station aimed at teenage males?

From Town to City to Metropolis and Syndication

Radio is similar to television news and talk shows in the manner in which on-air personalities and producers are seasoned into the business. Although there are notable exceptions, most people who want to get into radio have to start in minor markets, where audiences are small and pay is even smaller. On-air personalities in minor markets make demo tapes of their broadcasts and try to use them to secure positions in larger markets. To gain the attention of the programming directors in larger markets, they must have something on their demo reels that distinguishes them from the other applicants. Thus, out of the necessity to rise from the below-poverty wages of a small market, radio personalities must innovate and hone their skills and on-air personas.

It is not usually until after an on-air personality makes it to a major market that radio executives feel that he or she may be ready for syndication, where a show will be broadcast in numerous markets across the country. In this way, the small markets, where on-air personalities and producers cut their teeth and then move on, may later regain what they lost in the form of a syndicated show from the same on-air personality.

RADIO CAREER PATH: PHIL HENDRIE

(Reprinted with permission from www.philhendrieshow.com)

Phil Hendrie was born September 1st, 1952, and was raised in the Los Angeles suburb of Arcadia. Phil spent much of his youth traveling with his parents, transplanted Canadians, on lengthy road trips, during which he became enamored of the sounds of American radio coming through the car speakers. By the age of 5, young Phil knew he'd found his calling.

At 14, he discovered Dylan Thomas, and he considered a career as a writer. But as his interest in radio grew as well, he began hanging around Pasadena's KRLA, watching the likes of Casey Kasem, Bob Eubanks, and "Emperor" Bob Hudson.

Phil attended Pasadena City College for two years, but dropped out and moved with friends to Orlando, Florida, to work as a construction laborer/cement finisher in the middle of the early seventies Central Florida building boom, and contributed to building Walt Disney World as well. According to Mr. Hendrie, he ". . . still entertained ideas about being a writer but didn't really write anything."

Realizing that he'd need a job to support himself if he was ever going to get down to the business of writing, he unwittingly chose his career . . . "I landed a gig as a disc jockey at WBJW 1440 AM in Winter Park Florida, a suburb of Orlando. I never really did start writing anything. And for that matter never did anything of note as a disc jockey for some 16 years, drifting from Orlando to New Orleans to Miami and then home to Los Angeles, spinning records and hating it. Real waste of life . . ."

But despite "hating it," Phil rose quickly through the ranks as a D.J., until he was fired from his final job as morning man at KLSX in Los Angeles. It was then that he realized he had to find a position which would better serve his talents, and began his career in talk radio at KVEN in Ventura, California, in 1990. For the most part "fed up" with the business of radio, Phil accepted the position for a meager ". . . $1,500 a month at the age of 38."

According to one interview, his current show format was in part born from a lack of calls on the board. Once he discovered the enthusiasm his outrageous guests brought about in his listeners, he knew he had an intriguing new format with which to work . . . and it's been one which has served him well.

But for Phil, it's more than just parody of the medium. In fact, in many respects, Phil doesn't care for the very industry in which he works. For Phil Hendrie, as well as for many other listeners of the medium, talk radio itself has become too self-important and too self-congratulatory. Its hosts take on extremist viewpoints merely to keep calls on the board . . . from callers who often just parrot whatever the host says. Worse yet, talk radio believes it makes a difference in the issues, when it rarely if ever does.

And perhaps worst of all . . . if it's on the radio, people believe it as an absolute truth, despite the fact that most of what's on talk radio is simply opinion. What Phil Hendrie does on his program manages to demonstrate that rather accurately, each and every night.

In this respect, be forewarned—through often outrageous humor, Phil Hendrie regularly exposes the media for what it is. But most of all—Phil's show is about poking a little fun at ourselves . . . and he and his listeners have a damn good time doing it.

While Mr. Hendrie insists that he still has a longing to write . . . most of his fans would probably agree that he's already found his niche.

(In 2003 "The Phil Hendrie Show" was syndicated on stations in nearly 40 of the U.S. States and in Canada.)

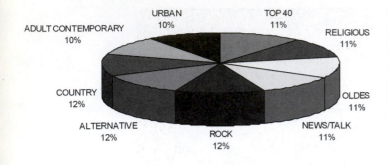

Figure 3.2
Radio music formats and the percentage of the market they occupy.
(Source: http://www.cyber college.com/frtv/ frtv022b.htm. Accessed July 22, 2004.)

Sources of Music Programming

The main product on most radio stations is music. The source for the music is record companies that willingly donate copies of their new releases to stations likely to program them. Although the records are free, stations must pay license fees to play music. These fees are paid to The American Society of Composers, Authors and Publishers; Broadcast Music, Inc.; and the Society of European Stage Authors and Composers, music licensing organizations that collect money from stations and pay it to music composers and publishers. The amount collected is an annual fee based on the station's overall revenue—about 1.4%. Each of these licensing organizations has jurisdiction over different music. Most stations find they must pay all three so that they can air whatever music they want. The licensing agencies periodically collect **playlists** from a representative sample of stations and feed into a computer the entries of musical selections from each playlist. Based on these, the agencies decide how much of the money collected should go to each composer and publisher.

In the early days of musical programming in radio, playlists were mostly determined by the deejays that spun the records. This deejay-driven strategy is still in existence to a limited extent, mostly on public radio and college stations. KCRW in Los Angeles, for example, offers numerous musical programs whose deejays have found loyal listeners both in the local market and on the Internet, such as their musically diverse morning program "Morning Becomes Eclectic," hosted by Nic Harcourt. Such deejay-driven programs have often introduced and popularized new artists, whose songs have then been picked up by commercial stations. In 1993, for example, "Morning Becomes Eclectic" was the first to broadcast the song "Loser" by then-unknown musical artist Beck.

Most stations, however, rely on program directors who select a consistent genre of music so that audiences know what they will hear from the station no matter when they tune in (Figure 3.2). Local radio stations conduct extensive testing and evaluation to discover what is hot and what is not with audiences, because songs tend to have a limited shelf life, especially in Top 40 radio. More on this process will be covered in the chapters on testing and evaluation.

Radio Consolidation and Music Programming. With the consolidation of radio station ownership that occurred after the 1996 Telecommunications Act, some worry that local programming decisions might be affected by a station's parent company. For example, in the lead-up to the 2003 war in Iraq, the country trio The Dixie Chicks made disparaging comments about President George W. Bush at a concert in Europe. Nearly overnight, their songs were dropped from many radio stations. Cumulus Media, which owns nearly 300 radio stations across the nation, briefly but officially banned The Dixie Chicks

(Figure 3.3) from the airwaves of their country music stations. Critics pointed out that many stations owned by the far bigger Clear Channel were no longer playing the until-then best-selling band. Critics also noted that some Clear Channel stations were taking part in war rallies, charging that the company had a right-wing political agenda. Clear Channel Radio CEO John Hogan, in a July 23 interview on the NPR program "Fresh Air," denied that Clear Channel or its stations were responding to anything other than local market forces when they stopped playing The Dixie Chicks. Hogan claims that all music programming decisions are left to the discretion of local program directors, based on research about what local audiences want and do not want to hear, and that there was therefore no concerted effort to ban the band. In fact, Hogan said, many Clear Channel stations continued to play the band's songs after their controversial statements.

Nevertheless, media observers worry that radio music diversity will, whether by design or by circumstance, be stultified by the conglomeration of radio ownership. As editorial observer Brent Staples wrote in *The New York Times* in February 2003, "independent radio stations that once would have played edgy, political music have been gobbled up by corporations that control hundreds of stations and have no wish to rock the boat."

Payola. Although program directors insist that their playlists are influenced only by audience preferences, this is not always the case. Throughout the history ·of music programming on radio, record companies have, to a greater or lesser extent, tried to influence which songs are broadcast, when, and how often—a practice known as **payola.** Record distribu-

Figure 3.3
The Dixie Chicks saw their airplay diminish after they made controversial comments. (Globe Photos, Inc.)

tors give money or special favors to those in radio programming in exchange for airing their music. Radio exposure is such an important factor in a record's success that distributors are willing to do almost anything to receive favorable, frequent airings. Payola was made illegal in the 1950s after it was discovered to be rampant in the radio business. But the antipayola laws only made it illegal for record distributors to pay stations for airing specific songs.

Soon, a new payola scheme was devised, that of the "independent promoter." In this scheme, the independent promoter is paid by a record company to promote the company's songs and artists to radio stations. The independent promoter, in turn, pays an annual fee to radio stations to have the "right" to promote songs to the station. In this way, record companies and radio stations can make two claims: (1) The record company and the radio station are not negotiating directly—instead, they are

Figure 3.4
Don Henley testified in the Senate about modern-day equivalents to payola. (Globe Photos, Inc.)

going through an "independent" third party. (2) The third party is not paying the station to play specific songs; it is only paying an annual promotion fee.

Complaints about this new payola scheme have surfaced many times since the 1960s, but evidence about the practice and how rampant it may be is hard to come by because those involved are not eager to disclose details. At one point, singer/songwriter Don Henley (Figure 3.4), best known as a member of the Eagles rock band, appeared before the Senate Commerce, Science, and Transportation Committee's hearing on media ownership. When asked about his firsthand knowledge of payola, Henley said, "I know there's payola because I get billed for it. My record company bills me back for the independent promotion monies they have to give to the independent promoter. And they have worked out a very sophisticated system to skirt the current payola laws; a very sophisticated system where the money

is paid to a middleman. And what happens after that is very privileged information. But I know that these things exist."[2]

Henley's appearance before the Senate committee was partly credited for the vow of the largest U.S. radio station owner, Clear Channel, to bar its radio stations from accepting money from independent promoters. Some lawmakers, however, looked upon this announcement with a jaundiced eye, having seen how quickly and consistently radio stations and record companies had circumnavigated the original intent of the payola laws. Senator Russ Feingold (D-Wisconsin) said, "I hope that Clear Channel considers this a first step toward reforming the industry, not a single concession aimed at pacifying Congress."[3]

Henley also warned against a new potential player in the payola game—the **concert promoter.** Record companies claim that profits have been hobbled in the late 1990s and early 2000s by illegal MP3 song file swapping over the Internet. Some critics say, however, that mergers in the record industry are to blame for sagging profits because they have made it difficult for interesting new musical acts to break into the business. As a result, these critics say, the public has soured on cookie-cutter megamusical artists who are more sheen than substance. Whatever the reason for drooping profits, the music industry has increasingly turned to live concerts for revenue, raising ticket prices markedly in recent years. To drive consumers to concerts, Henley warns that concert promoters might be trying to get the songs from touring artists into heavy rotation on radio stations. An ominous sign that Henley points to is that Clear Channel has become the biggest player not only in radio but also in concert promotion—and that its song playlists may therefore be determined, at least partly, by self-interest to support its touring artists.

Sources of News Programming

All-news radio stations have the same elaborate source structure as major TV news outlets. They subscribe to wire services, networks, and databanks, and they hire numerous reporters to roam the local streets and even travel nationally and internationally to cover stories. They must have a well-organized but flexible infrastructure to incorporate and update the latest happenings.

However, on many music-oriented stations, news is downplayed. Since the deregulation in the 1980s, radio stations are not required to program news, so many of them provide only a minimal amount. They do not have their own full-blown news staffs and choose instead to subscribe to a network (or several) to receive news. Sometimes the stations use the network newscasts just as they are, and sometimes they use the network actualities (interviews with people in the news) but surround them with copy read by a local announcer.

The downplaying of news, decreasing local origination and increasing automation in radio stations has meant that radio's place as a resource for timely or urgent local news has diminished. David K. Dunaway, an English professor and media analyst at the University of New Mexico, cites the derailment of a train as an example: "The best example of the importance and decline of local origination happened in a town of Minot, North Dakota, where last January a train derailment released a toxic cloud of ammonia . . . Emergency workers called the stations, but Clear Channel had fired the local reporters, and no one could notify the public about the toxic cloud."[4]

Sources of Talk Radio Programming

Nearly every radio station has an element of talk radio programming in it, whether it is a Top 40 music station with a special guest interview of a hot pop star, a soft hits station that reads romantic dedications at night, or one of the staple all-talk stations. All-talk stations have taken off in the last 20 years. In 1980, there were only 75 all-talk stations in the United States. By 2003, there were more than 1300.[5]

Members of the Public. Unlike television, many radio programs depend heavily upon audience contributions—call-in talk shows are built completely around audience contributions, even if only a tiny percentage of listeners call. This is not to say that call-in talk shows just open the phone lines and sit back. The content is driven by the production team and the on-air personality. Listeners tune in not to hear what callers will say but rather to hear how their favorite on-air personality will react.

Although there are many types of call-in shows, they usually involve the on-air host introducing a topic "ripped from the headlines," whether the headlines of a newspaper, a tabloid, or even an obscure article from a small publication. Often there is also an expert or someone directly related to the topic with whom the on-air personality discusses various aspects of the issue before throwing it open to audience comments or questions. Rarely do call-in shows simply go from caller to caller. Instead, the host, expert, or both have prearranged talking points about the topic to discuss between calls. In addition, there is usually a vigorous call-screening process because the point of call-in shows is less to let callers say their piece and more to provide interesting

Figure 3.5
Dr. Drew Pinsky plays the straight man to Adam Carolla's riffs on sexual topics in their syndicated talk show, "Loveline," but the show mainly focuses on call-ins. (Globe Photos, Inc.)

eventually was broadcast to about 125 stations nationwide. But in 1999 they ended their syndication run, concluding that they are most comfortable and effective when dealing with local and state issues.[6]

Other call-in shows, such as help or advice shows like the nationally syndicated "Dr. Laura" or "Loveline" with Dr. Drew Pinsky (Figure 3.5) and Adam Carolla are driven less by host-derived topics and more by the personal problems that callers bring to the shows. Again, call screening plays an important role in providing variety and interest to the content, and the hosts often talk between calls to comment on a topic brought up by a caller or to talk of other issues of interest to their target audience.

As noted before, most music format stations also include elements of talk derived from members of the public. Audience members request songs or dedicate them to loved (or hated) ones. Again, call screening plays an important role. Stations do not put on callers who request songs that diverge greatly from the station's format. WHOM-FM in Portland, Maine, for example, has run a show "Love Songs at Night" with Sandra Harris since the early 1990s. The operations and program manager at WHOM, Tim Moore, said that although the songs the station plays in the "Love Songs at Night" show are not that different from those it plays during the day, "There is a different flavor at night and Sandra's sending it out specifically to one person with that message is what makes it magical."[7]

material for listeners—especially in commercial radio. Some shows stick with topics for long periods; others might rifle through a dozen topics in an hour. Often the amount of time spent depends on the complexities of the topic.

Some nationally syndicated examples of this type of call-in show are "The Rush Limbaugh Show," "Radio Factor with Bill O'Reilly," NPR's "Talk of the Nation," and the fringe "Coast to Coast AM." Nearly every major market, and many smaller markets, also have their own homegrown local call-in shows. Many nationally syndicated shows started out as local shows that caught fire and then were retooled to appeal to larger audiences. Some talk show hosts, such as John Kobylt and Ken Chiampou of the "John and Ken Show" from KFI in Los Angeles, have made the trip from local to syndicated and back to local again. The pair's show, which started out in New Jersey, began syndication after they came to Los Angeles in 1992 and

Many radio shows also have sketches that play tricks on audience members or on the behalf of audience members. The syndicated "Phil Hendrie Show," for example, is an often-outrageous parody of a talk radio show. Unwitting listeners sometimes chance upon the show and are incensed by its farfetched content, calling in to lodge their complaints or spar with outlandishly concocted "guests." Hendrie and his "guests" then take the opportunity to milk these callers for all the comic, if off-color, interactions they can. In Rick Dees's "Candid Phone" sketch, an audience member calls in to request that Dees make a crank call to a friend or family member—providing Dees with information about the person that he can use to bait his victim.

Stars. Another source that radio taps for programming is known personalities, usually from television. With recent media mergers, this "transplanting" of talent is becoming more prevalent. Personalities who have developed national followings on television, such as Carson Daly (Figure 3.6) of MTV's "Total Request Live," now have syndicated daily radio programs, such as Daly's "Most Requested" and "Most Requested Rhythmic" shows. (Interestingly, Daly started out in radio before being picked up by MTV at age 24.) But this phenomenon is not limited to national television and radio. Many local television news personalities, after they are done with their morning television broadcasts then host radio programs. For example, Sam Rubin, an entertainment reporter for KTLA in Los Angeles's morning television news program, also has a 1-hour entertainment radio program on Los Angeles's 97.1 FM talk station.

On the other side of the coin, many radio personalities have made the jump from radio to television, although the results there have not been particularly impressive, showing that radio and television are very different mediums. Dr. Laura Schlessinger, whose radio talk show is syndicated on more than 300 AM stations across the country, made the move to television in September

Figure 3.6
In addition to his MTV show, "Total Request Live," Carson Daly parlays his celebrity into radio gold. (Globe Photos, Inc.)

2000. Although her radio program, which has been syndicated since 1994, is the second most listened to talk radio program on the air, it has stirred up considerable controversy—especially concerning comments she made about homosexuals, labeling them "biological errors." This pot of controversy, although simmering before, began to boil once plans for her television show were announced. A group of activists set up a website, StopDrLaura.com, and arranged for protests outside of the Paramount Studios, where the show was being taped. The protests and website received considerable media attention, scaring advertisers both from Schlessinger's new television show and her longstanding radio program. Less than a year after the television show began airing, it was canceled. The activists at StopDrLaura.com claimed victory, although Dr. Laura continues to broadcast her daily radio program and it still holds its place as the number two talk show on radio behind Rush Limbaugh's program, who also had his own short-lived television show in 1995 and 1996.

Shock jock Howard Stern, however, has had moderate and longstanding success on cable television's E! Entertainment Television network since 1994. His show, unlike the Schlessinger and Limbaugh shows, was hardly modified for television. Instead, cameras simply capture the radio show as it is produced, perhaps with a few "behind-the-scenes" sketches and interviews with guests before they enter the studio.

Sources of Other Programming

Most radio programming falls into the formats of music, news, and talk, but other programming exists on the periphery.

Many stations air play-by-play sports coverage of local teams on weekends. Play-by-play sports can be supplied locally, regionally, or nationally. Stations that program only sports use all three, but most stations, if they program sports, either produce the game coverage in-house or use the services of one network.

Radio drama never fell completely off of the airwaves. Golden-age radio dramas are still replayed in syndication. Equity Radio Network, for example, has agreements with 22 stations across the country. Equity Radio Network's president, Gary Nice, explained his interest in the shows from the 1930s and 1940s by saying, "I wanted to syndicate something different. I wanted to find a niche. Originally, I was syndicating talk shows, but they're a dime a dozen nowadays—especially conservative talk shows."[8]

New radio dramas have also been produced throughout the years, mostly on public radio. For writers and actors, radio drama can be an attractive medium in which to try something new without the budgetary nightmares inherent in film and television production. Although radio dramas are less expensive to produce than TV or film ones, they are still more expensive and labor intensive than most radio content. However, with the burgeoning billion-dollar "books on tape" market, often dramas produced for radio can see additional revenue in a CD after market or, more recently, on satellite radio.

Sources of Satellite Radio Programming

Unlike terrestrial radio, satellite radio closely resembles television. As a subscription service, the brand of the satellite radio network is extremely important. In 2003 there were only two network brands: XM Radio and Sirius. With upward of 100 channels to fill with content, these networks use both self-produced and syndicated material, some of which is also broadcast on terrestrial radio stations or the Internet. XM Radio, for example, broadcasts a feed of Los Angeles's KIIS-FM Top 40 station and NPR's daily offerings.

Satellite radio features some stations that are wall-to-wall genre-specific music. Other stations include deejay chatter between music and exclusive interviews or live performances by recording artists. Many talk radio, news, and sports stations are available. But satellite radio also provides stations that contain material not offered elsewhere, such as nonstop stand-up comedians, radio dramas, and niche programming, like Sirius's OutQ station, a channel of news, information, and entertainment programming aimed at the gay, lesbian, bisexual, and transgender communities. XM Radio also features Playboy Radio, a premium channel that subscribers must pay extra to listen to. Although many stations are commercial free, others include commercials to augment listener subscription fees.

Sources of Low-Power FM Programming

Provided for in the 1996 Telecommunications Act, low-power FM (LPFM) radio stations have a small broadcast radius, usually of about 10 miles. They are meant to provide opportunities for schools, churches, and other local organizations to use the public airwaves to make their voices heard.

The FCC's eligibility criteria for LPFM require the applicant organization be a not-for-profit educational institution or organization or an entity that has proposed a noncommercial public-safety radio service to protect the safety of life, health, or property. The applicant cannot have financial interest in any other television, radio, newspaper, or cable television operation (excluding public access) and must agree to broadcast a minimum of 36 hours per week, much of which must be locally produced programming. Therefore, sources of LPFM programming are mostly local, independent, and not for profit.[9]

The National Association of Broadcasters and even NPR have lobbied for strict controls to limit the proliferation of these stations, pointing to the possible signal interference that low-power stations might have on their own signals. Studies on signal interference by LPFM stations have been mixed, but they suggest that interference, in most cases, is insignificant. Some media watchers question whether established radio's objections to LPFM may be based more on wanting to eliminate possible competition than avoiding signal interference. As of July 2003, there were 744 LPFM permits issued and 220 stations on the air, according to the FCC.[10]

Despite its establishment of not-for-profit and community-based media opportunities such as LPFM, many have criticized the 1996 Telecommunications Act and other more recent deregulation of broadcast ownership because it allows much of traditional broadcast media to be swallowed by a few big corporations. Critics argue that fewer media owners means fewer sources of programming and fewer points of view expressed in the media. Publicly traded companies, many caution, have only three concerns—minimizing costs, maximizing revenues, and therefore generating profit.

Supporters of the 1996 Telecommunications Act say that without it, traditional media would have fallen into the red as a result of competition and the fracturing of the marketplace. Erica Farber, president and publisher of *Radio & Records,* said when she spoke at California State University, Fullerton, that the 1996 Telecommunications Act allowed radio to "finally function as a real business."

Although many supporters of the 1996 Telecommunications Act and subsequent deregulation agree that traditional media may see less diversity, at least in ownership, as a result of media mergers, they point to the new media opportunities available to the public, specifically the Internet.

SOURCES OF INTERNET PROGRAMMING

With the Internet, supporters of media deregulation say, diversity of viewpoints and sources of programming can grow exponentially. Indeed, the number of unique websites on the Internet, according to the Online Computer Library Center, continues to grow—from 2,636,000 in 1998 to 8,712,000 in 2002.[11]

PROGRAMMING FOR TV, RADIO, AND THE INTERNET

Every Computer a Potential Source of Programming

The Internet, developed by the U.S. government in 1969, is a vast network of computers that can, with permission, connect to each other to share digital files. Unlike radio or television, which is broadcast from one location to be received in the surrounding area, any computer connected to the Internet can serve as both a broadcaster and a receiver. Anyone with an Internet connection who follows the correct World Wide Web protocols can create content in the form of web pages. These can be viewed by anyone else with an Internet connection—provided that they know the correct **uniform resource locator** or address of the desired website.

The Internet was started as a military tool and soon spread to universities to aid in research. It did not really start gaining exposure to the general public until the early 1990s, but use and access to the Internet has quickly grown ever since. In 1995, Nielsen estimated the number of people in the United States with access to the Internet at 18 million, or 6.7% of the U.S. population. In April 2002, that number had risen to 167 million, or 59.1% of the U.S. population.[12]

Obstacles to Internet Mass Usage

These numbers, however, may be deceiving; they include people who use the Internet at work, at home, in Internet cafes, and in public libraries. Only an estimated 32% of the U.S. population had Internet access in their homes in April 2002. Comparing that to the 98.9% of households with a color television and the nearly ubiquitous presence of radios in U.S. households, the growth of the Internet, although impressive, has not been as quick or universal as that of early radio or television.[13]

Part of the problem with adoption of the Internet by the masses is inherent in the technology and the medium of the Internet. Radio and television receivers require little technical know-how or training to operate. The same cannot be said for the Internet, which, in most cases, must be received through a computer. Many people's computer skills and especially troubleshooting skills are limited. When a computer problem occurs, which it inevitably does, users may be turned off, especially if they are using the computer during their leisure time.

Although creating and publishing websites and Internet programming for consumption by others can be far less expensive and difficult than producing and broadcasting television and radio programs, it is still no walk in the park. Once Internet content is produced and made available to web surfers, there is still the problem of letting people know that the site exists and how to get to it. Web producers must submit their sites to **search engine** services, such as Google.com, AltaVista.com, and Ask.com. With millions of sites on the Internet, web producers must optimize their sites so that search engines can effectively index them—increasing the possibility that the site will be listed in the first few results in a search. In short, although the Internet certainly guarantees the opportunity for expression to anyone with a computer and an Internet connection, it does not as easily guarantee an audience for that expression.

Traditional Media Sources

Nowadays, nearly every media outlet, whether a newspaper, television network, or radio station, has a website. These websites may range from the perfunctory one-page site that serves as an online brochure to a full-featured, interactive website with regularly updated text, photos, audio, video, and motion graphic content.

Oftentimes, traditional media sources populate their websites with materials taken directly from their traditional outlets. A radio station may provide a live **stream** of the station's broadcast online or archived files of previous shows to which visitors to the site can listen **on demand.** This is especially true with talk radio programs, which are often broken into several files, each representing one of the topics covered in the live show.

For television, connection speeds are not yet fast enough to stream quality live video to most viewers. Television networks may provide short on-demand video clips of recent or archived shows. But it is often preferable to create video content specifically for the web. The file **compression** process used to make video files small enough for efficient Internet transmission favors images with minimal movement and detail. Although on television the busy background of CNN's newsroom provides an interesting visual environment, after file compression, most of the moving details in the background would look like distracting, blurry splotches (Figure 3.7). For this reason, video created specifically for the web usually consists of the proverbial talking head with a monochrome background. As better compression programs (codecs) are developed,

video on the Internet is becoming more robust, but it still has a long way to go.

One type of video Internet programming has taken off in recent years: music videos. As music video networks such as MTV and VH1 have moved toward programming shows, rather than the wall-to-wall videos they started out playing, viewers have turned more to the Internet to watch the latest videos of their favorite artists. Yahoo's Launch.com features thousands of music videos dating back as far as "Video Killed the Radio Star," the video by The Buggles, which inaugurated MTV in 1983.

Another type of content that traditional media outlets provide on their websites is material that supplements their regular programming. Radio stations may feature biographies of on-air personalities, "unedited" versions of interviews broadcast over the airwaves, or other resources for their listener community, such as calendars of events, chat rooms, and message boards. Television networks may provide "backgrounders" on specific shows. The website for CBS's hit show "CSI: Crime Scene Investigation" contains a section called Case Files, which shows details of each of the crime scenes featured on the show. A Personnel section gives background about each of the show's characters. Among other content on the site is a Handbook with definitions and descriptions of the various methods

Figure 3.7
Compression can significantly degrade the quality of video streamed over the Internet.

and tools of crime scene investigation and pictorial maps of crime labs. On some television shows, characters mention fictitious website addresses and viewers flock to the addresses to see what is there, just as they inevitably call phone numbers mentioned on television shows, causing nightmares for the unlucky individuals or businesses to whom the numbers belong. On the NBC show "Will & Grace," the character Jack mentioned his website Just-Jack.com several times on one episode. When viewers went to the site, they found a modest number of pages detailing Jack's frothy "private thoughts."

Some television and radio shows use their Internet sites to allow audience members to play along, interact with, or even determine the direction of a show. The ABC prime-time game show "Who Wants to Be a Millionaire" featured an option for audience members to play along at home, and some reality television shows have relied on Internet audiences to determine who stays and who goes. News and talk programs on television and radio often ask their audiences to go to the show's Internet site to vote on issues of the day, disclosing the "polling" results at the end of the program.

Internet-Only Sources

Outside of traditional media sources, the Internet is host to programming from all manner of other sources. As stated previously, any person who hooks a computer up to the Internet can become a source of programming—whether text, photography, audio, video, static or motion graphics, or a multimedia combination. Nowadays, nearly every business has a website, and increasingly individuals have set up their own websites. The purposes behind personal websites include sharing personal photos and other media with friends and family, serving as an online resume or port-

folio, expressing opinions or observations, or broadcasting personally produced forms of entertainment, perhaps with the aim of gaining notice from traditional media, making money off of the endeavor, or both.

If a person or entity wishes to have an endeavor reach an audience, however, just as with radio and television networks and stations, associating with a known quantity on the Internet will greatly help the process. Search engines, **web rings, link sharing,** and **email marketing** are just a few ways to associate websites online.

Private vs. Public Sources of Programming

In the early days of the Internet, most programming was public. Anyone could view most websites without permission or payment. As the years have gone by, the percentage of public and private sites has evened out. In 1998, 55% of all websites were public, with 12% private and the remaining 33% "under construction." By 2002, the percentage of public sites had dipped to 35%, with the private percentage rising to 29% and "under construction" sites staying nearly unchanged at 36%.

Often services on the web start out free; after viewers have become accustomed to the service, the website starts to charge a fee for access to the site or for access to "premium" content on the site. Perennial Internet service provider AOL offers its members many services and content available only to members.

Thus, the sources of programs are many and varied, and ideas are brought to buyers in a range of forms. Sometimes they are expressed in a single sentence; more frequently they are typed out in two or three pages. Occasionally, a program creator will present a few minutes of tape or film to communicate the core of the show. Sometimes, as mentioned previously, they strike out on their own, creating content, perhaps on a website, to draw attention to their ideas and talent.

When buyers like what they see or hear, they start a chain of events known as **development.** This important process is addressed in Chapter 4.

EXERCISES

1. Find an article that you think would make a good topic for a radio talk show segment. Identify an expert or person involved in the story who might make a good in-studio guest. Come up with talking points to discuss between callers.

2. Design a new music radio format. What type or types of music would the station play? Argue why a radio station should give the format a try.

3. Select a popular television drama or comedy and come up with Internet content that might interest audience members. Think of ways to incorporate fictitious websites into the storylines.

REFERENCES/NOTES

1. Peter Spellman. "McRadio," http://www.mbsolutions.com/biz/Info30.html. Accessed July 15, 2004.

2. "Testimony from Senate Commerce, Science, and Transportation Committee hearing on media ownership: Radio industry," http://www.azoz.com/news/0019e.html. Accessed July 15, 2004.

3. Chuck "Jigsaw" Creekmur. "Clear Channel Rejects 'Payola' Practices," http://www.bet.com/articles/0,c3gb6009-6758,00.html. Accessed July 15, 2004.

4. TV Times. "FCC Deregulation Decision Draws Controversy," http://tvitimes.tvi.edu/archives/030617/030617_fcc.htm. Accessed July 15, 2004.

5. Hendrik Hertzberg. "The Talk of the Town," *The New Yorker,* August 11, 2003, p. 23.

6. Steve Carney. "Crusading for Truth, Justice, on Weekday Afternoons," *Los Angeles Times*, May 6, 2003, p. PE-1.

7. "Ten Years of Love Songs," http://www.fishlakia.com/LoveSongs/default.htm. Accessed July 15, 2004.

8. Radio Guide Magazine. "The Return of Radio's Golden Age," http://www.radioguide.com/sdrad/mag19/goldyear.html. Accessed July 15, 2004.

9. The Microradio Implementation Project. "National Microradio Advocate Celebrates Two-year Anniversary of New Radio Service; Close to 100 Applicants in Oregon, 70 in Washington, 3,000 Nationwide," http://www.microradio.org/mr021202.htm. Accessed July 15, 2004.

10. Mario Hieb. "LPFM: All That Fuss for Nothing?" http://www.radioworld.com/reference-room/special-report/01_rw_lpfm_4.shtml. Accessed July 15, 2004.

11. Edward T. O'Neill, Brian F. Lavoie, and Rick Bennett. "Trends in the Evolution of the Public Web," http://www.dlib.org/dlib/april03/lavoie/04lavoie.html. Accessed July 15, 2004.

12. Michael Pastore. "At-Home Internet Users Approaching Half Billion," http://www.clickz.com/stats/big_picture/geographics/article.php/986431. Accessed July 15, 2004.

13. Stephanie Battles. "The Effect of Income on Appliances in U.S. Households," http://www.eia.doe.gov/emeu/recs/appliances/appliances.html. Accessed July 15, 2004.

4   Development

In this chapter you will learn about the following:

- What future programmers need to know about the inner workings of the development process
- Ways to pitch a story
- The role finance plays in the development process
- Strategies professionals use to get a project into development
- The role globalization plays in development
- Format development in radio
- What development means in public broadcasting
- How Internet program development is seeking to maximize the potential of the wired world

Development, sometimes called "development hell," is an essential step in readying a program for broadcast. Shows do not appear ready for public consumption. An idea has to be shaped, fine-tuned, and perfected during the development process. The daunting blank page that creative people confront has to be filled with ideas that translate into an effective radio format, a successful series that has the potential to make millions of dollars in syndication, a reality program that can make a network No. 1 instead of an also-ran, or a way to raise Internet usage to greater levels. Such are the challenges producers, writers, and performers face when they become sellers seeking entry into development.

Many people find the development process hellish because it is time intensive and extremely costly. The odds for success are also exceedingly slim. Hits do not come easily, and the mandate of a programming chief often is to find a single hit show, one that functions as a building block for a network. One hit. How hard can that be? As the development process reveals, it is extremely difficult. Although the odds of developing a show that succeeds out of the hundreds developed each year are not good, the few that do succeed keep people trying to hit the jackpot.

Many people are involved in development: programming executives, researchers, producers, **showrunners** (individuals who are in charge of all day-to-day aspects of a show), performers, financial advisors, and, perhaps most importantly, writers. Writers usually are paid once a project is put into development by a network, but producers do not earn money until the start of production, causing some producers to rush the development process and to present a show before it is ready.

Development cycles are also apt to change quickly. What is hot one moment can grow cold quickly, leaving the creative team developing a show that misses the mark. Although development can vary from medium to medium, the process nevertheless consists of a series of established steps. These steps are carefully followed until a buyer believes the project has a chance for success and a green light can be justified.

In this chapter, we examine how the all-important development process functions.

TELEVISION DEVELOPMENT

When producers, writers, and the creative team come up with a **concept** that seems promising, they spend a great deal of time reviewing it. Many questions are asked. For example, does the idea have "legs"? Does the series, for example, have the potential to generate enough story lines for 88 episodes, the "magic" number that leads to syndication gold? Are the characters strong enough to maintain interest? Can the show be produced in a way that makes sense financially—that is, will a network determine that the show can be produced under its budget guidelines? If it is based on a book, an article, or a true story, are the rights available? How can the concept be made more salable? Is another element needed? All these considerations, and others, have to be taken into account during the development process.

Securing the Rights

If your project is based on a book, you will need the rights to the book before the start of production. Similarly, if your project is based on a real person, you will need the rights to that person's story—that is, the permission to portray that individual on television.

This seems simple enough, but when and how should you go about securing these rights during the development process? It is best to option the necessary rights before you venture into the marketplace. This is the most prudent approach, because it protects you from having the rights fall out from under you.

Securing rights options, however, often necessitates up-front money, and many producers do not want to put up any cash until they know they have a sale. These producers will often develop a project and even risk submitting it to buyers without the necessary rights as long as they know that the rights are available.

How do you know what rights are needed, and how do you know how to acquire those rights? Established producers have lawyers and business affairs executives to advise them. They can also sometimes get a book agent to give them permission to take a book to potential buyers for a limited time without putting up option money. But how does a newcomer go about the process of securing rights?

There are several resources available, including Howard J. Blumenthal and Oliver R. Goodenough's *This Business of Television*[1] and Enterprise of Hollywood.[2] The latter has sample contracts for a range of contingencies, including the basic option acquisition agreement, music assignment of all rights agreements, and artist performance agreements. Remember to keep any option agreement simple to avoid making individuals wary of signing on the dotted line. Once you are comfortable that you have taken care of the rights, you can continue the development process.

An option acquisition agreement should include the following:

- The names of the individuals involved in the agreement
- The date of the agreement
- The nature of the option agreement and the duration of the option
- The compensation, including how the compensation will be distributed
- Verification that the individual granting the option has the right to do so
- Agreement about how the credits for the project will read

- What happens if the individual purchasing the agreement does not pay on time
- Whether the purchaser of the agreement can assign the rights to another party
- Any miscellaneous stipulations of importance to either party
- Signatures

Attaching a Star, Writer, or Showrunner During the Development Process

The question of whether to add another element, such as a star, is a difficult one to answer. Enlisting the services of a major performer may be just the addition necessary to push the project into the win column. For example, the word on the street may be that Les Moonves at CBS is looking for a vehicle to star Jason Alexander, and thus attaching Alexander to your show might seem like a good idea. But there are significant risks to star attachments. The performer, for example, may not be right for the part. The star in question may not fit the format of the show. Should the entire concept be distorted to accommodate the style of a star with reputed "heat"?

There have been so many star failures (Figure 4.1) that attaching even the seemingly most-bankable star is risky. Also, although some networks, such as CBS, are consistently star driven, many, such as TBS, do not want stars attached during development, making the decision about attachments even more complex. If you attach the "wrong" star, your project is dead at the start.

Some networks, such as ABC, are reluctant to entertain projects with stars attached; they do not want to ruffle egos by passing on a performer because they do not like a project. They do not want to hurt their chances of casting that performer in a show they like.

Star	Program	Network	Season
Sally Field	The Court	ABC	2001–2002
Richard Dreyfuss	The Education of Max Bickford	CBS	2001–2002
Joan Cusack	What About Joan?	ABC	2000–2001 2001–2002
Jason Alexander	Bob Patterson	ABC	2001–2002
Geena Davis	The Geena Davis Show	ABC	2000–2001
Bette Midler	Bette	CBS	2000–2001
Nathan Lane	Encore! Encore!	NBC	1998–1999
Chevy Chase	The Chevy Chase Show	Fox	1993–1994

Figure 4.1
Recent star failures on television.

Also, many believe that television creates its own stars. For example, NBC's hit comedy "Friends" made stars of its "unknown" cast, catapulting them to salaries of $1 million per episode in the show's final year. Most mass-market movies are wary of unknown performers, preferring to cast established names. Many of these became stars through television—for example, Robin Williams, a graduate of ABC's "Mork & Mindy," and Eddie Murphy, a graduate of NBC's "Saturday Night Live."

Similarly, attaching the wrong showrunner or the wrong writer to a project can hurt your chances before you leave the starting gate. For example, a producer who did not do his homework about who was "in" and who was "out" was surprised that Lifetime passed on his high-profile project based on a bestselling book. His project was passed on because he had attached a writer who was out of favor.

The Role of Agents

Agents play a significant role in the early stages of the development process for cable and commercial television. Agents are aware of the needs at the cable and commercial networks. If ABC, for example, needs a drama for 10:00

Thursday nights, if CBS needs to fill a hole on Friday nights at 8:00, or if Showtime wants to get out of the comedy series business, the agents are able to guide their clients accordingly. Agents also have access to material, and they can "package" a program by bringing key creative elements together.

Packaging is a complex art and a lucrative one for the agencies. Agents collect a 10% fee for representing a client, but if a **package commission** is added, the agency receives additional income. For example, if a director, star, and writer are packaged, the agency receives a 10% commission on all three salaries plus a package fee ranging from 3 to 5%. Many credit the Creative Artists Agency (CAA) under Bill Haber and Mike Ovitz with perfecting the art of packaging.

When packaging was conceived in the 1970s, the package commission was justifiable and generally accepted by production companies and distributors. But over time, agencies sometimes insisted on a package commission even when they only represented one creative element. They reasoned that their client (a major star, for example) made the project viable; therefore, they were entitled to a package commission. This was interpreted by buyers as a power play in which an agency used the appeal of a client to extract a higher commission for itself. The device still raises hackles when it is employed with marginal validity, but most agencies happily engage in this profitable practice.

Development Deals

Everyone in the entertainment business wants to have an edge when it comes to development. Producers, in particular, spend many hours figuring how they can best beat the system. Some producers develop many projects, figuring that the more projects they have, the better their chances of striking pay dirt; others internally develop a limited number of projects, figuring their chances are better if they focus on their "passion" projects.

In recent years, the major studios have sought to beat the development odds by striking development arrangements known as **pod deals.** These are seven-figure deals, such as those Gavin Polone's Pariah Productions and Dream-Works made with NBC Productions in 2002. NBC hopes to get a lock on some successful shows with high-profile, quality production companies, enabling it to avoid prolonged stays in development hell, although the deal with Pariah was terminated in 2004 over disagreements about comedy development.

Getting Ready for the Pitch: Creating a Log Line

Lots of research and planning goes into preparing to **pitch.** First, all aspects of the story have to be worked out: What is the genre? What is the opening scene? Is the start of the story going to capture an audience? Are the conflicts clearly established? Is the resolution of the story satisfying? Are there any "jumps" in the story—that is, logic leaps? The creative team has to know all aspects of the story to be prepared to answer any questions that come up in the pitch meeting.

The pitch must then be rehearsed and perfected, often in front of a critical audience or a mirror. Mock dialogues are played out: "If we're asked where the conflict is between the mother and daughter, Irv will respond by pointing out that . . ." Or, "If we're asked where the character of Amanda worked before the start of the story, we have to have a ready answer: She worked in St. Louis."

One of the most important things in preparing a pitch is coming up with a strong **log line.** What exactly is a log line? Many writers and producers have stumbled when it comes to defining a log line. It is not a straight summary of the project. It goes to the heart of what a project is about in one or two sentences, defining the theme of the project. Thus, saying that your project "deals with a man who lives in the woods and finds true love when a tourist shows up" is more of a plot summary than a log line. A log line would take the same story idea and suggest a bigger meaning. For example, "When a man who has lived on his own in the wilderness meets a woman who is on a wilderness trek, he realizes that his cherished loneliness is a facade that hides his fear of commitment. It's *Jeremiah Johnson* meets *Sleepless in Seattle.*"

Writing an Effective Log Line

Time spent fine-tuning a log line is time well spent. The log line usually introduces a project; it is extremely important for a seller to get it right. The log line has to suggest a connection to what is going on in society and, possibly more importantly, what is going on in movies and television. This is why so many effective sellers describe their projects as "successful movie No. 1 meets successful movie No. 2." This is shorthand that buyers understand. Referring to successful television programs can also work ("Friends" meets "That '70s Show"), although most "meeting" in television pitches is done with theatrical films. Cynics might say this is because buyers do not watch much television and they might miss the intended connection; others believe that a movie reference is an easier, more universal connection.

Even if the meeting you have selected does not make a great deal of sense upon close inspection, it can generate interest. For example, "*Jaws* meets *Saving Private Ryan*" may not make sense, but it might be enough to get the buyer's attention. You would hope that no explanation would be requested about *how* that particular meeting works.

In one or two sentences, the log line has to suggest change, such as a character's growth from one set of values to another. It also needs to suggest action. Starting with the words "when" or "after" is helpful in this context. For example, "When a 20-year-old virgin decides to find the perfect man to marry, she must reject many inappropriate suitors who are interested in her for the wrong reasons." This log line suggests that changes will take place in the woman's life.

A log line such as "When a teenager's life is threatened, he feels he must take the law into his own hands until a stranger shows him a better way" suggests change and action: the teenager will take the law into his own hands until he learns the better way at a turning point in the story. A log line such as "After a woman's husband of nearly 50 years dies, she must learn to live on her own with the help of the neighbor she previously ignored" coupled with "It's *Terms of Endearment* meets *Driving Miss Daisy*" might generate buyer interest because it indicates changes in the woman's life and because she will see her neighbor in a new light, something many people can identify with.

Many successful pitches start with the words "when" or "after;" a second sentence uses the "meets" analogy. Practicing coming up with log lines that "flow" is worth the time spent. Buyers need a strong log line to use with all the people who will be evaluating the project's potential (schedulers, members of the promotion department, the business affairs department, the research staff who will use the log line to test the viability of a project, etc.). Sellers who provide strong log lines for buyers greatly facilitate the development process.

Getting a Meeting

Before a producer can go in to pitch, however, a meeting has to be secured. To request a pitch meeting, you generally must prepitch the story. What this means is that a preview, that is, a teaser, has to be offered to the prospective buyer. A call simply asking for a meeting without providing any information about the proposed "arena" of the pitch usually fails to get you in the door. Unless you are a producer–writer with an incredible track record, you rarely will be invited to make a formal presentation without "clearing the arena." It is regarded a real compliment to be told that no prepitch is needed. "Just come on in and we'll sit down and talk" are the words producers–writers long to hear.

A successful prepitch is short, just enough to whet the appetite. "It's a dramedy about doctors with issues along the lines of FX's 'Nip/Tuck' but with more of a reality base" might be enough to generate interest, particularly if a well-placed agent has discovered that the targeted network is in the market for a "hip" show about doctors.

The goal of the over-the-phone prepitch is to get an in-person meeting. Being told that the arena shows promise but is not what the network is looking for ("I don't want to waste your time coming in" is the way the buyer will generally phrase the rejection) sends a producer back to the drawing board. Being told to send a few pages without being granted a meeting is only a half victory. The pages could sell themselves, but the in-person meeting provides a much better platform.

Some producers, however, have perfected the phone pitch and prefer to do their selling over the phone. These producers are happy to send the pages and any other requested information. Not scheduling a meeting can save several weeks, and a project's heat can cool in these weeks. Not taking 3 or 4 hours to attend a meeting can also allow more time for additional phone sales.

STEPS TO SUCCESSFUL PITCHING

Judith A. Polone, president of movies and miniseries at Lions Gate Entertainment, has been one of television's most successful sellers for more than 20 years. Her impressive string of credits includes "JFK: Reckless Youth" (1993), "Riot" (1997), "Wildflower" (1991), and "Malice in Wonderland" (1985). Polone believes strongly that "We are all sellers, and we have to be good at it." A master of the phone pitch, Polone has the following suggestions for making successful pitches:

- Approach the pitch with confidence.
- Be passionate about what you are pitching.
- Know your material.

- Be brief. If you know your material well, you can pitch it succinctly and effectively.
- Be aggressive, but temper your drive and ambition with humor.
- Refer to a successful project similar to yours.
- If you are pitching a book, read it. Do not rely on coverage that may misrepresent the book. (Polone once got a development deal for a book that had been turned down "all over town" because the coverage used was bad. She read the book herself and found the appeal that the coverage ignored.)
- Do your homework. Know what the buyers are looking for and locate material that suits the marketplace.

- Prepare "leave behind" pages for the buyer that clearly describe the project. Revise the pages as many times as necessary.
- Create a solid log line.
- Get to know your buyers as individuals so that you can engage them on a topic of mutual interest before you start your pitch.
- Occasionally, try a "reverse sell" by teasing the buyer with opening salvos such as "This project may not be right for you," "This project may be a little highbrow/too edgy for you," or "This project is too good for you." The reverse sell is tricky and it can backfire, but, used effectively, it can challenge the buyer to question why the project is not right or is too edgy, enabling you to segue into a strong pitch. Telling a broadcast network executive that the project you are pitching is too edgy, possibly a better fit on HBO, can be effective when the broadcast networks seek to be more like cable.
- Also occasionally, challenge the buyer with closing remarks such as "I want you to know that I am going to sell this project and you will have to program against it" or "After you have seen this tape, tell me you don't want to make this movie."

The Pitch Meeting

Sellers usually do not have much choice about to whom they will be pitching. Most often, the network hierarchy determines the protocol, and sellers go to assigned development executives. If, however, a member of the selling team is a major player, appeals can be made to pitch to the executive who has the power to say "yes" in the room.

Most sellers agree that pitching to the top gun is best; they will go to great lengths, calling in favors and jockeying for position, to get a meeting with the "right person." For example, when an agent found out that his client was going to pitch to a midlevel executive, he complained that the project was "seriously being undermined" by this faux pas. The agent made a quick, personal call to the head of the department, asking her to sit in on the meeting that same afternoon as a courtesy to him and to the client.

There are, however, some sellers who prefer to pitch to an underling because they feel the lower-level executive will fight harder on their behalf. They believe that department heads have so much on their plates that a single project does not warrant their full attention.

At the appointed hour, the sellers travel to the office of the designated buyer to present their idea. The composition of the selling team may range from two to six people. Small production houses will usually be represented by just a major executive of the company and the chief creative person (writer or producer) connected with the concept. Large companies will arrive with some combination involving a major executive, a development person, the executive producer, the line producer, the writer, and possibly an agent or, if it is CAA, two agents (CAA likes to show its muscle by frequently sending a couple of key agents).

The buyer may be represented by just one person or by an ensemble, usually depending on the stature of the producing company. If a superstar producer or writer is making the presentation, the audience can include the president of the entertainment division, the head of all development, and the entire staff of whichever department is appropriate—comedy, drama, reality, etc. Networks are eager to be ingratiating with superstars, and a large turnout for a pitch is a way to demonstrate respect and affection.

The meeting never starts immediately. No matter how gigantic the project, it is obligatory that the first few minutes be devoted to trivia. ("How 'bout the breakup of the Lakers?") Eventually, one of the sellers, most likely the senior executive, will begin the presentation with a few scene-setting remarks such as the talent of the writer, the appeal of whatever story form they are about to present, or the time needs of the network. The presentation is then turned over to the principal architect of the show, who describes its concept, characters, and appeals.

A successful pitch presentation transforms a room into the world of the proposed show, with fully realized characters and well-laid-out sample scenes. The pitch will reveal the show's solid structure and the potential for future episodes. Agents often point out why the show has the necessary goods. Everyone on the selling side is there to lend support to the project.

Most buyers wait for the presentation to be completed before they offer questions and observations. At this point, the seller's hours of preparation can pay off. The more buyer doubt removed, the better the chance of a pickup. Any suggested improvement by the buyer should be treated with the utmost enthusiasm; the time to quibble over changes is *after* the deal has been secured.

Some sellers are brilliant at pitch meetings and can make a program sound like another "Frasier." Frequently, the verbal virtuosity conceals conceptual weaknesses. The buyer is well advised to enjoy the performance but remain vigilant; viewers will be watching the flawed show not the dazzling pitch. On the other hand, many program creators are not born sales people, and their presentations fall short of the shows'

potential. Buyers must train themselves to pierce through the bungled rhetoric and find the essence of the idea.

Many sellers and some buyers do not like the pitch process. Even a production legend such as David Susskind, whose programs won so many Emmy awards he was elected to the Television Academy's Hall of Fame, loathed the pitch process. He called it "demeaning, nerve-wracking, and exhausting." Despite his revulsion, he was an effective spokesperson for his projects and enjoyed more than 30 years of prosperity and prestige.

Allen Sabinson is a programming executive who has had successful runs at NBC, ABC, and A&E. Sensitive to the torment some individuals experience pitching, he once cut short a writer's pitch because the writer was sweating profusely, failing to put words together, and dropping his disorganized notes on the floor. Not wishing to see the writer in such distress, Sabinson offered to read some pages "as soon as they were ready."

Some buyers seriously question the pitch process. For example, Susan Baerwald, while head of miniseries at NBC, never embraced pitches as a way to tell whether a project had the makings of a successful movie. For her, pitching reflects a seller's personality and salesmanship, not a project's value. Many networks and studios internally develop shows, limiting the need for producers to come in and pitch. During internal development, the buyers come up with the concepts and "break down the stories," later "kissing in" an outside producer or turning the project over to a producer with a deal with the studio or network. Nevertheless, pitching remains one of the primary ways projects can ignite the interest of buyers.

For additional information about pitching, see Kathie Fong Yoneda's helpful *The Script Selling Game: A Holly-*

wood Insider's Look at Getting Your Script Sold and Produced.

"Laying Pipe" for a Pass

Following the seller's presentation, the buyer will generally ask several questions and then make some sort of pronouncement. If the pitch stands little chance, the buyer will most often "lay pipe," as the practice is called, by saying the project, although "very interesting," may not be what the network is looking for at that time. Many buyers prefer to lay pipe than to "pass in the room." A quick pass may be more efficient, but some buyers do not want to burst a seller's bubble, especially right after a heartfelt pitch.

Some buyers, however, make the mistake of being too positive at a pitch meeting by praising the project too highly. This leads sellers to believe that a sale has been made when no sale was in the offing, causing many a disgruntled seller to face the reality of a pass several days after a pitch meeting. Thus, inexperienced programmers are instructed by their in-house mentors to lay pipe. By doing this, the buyer has something to fall back on if sellers complain they were misled.

One producer who heard the head buyer talking about "finding the right writer" for the proposed project assumed she had a deal. When the junior executive called to pass on the project, the producer complained loudly that there had been no hint of a pass, that everything said by the department head indicated a "go." This kind of situation benefits no one. Bruised egos ensue, and the authority and management savvy of the network come into question, again reinforcing the need to lay pipe.

If the buyer is convinced there are no fundamental flaws and the production, with proper scripting, casting, and execution, has a chance, he or she will most likely pitch it to the head of the department. This leads to another kind of pitch meeting, specifically, a department meeting where all the executives pitch the projects they like to the boss. These midlevel or junior buyers often have less time to do their pitching than the sellers. They have to select the strongest selling points. They also have to make sure the log line that describes the project's premise is on target; this often requires them to revise the seller's original log line to make it work for the boss.

At other times, a detailed **bible** or **treatment** that outlines the concept, major characters, and future plot lines is requested by the head buyer. Sometimes, a follow-up meeting with the sellers is required for the pitch to be repeated for the department or network head. If the show's potential is subsequently embraced, the parties enter negotiations to close a deal.

Fundamentals of the Deal

No money will ever be handed by the buyer to the seller until a contract is in place. Thus, when an executive says, "I like it, let's go forward," it means, "Let's go forward to the business affairs department where your lawyer and our lawyer will discuss terms and conditions." It is not within the province of this book to cover the range of program deals, some of which weigh slightly less than an air conditioner.

Development is an expensive process. NBC, for example, is estimated to have spent $40 to $50 million on development for the 2003–2004 season.[3] Buyers have many concerns when they seek to protect their investments. These include license fee cost per episode, the length of time their **hold** is exclusive (cannot be taken to another buyer), **right of**

first refusal (the ability to match the best offer of a competing buyer when the initial term is completed), who pays cost overruns, and creative control. The sellers are equally interested in these matters and attempt to preserve their profit potential.

When the contract is essentially agreed upon, the project can proceed. In the real world, work gets under way long before papers are signed. If it did not, few shows would ever get on the air. Companies that have dealt with each other many times are sufficiently confident that a deal will eventually be made. Unless substantive disagreements emerge, the parties proceed as though the documents will eventually be signed. At times, the decibel levels go ballistic and the cage rattling is deafening, but nobody makes money unless there is a picture on the screen, a fact both sides are aware of. Most deals eventually close, although a tight money climate can stymie a deal, greatly increasing everyone's anxiety level.

Public Television Development

The word "development" has a different connotation in the noncommercial structure. Most public broadcasting organizations have a department of development that is responsible for obtaining grant money. This department is often compared to the sales department of a commercial broadcaster because it is responsible for bringing in revenue. As the "public" television name suggests, some of the operating budget is derived from the public (i.e., tax money allocated from the federal government), but public money has steadily become scarcer. From 1998 to 2003, for example, according to PBS's annual report, public funds made up roughly 10% of the network's operating budget.[4] Most funds (more than 60%) came from

"program underwriters," corporations, and other organizations. Theoretically, the organizations that donate money to public broadcasting do not influence the content of the programs, but sometimes whether or not a program reaches the airwaves depends on the financial resources. So, in that way, the fundraising undertaken by development departments affects program decision making.

Public television prides itself on being different from commercial television, seeking to air programming that avoids sinking to the lowest common denominator; however, the expanding world of cable has cut into public television's long-held dominance of quality programming, adding to the difficulties public television is experiencing.

A writer or producer seeking to develop a show for public television needs to survey the programming landscape carefully to come up with a show concept that coincides with public television's mission to promote quality. In addition, because of the financial crisis public television is experiencing, it is becoming almost essential to have the grant money in hand when the proposal for a show is made.

Syndication Development

In syndication, the process is different from that in cable, commercial, and public television. As explained in Chapter 2, syndicators sell their shows directly to stations. They need to clear close to 80% of national coverage before deciding to proceed to full-production mode. According to Mike Stornello, senior vice president of development for major syndicator King World Productions ("The Oprah Winfrey Show," "Dr. Phil," "Jeopardy," and "Wheel of Fortune"), it takes most of 2 years to develop a show for syndication.

Stornello adds that there is lots of tweaking and changing during development to ensure success. Syndication development often revolves around a strong personality in a talk format, but syndication development can also focus on a strong idea as syndication seeks to move into cable.[5]

Once the prototype of the show is completed and the decision has been made to go to market, the show is basically in the hands of the marketing specialists. Occasionally, the programmers will be asked to participate in the selling effort, particularly with executives of station groups or stations in large cities. These buyers like to hear about series plans directly from those responsible for the production. The programmers will no doubt have to attend the NATPE convention.

NATPE was founded in 1963 to bring together station program directors for an exchange of ideas and viewpoints. By the mid-1970s, the NATPE convention had become the most important event in the business life of syndication producers and distributors. All pilots, demonstrators, and promotion campaigns were geared for the big push at the convention. With such spirited competition among highly creative and aggressive personalities, the convention gradually took on a carnival atmosphere. A buyer could not walk 30 paces without being invited to a seller's suite by a trio of sideshow barkers, models in nuns' habits, or a pair of gorillas. The taste level plunged to unacceptable depths, and in the 1980s, NATPE officials took steps to curb some of the more outrageous promotions.

Syndicators have spent hundreds of thousands, even millions, of dollars to construct exhibition areas designed to attract buyers into screening rooms to view pilots. A syndicator's principal objective is to build a sales momentum that will overrun the convention. To encourage this momentum, syndicators make frequent and imaginative use of hyperbole. Every show is "snowballing," all station lineups and coverage are "growing too fast to calculate," and every "I'll think about it" becomes "It's a wrap." Announcements at NATPE can be politely referred to as an excess of exuberance.

In recent years, the convention has become somewhat less pivotal to a syndicator's survival. Many distributors discovered that if they waited for the convention (usually held in January or February) to launch their major sales effort, they would be too late. Competitors would have contacted key markets months earlier and picked up all the best clearances. At NATPE, syndicators often do not set up exhibition booths on the convention floor and instead hold meetings in suites at the convention hotels. This practice reduces costs and lessens the carnival atmosphere that characterized NATPE for so many years.

Now NATPE is used more for muscling the wafflers and establishing those all-important relationships, because the entertainment business still operates in terms of who you know and who will take your calls. For in-studio producers who are attending their first NATPE, it can become puzzling. When they hear that the syndicator cleared Chicago, they become euphoric. Then they notice that the sales staff is somber.

"Why aren't you excited?"
　"Because it's a **tier deal.**"
"What's that?"
　"It means we've got prices for six different time periods."
　"So?"
　"So, if they run it at 2:00 A.M., you won't get any viewers and we won't make a dime."

Station Development

When stations decide to program a local show, they do not go through the elaborate development process engaged in by the networks. The ideas usually come from within the programming department and are in response to some need in the community. As the amount of local programming has dwindled in the last few years, so has the amount of development.

Another reason for downgrading local development is that many stations now belong to large groups: Fox, Tribune, Westinghouse, etc. The creation of new programs is the responsibility of a corporate production unit rather than the program directors at the individual stations.

One variable that could cause a resurgence in local nonnews production is changing **station compensation.** As the trend continues toward reducing or eliminating the network's financial contributions—in the form of payments by the networks to stations for airing a show—the possibility of station defections from certain times and **dayparts** grows. Some stations may conclude that a locally produced program in which the station keeps all the revenue may be a better risk than a network-supplied show for which there is no compensation and just a few spots in and around the program for local sale. If this were to happen, the program director could quickly become a busy person in the creative field.

Figure 4.2
"Oprah Winfrey Presents: Tuesdays With Morrie," starring *(a)* Jack Lemmon and *(b)* Hank Azaria, *illustrates the complex television development process.* (Photo courtesy the Academy of Television Arts & Sciences.)

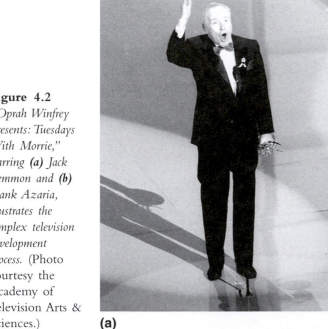

(a)

(b)

THE DEVELOPMENT OF "OPRAH WINFREY PRESENTS: TUESDAYS WITH MORRIE"

The development of the television movie "Oprah Winfrey Presents: Tuesdays with Morrie" (Figure 4.2) can be used as a representative case study. Kate Forte, the president of Harpo, Oprah's production company, had an advance copy of the manuscript of *Tuesdays with Morrie* by Mitch Albom about his relationship with his former teacher, Morrie Schwartz. Forte sent it to her executive at ABC with a note saying she saw something special in the book and wondered whether ABC would be interested in putting it into development.

The executive agreed and pitched it to his boss, who passed on it, saying it was about two men sitting in a room talking and would be of little interest to viewers. Refusing to take no for an answer, the executive and Harpo's director of development, Susan Heyer, redid the pitch pages, stressing Albom's life as a sports writer to "open up" the movie and get it out of Morrie's house. The revised pages did the trick and the project was put into development. A-list writer Tom Rickman, whose credits include *Coal Miner's Daughter* and *Everybody's All American*, was hired to write the teleplay. After the book became a bestseller and Harpo was wooed to abandon television and produce the film as a feature, Forte refused, saying ABC had backed the project when only a manuscript existed and she was not going to switch from television to features. The movie went on to win an Emmy Award as the best television movie of the 1999–2000 season, helping ABC break HBO's hold on the category.

The Pilot

Once the buyers in cable and commercial television are satisfied that the program is fundamentally sound, the creative team is equal to the creative challenge, and the script is in shooting shape, they face a key decision: to make or not to make a **pilot,** that is, an episode that will enable buyers to judge how the executed script plays on the small screen. This decision is not an easy one. At risk is an enormous outlay of money. A half-hour pilot in 2003 cost between $1.6 million and $2 million.[6] Pilots cost more than the average episode of a series because there are no economies of scale and anything done for the first time is more time-consuming and expensive. Furthermore, if a pilot goes to series, the cost of the sets and props can be amortized, that is, spread out over the length of the commitment. But if the show is not picked up for more episodes, the entire expense of the pilot must be laid against the program development budget.

It is not uncommon for the cost of the pilot to be greater than the network's financial contribution. The production company must either cut corners to deliver the pilot within budget or cover the additional costs. Usually they choose the latter. A downsized, on-the-cheap pilot might quickly become a dead pilot. Because this is the only sales opportunity the project will have, the producers, amid much muttering, often spend the extra money.

However, because costs have risen so drastically and network revenues have dropped so precipitously in recent years, network executives increasingly order **minipilots,** or **presentations,** (selected scenes) instead of full episodes. The argument in favor of these truncated prototypes is that they reveal enough of the core idea and the staff's execution to make a sound judgment at a substantially reduced price tag. The argument against them is that the chosen sample may be "loaded" (with guest stars, action scenes, etc.) and not be indicative of the series. Minipilots sometimes become more useful as sales tools than as a basis for program decisions. "I'd much rather do a minipilot," said Saul Turteltaub, veteran writer–producer of network

Figure 4.3
ABC developed "Karen Sisco" for the 2003–2004 season, hoping that it would appeal to its target audience. (Photo © ABC Photography Archives.)

but some failed pilots air on cable channel Trio's "Brilliant, But Cancelled" or as summer "specials;" most of the time, however, they simply disappear, failures on the development highway. Clearly, the pilot process is fickle, expensive, and draining, rather like gambling in Las Vegas. Sometimes it takes a lot of spins before hitting the jackpot. For example, George Clooney was cast in 15 failed pilots before he hit television gold with "ER" in 1994, and Don Johnson was in 5 before "Miami Vice."[8] But when the right pilot comes along, the payoff can be huge, which is why so many producers, writers, and performers continue to put themselves through pilot hell every year.

comedies. "It's much easier to be terrific for 8 minutes than for 30."

Even though the minipilot has its flaws and can lead to blundered program choices, it is here to stay because of the new economic realities facing the industry.

In his article "The Wasteland," about the 2001 pilot season, Austin Bunn provided an in-depth examination of the pilot process. He wrote, "A network will buy 100 pitches to make into scripts and spend millions turning 20 into 'pilots.' These pilots are all made during the same three months in the spring, which creates, as one producer called it, 'a climate of fear' that descends on Los Angeles—'fear' because in that mad dash to delivery, these pilots, despite staggering infant-mortality rates, begin inevitably to matter to their creators. In mid–May, each network usually 'picks up' somewhere between 5 and 10 pilots to become series for the fall. Roughly two thirds of the pilots, the best efforts of each network, are stillborn."[7]

Presentations cannot be broadcast because they are not polished enough,

Development Ratios

Broadcast outlets develop on different ratios depending on their specific needs. The standard **development ratio** used to be four shows for every one that makes the final cut, but the development ratios can vary greatly. For example, in 2002, ABC developed about 90 drama scripts for possibly four or five slots because the network needed a bona fide drama hit. For the 2002–2003 season, NBC heard more than 200 comedy pitches, 54 scripts were ordered, and 15 pilots were made.[9] For the 2003–2004 season, ABC was still in need of a hit and had high hopes for its series "Karen Sisco" (Figure 4.3), although it turned out that its comedy development got better viewer response.

Some networks tend to go overboard when it comes to pilot development. Allison Romano, in "MTV: Operating Without a Net," observes MTV's unconventional style. She writes, "In a busy year, most basic-cable networks might greenlight just five pilots, putting two or three on the air as regular series.

A broadcast network might make 20 pilots. MTV moves at lightning speed, pumping out 50 potential projects. The mantra, quite simply, is that more is more."[10] This method produced the biggest hit of the 2001–2002 cable television season, the reality series "The Osbournes" (Figure 4.4).

Testing

Gone are the days of the fabled, gut-instinct buyers who watched a pilot and before the lights came up said, "I like it. Put it on," or "It's lousy. Bury it." Today when the pilot or minipilot is screened by network executives, it is just the start of a lengthy process of assessment through research. This phase of program selection is dealt with in detail in Chapter 5.

The reasons buyers require extensive statistical support before they make a program choice has been the subject of many conferences, panel discussions, and print interviews. The cynics say the buyers have no faith in their own judgments and need mounds of data to justify their decisions. They also claim buyers engage in research to avoid later criticism. If a program goes on the air and bombs, their excuse is that the research was faulty and misleading.

Not so, counter the defenders. The stakes are high and the criteria for success are inexact. Furthermore, as objective as network executives try to be, they are products of their backgrounds, which may not be representative of national tastes and interests. Why should they not sound out the opinions of those who will be watching (or ignoring) the product? Every manufacturer in the country test-markets products before launching them nationally—why not networks?

Figure 4.4
"The Osbournes" was a phenomenon when it aired on MTV, changing the face of reality television. (Globe Photos, Inc.)

The Decision

In most cases, before a final judgment is made, several company executives are consulted. These usually include people from programming, sales, research, promotion, production, scheduling, finance, planning, and top management.

The need for each of these disciplines is obvious. The show is worthless if the sales department cannot sell it, the promotion department has no hook on which to hang a campaign, or both. There is no sense in proceeding if the finance people say it is too expensive to ever be profitable or if the research staff says there is only a small audience available at the intended time. In many instances, experts in a specialized aspect of the company need to be consulted, for example, the standards and practices division if the program contains borderline scenes and language. Although censors are involved in the pilot process, the finished product can often present unforeseen concerns that need to be addressed before a show is given a 13-week order.

But the pilot process, as unwieldy as it may seem, is soundly constructed. Without input from all affected parties, a programmer could blunder fatally because of some overlooked item. Still, the final decision is rarely a consensus of all the viewpoints. Often, there are two or more screening rooms; senior executives are situated in the A room and junior executives are in the B room. The executives in the B room may have lots of opinions and be willing to voice them with passion, but it is what goes on in the A room that matters. After a program has been thoroughly discussed in both the A and the B rooms, two or three top members of the inner circle will usually go off for a private conclave where *the decision* is made.

Globalization

Although the global market may not be the primary concern during the development process, it should never be ignored. Success abroad is necessary for a show to generate positive cash flow. The foreign market may be in constant flux, but, as explained previously, it should not be overlooked. To do so limits a producer's financial options.

Some markets, such as China, are tolerant of violence but adverse to sex and nudity. In Germany, bloody scenes are taboo but even frontal nudity is fine. During the development process, producers have to be aware of the adjustments that might be needed for different markets to maximize foreign sales.

This holds true for franchises and video games. For example, "American Idol" started in the United Kingdom as "Pop Idol." It was a major success, becoming a likely candidate for export. When franchises of this show were set

up in approximately 19 countries, some key changes to the format had to be made to avoid clashing with local customs. As Charles Goldsmith points out in his article "How 'Idols' Around the World Harmonize with Local Viewers," the word "idol" cannot be used in Germany because it carries Hitler-like connotations. Thus, the show is called "Germany Seeks the Superstar."[11] Each version of "American Idol" needs to be adapted to suit local tastes "while keeping the show recognizable as the 'Idol' franchise." Savvy producers who envision franchises around the globe have to develop a concept that can successfully be adapted for many countries, as with the 100 or so versions of "Who Wants to Be a Millionaire" that existed in 2003–2004.

Similarly, the $25 billion video game industry has to adjust its games to meet the demands of individual countries. Topless women in games distributed in Europe sport bikini tops in the American versions.[12] Violent sex scenes in the games distributed in Japan are toned down for the American versions.

Sellers lucky enough to see their shows journey successfully through the development process may not readily admit to the networks that the "tweaks" made during production are being done to adjust to the foreign market, but this is often the case. Network programming executives care about the audiences *in* America, not the audiences abroad, but savvy producers have to adjust their development toward foreign audiences. This is particularly true in the development of one-shot television movies, where introducing a German character as the fourth or fifth lead can help the German sale. It also applies to series development—an element introduced in a pilot that makes it to air could turn out to be the key ingredient that guarantees success abroad.

Format	Number of Stations March 1996	Number of Stations March 2001	% Change
Country	45	30	−33.3
Urban adult contemporary	11	12	+9.1
Hot adult contemporary	20	20	0
Alternative	40	39	−2.5
Urban	28	28	0
Contemporary hit radio—Rhythm	15	15	0
Rock	20	20	0
Adult contemporary	18	20	+11.1
Active rock	20	19	−5.0
Adult alternative	20	20	0
Contemporary hit radio—Pop	45	45	0
Jazz	20	20	0
TOTALS	302	288	−4.6

(a)

Formats from fall 1996 that no longer existed in fall 2001	Formats in fall 2001 that did not exist in fall 1996
'70s hits	'70s and '80s
Adult hits	'80s and '90s
Black adult contemporary	'80s hits
Christian country	Classic middle of the road
Urban inspirational	Hip-hop
	Kids
	Mix adult contemporary
	Modern adult contemporary
	New age
	New rock
	Tropical

(b)

RADIO DEVELOPMENT

Development in radio deals more with formats than with individual shows. Much of the programming develops itself once the format is decided. For most radio stations, the format is a particular type of music, but talk formats such as all news, all sports, and all talk can be chosen. Selecting a format involves thinking about the type of peripheries, such as news and features, that will be used with the basic format.

Developing a Format

One of the problems with selecting (or maintaining) a music format is that music is constantly evolving. "New wave" does not stay "new," "progressive rock" might not "progress," and "alternative music" may enter the mainstream (Figure 4.5). When a particular type of music, such as rock, becomes popular, it tends to be subdivided into categories

(hard rock, soft rock, classic rock, album-oriented rock, etc.) so that stations can have a unique sound.

Nevertheless, format names exist, and format changes are made with fairly regular frequency, partly to take into account the newer forms of music. The job of determining format is usually undertaken by top management that may or may not include the head of programming. Often the program director is hired after the format decision is made so that someone with knowledge about that particular type of music can be chosen. In some stations, a format change is made without the program director's involvement. If, for example, a station switches from easy listening to country, it simply fires the old program director (and disc jockeys) and hires a new one.

When a station first comes on the air, it must select a format. Few open frequencies are left in the United States, however, so few new stations come from

Figure 4.5
(a) Music formats through the years. The major music formats and the approximate number of major market stations playing them in 1996 and 2001, as compiled by the FCC. The "% Change" column illustrates the shifts in formats over time. Some formats have seen much change; others have seen none.
(b) Some radio formats have disappeared from the airwaves between 1996 and 2001; others have been added.

scratch. Format changes are common among established stations that are not doing well in the ratings and among stations recently purchased by new management (often because they were not doing well in the ratings and were about to go under financially).

THE DEVELOPMENT OF URBAN AND HIP-HOP RADIO

No radio format has seen a more dramatic rise in the last decade than the urban and hip-hop format. Rap or hip-hop began in the New York club and party scene in the 1970s, when deejays speaking on microphones over music would make "party shouts" either touting their own deejay talents or welcoming newcomers to the party. One of the first of these deejays, (later called emcees because they served as the "master of ceremonies" at the party) Kool Herc (a.k.a. Clive Campbell), would do a party shout such as "Kool Herc is in the house and he'll turn it out without a doubt." Over time, these shouts expanded into raps.

In 1979, the first commercial hip-hop song, "Rapper's Delight" by The Sugarhill Gang, was released. The song reached No. 4 on the black singles chart and received airplay on many black radio stations. Hip-hop sold its first gold album in 1984 with Run-DMC's self-titled album. The next year Run-DMC's *King of Rock* album reached platinum status, and 1986 saw Run-DMC collaborating with heavyweight rockers Aerosmith for the first hip-hop song, "Walk This Way," to reach Billboard's Top 10 pop singles, attesting to both the song's strong sales and its radio airplay.

In the early 1990s a few radio stations, notably those controlled by black-owned Radio One, switched to an urban format that prominently featured hip-hop music. But by 1993, there were only six hip-hop and rap radio stations in the United States. The years between 1993 and 2003, however, saw a meteoric rise in hip-hop's popularity, especially after hip-hop co-opted some of the more palatable melodic trappings of traditional pop music. Some point to white rappers, such as Vanilla Ice and, more recently, Eminem, entering the fray as forces that made hip-hop more acceptable to nonblack audiences.

By 2003, there were more than 150 hip-hop stations across the country, with hip-hop stations dominating the airwave ratings in each of the top 11 U.S. radio markets. In October 2003, the Billboard charts saw a first: their entire Top 10 pop singles list was occupied by black hip-hop artists, such as Beyonce, P. Diddy, Lil' Kim, Ludacris, Jay-Z, and 50 Cent. Even corporate America has gotten on the hip-hop bandwagon; McDonald's, Dr. Pepper, Sprite, and Kool-Aid have all used hip-hop jingles to reel in young consumers.[13]

Seeing the cash cow that companies such as Radio One were milking, major radio players such as Clear Channel and Cox Communications have dipped into the pot of gold, putting their own urban-flavored radio stations up against existing hip-hop stations in major markets. The competition, many commentators note happily, has forced old and new radio players alike to innovate and keep their ear out for the next big thing.

Management and Consultants

A booming business of radio doctors (consultants) has arisen to help stations make the decision regarding a format change. Some big companies that own numerous stations now have their own internal format "consultants." Often programming directors who preside over many different stations owned by one company in one area rely on outside consultants to help them navigate the formats they may be overseeing, from adult contemporary to pop to talk radio. Many smaller radio station owners or general managers do their own research to determine what format would be best, but some hire one of the consulting firms to assist. These consulting companies, or their equivalents within large companies, have run research studies in many cities and have developed a basic procedure that usually works.

They have developed a knowledge of the radio business that includes the following:

1. The appeals of various formats— They know, from studies they have conducted and from general industry reading, the pros and cons of the various formats and the type of people each appeals to.
2. Cost effectiveness of the various formats—Again through experience, they can fairly easily determine the costs of differing types of programming for specific markets. For example, all-news programming is more expensive than middle-of-the road music and can only be undertaken in markets large enough and rich enough to support it with advertising.

When the consultants come to town, they check out the area, looking mainly at the following:

1. Demographics—If the community contains many young people, their presence might be a determinant in planning for a format. If a large ethnic group is within the station's reach, this presents the possibility for a particular type of programming aimed at those people. The consultants use census data, Chamber of Commerce data, and personal tours of the community to determine demographic information.

2. Lifestyles—If the schools are on a split shift and, as a result, young people are available as listeners during the morning, this could affect the format and its accompanying features. If a city has massive traffic jams, this could mean more time needs to be devoted to traffic information than might otherwise be planned. Interviews with station management and with citizens of the community and trips to shopping malls, restaurants, and parks can give insight into lifestyles.
3. Sales of records and CDs—Although Internet sales and illegal swapping of music has cut severely into the business of local music stores, consultants may nonetheless visit music stores and talk to employees and customers to determine who is buying what type of music when and where. The age and sex of types of music purchasers is noted.

Consultants also thoroughly examine the competition by noting the following:

1. What is aired on all the competing stations—Consultants usually spend at least one full day listening to each station in the market. They log everything they hear—station identifications, disc jockey comments, news stories, editorials, features, etc. They make careful note of all the formats and features on the air.
2. The ratings of all stations—This consists of a thorough breakout of ratings data for each station that gives not only its overall rating number but also its rating according to specific demographics and specific times of day.
3. The **reach** of all the stations—Some stations are more powerful technically because of FCC requirements and therefore reach a larger geographic area. A weak station with a popular

format might not reach the whole market, so a more powerful station with the same format could attract listeners on the outskirts.

The consultants must consider the opinions of the top station management, including the following:

1. Programming biases—If the station owner abhors country western music and has stated that he or she does not want to be associated with a country music station, that alternative is ruled out, even if it seems to be the most economically viable one.
2. General objectives—Sometimes managers have specific personal or station goals. If someone wants the station to earn as much money as possible, a different approach can be used by the consultants than the one used for someone who wants to make a reasonable profit but to ensure that the station participates fully within the community.

Once the members of the consulting team have gathered and analyzed the information, they discuss it with the management and make recommendations. Perhaps they think the station should program adult contemporary with 10-minute news updates on the half hour. To support this, they might include that a large number of middle-aged people spend a great deal of time in their cars traveling between office and factory locations of a large employer whose business is spread over town. They want information mixed with relaxation. Although two other stations in town might program adult contemporary, one of them could be low powered and unable to be heard at two of the company's locations. The other could be the second highest-rated station in the market, with news for 2 minutes on the hour, so some of its

audience could be attracted by the longer news.

Management is free to ignore the advice of the consultants, and sometimes the chemistry between consultant and management is such that the two never come to an understanding. But usually management will listen to the advice it has paid dearly for and go with what is suggested. If it does not work—well, there are always other consultants.

Developing Programming

Once management, a consultant, or both have determined a format and an overall programming philosophy, individual programs must be developed. For many music stations, the switch from one program to another is virtually seamless. The disc jockey may change, but the sound of the music remains the same. The programming is not really developed; it is supplied. Someone has to select the music to be played from all the new submissions and old songs available. At most stations, the program director takes total charge of this; at other stations, the disc jockeys have a say as to what gets played. Stations that specialize in the newest of the new may have a person who does nothing all day but listen to submissions and winnow them down to a smaller stack that is passed to the program director.

For all-news stations, the programming is also supplied—in this case by daily events. A news director must decide which news services to use, which stories to cover, which stories to put on the air, and how much time to allot each story.

Talk stations give thought to the development of specific programs. Hosts and their topics of conversation are thought through, usually by the stations' programmers. Occasionally, potential talent will pitch an idea to a talk station and then be hired to conduct the show.

Profit and Other-Than-Profit Motives

Overall, radio development is different from that of television. The great degree of content fragmentation and the less expensive nature of radio separate it from its visual cousin. Despite media consolidation after the 1996 Telecommunications Act, many radio owners are still not publicly owned entities, unlike most television owners. For example, according to Michiguide.com, there are around 500 radio stations in the state of Michigan. More than 30% of those 500 stations are owned by 10 companies, with Clear Channel alone owning more than 5%. But the remaining 350 odd stations are owned by more than 100 companies, many owning just 1 or 2 stations.[14] Although many of the stations owned by smaller entities may be in smaller markets, their programming still goes on the air, and if it connects with listeners, it can still be successful. "Success" for smaller radio owners may be defined much differently than in the dollars-and-cents terms of big radio companies who have stockholders to satisfy.

Some commercial radio developers have goals that favor ideological or community service agendas over financial ones. For example, many liberal and Democratic groups and individuals, dismayed by the dominance of conservative voices in talk radio, such as Sean Hannity, Michael Savage, Michael Reagan, and Rush Limbaugh, have put up large sums of money to develop equivalent liberal shows. Many such shows have been commercial failures, such as those of former Texas agricultural commissioner Jim Hightower and even former New York Governor Mario Cuomo, but Democrats have not given up on their search. They started a radio network in 2004, Air America, with comedian, writer, and right-wing baiter Al Franken as its star host. In a similar vein, some nonprofit social advocacy groups have bought radio stations to provide content that aims to both entertain and empower. The Black United Fund of New York, a nonprofit organization that promotes social and economic development for the African-American community, bought WCKL 560 AM in Albany, New York. Kermit Eady, the organization's founder and president, said that the station "will surely aid in the empowerment process and could be our most valuable asset."[15]

With so many radio stations still in the hands of smaller organizations and "Ma and Pa" operations, there are many opportunities for people to pitch ideas for radio programming to these more accessible commercial radio station owners. There is also the opportunity for LPFM radio stations, which, according to the Center on Democratic Communications National Lawyers Guild, can be set up for as little as $2000, although the bureaucratic process of securing a license can be taxing and lengthy for a small operation.

Satellite Radio Development

Satellite radio, a subscription service providing a multitude of "stations," has different concerns than terrestrial radio. Even with the draw of satellite radio's superior sound quality and ubiquitous signal coverage, listeners can pick up terrestrial radio stations for free, so satellite radio must provide content attractive and different enough from terrestrial broadcasts that consumers will be willing to pay for it. Satellite radio, with its many stations, can pursue many avenues of development.

Because at least some of the operating costs of the network are covered by subscription fees, satellite radio can afford to offer stations with no or fewer

ABC News & Talk Channel	Electronica	The '90s Live on 9
Adult Contemporary Christian	Escape into the Movies	No Compromise African-American Talk
All Love Songs 24/7	Everything Funny	Old School R&B
Alternative Hits	Exciting Fox Style News 24/7	Old Time Country
America's First Trucker Channel	The Exclusive Satellite Radio Service of NASCAR	Politics & Business Coverage
America's Hottest & Most Controversial Talk Stars	Experts Talk	Pop Music Mix
Anything Can Happen...Really, Anything!	Family Laughs & Fun	A Premium Adult Channel
Audio Books & Radio Dramas	From Bluegrass to Newgrass	Progressive Country
The Authentic '60s Sound	From the World's Pop Charts	Progressive Rock & Fusion
The Awesome '80s	The Full Spectrum of BBC's News & Entertainment	Regional Mexican
Beautiful Music	Glorious Gospel	Rock en Español
Best of the '70s	The Golden Age of Radio	Round the Clock Country Hits
Big Bands & Hits of the '40s	The Greatest Music of the Last 1000 Years	Sinatra & Friends
Breaking Stories from Around the World	Greatest Soul Music of All Time	Singers & Songwriters
Broadway & Showtunes	Hard Alternative	Spanish Pop Hits
Capital of the Blues	High-Energy Combination of Sports News & Talk	Sports News & Play-by-Play Coverage
A Celebration of Folk Music	Hip-Hop from Day One	The Sound of Africa
Cerebral New Age	I Want My MTV—Radio!	Stadium Rock & Hairbands
Christian Music that Rocks	Industrial Strength Metal	The Tech Station
Christian Talk	Interactive Top 20 Countdown	Tejano
Classic Album Cuts	Kids & Disney	Top 40 Hits from Los Angeles
Classic Alternative	Latest Entertainment News & Celebrity Gossip	Traditional Jazz
Classic Country	Latin Jazz	24-Hour Crazed Morning Shows
Classical's Greatest Hits	The Lounge Lifestyle Lives On	24/7 Business & Finance Coverage
Club Hits	The Magic of the Human Voice	U.S. Government Hearings & Public Affairs
CNN in Spanish	Mellow Alternative	Uncensored Hip-Hop
Concerts & Interviews	The Most Mighty, Wicked, Dangerous Reggae Ever	Underground Dance
Contemporary Electric Jazz	Music First...Everywhere!	Unsigned Bands Only!
Deep Album Cuts	Music from the Caribbean	Urban Adult
The Definitive 24-Hour Sports News Network	The Nation's Premier Provider of Weather Information	Urban Top 40
Discovery Channel Comes to Radio	Neo Soul	Where Disco *Doesn't* Suck
Early Rock 'n' Roll	New Music...Now	World Music
Easy Jazz	News	
Eclectic Mix from Celtic to the Blues	The Next Generation of Radio For the...Next Generation	

(Xmradio.com.)

Figure 4.6
Station listings for XM Radio.

advertisements than terrestrial broadcasters. This can be a draw for listeners fatigued by commercials. But playing wall-to-wall music, for example, can also become fatiguing for listeners, so many satellite music stations, like terrestrial stations, have deejay patter between sections of music to mix things up.

Another way that satellite radio develops programming to attract subscribers is to provide programming unavailable elsewhere. Many satellite radio music stations feature interviews of and live performances by musical artists that far exceed the scope of such interviews and performances typically broadcast by terrestrial stations. There are also stations that feature lesser-known songs by major artists, music from independent record companies, and tighter niche programming than terrestrial stations. Terrestrial stations, to appeal to larger audiences and larger advertisers, must, for example, combine pop music from the 1990s with the 1980s and 2000s; satellite radio can set aside a station for each decade, even subdividing the decades into genres (Figure 4.6). But it is not as if there are unlimited stations on satellite radio, so strategic and researched choices must be made—on a national level.

Satellite radio can also attract listeners by providing niche programming aimed at a specific segment or group of the national population. Perhaps on a local level, this group or segment would not be big enough to justify the expense of a 24/7 radio operation. With satellite radio's national reach, a minority-population audience can reach significant numbers of listeners. The Sirius satellite network, for example, airs a station, OutQ, targeting the gay and lesbian community. The network's controversial decision to develop the station in 2003 garnered significant media attention, helping the lesser-known network to gain visibility under the shadow of its more well-known competitor, XM Radio. It also helped Sirius to distinguish itself from XM Radio, since the two networks mostly offer similar programming choices.

Public Radio Development

Where commercial radio networks develop programming designed to more strictly follow what audiences want, public radio networks, like some of the smaller, nonprofit commercial radio owners, have more idealistic goals. NPR's mission statement states that it aims to develop programming that creates "a more informed public—one challenged and invigorated by a deeper understanding and appreciation of events, ideas and cultures." Jay Kernis, NPR's senior vice president for programming, said that he is focused on two concerns, "what public radio audiences across the nation want—and need—to hear on their local stations."[16]

There is debate about whether NPR achieves its lauded development goal of an evenhanded approach to the day's events and ideas. Popular commercial radio talk-show hosts, such as Rush Limbaugh and Bill O'Reilly, have vilified NPR for, in their words, using public money to push a lopsided liberal agenda. As Bill O'Reilly said in a contentious interview with NPR's "Fresh Air" host, Terry Gross, "You're easy on [liberal political satirist Al] Franken and you're hard on me . . . this is NPR . . . you should be ashamed of yourself."[17]

Although NPR receives some public funding, less than 2% of its operating budget comes directly from government sources. Nearly half of its funding comes from member stations (13% of whose overall funding is derived from government agencies, some of which filters through to NPR); the rest is gleaned from grants and support from private foundations and corporations. So NPR's vice president of development, Barbara Hall, is mainly preoccupied with raising nearly $50 million per year to support programming that NPR's think tank of intellectual and cultural advisors devises to serve the organization's mission statement.[18]

For the other major public radio network, PRI, development is directed more by the missions of individual member stations, many of which are also member stations of NPR. But most PRI member stations share the idealistic goals of NPR: to provide both what they know their audiences want and what they believe their audiences need. With PRI, the difference is that development is not centralized as it is with NPR.

PRI stations and, to a lesser extent, NPR are open to "pitches" for new program development, even from members of the public. Some NPR cultural shows, such as "This American

Figure 4.7
*With a smart
combination of
regular contributors
and stories
submitted by the
public, "This
American Life,"
hosted by Ira
Glass, has become
a weekly staple on
NPR. (Jon
Hughes/
Photopresse.)*

Life" with Ira Glass (Figure 4.7), solicit submissions from their listening audience and receive nearly 50 submissions per week, some of which, often with editing and additional postproduction, they broadcast.

INTERNET DEVELOPMENT

With the Internet, development of programming can take a mind-numbing number of routes, from the proud parents of a newborn placing pictures of their child on a web page for viewing by relatives, to a garage band uploading songs to a music website such as MP3.com for exposure, to a social or political activist creating a web log (or "blog") of their personal thoughts and observations about life and the world, to a television or radio network such as CNN or Clear Channel developing web content to support its brand, to a film producer creating an oft-updated website to build buzz for an upcoming theatrical release.

History of Internet Development

The "democratic" development of the Internet as a technology practically anyone could use to create and obtain

content charged the imaginations of all who came in contact with it in its early days. The possibilities seemed endless. Perhaps, many thought, the Internet could break the hegemony of media companies, displacing radio, television, and newspapers as the dominant sources of news and entertainment. The Internet, many thought, could also revolutionize commerce. The opportunities for development seemed to have no bounds.

The relatively brief history of the Internet has thus been marked by tremendous hype, hope, and speculation. Most notably, the late 1990s saw what U.S. Federal Reserve Chairman Alan Greenspan called "irrational exuberance" for investment in Internet ventures. Investors contributed billions of dollars to start Internet companies, most of which never turned a profit before imploding. When the bubble burst, the field of Internet developers was decimated and their investors, many of whom were individuals, were badly burned.

But this is not to say that the hype was divorced from reality. The Internet has and continues to unquestionably transform the face of media and commerce. It has just settled into doing it less stridently than many had predicted or hoped. Instead of sucking the real world into cyberspace with one long slurp, the Internet has come to coexist with the real world, taking over and improving upon aspects it can perform more efficiently and conveniently.

Before the advent of the Internet, for example, personal letter writing was a dying art usurped by telephone conversations. Now email and instant messaging have taken a significant bite out of telephone and fax communications, although the quality of email communication, many would argue, often falls far below the standards of telephone conversation and handwritten communications.

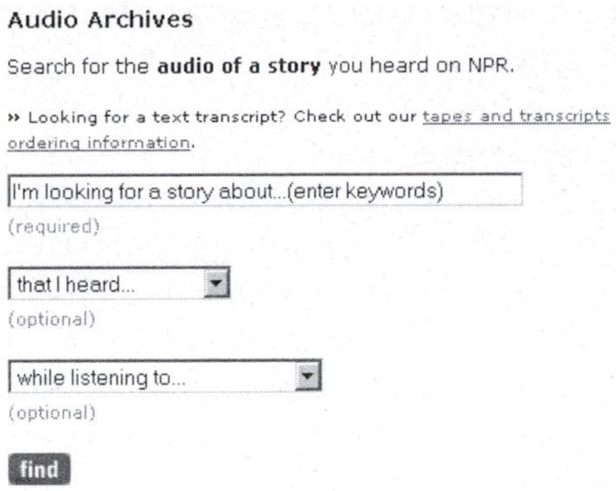

Traditional Developers Adapt to the Internet

Just as email streamlined the diffusion of personal messages, the Internet allows companies and organizations to push their message or product more effectively and widely to consumers. The traditional newsletter, broadcast, or storefront can now have both a **brick-and-mortar** version and a cyber version—the cyber version available on demand by consumers across the globe.

With this dual strategy, the development cost for Internet content is often far outweighed by the additional exposure a website can provide. Because entities can simply retool into a website what they have already created for their traditional outlets, the development costs are chiefly technical, not creative. Numerous radio stations, for example, now broadcast the same content simultaneously over the air and an Internet stream.

Closely related to the simulcast idea is the development of Internet archives. With the cost of digital storage dropping exponentially, it is increasingly economical to archive nearly anything broadcast, making it available on demand at a later date. Internet connection rates are not yet fast enough for the feasible wholesale distribution of quality video, but audio archives of radio programs are nearly ubiquitous for syndicated radio programs. The only cost associated with the development of this material is the technical process of breaking material into specific subjects or segments and indexing the material so that it can be easily found by Internet surfers.

In recent years, the trend has been for many of these radio archives to become

Audio Archives

Search for the **audio of a story** you heard on NPR.

» Looking for a text transcript? Check out our tapes and transcripts ordering information.

I'm looking for a story about...(enter keywords)
(required)

that I heard...
(optional)

while listening to...
(optional)

find

Figure 4.8
Online archives allow visitors to easily find content using various criteria.

subscription services, helping to generate revenue that covers archiving costs and, many undoubtedly hope, to generate profits. Public radio, on the other hand, offers staggering amounts of archived material, nearly all without subscription fees (Figure 4.8).

It is doubtful whether, even when Internet speeds greatly improve, we will quickly see mass on-demand offerings of archived television programs. The syndication market is too robust yet for television executives to risk eroding interest in broadcast reruns by making them available online. There are, however, notable exceptions. News or other time-sensitive programming that cannot be rebroadcast is increasingly archived and available online, either free or by subscription. But perhaps the most widely archived and viewed online video content, especially by the advertiser-cherished young demographic, is music videos. As MTV and other music-video television networks have moved further from their roots of broadcasting wall-to-wall music videos, videos have moved onto the Internet. Viewers can see what they want when they want it after sitting through short advertisements before each video. Standouts are Yahoo's Launch.com and America Online's music channel, which features some content, such as live streaming concerts, that only subscribers to America Online can view.

Another web-based video service making waves and significant revenue is in the area of sports. Major League Baseball, for example, runs a site, MLB.com, that offers several services for diehard baseball fans. It sells live video and audio streams of games and abridged game recordings that can be watched in just 20 minutes, cutting the game down to its action essence. MLB.com and Yahoo have also developed free graphical simulations of baseball games, in which the graphic of a baseball diamond is populated by representations of players coming up to bat and moving around the bases in real time.

But even if television producers are not likely to voluntarily make their programs available online until the economics make sense, a growing number of television programs are being recorded, placed in the digital format, and made available illegally over the Internet. The music industry was the first to have to confront this online piracy problem—both by going after illegal song-file-swappers and by developing legal, fee-based alternatives. Consumers, whether through legal or illegal means, have become accustomed to the on-demand nature of the Internet. Traditional media producers and developers will have to respond or be circumnavigated.

Traditional media also develops material supplemental to its broadcast offerings. Commercial radio and television networks use the Internet to build upon their brand identity and to give fans additional opportunities to bond, and even interact, with products. Development of these materials often occurs in tandem with development of the original broadcast show. Some shows, such as

reality and game shows, lend themselves easily to supplemental websites. CBS's multiseason ratings performer, "Big Brother," for example, has from the beginning had an extensive website that both gives additional information to loyal fans and helps newcomers to get their bearings if they start watching the serial "reality" series midseason. Although the show broadcast on television is extensively edited before it hits the airwaves, the show's website offers a bevy of 24/7 video feeds from the house. The website also allows viewers to weigh in on and chat among themselves about what they think the outcome of each episode will be—who will be evicted and who will stay for a chance at the cash prize.

For other shows, most notably sitcoms, the development of supplemental websites has been much less robust. Because sitcoms rely heavily on single-episode plots, there is not a lot of between-the-episodes intrigue. The NBC comedy "Scrubs," for example, has a website limited to roughly 10 pages of content, most of it in simple text: Main, About, Bios, Credits, Photos, and Episodes. CBS's successfully syndicated show "Everybody Loves Raymond" has even less: Home, About, and Cast.

Websites developed for dramas tend to be more complex. The perennial crime or legal show format allows plenty of supplementary material: explanations of forensic techniques, real-world legal precedents, detailed descriptions of crime scenes and evidence, and so on. Some ongoing dramas, such as PBS's "American Family," provide insights into the characters on the shows. In the case of "American Family," the character Cisco keeps an online interactive journal (Figure 4.9), which was developed by Artifact, an independent integrated content creation company. Artifact CEO, editor, and creative director Steve Armstrong said that the goal of the online journal is to give the audience "a glimpse of this guy figuring things out."[19]

With the future of the web and of its effect on traditional media still developing, traditional media wants to be sure not to miss the boat. Experimenting with web development and testing its outcomes is something that programmers must take into account in today's programming landscape.

Figure 4.9
Cisco's journal, mostly composed of images, is updated with clues about the "American Family" character's inner motivations, thoughts, and impulses.

A New Venue for Independent Developers

There is plenty of Internet content, produced by individuals or collaborations, that is not directly associated with a traditional media or commercial entity. Development of this material arises with numerous motives, depends on various resources, and results in wide-ranging outcomes.

Chief among the motives of independent web content developers is the desire for self-expression. Many individuals have set up web pages with information about themselves, their interests, and their pursuits. For some, these sites have no other goal than to inject a personal mark into the global community of the Internet. An ever-growing and -contracting group of companies provides "free" advertisement-supported web hosting services that allow users to create their own websites. The craze of Internet dating or just simple chatting would be hobbled without the ability of potential mates to post their pictures and information about their personal attributes onto easily accessible websites. They may trade the addresses of these with chatting partners to become better acquainted, even if many suspect and many more discover a rampant element of false advertising.

For others, self-expression bleeds into self-promotion. Some personal websites have become calling cards, promoting job skills and especially artistic endeavors in ways that were much more difficult before the Internet. In 1981, artist Keith Haring, bypassing the exclusive art gallery system, took to the New York subways armed with sticks of chalk with which he drew his soon-to-be-famous unmistakable artworks on the walls of the underground rails. The notoriety afforded him by this public art soon brought offers to show his works in the very galleries he had been flouting by going directly to "the people." Today, artists, independent film producers, musicians, writers, and animators use the Internet, hoping it will provide them the kind of public exposure that the subways did for Haring.

Putting content on the Internet is easy. Getting someone to see it is another matter. Had Haring put his chalk drawings in the sewage system of New York rather than the subway, no one would have seen them. Among the

Figure 4.10
Screenshot of the Ifilm.com website.
(Courtesy ifilm.com.)

millions of websites on the Internet, people who wish to have their material seen must develop a plan for doing so. After a website is up on the web, the easiest first step in bringing the site to the attention of web surfers is to submit the site to search engines, such as Google.com, Yahoo.com, and AltaVista.com. A computerized program called a **spider** will visit the address provided and index all of the words on the site. Then, when someone puts some of those words into a search engine, the engine will return all sites that contain those words as potential matches.

Although those are the basics of how a search engine operates, behind the scenes things are more complex. Website developers are always vying for top placement in search engines, and search engine companies are always trying to fight off tactics that developers use to trick their spiders into giving them top placement, even if their sites may not be the most appropriate match for a search. One of the many criteria that search engines may use in ranking sites is to index how many other websites contain links to a specific site. The idea here is if a lot of other websites are linked to a specific site, that site must be popular or at least of interest—so the search engine might rank that site higher than other sites that contain the same indexed words. So, along with making sure that a site contains the correct words, it is a good idea to exchange links with other websites. There are entire books written about search engine strategies, so we will not go into them here.[20,21]

Another way for independent producers to have their programming seen on the Internet is to submit to sites that review submissions and place those that meet their qualifications on their own sites. The granddaddy of these sites is Ifilm.com (Figure 4.10), which has launched the careers of many film and television makers. In some ways, the Internet has become like a big, ongoing film and television pilot festival—but like a film festival, it is not necessarily a free-for-all. If sites want to maintain their audiences, they must exercise some editorial quality control. There are dozens of reputable sites that accept submissions from many genres and interests and many more less-reputable ones. With film sites that accept submissions there are animation sites and even sites that target radio. Transom.org is a website with a goal, founder Jay Allison says, of getting new and unsolicited voices on the radio (Figure 4.11). The site not only accepts submissions but is set up to operate as an online workshop where material can be refined through comments from other site visitors and contributors and from radio professionals.[22]

Another factor in the development of independent content for the Internet is the resources at the developer's disposal. With the cost and technical difficulty of video, audio, and animation hardware and software continuing to plummet, producing quality content at home and as a hobby or a vocation has become more possible. Handheld digital video cameras and robust desktop editing software such as Final Cut and Adobe Premiere, with simple animation programs such as Macromedia Flash, have put visual storytelling, as long as there is a good story to tell, within reach of even those with very limited budgets.

Although the development of some projects is more costly than that of others, all development is a gamble. Decisiveness, confidence, and persistent commitment, however, are qualities that serve all programmers well. Successful programming does not spring fully grown from the ether, like Athena from the head of

Zeus. There are always obstacles and periods of doubt. A strong collaborative spirit can make the process less lonely, and a willingness to think outside of the box for solutions to inevitable snags can yield fresh ideas. The ability to lay the bodies of failed projects before your feet and use them as gruesome stepping stones on the way to the next development endeavor will also help.

Figure 4.11
Screenshot of the Transom.org website. (Courtesy Transom.org.)

EXERCISES

1. Come up with a drama or comedy series that you feel fills a void in the television programming landscape. Write a log line for this show. Develop some story lines for the show that indicate the potential for the show to last several seasons.

2. Prepare the pitch for your show. Make a list of ways to get the all-important pitch meeting (websites, agents, personal contacts, recent graduates of your school, production companies that produce similar shows, etc.).

3. Prepare a strategy to counter any reservations about your show. How can you make your presentation stronger by anticipating these reservations?

4. Envision a reality program that you think will have franchise possibilities all over the world. What about your show makes it possible to adapt to different territories?

5. Write letters to 10 producers of shows you have enjoyed. Tell them specifically why you liked the show. Do not pitch them an idea in this initial letter. Wait a few weeks; contact these same producers, referring to your previous letter; and request a meeting to pitch your idea.

6. Review your local market radio offerings. Come up with a music radio format that you feel fills a void in the local programming landscape. Come up with a sample song list and a description of the type of on-air personalities appropriate for the format.

7. Look at the XM Radio channel listings in Figure 4.6. If you were asked to consult with the network on how to attract additional college-age listeners, which three stations would you eliminate? With what formats would you replace those three channels?

8. Look at the website supporting one of the television shows you watch frequently. Critique the efficacy of its content. Is it easy to navigate? Does it offer what you, as a viewer, expect and hope that it will? How might it better enhance your involvement with the show?

REFERENCES/NOTES

1. Howard J. Blumenthal and Oliver R. Goodenough. *This Business of Television* (New York: Billboard Books, 1991).

2. Enterprise of Hollywood, http://www.enterpriseprinters.com.

3. Marc Gunther. "Jeff Zucker Faces Life Without Friends," *Fortune,* May 12, 2003, p. 96.

4. PBS. "PBS Financial Highlights 2003," http://www.pbs.org/aboutpbs/content/annualreport/2003/FY03FinHighlightsPublished.pdf. Accessed July 15, 2004.

5. Roger Strauss. "Quest for TV Magic," *Los Angeles Times,* November 16, 2003, p. E-32 through E-33.

6. Gunther, p. 96.

7. Austin Bunn. "The Wasteland," *New York Times Magazine,* June 23, 2002, p. 33.

8. Bunn, p. 35.

9. Gunther, p. 96.

10. Allison Romano. "MTV: Operating Without a Net," *Broadcasting and Cable,* May 27, 2002, p. 21.

11. Charles Goldsmith. "How 'Idols' Around the World Harmonize with Local Viewers," *The Wall Street Journal,* September 29, 2003, p. B-1.

12. Alex Pham and Scott Sandell. "In Germany, Video Games Showing Frontal Nudity Are OK, But Blood Is Verboten," *Los Angeles Times,* June 6, 2003, p. C-1.

13. Jego R. Armstrong. "Hip-Hop Radio War—Good for Fans," http://www.sohh.com/thewire/read.php?contentID=4917&highlight=radio%200ne. Accessed June 16, 2004.

14. "Michigan Radio and TV Ownership Guide," http://www.michiguide.com/dials/owners.html. Accessed July 10, 2004.

15. Barbara Pinckney. "New Owner Black United Fund Changes Format of Radio Station," http://albany.bizjournals.com/albany/stories/2003/06/30/story8.html. Accessed July 15, 2004.

16. NPR. "Jay Kernis, Senior Vice President for Programming," http://www.npr.org/about/people/bios/jkernis.html. Accessed July 15, 2004.

17. Bill O'Reilly, quoted on "Fresh Air," October 8, 2003, archived at http://freshair.npr.org.

18. NPR. "NPR Annual Report 2002," http://www.npr.org/about/annualreports/npr2002.pdf. Accessed July 15, 2004.

19. Paul Bond. "Family Secrets a Click Away," *Hollywood Reporter,* January 28, 2002, p. 14.

20. Shari Thurow. *Search Engine Visibility,* 1st edition (Berkeley, CA: New Riders, 2002).

21. Tara Calishain and Rael Dornfest (editor). *Google Hacks: 100 Industrial-Strength Tips & Tools,* 1st edition (Cambridge, MA: O'Reilly & Associates, 2003).

22. Cody Ellerd, Associated Press. "Web Site Helps Get New Talent on the Air," http://www.miami.com/mld/miamiherald/business/6939697.htm. Accessed October 5, 2003.

5 Testing

In this chapter you will learn about the following:

- The importance of testing in making programming decisions
- The significance of sample selection
- The four primary types of testing
- How the effectiveness of testing is measured
- Why Las Vegas is considered an ideal testing location
- Individual song and listener-lifestyle testing for radio
- User-friendliness testing of Internet programming
- Different views on the efficacy of testing

Research is a heavily used device in the programming process. Programmers are reluctant to commit huge amounts of money to productions without some evidence from the public that the project has a reasonable chance of success. That would seem to be unassailable prudence. But it is routinely assailed. Doubters ask the questions: Who is being researched? How reliable are these potential viewers? Who is doing the interpreting? What is the track record for all this statistical stuff?

According to some critics, the history of predictive research in television is abysmal. Dan Enright, a producer of programs since the medium's inception, stated, "Nearly every network program that sees the light of television has been tested by focus groups and other mass devices. And each has passed its test with flying colors. However, once they hit the air, more programs fail than succeed, contradicting the test findings. Why do we continue to resort to TV program testing when its failure is so monumental? Testing [is] the bane of programming. It's amazing how we still cling to it."[1]

Supporters of research may argue that failure cannot always be ascribed to faulty testing. Many cancellations are the result of poor execution, inept scheduling, unrealistic expectations, misdirected promotion, or murderous competition. And so it goes, attackers vs. defenders. In this chapter, we examine the various techniques used by researchers and explore the strengths, weaknesses, and interpretations. No matter what side of the argument a programmer adopts, knowledge of the testing systems and procedures is essential.

TELEVISION TESTING

All network programs and most syndicated programs, regardless of the daypart, are subjected to some testing. Less attention is paid to testing in cable, possibly because cable tends to keep its testing under the radar. For example, Chris Albrecht, HBO's programming chief, says he does not believe in testing, particularly after "The Sopranos" testing was not promising and HBO decided to go ahead anyway, creating one of television's biggest hits. Programmers wishing to start a cable niche channel will more than likely test to see whether the concept has potential. In general, however, testing is not as prevalent in cable as it is in broadcast television because programming is supported, at least partly, by viewer subscription fees instead of by advertising.

Because the advertising stakes are so high, prime-time network shows go through a constant testing process from the initial concept through the first year on the air and sometimes even later. There are several companies that do this type of research, the most active of which is Audience Studies Institute (ASI), a company that claims to be able to test virtually anything. ASI bills itself as the largest communications-specialist data-research organization in the country. According to David Castler, president and CEO, the full-service testing facility includes the following client services:

- Broadcast and cable television pilots and programs
- Continuing series
- Title, concept, and script appeal
- Movies made for television
- Children's programs
- Target audiences
- Program scheduling
- Commercials
- Gaming
- Sports
- Personalities—News anchors and program hosts
- Competitive environment
- Station image
- Brand image
- Tune-in campaigns
- Program and channel awareness

Awareness Testing

The last item, program and channel awareness, is important because viewers have so many choices and because shows are given so little time to establish themselves. **Viewer awareness** of a show has become essential. If viewers are not aware that a show is on the schedule or about to premiere, that show's chances for success are significantly diminished. Testing awareness has thus taken on great significance. At a 2003 presentation to a class of radio and television majors at California State University, Fullerton, Howard Schneider, then vice president of promotions at the Fox network, sought to determine whether the students were aware of shows coming to the Fox lineup. He showed on-air promotional spots to the class to get a sense of what did and did not work, but what he really wanted to gauge was the students' awareness of upcoming programs.

Promo tests become a key gauge of audience awareness. However, before a new show airs, the promo developers only have the pilot to work with. Therefore, there may not be a lot of footage available to create a promo that will generate excitement and audience awareness. It thus becomes important to use promo testing to evaluate what will get a show recognized by viewers. If the promos do not connect with the audience, the show's awareness suffers significantly.

With the increased importance of awareness, a company such as ASI provides "customized" research. For example, Castler said that ASI will conduct studies for a client to determine an audience's awareness of a program's existence. Then it will probe to see whether those who know it is on have sampled it and, if so, whether they are watching more or less than they used to.

Sampling

A research design can be developed to investigate any problem confronting a programmer. Its value and reliability are subject to a host of variables, the first of which is the quality of the test sample.

Program testing requires the recruitment of groups who represent the universe to be measured. For example, if a producer wishes to test the effectiveness of a program with the 18- to 34-year-old female audience, the testing service must locate a sufficient number of viewers in this category to draw reliable conclusions. In addition, the survey group must offer a balance of economic, social, ethnic, and geographical considerations to prevent tilted or biased results.

Beverly Bolotin, executive vice president of client services at ASI, says the sampling selected for a test reflects the demographic of the targeted network. A network that caters primarily to a young demographic will be tested by that specific group.

According to Paul S. Lendburg, ASI's chief consultant, "**Sampling** isn't the most important thing in research today; it's the only thing." The reason is apparent. Even the most carefully constructed questionnaire or the most skillfully conducted discussion session will yield worthless results if the respondents are not representative of the whole. Examining 40 18- to 25-year-old females, all of whom come from the same ethnicity and church group in a community of $300,000 homes, is not going to help a producer develop a format for a television show intended for a broad national audience.

Respondents are usually selected by phone. Data available from many sources enables a recruiter to establish the general socioeconomic level of each home to be called. The respondent is taken through a detailed questionnaire, and if the answers fit the needs of the study, the person is asked to participate. There are financial and practical limitations to assembling a perfectly balanced sample group.

Figure 5.1
CBS has found Las Vegas to be an excellent place to test shows because of the large cross section of individuals available to take part in testing at their Television City. (Courtesy Donny Sianturi.)

To achieve the optimal sampling, CBS established a testing center in the MGM Grand Hotel in Las Vegas in 2001. Dubbed CBS Television City (Figure 5.1), the research center uses A.C. Nielsen's Reel Research online system; every seat has a touch screen, allowing network executives near and far to track viewer responses. The facility is geared for maximum efficiency. Equipped with two screening rooms that can accommodate 25 people each, it is also set up to handle **focus groups,** where participants discuss the merits and deficits of a show. Two-way mirrors enable executives to observe these discussions. Video conferencing is also available. Serving as a magnet to attract test subjects to CBS Television City, next door to the testing facility there is a retail shop that sells merchandise from CBS/Viacom shows: T-shirts, hats, cups, etc. Coupons for items in the retail shop are given to individuals who watch the shows being tested.

According to Eric Steinberg, senior vice president of research at CBS, Las Vegas provides an excellent cross section of the population for testing purposes. Visitors from across the country visit Las Vegas, and many of them have free time in the afternoons to engage in program testing for CBS. The CBS Las Vegas testing center proved so successful and cost effective that NBC opened its own testing center at the Venetian Hotel in 2004.

After the sample is selected, the research is conducted. There are four primary methods of conducting program research: focus groups, **minitheater tests, cable-based studies,** and **telephone research.**

Focus Groups

For this method, the research company brings together a small group (usually 10 to 12 participants) to discuss a programming matter under the guidance of a trained moderator. The subject of the focus group might range from the appeal of potential hosts for a game show to the acceptability of the language used in a sitcom pilot.

In some cases, the session will begin with a screening of the program to be studied, although focus groups have been used to test program concepts that have not been committed to paper, let alone videotape. The conversation typically lasts about 2 hours. The moderator will have a carefully prepared list of topics but will not slavishly follow it. The goal of the session is to stimulate candid comments that will allow a client to hear what the audience really thinks. For later reference, the sessions are generally videotaped by an unobtrusive camera.

One of the virtues of focus groups is that they can be conducted in any city with a minimum of equipment and expense. TV sets and VCR or DVD units are available everywhere, and the moderator only needs to bring a copy of the show and a pad to be in business. The chief value of a focus session is that the producer or programmer can gain reactions directly from the consumer;

the words are not filtered through a computer or hidden in a welter of statistics. The passion, or the tepidness, of the consumers' reactions can serve as guidelines for format adjustment and improvement. Because there are only 12 participants, the findings are never quantified. However, any unanimously negative expression would be a clear signal for remedial action. A focus session is a hunt for clues and should be used as such.

There are three major concerns about this form of research: the limited size of the group, the potential for a strong-willed participant to unduly influence the opinions of others, and an analyst who does not connect with the members of the focus group. The size of any group cannot be enlarged without risking a loss of control and candor. However, clients who wish a greater range of responses can lessen the effect of the small sample by ordering additional sessions. The second concern can be more damaging. Dominant personalities do not always reveal themselves in a preinterview and can burst open during the session to the surprise and chagrin of all. Experienced moderators are frequently able to cope with this dismaying situation by repeated appeals "to let everyone have a fair chance to speak." When the dominant personality simply will not cooperate, the session has to be invalidated and a new one scheduled—a waste of time and money to all involved.

Scott Gimple, the creator of the children's television show "Fillmore," experienced the third situation firsthand. He was stationed behind the two-way mirror to observe the focus group that would help to determine the fate of his show. He quickly became concerned with the moderator's approach when he adopted a military style of barking questions at the 6 year olds in the group.

One little girl even started to cry when she was commanded to answer a question. The test results were more positive than Gimple had expected, but he spent a few anxious moments observing the confrontational style of the group moderator and had to take the moderator's approach into account when interpreting the results.

More than any other method of research, the focus group must be interpreted by a seasoned analyst. After conducting hundreds of these sessions, most moderators, with the possible exception of the one who conducted the "Fillmore" session that Gimple observed, become sensitized to group dynamics and are able to detect the most subtle undercurrents. Many times the subtext of the commentaries will be more valuable than the boldly stated opinions. Programmers are advised to listen carefully to the savvy moderator to learn what the group is really saying.

Figure 5.2
"Everybody Loves Raymond" initially tested poorly. (Courtesy the Academy of Television Arts & Sciences.)

PERSONAL OBSERVATIONS ABOUT MINITHEATER TESTING

Lynn Gross has conducted minitheater testing sessions. Here are some of her observations.

For several years in the 1990s, I tested CBS pilots at CBS Television City in Los Angeles. We obtained our participants from people waiting to see the taping of "The Price Is Right" and from tourists visiting the farmer's market next to Television City. There were more volunteers from Los Angeles than anywhere else, but drawing from these two pools yielded people from throughout the United States. If there were too many people from Los Angeles participating in the testing, we just threw out their answers. If there were too many of anything, we did not use their questionnaires. A production company might, for example, only be interested in the responses of midwestern men between 24 and 54 who had blue-collar jobs. All 25 people would watch the pilot and fill out the questionnaire, but the only answers that would make it into the study would be those from the targeted men. If anyone with ties to the entertainment industry showed up in the sample, their answers were perfunctorily discarded. We did not tell people we might not use their questionnaires, and we certainly did not prevent anyone from watching the show.

One of the programs I tested was "Everybody Loves Raymond" (Figure 5.2). It tested low. The comment I remember occurring most often was that it was a one-joke show—nothing but a bunch of mother-in-law jokes. It became a stable hit. Our testing was not always to determine whether a show would make it on the air. Some-

continued

times the producers were trying to fine-tune the series to make it better. Such was the case when we tested "Ink." Ted Danson, "Ink's" star, had a contractual arrangement with CBS, so the series was going to make it into the schedule regardless, but the producers hoped to ensure its longevity through testing. Such was not the case—it did not last long.

I found that the actions of one person or a small group could affect the results of the overall minitheater testing session even though each person filled out his or her own questionnaire. For example, one program I tested started with a woman doing a striptease in a courtroom (probably in an attempt to **bounce the needle**). During one testing session, a woman said, "This is disgusting," and got up and walked out. The show scored much lower overall in that session than in any other sessions.

Another potential series I tested was a comedy about a computer genius that included plays on words related to computers, such as "log on," "boot," and "crash." One time I showed it, about 10 of the participants were students from a local college and the rest of the group was a mixed demographic. The college students loved the show and laughed enthusiastically at the jokes. All the people in the room rated the program high. The next time I showed it, about 10 of the participants were from a retirement community and the rest were similar in demographics to the people in the group with college students. The senior citizens did not enjoy the program and probably did not understand most of the jokes, but the whole group rated it low. Being in a room with people who either like or do not like the show seems to affect those who might otherwise be more neutral.

The minitheater session leaders, other than myself, were primarily actors. Everyone was cooperative about switching shifts if someone had an audition. It is an excellent job for actors because it gives them experience in front of people and the opportunity to make a repeated canned speech sound spontaneous.

Minitheater Research

For minitheater research, a sample group of people from the desired universe are brought to a small theater where they record their likes and dislikes. Within commercial television, the main use of the minitheater is to study series pilots. These tests allow the programmer and the production staff to see whether the concept is sound and the execution is satisfactory. Although many of the directorial flaws, casting mistakes, and other production missteps become apparent when the pilot is privately screened, the executives and producers still have no way of knowing whether the public will find the show appealing. For that, some expression from potential viewers is required.

ASI attempts to fill this need with their minitheater research service. It invites 42 carefully selected individuals who receive $50 to $75 each to a specially equipped facility. On the arm of each seat is a small electronic device that contains a dial participants can turn to any setting between ++ and −−. The dials are connected to a central computer that records the consumers' choices. Responses can be broken into virtually any demographic configuration desired by the client. Also on the dial at ASI is a button that respondents can push at the point they would turn to another channel. This is the "tune out" button. The dial also has a "buy" button that respondents can push at the point they are ready to buy a product offered by a commercial. The ASI dial was created by Castler, and it is the only dial that has the "tune out" and "buy" buttons.

After participants have been comfortably seated and a moderator has explained the operation of the dialing device, the pilot is presented on a large screen. The dials are preset exactly between ++ and −−. As the show unfolds, consumers twist the dial to signify their pleasure or disinterest in the events on the screen. The sum of their reactions is instantaneously calculated by the computer and converted into a running graph, not unlike an EKG readout. The people who have commissioned the study are seated in client booths, watching the same film on a special monitor on which the graph plays along the bottom of the screen. Clients are immediately able to see the joke that worked, the scene that failed. The entire picture, including the graph, is taped and made available for subsequent second-by-second study.

Following the screening, consumers are asked to fill out questionnaires that contain personal information and supplementary inquiries about the program. The questionnaires are coded by seat number and can be linked with the computer readouts of the dial responses. Thus, the client can obtain the reaction of any demographic subgroup in the audience.

After the screening, approximately 24 individuals are asked to stay behind to participate in follow-up focus sessions, two sessions of 12 people each. The purpose of this final phase is to probe the feelings and reasoning behind the reactions of the respondents. The moderator has seen the graph and can explore highs and lows in greater detail. One potential drawback to having the creators or performers in the client booth can occur if the focus group is going badly ("How can someone of his stature be a part of something as awful as this?"). Castler says that often a creator will storm out of the client booth, rush into such a focus session, and take it over to see whether the negative comments can be redirected.

Castler adds that he would prefer for emotionally attached performers not to witness the testing sessions, but this is not something he can control.

For many years, ASI conducted its theater research on a much larger scale. Approximately 400 consumers were invited to react to programs in a large theater. Approximately 50 of the participants were hooked up to special sensing devices that measured their pulse and perspiration as the show evolved. The greater these emotional responses, the more effective the show was judged to be. However, the results were ambiguous and difficult to interpret, and the technique was subsequently shelved. The minitheater replaced large-house testing for two reasons: (1) When there were basically three networks, people were excited and willing to participate in testing on a voluntary basis; television was fresh and it was fun to be part of the process of determining what was going to be on the air. Today, however, it is necessary to compensate respondents for the 2 hours they devote to testing. Thus, the cost of testing large groups became prohibitive. (2) It is possible to achieve essentially the same reliability with a smaller group for substantially less cost.

Also, the smaller sample helped to eliminate a misuse of the service. With 400 consumers in the survey, clients were tempted to seek one number, the average score of all the dials over the course of the screening. ASI has always cautioned against such a simplification of the system, but programmers and producers found it a short, convenient way to interpret the findings. Producers quickly learned that decision makers were placing great emphasis on that one figure and hit upon a technique to make it work for them. The trick was to insert a high-powered scene early in the show. The earlier the viewer could be moved off the middle reading and toward the ++ side, the better the chances that the overall rating would be impressive. Consequently, veteran producers inserted rousing action or sex scenes at the beginning of programs, many times with little or no relevance to the drama, just to bounce the needle.

They would test the show, edit (or reshoot) scenes, test it again, edit again, and keep up the process until they had engineered a lofty overall score. Then the pilot would be turned over to the buyers for evaluation. The first thing they did was test it at ASI. Sure enough, there it was—a whopping number. A hit was assured; everyone was delighted. Unfortunately, many of those "guaranteed" smashes quickly wound up in the Nielsen graveyard. ASI ended the game by reducing the sample and withholding any composite number. Clients were encouraged to use the service for its original intent, spotting flaws and discovering targets or opportunity.

Cable-Based Research

One of the major drawbacks of theater research, at least as perceived by many clients, is the unnatural setting of the test. Television is usually a solitary or family experience, most frequently occurring in the comfort of a home. Yet, the testing takes place in a public facility with the ever-present possibility that crowd response and other distractions might influence judgments. This dissatisfaction led to a search for a method by which people's opinions could be solicited in the normal viewing environment. The solution was cable-based research.

Companies that offer this service develop relationships with cable operators throughout the country. Through these connections, they are able to recruit the desired number of sub-scribers willing to participate in a survey. The consumers are asked to watch the program that will be fed on a certain channel number at a specific time. A reminder call is usually made the day of the test. Upon the conclusion of the program, an interviewer phones the consumer and administers a detailed verbal questionnaire to obtain the information most desired by the client.

As in other forms of testing previously described, a consumer sample can be assembled to meet any demographic need. Without the distraction of other participants and within the environment of his or her own living room, a participant is more likely to offer reliable responses.

Telephone Research

Phone research has limited value for determining reaction to proposed television programs because the consumers cannot simultaneously watch a program and answer a questionnaire. However, phone research can be used effectively to find out information about programs on the air.

Interviewers call appropriate samples of people and gather their responses to set questionnaires. Sometimes the interviewers merely screen and obtain the permission of the people over the phone then mail them the questionnaires. This method usually requires numerous follow-up calls to remind the participants to fill out and mail in the questionnaires.

One of the major phone–mail research studies is **TVQ,** a popularity evaluation service. These periodic studies, provided by Marketing Evaluations, measure the audience's familiarity with programs and personalities and the intensity of their appeal. A nationwide panel of 1800 viewers completes a mailed questionnaire (Figure 5.3) that

PROGRAM POPULARITY POLL 0798-0203 PP 644

a) Your Sex: 1▢ Male 2▢ Female
b) Your Age: 1▢ 6-11 2▢ 12-17 3▢ 18-34 4▢ 35-49 5▢ 50+

We'd like to know your **overall opinion** of each of the television shows listed, as well as the **number of times**, if any, you have watched **each one** in the <u>past 4 weeks</u>.

FIRST, answer the shaded column under "Your Opinion".
- If you have **never** watched the program, write in an "N"
- If you have **definitely watched** the program, write in a 1, 2, 3, 4, or 5, depending on how you feel about it.

THEN, for each program you have **ever seen**, place an "X" in the appropriate box to indicate **how many times** in the past 4 weeks you have watched the program.

YOUR OPINION

Write In:	If The Program Is:
1	One of your favorites
2	Very good
3	Good
4	Fair
5	Poor
N	A program you have never seen

NUMBER OF TIMES WATCHED IN PAST 4 WEEKS

- 0 = Didn't watch in past four weeks
- 1 = Watched 1 time in past four weeks
- 2 = Watched 2 times in past four weeks
- 3 = Watched 3 times in past four weeks
- 4 = Watched 4 times in past four weeks

("x" the appropriate box for each program)

MONDAY NIGHT

The Practice, The King Of Queens, Boston Public, Half And Half, One On One, Joe Millionaire, 7th Heaven, Monk on ABC, Third Watch, The Parkers, Crossing Jordan, CSI: Miami, Yes, Dear, Fear Factor, Miracles, Everybody Loves Raymond, Still Standing, Girlfriends, Everwood, Veritas: The Quest

TUESDAY NIGHT

Buffy The Vampire Slayer, According To Jim, A.U.S.A., 8 Simple Rules For Dating My Teenage Daughter, Hidden Hills, Just Shoot Me, Gilmore Girls, The Guardian, Smallville, Life With Bonnie, JAG, Abby, NYPD Blue, Judging Amy, In-Laws, Frasier, 24, Less Than Perfect

WEDNESDAY NIGHT

That 70's Show, Enterprise, The West Wing, My Wife And Kids, The Bernie Mac Show, The Price Is Right Million Dollar Spectacular, Presidio Med, Birds Of Prey, Law & Order, The Bachelorette, Dawson's Creek, Angel, Celebrity Mole: Hawaii, Cedric The Entertainer Presents, Ed, 60 Minutes II, George Lopez, The Twilight Zone

THURSDAY NIGHT

Friends, Will & Grace, FOX Thursday Night Movie, WWE Smackdown!, The Pulse, Without A Trace, Primetime Thursday, Good Morning Miami, JKX:The Jamie Kennedy Experiment, ABC Thursday Night At The Movies, Surreal Life, ER, CSI: Crime Scene Investigation, Scrubs

Please Be Sure You've Written In Your Opinions

Figure 5.3 *A sample of a TVQ questionnaire.* (Courtesy Marketing Evaluations, Inc.)

Figure 5.4
Some past and recent shows that began as borderline programs that survived because of strong TVQ scores. (Courtesy Marketing Evaluations, Inc.)

Past	Recent
"All in the Family"	"Friends"
"Hill Street Blues"	"X-Files"
"Cheers"	"Everybody Loves Raymond"
"St. Elsewhere"	"Ally McBeal"
"Seinfeld"	"Touched by an Angel"

Following are examples of the early detection of potential "Winners" and "Losers."

Early Detection of a Potential "Winner"

Adults 18-49

As can be seen below, **Ally McBeal** built its sampling with a dramatic increase in its appeal and significant reduction in its negative reaction. The audience ratings eventually caught up with the strong loyal following indicated by TvQ.

Ally McBeal

	FAM	TvQ Score	Drama Index	Negative Q Score	Drama Index
October 1997	19	24	109	33	127
December 1997	31	33	150	24	92
April 1998	40	33	150	25	96

Early Detection of a Potential "Loser"

Adults 18-49

The following chart reveals that **Hiller and Diller** was unable to build sampling primarily due to very weak inherent appeal and growing negative reaction. Even with strong lead-ins, the early season detection of a qualitative weakness could not be overcome and ultimately lead to poor audience ratings for the show.

Hiller And Diller

	FAM	TvQ Score	Comedy Index	Negative Q Score	Comedy Index
October 1997	18	1	5	52	163
December 1997	18	7	33	55	172
April 1998	15	4	19	57	178

Figure 5.5
How TVQ scores can predict potential winners: if the TVQ score is higher than the familiar score, that is a positive sign as opposed to a high familiarity and a low TVQ score. (Courtesy Marketing Evaluations, Inc.)

lists up to 1700 personalities (Performer Q), 350 broadcast television programs (TVQ) and 175 cable programs (Cable Q).

Results are distributed to clients in the distilled form of two scores, Fam (the percentage of respondents familiar with the subject) and Q (the percentage who checked "one of my favorites"). Demographic breakouts according to age, gender, education, household income, employment, race, and religion are also offered in the report. In addition to Performer Q, TVQ, and Cable Q described previously, Marketing Evaluations offers Sport Q, Cartoon Q, Product Q, Kids Product Q, and Dead Q (performers of the past).

Subscribers primarily use the data to determine the intrinsic appeal of a show. When the Nielsen rating is low but the quality of the production seems to be first rate, the programmer will frequently look to the TVQ for glimpses of encouragement (Figure 5.4). If the Q score is high but familiarity is weak, it suggests that those who have seen it like it but that too few have seen it. An expansion of audience awareness through a heavy promotion campaign might result in success. If the ratings are low but the Q score for a particular demographic unit is high, it could mean a time change is called for (Figure 5.5).

In terms of television history, David Poltrack, CBS's head of research and planning, noted that in the 1988–1989 broadcast television season, "without the TVQ ratings, 'Tour of Duty' and 'Wiseguy' would not have been on this season's schedule. Their Q scores helped to get them renewed despite low Nielsen ratings."

The application of TVQ findings to casting decisions can be the cause of great concern among performers. The Screen Actors Guild has railed against the service for more than a decade. Kathleen Nolan, former president of the guild, called it an infuriating catch-22: "If you're not on the air, you're not familiar. If you're not familiar, you're not on the air." Performers believe that a good Q score is a function of the part being played. The actor who plays Saddam Hussein will be less liked than the one who portrays a hero fighting tyranny.

Program executives generally deny a reliance on TVQ for casting decisions.

Actors and other on-air people remain skeptical. "They shouldn't be," said Tony Barr, a former vice president of dramatic programs at CBS. "In my 11-1/2 years at CBS, I never once even heard the phrase 'TVQ' mentioned. It simply was not a factor in any talent decisions." This is a position many current programmers and casting directors continue to support, at least in public.

Station Testing

Little program testing is done by either affiliated or independent stations, primarily because there are so few locally originated shows. Research is confined almost exclusively to news productions. "We do quite a number of focus sessions over the course of a year on our news personalities," said Bob Brooks, program director of KFOR in Oklahoma City. "It helps us to see if they're in tune with our audience."

Newscasters historically have resented being submitted to focus group scrutiny. They feel they should be evaluated as reporters, not showpeople, and that focus research places too much emphasis on appearance and not enough on journalistic skill. In a perfect world, program executives might tend to agree. But many viewers base their news selection on the clothes, hairstyle, mannerisms, and personality of the anchors; as long as that is so, decision makers will take steps to ensure these qualities are present.

When local stations need to make decisions about the inclusion of syndicated programs in their lineup, almost all syndicators can produce research by the ton to show why their programs cannot miss in any market. Station program directors see no need to conduct their own studies to confirm or deny the syndicator's data. They usually examine

the figures and come to their own conclusions.

Public Broadcasting

Testing is not a high priority in public broadcasting, partly because of its cost and partly because public broadcasting shows do not live or die by ratings. Sometimes the producers of PBS programs (primarily the public TV stations) will test shows just as commercial producers do, but many shows hit the airwaves without the benefit of testing.

One major exception to this is the programming that comes from the Children's Television Workshop, for example, "Sesame Street." This organization undertakes major statistical pretesting to determine not only how well children like their programs but also how much they learn by watching (Figure 5.6). Interestingly, Nickelodeon's successful

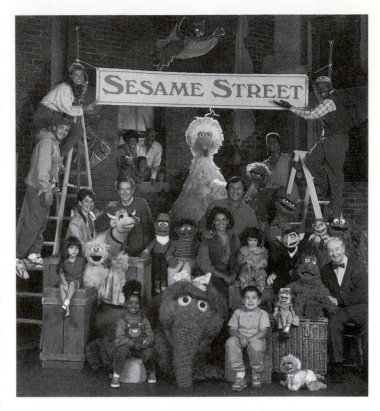

Figure 5.6
"Sesame Street" underwent intensive testing before its debut in 1969, and elements of it are still tested on a regular basis. (Courtesy Children's Television Workshop.)

Figure 5.7
Nickelodeon's "Blue's Clues" uses testing successfully. (Globe Photos, Inc.)

gramming. Advisory boards, although they do not constitute a formal testing audience, are often used as a sounding board for ideas and programs.

RADIO TESTING

Commercial radio makes extensive use of testing to determine the effectiveness of potential formats, music mixes, on-air personalities, contests, and promotions. Many companies exist to assist radio stations, networks, consultants, or station group owners with their specific needs. Some of these specialize in specific aspects of radio programming, such as adult contemporary music, small markets, news, or talk, but most of them will conduct research studies into anything the client requests.

Sampling

Radio stations test potential broadcast material to answer two questions: Will it keep our current listeners tuned in? And will it attract new listeners?

Current listeners are broken into two segments: **preference 1 (P1) listeners** and **preference 2 (P2) listeners.** P1 listeners are considered to be a station's core listeners—those who respond with the name of your station when asked, "What radio station did you listen to the most over the past week?" P2 listeners are those who name your station as another station they tuned in to over the past week. Usually the other station named is a competitor of the P1 station that the listener tunes in to when he or she does not like what is playing on the P1 station or tunes in to "for a change."

Radio listeners who are not part of a station's core P1 or P2 are called the **cume,** or the cumulative size of an area's radio audience for all stations during a given period. A radio station's goals, then, are to maintain its P1,

children's show "Blue's Clues" (Figure 5.7) undertook much of the same research as "Sesame Street" at a more intense level. As Malcolm Gladwell wrote in *The Tipping Point,* "Where Sesame Street tests a given show only once—and after it's completed—Blue's Clues tests shows three times before they go on the air. And while Sesame Street will typically only test a third of its episodes, Blue's Clues tests them all."[2]

Occasionally, a public TV station will pretest a local concept. For example, in 1991, WGBH in Boston decided to program a talk show without a host. Because this was a rather revolutionary idea, the station tested the idea all summer and made many changes before launching the show in the fall.

The CPB holds focus groups around the country to discuss the overall effect of certain programs and how public broadcasting can better serve the public. Sometimes local stations piggyback onto these focus groups and arrange to have the participants queried about local pro-

convert its P2 into P1, and attract new cume listeners, ideally converting them into P1 or P2 core listeners.

To test what broadcast material might accomplish these aims, radio stations must be able to target their testing to specific segments of the radio-listening population. A radio program director trying to learn the type of news items that appeal to the station listeners, most of whom are 12- to 24-year-old males, would obtain little value from a research study if the research company used the general population as a base.

Research companies often call many people and administer a prequestionnaire before they solicit people for radio testing. This prequestionnaire consists of lifestyle elements such as age, income, and general radio-listening patterns. When more than enough people have been found to fulfill the needs of the particular study, a random group of these people is asked to participate in the research. Or sometimes, when a person has been identified from the prequestionnaire as appropriate for the research, he or she is administered the research questionnaire immediately. If the research is being conducted for a local station, as opposed to a network, the sample should be drawn from a particular market.

To solve the sampling problem, research companies or radio stations themselves sometimes use only known station listeners as the universe from which to select the sample. Stations keep lists of people who call in, write, or e-mail and contact them when research needs to be undertaken. This sample base is not effective if the station is trying to gain new listeners from the cume, but it is effective if the goal is to please P1 and P2 listeners.

Testing Methodology

Telephone research is the most common methodology for radio testing. Unlike video programs, audio musical selections can easily be played over the phone, so people do not need to be brought into a theater where the artificiality of the situation can corrupt the findings. Phone research is usually conducted from a research company's central office that can be located anywhere in the country. The people undertaking the phone interviews are all in one location where they can be carefully trained and supervised. This type of testing is relatively inexpensive.

However, people are not usually willing to spend much time on the phone answering questions and listening to musical selections. Also, the low fidelity of the phone system can interfere with a listener's enjoyment of a song that might sound more acceptable on stereo FM. As a result, minitheater testing (usually called **auditorium testing** in radio jargon) is also used for radio, particularly when numerous musical selections need to be tested. Typically 75 to 125 people are brought into an auditorium to listen to music.

Focus groups of 10 to 12 people are also used, especially to discuss broad concepts such as proposed format alterations or changes to call letters. Often, questionnaires are distributed to participants before the focus group to minimize the group psychology or the effects of a dominant personality. These questionnaires are used during the focus groups to bring up ideas that may have been expressed on paper by the more reticent members of the group.

A growing number of radio stations also use the Internet to conduct testing. On a radio station's website, listeners can voluntarily weigh in on, among other things, which songs they think should be played more or less often on the station. Uses for and of Internet testing will likely continue to evolve and expand, although the Internet poses inherent integrity quandaries because it is difficult to verify the identities of respondents. One person could undetectably answer the same survey multiple times out of enthusiasm for a favorite artist, through mischief, because of boredom, or with a more malicious intent, and skew the results.

Some phone testing companies, such as Music-Tec (http://www.musictec.com), combine the old standard of phone testing with new technologies to create a less-expensive, automated system that still offers a strong, if not foolproof, ability to validate its data. With Music-Tec's system, targeted audience members who have agreed to participate in testing are given a toll-free number and an identification number. When they call the system, they enter their unique ID number, are given instructions about how to use the system, and then are played samples of songs and asked to rate the songs by pressing a key on the phone from 1 (hate) to 5 (favorite). Occasionally, as they go through the songs, respondents are asked to speak their names into the phone, which records them to validate their identity. An added advantage of this system is that respondents can rate as few or as many songs at a time as they like, hanging up whenever they become fatigued and then calling back to pick up where they left off.

Research Areas

Radio stations, because of their local and individualistic nature, have a variety of research needs. Some of the most commonly tested topics include the following:

- **Format**—When a station is contemplating a format change and wants to find out what direction to take, it will commission research to explore community response to a variety of structures. In addition, participants usually listen to sample material of various formats and are asked their opinion of each. Usually this type of research is conducted in focus groups, although a station that has narrowed the format choice to three or four can use phone or auditorium research to tabulate opinions.

- **Music within format**—Although a good program manager will have a feel for which new releases fit within the station format, his or her judgment should sometimes be checked or enhanced by playing the new releases for audience members and seeing which they feel belong. Usually this research is auditorium-based because entire selections are presented, although short samples of the music can be played over the phone.

- **Music mix**—The order in which various musical selections are offered is another element that lends itself to auditorium research. Do the listeners like three oldies between each new release, or would they rather have a stronger emphasis on new recordings? How often should there be commercial breaks? For this type of research, participants usually listen to several samples demonstrating different music mixes and indicate a preference.

- **Music callouts**—These are conducted to determine which songs should be taken off a station and which should be added. Even though people like to hear their favorite songs, popular music tends to burn out after a short period. Listeners switch the dial when something they have heard too often comes on. By determining ahead of time which songs are about to burn, a station can engage in guardian maintenance and save itself lost listeners by removing

ALPHABETICAL BY ARTIST

(SCORE / BURN% / UNFAMILIAR% / RANK)

	TOTAL RESP.	TOTAL MEN	TOTAL WOMEN	TOTAL 18-24	TOTAL 25-34	TOTAL 35-44	WXXX CUMERS	WYYY CUMERS	WZZZ CUMERS	WXXX FANS	WYYY FANS	WZZZ FANS
B-52's	70.83	73.75	69.11	70.00	66.17	76.47	70.83	77.27	53.12	75.00	70.19	57.14
ROAM	0.00	0.00	0.00	0.00	0.00	0.00	0.00	0.00	0.00	0.00	0.00	0.00
	27.02	35.48	20.93	33.33	15.00	29.16	27.02	35.29	11.11	30.61	21.21	41.66
	7	3	7	7	7	3	7	2	7	4	6	7
Bad English	73.61	71.05	75.00	80.00	66.66	72.36	73.61	68.75	78.57	73.12	73.80	68.75
PRICE OF LOVE	5.40	6.45	4.65	3.33	15.00	0.00	5.40	17.64	0.00	6.12	3.03	16.66
	27.02	38.70	18.60	33.33	25.00	20.83	27.02	29.41	22.22	18.36	36.36	33.33
	3	4	4	1	6	6	3	5	3	6	3	6
Jackson, Janet	79.05	76.61	80.81	78.33	77.50	81.25	79.05	80.88	86.11	81.63	77.27	75.00
ESCAPADE	8.10	9.67	6.97	6.66	10.00	8.33	8.10	11.76	0.00	8.16	9.09	8.33
	0.00	0.00	0.00	0.00	0.00	0.00	0.00	0.00	0.00	0.00	0.00	0.00
	1	1	1	2	2	1	1	1	1	1	1	3
Madonna	73.10	61.53	80.62	71.29	73.43	75.00	73.10	68.33	85.71	73.93	70.53	77.77
KEEP IT TOGETHER	4.05	9.67	0.00	6.66	0.00	4.16	4.05	5.88	0.00	4.08	0.00	8.33
	10.81	16.12	6.97	10.00	20.00	4.16	10.81	11.76	22.22	4.08	15.15	25.00
	4	7	2	5	3	4	4	6	2	5	5	2
Motley Crue	72.45	69.79	74.28	78.12	70.00	67.50	72.45	75.00	78.57	71.15	75.00	69.44
WITHOUT YOU	6.75	9.67	4.65	10.00	5.00	4.16	6.75	5.88	0.00	6.12	6.06	0.00
	20.27	22.58	18.60	20.00	25.00	16.66	20.27	17.64	22.22	20.40	24.24	25.00
	5	5	6	3	5	7	5	3	3	7	2	5
Myles, Alannah	77.04	76.04	77.70	72.00	82.81	78.75	77.04	71.42	75.00	80.48	71.15	79.16
BLACK VELVET	6.75	6.45	6.97	13.33	5.00	0.00	6.75	11.76	0.00	8.16	6.06	8.33
	17.56	22.58	13.95	16.66	20.00	16.66	17.56	17.64	11.11	16.32	21.21	50.00
	2	2	3	4	1	2	2	4	5	2	4	1
Penn, Michael	72.41	69.00	75.00	70.45	73.21	73.86	72.41	65.38	66.66	76.19	67.39	75.00
NO MYTH	2.70	3.22	2.32	0.00	10.00	0.00	2.70	0.00	11.11	2.04	6.06	8.33
	21.62	19.35	23.25	26.66	30.00	8.33	21.62	23.52	33.33	14.28	30.30	41.66
	6	6	4	6	4	5	6	7	6	3	7	3

Figure 5.8
Example of a music callout results sheet.

the song before it chases away the audience. In a similar vein, listeners can choose the new releases they would most like to hear, and the station can quickly add these to the playlist. This type of research is usually conducted over the phone with small bits of the old and new songs being played and listeners being asked their opinion (Figure 5.8). For most formats, this research must be directed specifically at people who listen to the particular format and must be conducted weekly. There are those who think music callouts are useless because of fast burnout.

- **Perceptual callouts**—The term "perceptual" is used to refer to the research of items other than music. For example, phone calls to people to determine the popularity of a new

disc jockey, the effectiveness of a currently running contest, the likeability of a talk show host, or the desirability of news on the half hour would be considered perceptual callouts. All of the respondents must be people who listen to the station.

- **Lifestyle research**—Wise radio station program managers will want to know something about how audience members live their lives when the radio is off to better serve them when the radio is on. Lifestyle research explores such characteristics as education, income, hobbies, opinions on social issues, use of various media other than radio, major purchases, and personal values. Through this type of research, program directors can not only learn those characteristics that set their audience members apart from rival stations but also discover particular segments of station listeners who differ on important attributes. For example, a sizable group of people available on weekends might like sports, and those available at 10:00 AM weekdays are neutral or negative toward sports. This knowledge might lead the station to adopt a block of weekend sports programming. Lifestyle analysis is easily done through telephone interviews.

In addition to these major forms of research, radio stations often want to explore other areas. They may desire research regarding new call letters, a new logo, the feasibility of a particular promotion campaign, or any other of a variety of subjects related to the overall programming.

Qualitative research is important to the radio business, especially in markets where the competition is keen. Program managers who do not keep up with the latest thoughts and preferences of the listening audience will quickly lose touch—and their jobs.

Satellite radio also conducts testing in many of these areas, although with different emphasis. Akin to cable television, satellite radio programming is, at least partly, supported by consumer subscriptions instead of advertising. Programming concerns are therefore less about keeping listeners tuned in to a specific station at a certain time (to hear specific advertisements) and more about keeping the audience satisfied with the selection and content of the service as a whole. This is especially important as the service tries to gain more of a share of the radio market. Recommendations to friends from satisfied current subscribers are the pot of gold at the end of the satellite radio programming rainbow. So programmers must exert significant

judgment and testing to get the colors just right.

Public Radio

Public radio, on the other hand, plays much looser with the testing ball, often dropping it altogether. A limited number of focus groups may comment on new programs, some before they air. Networks may conduct separate focus groups for audience members and for station program directors. Often, different results emerge from these two groups, thus proving to some program directors that they should not program for their own taste.

But public radio also may not test programs until they are already on the air. As NPR's Peter Pennycamp explained, "The program is given several months to develop and shake out, and then focus groups are brought in." This time factor constitutes a major difference between commercial and public broadcasting. Because public radio is not dependent on advertiser support and ratings, it has the luxury to let something grow on its own.

Still, PRI, for example, asks independent producers who are considering submitting program material to have answers for the following questions before submitting:[3]

- What is my program idea?
- What makes my perspective unique?
- Why would a national audience be interested in my program or series?
- Why would a program director want to broadcast this program or series?
- What marketing strategies make good sense for this program?

INTERNET TESTING

As we explained in previous chapters, Internet content can be generally broken into two groups: content **simul-cast** over the Internet, such as the live streaming of traditional radio or television station broadcasts, and content available only on the Internet, which can include archives and web-only media from traditional broadcasters and content created by independent developers.

Testing (Or Not) Simulcast Content

Simulcast content mostly relies on the testing that radio or television entities have already conducted before the traditional broadcast of the content. Programmers of radio stations that are simulcast over the Internet (a growing roster) rarely concern themselves with what the potential worldwide Internet audience might like to hear on a live webcast. Their advertisers are targeting the local audience, so that is the audience programmers target. The proportion of local to out-of-area Internet audience members, especially to commercial radio and television, is probably negligible. It mostly consists of ex-residents who listen out of habit or nostalgia or locals who are not near a radio, are out of the broadcast range, or for whom it is easier to listen on the computer—at work, for example.

Noncommercial simulcasts, however, are more likely to garner a more international audience. The United Kingdom's BBC, for example, offers a live feed of its television news broadcasts, and public broadcasting networks from the United States, Canada, Norway, Sweden, and so on all offer live radio feeds (many in English) that world news wonks tune in to regularly to gather different perspectives from around the globe. But where there is little to no testing of local populations done by public radio stations before

they air local programming, there is even less done to gauge the likes and dislikes of an international Internet audience.

Testing Archived and Independently Produced Content

Archived content, likewise, does not need to go through additional testing before being placed on an Internet site. Even with independently produced web-only content, the interactive and choose-your-own-path nature of the Internet makes content testing largely unnecessary.

Radio and television stations, unlike Internet entities, must make difficult choices about what to air when to gain optimal market share of the available audience. But the interactivity of the Internet allows audiences to request and experience the content of their choice whenever they want it. Although MTV (in its ever-diminishing lineup of solid music video programming) must play one music video after the other, risking that the second will turn off the viewer who was interested in the first, a website such as Launch.com can place thousands of music videos on its website and a viewer can choose which videos will come first, second, third, and so on.

As long as descriptions of content and hyperlinks are accurate, audiences will approach only content in which they have an interest. If, however, descriptions and hyperlinks are misleading, web surfers will quickly become frustrated and likely abandon a site forever—so accuracy and truth in advertising is highly advisable. A website is only as strong as its weakest link. Some audience members may have an interest in amateur-produced content; let them know that beforehand and they will not be disappointed with subpar production values.

Testing User Friendliness

Although testing of content before it goes on the Internet is a minor concern, another kind of testing is essential—the testing of functionality and usability. The term **user friendly** was coined in the 1990s when the Internet was going through an awkward puberty. The term did not describe most websites of the period but was a guide to what they should aspire to be. Thousands of websites were being rushed to market—developers trying to get their content to the public as quickly as possible. Although a baffling array of content became available on the Internet, trying to navigate through the content was even more baffling. With poor navigation plans, buttons that did not do as advertised, hyperlinks that led nowhere, sites crowded with superfluous graphics, time-consuming and useless introductory pages and doodads, and especially discouraging experiences of devoting tens of minutes filling in forms only to have the site malfunction upon pressing the final submit button—if it was not for the novelty of the Internet, users would have long abandoned it in frustration.

But user friendliness became more of a reality as web developers realized that, although they may have desirable and customizable content, if web surfers have to exert too much effort to get to that content, they will give up and turn to other more manageable sites. Worse yet, audiences may return to their radio or television, where they can consume without heartburn even if the flavor may not be as consistently to their individual tastes.

Today web developers test their **user interfaces** and designs before they go live with their sites—if they know what is good for them. Even the most seasoned web designer is often surprised, and somewhat befuddled, when he or she observes a test subject's first approach to a new design. What seemed a straightforward design can become an incomprehensible maze to a web neophyte.

Along with conducting their own tests, web developers can turn to numerous consulting companies that will conduct testing for them. As in television and radio, the consultant will want to first determine the target audience then to gather a sample and ask them to rate the proposed site based on various criteria.

Website usability analysis usually answers the following questions:

- How does the target audience use the site?
- Will a redesign make the site more appealing or easier to use?
- How does the site's usability compare with that of other sites serving the same audience?
- Can a visitor find what he or she came for, or do users leave without satisfaction?
- Will the site attract the right audience?

When it comes to advertising space—where, when, how much, and what type—web developers must find ways, often through testing, to answer many of the same questions that radio, television, and print media must answer. How much advertising is too much? What type of advertising is more frustrating to users, turning them off from the whole site? For example, as more Internet users switch to broadband Internet connections, web advertisers are finding new ways to use this bandwidth, replacing static banner advertisements with streaming video, glitzy motion graphics, and even animations that drop down or dance across the content of the website. Each new advertising format must be tested, both for its effectiveness in gaining the audience's attention and in conveying the intended message and for the level of frustration it may cause for viewers.

Another cause for testing is required by law of websites for nonprofit and governmental agencies because there are set federal accessibility standards to assist users with vision or other impairments. Many consultants offer these services, both to check for compliance and to fix those elements that do not comply.

DOES THE RESEARCH WORK?

Although usability tests for websites do not raise much controversy or debate, attitudes toward whether or not research works in radio and television differ widely and sometimes passionately. Some producers consider qualitative research a valuable tool in the shaping of their productions. Others think it is a pestilence. They would rather put their faith in the opinion of one experienced staff member than in a battery of audience tests. Gene Reynolds, producer of many popular shows, including "M★A★S★H," a multi-Emmy award winner, refused to even read a packet of research material that a network had provided on a new series he was about to launch. He had his own vision of the series and was more confident in his own instincts than in the reactions of untrained critics.

The pilots of two of the biggest hits in the history of network television received moderate to low test scores. "Batman," a late-1960s weekly prime-time series based on the cartoon character (later converted into a major motion picture success), was produced in a broad, tongue-in-cheek fashion. With its colorful villains and larger-than-life leads, it zoomed to the No. 1 position in weeks. But before its premiere, it fared abominably in a large theater test. As one ABC program executive recalled, "The theater audience was puzzled about what they were looking at. Was it a comedy, an adventure, a combination of both, or what? So we ordered a second test and had the moderator come out before the screening to tell them it was a put on, it was fun, it was OK to laugh. And they did. The second score was very good. We changed all our promos overnight to stress that the shows were fun. The spots positioned the audience properly and we had an instant hit."

"All in the Family," which premiered in 1971 on CBS, was a show unlike any other that had ever appeared on television (Figure 5.9). The protagonist, Archie Bunker, was a bigoted, racist male chauvinist who referred to minorities in derogatory phrases and told his wife to "stifle" herself. The reaction of the test audience was primarily bewilderment with touches of outrage, and the scores were decidedly subpar. Nowhere in the survey findings was there indication that the show would become an enormous hit.

When people seek to emphasize the flaws of testing, they often point to "Seinfeld," a phenomenally successful show that tested poorly. But, as CBS's

Figure 5.9
"All in the Family," with Carroll O'Connor playing the "lovable bigot" Archie Bunker, dominated the prime-time ratings in the 1970s. But when the pilot was tested, the show's breakthrough language and story lines puzzled and annoyed respondents, who gave it a failing grade. (Courtesy the Academy of Television Arts & Sciences.)

Figure 5.10
Testing paved the way for the success of "Joan of Arcadia" in the 2003–2004 season. (Globe Photos, Inc.)

Steinberg observed in defense of testing, people often fail to consider key factors when discussing so-called testing failures. He points out that the tested "Seinfeld" episode was very different from the show that aired and that became one of television's landmark shows. For example, the "Seinfeld" episode that tested poorly did not include the pivotal character of Elaine, played in the series by Julia Louis-Dreyfus.

Another show often singled out as a testing failure is CBS's "Everybody Loves Raymond." Television commentator Brian Lowry in an article questioning the effectiveness of focus groups notes that the show, which became a powerhouse for CBS, was dismissed by focus groups as "too thin" and "not current" with a "weak" main character who has a wife who "lacks charisma."

The show, which began in 1996, posted "average" or "below average" scores at ASI. Research found testing groups complaining that the show contains "nothing fresh or new."[4]

One of the reasons "Everybody Loves Raymond" has succeeded as well as it has on air and in syndication is that it contains no topical references, references that can date a show quickly. The early testing questioned the lack of topicality, but creator and executive producer Phil Rosenthal refused to alter the show, resisting topical issues and calls to give the show more edge.

In terms of **concept testing,** respondents will sometimes take the high road, indicating they would rather see a serious piece about the Civil War than a piece of fluff about three co-eds who have to pretend to be strippers to save their beloved sorority. The network executive who sees a potential hit in the Civil War movie based on testing might be disappointed in the ratings if he or she goes ahead with it, particularly if it is programmed against the show about the three co-eds. Failing to take into account that respondents do not always watch what they say they are going to watch can be a costly lesson.

Nevertheless, testing professionals maintain that testing can be an indispensable tool and that testing interpreted correctly rarely fails to be an accurate barometer. Interpreting testing correctly means not looking at testing in isolation but rather evaluating it in terms of other factors, such as scheduling, **audience flow,** and promotional marketing strategies and budgets.

CBS's Steinberg believes strongly that programs need to "buy the equity of the audience," and he points to the success of CBS's 2003–2004 drama "Joan of Arcadia" as a show that benefited greatly from thorough testing and testing evaluation (Figure 5.10). The show, about a teenage girl who sees God in various incarnations, sometimes as a cute teenage boy or sometimes as an African-American cafeteria worker, had to be positioned to avoid preaching at or to the audience. Nor could it offend the audience. Thus a potentially controversial show about the sensitive topic of religion avoided pitfalls as a result of testing.

Similarly, the testing of the promos of "Hack," a CBS drama that premiered in the 2002–2003 season, revealed that the initial promo, which touted the show as "from the writer of 'Spiderman,'" was using the wrong approach. This is because the promo caused viewers to expect a superman-type story instead of a gritty drama about a former Philadelphia cop who solves crimes from the vantage point of the cab he drives.

Although budget constraints may preclude this from happening, testing can also be useful in recasting if a particular performer in a pilot fails to connect with a test group.

Test findings are most reliable when they are measured against the norms of other programs of similar and familiar content. Attempting to evaluate unique program concepts for which no normative values have been established proves difficult. The system can be unreliable if the show departs too radically from the norm. Or, as Ken Auletta reports in his book *Three Blind Mice,* breakout shows such as "Hill Street Blues" test poorly because they are not familiar.[5]

Because song callouts for radio usually consist of playing the short hook of a song to a test subject in an unnatural environment, usually over the phone, some question the efficacy of callouts, especially when evaluating how receptive the audience may be to an unfamiliar, newly released song. Radio programmers want new songs to succeed with audiences, even though they may have no personal stake in the production of a song as a television programmer may have in a television program. A radio station will be unable to keep sounding fresh without introducing fresh material, hoping that songs will catch on with listeners. But programmers know that it only takes one lame song to make many audience members change the station, so they cannot go too far out on a limb when introducing new songs to audiences. Therefore, commercial radio programmers often rely on public radio stations to break new acts or songs, such as Beck's "Loser" in 1993 and Kelis's "Milkshake" in 2003, both of which saw their first spins on Los Angeles public radio station KCRW.

But programmers also rely on an artist's reputation, combined with testing, when deciding to air new material. This strategy, however, can have inconsistent results. After Pink's 2000 debut album, with the hit song "Most Girls," programmers held their breath for the dreaded sophomore album, where so many artists with great debuts fall, never to be heard from again. The lead single on Pink's 2001 *Missundaztood* album, "Get this Party Started," had mixed testing results, but as Sean Ross, Edison Media Research vice president of music and programming, said, "Top 40 programmers, thrilled to have some actual, by God, pop/rock balance on their stations, held their breath and waited—playing it a rotation, or two, higher than it might have deserved initially, because it was a record they *wanted* to work." Eventually it became one of the biggest singles of the year and yielded two more hit singles from the album. But when Pink's third effort was released in 2003, the first single, "Trouble," got immediate airplay from programming directors who thought, after striding over the sophomore hurdle, Pink's third album would be programming gold. "I thought the record would be so big, I added it straight into subpower out of the box. Wow, did I miss on that one," said WAKS Cleveland Programming Director Dan Mason. Unlike Christina Aguilera's "Dirrty," which had a rough start too, Mason says, "This isn't even the case of a huge phone record that took a minute to call out. Our audience was just apathetic about [Pink's new song "Trouble"] from the start." Nonetheless, some testing showed signs that the song might eventually catch on, so many stations continued to give it strong rotation. It turned out to be throwing good airtime after bad until programmers realized that the positive callouts probably reflected the test subjects' desire to see Pink's song succeed more than the song's ability to succeed on its own merits.[6]

This is all to say that testing programming is an inexact art. The process is filled with hunches, feelings, guesses, and prayers. Any hard facts that can be introduced into the mix can help to reduce the number of variables and lead to more reliable decision making. Solid data should be encouraged. So-called visceral programmers should welcome information that will contribute to more enlightened judgments. But programmers would do well to heed the words of ASI's Paul Lendburg: "The purpose of qualitative research is to identify opportunities and help to eliminate flaws, thereby reducing risks."

Research holds a potential danger: any number, no matter how questionably arrived at, may be considered more valid than a seasoned opinion unsupported by charts and graphs. All research data should be given its proper weight and added to the host of other considerations that enter a programming decision. Many of these other factors are dealt with in the following chapter, which describes elements that help make successful programming.

EXERCISES

1. Watch a television show, listen to a radio program, or visit a website. Make up a series of focus group questions. Administer your own focus group based on the questions you prepared.

2. Come up with an idea for a niche cable channel. Prepare a concept test to see whether your channel is viable in today's marketplace.

3. Research a program that has tested poorly and done well in the ratings. Then analyze the discrepancy between the show's weak testing and its successful performance.

Do the same with a show that tested well and performed poorly.

4. Ask your local testing service if you can observe a testing session. Write a paper detailing what you witnessed.

5. Pick an Internet neophyte in your acquaintance and ask him or her to achieve a specific goal on a site that you use often. Observe, but do not assist, navigation of the site. Note any difficulties and come up with suggestions for a redesign of the site that might help to alleviate these difficulties.

REFERENCES/NOTES

1. Dan Enright. "Let's Replace TV Audience Testing with Ingenuity and Daring," *Los Angeles Times,* March 23, 1992, p. F-3.

2. Malcolm Gladwell. *The Tipping Point* (Boston: Little Brown, 2000), p. 127.

3. PRI. "Producing for PRI," http://pri.org/PublicSite/inside/text_producing.html. Accessed December 20, 2003.

4. Brian Lowry. "When Not to Trust the Feedback," *Los Angeles Times,* July 9, 2002, p. F-1.

5. Ken Auletta. *Three Blind Mice* (New York: Random House, 1991), p. 515.

6. Edition Media Research. "Ross on Radio," http://www.edisonresearch.com/ross_on_radio_trouble.htm. Accessed December 26, 2003.

6 Elements of Successful Programming

In this chapter, you will learn about the following:

- How industry professionals create successful programming
- The importance of prestige and awards in determining a program's success
- How timing, trend awareness, and other key factors influence success or failure
- The important difference between star-dominant programming and format-dominant programming
- Radio's focus on being locally relevant, creating a mood, and maintaining innovation
- The Internet producer's need to keep content fresh, consistent, and innovative
- The Internet's unique ability to target content to individual audience members

How does a programmer create product that has a reasonable chance at success? Where does he or she start? What factors are involved? What has worked in the past, and what is likely to work today? In this chapter, we examine elements that programmers must take into consideration if they hope to achieve success. We look at past successes to gain an appreciation of the influences that have shaped the contemporary landscape.

In one respect, programming for television, radio, and the Internet is no different from any other marketed product: success is measured by the achievement of an objective. In most cases, the goal of programs is to attract the largest possible audience—but not always. As you shall see, some shows have a different purpose.

After an objective is established, the programmer must decide how to attract the audience. Can viewers, listeners, or Internet users best be reached by laughter or adventure, drama or interactivity? Once that decision is made, what elements should be emphasized to give a programmer a solid chance at success?

Even if these questions are carefully considered by the programmer, there is no guarantee of success. Audiences are notoriously unpredictable, and their tastes mercurial. But one thing is certain: no show ever succeeded by ignoring its objective or dismissing essential elements.

TELEVISION PROGRAMMING

Because commercial television and **basic cable** must be responsive to advertisers, the overriding elements for success have to do with delivering an audience for the advertisers. In addition, basic cable has to provide programming that keeps subscribers paying their monthly subscription fees. **Premium cable** channels such as HBO, Cinemax, Starz, or Showtime, which do not have to contend with advertisers, must provide the type of programming that justifies the additional subscription fees charged to the subscriber. Cable system managers and consumers alike complain about rising costs. Cable **multiple system owners (MSOs)** complain because cable networks are charging high rates for the MSOs to carry their programming, even if the ratings are falling. Consumers complain because the increasing fees MSOs pay are passed on to them in subscription fees that seem to rise too frequently. The five most expensive television networks for MSOs to carry in 2003 were, in order, ESPN (charges $1.76 per household), Fox Sports ($1.16), TNT ($0.78), the Disney Channel ($0.74), and USA ($0.40).[1]

Programming Objectives

Various goals may be established for a program. These are described in the following sections.

Widest Possible Audience. Television is a mass medium. It is the principal leisure-time activity of the nation. It is also a mass advertising device. Corporations spend hundreds of millions of dollars to stimulate desire for their products. Therefore, the objective of most shows is to attract the largest possible audience. The more viewers, the higher the advertising rate, the greater the gross revenue, and the larger the profit. Conversely, no audience, no advertisers, no profit, no broadcaster.

But not all segments of the audience watch the same shows. Children, ethnic groups, and infrequent viewers are all part of a broadcaster's constituency. Each will probably have different viewing habits. It thus follows that programs designed for the interests of these groups must be represented on the schedule if a broadcaster truly wants to reach the largest number of viewers.

Frequently, however, a broadcaster (or advertiser) is more interested in reaching a particular segment of the audience rather than a large body count. Not all segments of the audience watch the same programs. For example, a luxury automobile company may have affluent males as its principal advertising target. This marketing goal will be better achieved through commercials in a golf tournament than in a broad-based sitcom whose larger audience consists primarily of women and children of lesser means. However, broadcasters must be careful about scheduling programs tailored to fit the specialized needs of a sponsor. The "demographic show" with its highly focused but limited appeal may substantially reduce the audience size of the programs that follow it. The consequent revenue loss may exceed the profit from the specialized presentations.

The Fox network was founded on demographic programming. To attract a commercially successful audience, Fox had to reach viewers who were not being satisfied by the three long-entrenched networks, ABC, NBC, and CBS. The company focused on the 18 to 34 year olds, the demographic group most desired by advertisers. In many ways, there is nothing particularly new about Fox's approach. Leonard Goldenson, former president of ABC, said it reminds him of the early days of his network, in the mid-1950s, when he began with 14 stations and both CBS and NBC had more than 70 affiliates. Fox is "really copying the same thing we did when we started," he said. "It's a sound principle—going after young families, trying to counter program wherever you can, trying to come up with some kind of innovation—and take chances."[2]

The WB, with shows such as "Dawson's Creek" (Figure 6.1), "Gilmore Girls," "7th Heaven," and "Everwood," similarly attracted the coveted younger demographic as it established itself as a new network. This allowed the WB to charge high advertising fees on shows that generally had low household ratings. Advertisers crave 18 to 34 year olds, and the WB was able to position itself as the place to be to appeal to this demographic.

The top 10 shows for 18- to 49-year-old viewers are different from the Top 10 shows for 50+ viewers, as are the top shows for African-American and Caucasian households. From September 22 to October 26, 2003, the top shows for 18 to 49 year olds were "Friends," "CSI," "ER," "Will & Grace," "Scrubs," "Survivor," "Monday Night Football," "Coupling," "CSI: Miami," and "Law & Order." The top 10 shows for 50+ viewers for the same period were "CSI," "Everybody Loves Raymond," "60 Minutes," "Cold Case," "JAG," "CSI: Miami," "Navy NCIS," "Law & Order," "Without a Trace," and "Two and a Half Men."[3] Note that only the two "CSI" shows and "Law & Order" overlap.

The top 10 shows for African-Americans for the fourth quarter of 2002 were "Cedric the Entertainer Presents," "One on One," "Girlfriends," "Half & Half," "The Parkers," "My Wife and Kids," "The Bernie Mac Show," "Monday Night Football," "Fastlane," and "CSI." The top shows for Caucasian

Figure 6.1
Katie Holmes and James Van der Beek starred in "Dawson's Creek," a show that captured the targeted audience for the WB. (Courtesy the Academy of Television Arts & Sciences.)

households for the same period were "CSI," "Friends," "ER," "Everybody Loves Raymond," "Survivor: Thailand," "Law & Order," "Will & Grace," "CSI: Miami," "Scrubs," and "Monday Night Football."[4] Note here that only two shows, "Monday Night Football" and "CSI," overlap.

Narrowcasting. Cable differs from commercial TV in that most of the networks do not attempt to gain the widest possible audience, preferring instead to go after a smaller, niche audience. Because of the high degree of narrowcasting within cable services, particular cable networks are more likely to aim for very specific demographic audiences, particularly when viewers have so many choices. Being all things to all people in the true sense of *broad*casting becomes increasingly difficult.

MTV's target audience is different from that of Nostalgia Television in terms of age and general lifestyle. Nickelodeon caters to the young; Black Entertainment Television targets African-Americans. Spike TV goes after men; Lifetime is aimed at women. Each of these services must consider its target audience as it assesses program ideas and its advertising possibilities.

Attracting Subscribers. For cable services that do not deal with advertisers, the story is a little different. Pay movie channels, such as HBO and Showtime, receive their money directly from cable subscribers who decide to pay for their programming. Therefore, their specific audience is the people who have subscribed. The services must program in such a way that they keep these people happy so they do not become disenchanted and disconnect. One way they accomplish this is by providing programming that the "free" television networks cannot match, such as feature films fresh from their theatrical releases, made-for-TV movies, and miniseries with large budgets and with stars such as Tom Hanks or Annette Bening who tend not to do commercial television. Premium cable networks may also offer high-profile sports events and series with adult themes and language such as "G-String Divas." Pay-per-view movies or specials are successful if enough people sign up to bring a profit. As media critic Allison Romano wrote, with premium cable, "It's not just about viewers tuning in. It's about their paying up."[5]

The "In-and-Out" Audience. Another type of specific audience that some cable systems try to attract is an in-and-out audience. The Weather Channel, for instance, does not presume that people will sit and watch it for hours, although they will happily accept someone who does. CNN and the various shopping channels are likely to capture audience members for a limited amount of time. What they are aiming for is a large total number of viewers, even though any one person might not stay with the service for a long period.

Attracting the Elite. The noncommercial nature of public broadcasting makes it unique because, although it must have enough money to cover costs, it does not have to concern itself with profit or advertising. It does, however, need to provide programming that **underwriters,** corporations that provide funding in exchange for a brief mention of their support, will find attractive.

In general, public broadcasters do not seek (or attain) a large audience. The broadcasters need to prove their worth to their funders, but they do not need to do so by delivering an overall enormous audience. They want to attract a large enough audience to make the costs worthwhile and to have a base of people who will donate to a station, but the nature of the audience is often more important than its size.

For this reason, the most important of the objectives to public broadcasters involves a specific target audience, a particular local or national purpose, and a unique objective that public broadcasters refer to as **units of good,** a public broadcasting term used to designate the inherent, uplifting worth of a program. Public broadcasting audiences are generally intellectually elite and politically influential. PBS compiles data each year that highlights the upscale nature of its audience (Figure 6.2).

Public television no longer has a monopoly on quality programming geared to the elite. The financial pressures of the FCC mandated convergence to digital, and many channels such as A&E, the Discovery Channel, and Bravo, have made inroads into public broadcasting territory. These channels and others have attracted high-end audiences and forced public television to redefine its concept of successful programming. For one thing, public television now offers more programs with American themes and locations and fewer British shows.

Making Noise. With the explosion in viewer choices that followed the deregulation of the entertainment industry in 1996, it became increasingly important for shows and networks to distinguish themselves from the clutter. In 2003, it was estimated that there were 287 cable networks. That is a lot of choices. Thus, "making noise," that is, drawing attention to a product or network, became in and of itself a sign of success.

A producer like Mike Fleiss, who created "Who Wants to Marry a Multimillionaire" for Fox (a show that caused considerable controversy when it was discovered that the groom in question had a restraining order in his past), "The Bachelor," and "The Bachelorette" became sought after precisely because of his ability to create noise.[6]

Similarly, FX's "The Shield," which premiered March 12, 2002, created instant noise with its realistic depiction of violence and its use of strong language. The show cemented its ability to garner attention with an Emmy Award win for its lead, Michael Chiklis. The show helped shine a spotlight on FX as it attempted to steal some of the thunder from cable rival HBO. FX's

The Public Television Audience

- The public TV audience reflects the social and economic makeup of the nation.
- 70.9% of all American television-owning families - 75.7 million households representing 143.6 million people - watched public television in October 2002, with the average home tuning in for approximately eight hours during the month
- From October to December 2002, 88 million viewers in 50.6 million households watched public TV each week, according to the Nielsen Television Index (NTI). This represents 47.4% of America's 106.7 million households with TVs.
- During prime time in this period, public TV was watched each week in 27.0 million households by 43.8 million people.
- During the October-December 2002 period, public TV's average prime-time rating was 1.7, compared with 1.4 for Lifetime, 1.3 for USA, 1.3 for Nick at Nite, 1.2 for TBS, 1.0 for Fox News, 0.8 for Discovery Channel, 0.7 for CNN, 0.7 for A&E, and 0.6 for the History Channel.
- The average viewing household during this period watched three hours of public TV in the course of a week; of this amount, and almost an hour and a half was spent with prime-time programming.
- 99% of all U.S. homes with a TV can receive a public TV station. The most widely available cable networks can be seen by only 82%. Public TV is freely available to viewers; cable costs about $600 per year.

Audience Breakdown

Below is a breakdown, by TV household characteristics, of the full day public TV audience for an average week from October 2002 and November 2002. National persons demographic figures are also provided by sex/age. (Source: Nielsen Television Index.)

* — Head of household

Characteristic	Total U.S. TV Households %	Public TV Audience %
Race *		
Black	12.0	10.7
Spanish Origin	9.1	8.5
Education *		
Less than 4 yrs. high school	14.9	14.6
4 years high school	30.5	29.1
1-3 years college	27.6	27.4
4+ years college	27.0	28.9
Occupation *		
Prof./Owner/Manager	25.8	25.1
Clerical & Sales	16.3	15.9
Skilled & Semi-skilled	26.7	23.9
Not in labor Force	31.2	35.2
Household Income *		
Less than $20,000	20.0	19.7
$20,000-$39,999	23.9	23.3
$40,000-$59,999	18.2	18.0
$60,000+	37.9	39.0
Age		
Children (2-5)	5.7	9.0
Children (6-11)	9.0	8.3
Teen-agers (12-17)	9.1	4.7
Women		
(18-34)		
(35-49)	12.0	8.3
(50-64)	12.0	11.8
(65+)	8.7	10.1
	7.1	11.3
Men		
(18-34)	11.8	7.4
(35-49)	11.5	11.3
(50-64)	8.0	9.7
(65+)	5.1	8.2

http://www.pbs.org/aboutpbs/aboutpbs_corp_audience.html (January 19, 2004)

Figure 6.2

2003 public television audience statistics from the PBS website. (http://www.pbs.org/aboutpbs/aboutpbs_corp_audience.html. Accessed January 19, 2004.)

Figure 6.3
*"The West Wing"
earned nine
Emmys in 2000.*
(Courtesy the
Academy of
Television Arts &
Sciences.)

subsequent show, "Lucky," may have been a more complex, more original program, but it did not succeed in creating the kind of buzz "The Shield" did and it quickly disappeared. The ability to make noise may not change the world of television (see, for example, Fox's surprise reality hit of 2003, "The Simple Life," starring Paris Hilton and Nicole Richie, in which two rich girls abandon their pampered lives to rough it on a farm, à la "Green Acres"). But any show that generates awareness in a crowded field has achieved a significant level of success.

Prestige and Awards. Prestige and awards raise the stature of the network or station and are thus much sought. Commercial broadcasters will occasionally keep a poorly rated show on the air for prestige and awards. For example, NBC kept its series "American Dreams" for several seasons despite weak ratings because of its quality and its prosocial values. Some series on commercial networks have even been known to invest additional money in an episode in an attempt to make it worthy of award consideration. These efforts are not just for ego gratification. They can produce highly tangible results. "Hill Street Blues," a superbly produced and acted series, was faring poorly in the ratings in its first season (1981). However, at Emmy time it walked off with eight awards. The subsequent excitement attracted many viewers, and the show went on to enjoy a healthy 6 year run. It held the record for Emmys until "The West Wing" (Figure 6.3) earned nine in 2000.

Prestige and awards are important to the commercial networks (at one point, CBS even had a special department charged with creating shows that would win awards, and many performers cleverly cast themselves as guest stars in network drama and comedy series to be recognized at Emmy time). But it is the premium networks that really go after this kind of recognition. Showtime, for example, lets producers know that what they want is "controversy and awards."

HBO, in particular, has gone after awards with a vengeance ever since cable was successful in lobbying to be allowed to submit programs for Emmys in 1987.[7] Because HBO attaches such importance to awards, it sends lavish packages of its high-end programming to members of the Academy of Television Arts & Sciences. Network executives are not hesitant to claim that it is unfair for them to have to compete with HBO because HBO has larger budgets and different programming objectives, creating an uneven playing field. Many feel that HBO, which has the slogan, "It's not TV, it's HBO," should not be competing with "regular" television programs for recognition from the Academy of Television Arts & Sciences.

Public television often supplies award-worthy programming. Underwriters in particular like to be associated with prestige productions, and many public television programs win prestigious awards, such as the George Foster Peabody Awards. But public television does not have the visibility (or HBO's promotion budget) to be a major player at many awards presentations (see sidebar on awards).

SOME AWARDS TELEVISION PROGRAMMERS STRIVE TO ATTAIN

Academy of Television Arts & Sciences Daytime Emmy Awards: For outstanding achievement in daytime television

Academy of Television Arts & Sciences Primetime Emmy Awards: For outstanding achievement for nighttime programs shown nationally

Achievement in Children's Television Awards: For significant contribution toward improving children's radio and television, presented by the media watchdog group Action for Children's Television (ACT)

The American Comedy Awards: For excellence in comedy on network programs, syndicated programs, and cable shows as voted by comedians

American Women in Radio and Television Awards: For excellence in portraying a positive and realistic image of women

The Annie Awards: For distinguished work in animation

The Director's Guild of America Awards: For television directing

First Americans in the Arts: For outstanding achievement by Native Americans

Freedom Foundation Awards: For television and radio programs that enhance America's image

The Gay & Lesbian Alliance Against Defamation (GLAAD) Awards: For positive portrayal of gays and lesbians on television

George Foster Peabody Awards: For achievement in news, entertainment, education, programs for children, documentaries, and public service

The Golden Globes: Frequently undermined for their fan-like approach and their limited membership but nevertheless coveted by stars and their publicists, possibly because the Golden Globe presentation party is such a good time and the goodie bags are filled to capacity with lavish gifts

The Humanitas Awards: For writers in the entertainment industry whose work enriches and enlightens audiences

Iris Awards: For outstanding local television programs

Media Access Awards: For realistic portrayals of people with disabilities

The People's Choice Awards: One of many awards that the public votes on, this is determined by a Gallup poll of more than 5000 people nationwide

Time magazine's "TV Most" Awards: For the best and worst that television has to offer

The Writer's Guild of America Awards: For good television writing

Figure 6.4
"The Six Million Dollar Man" was a perfect example of a format-dominant show. (Courtesy MCA Television Group.)

The Search for a Successful Formula

Since television's early days, programmers have sought a "formula" for a hit. They have tried to research a winning combination, they have attempted to promote their way into success, and they have even consulted clairvoyants. For example, ABC's Fred Pierce secretly hired a Hollywood psychic, Beverlee Dean, at a salary of $24,000 a year in 1978 to consult with her about programming decisions.[8] To this day, Dean maintains that all she did was give some opinions about scheduling and which shows she liked, that she really was not a psychic, but hiring her caused Pierce significant embarrassment: "Hiring a psychic, what next?" The magic key to programming success has long remained elusive, for a good reason. There is no key, and there are no shortcuts.

Success is a strange alchemy of timing, hunch, hard work, anticipation, professionalism, and luck. This is true for one particular show, a series, or an entire programming concept, and it holds true whether the program is format dominant or star dominant (see sidebar on programming forms).

TWO BASIC FORMS OF PROGRAMMING

All programs, regardless of their objectives or their appeals, originate in one of two forms:

1. **Format dominant**—The concept of the show is the key to its success; performers are selected to fulfill the requirements of the core idea.
2. **Star dominant**—The star is the key ingredient; a format is designed around the skills of the lead performer.

A classic example of a format-dominant, **high-concept** (a show whose premise is quickly and easily understood) program was "The Six Million Dollar Man" (Figure 6.4), an action–adventure series in the late 1970s. The show was based on the idea that a badly injured astronaut could be rebuilt with atomic-powered electromechanical devices that would make him capable of superhuman performance. Stories were developed more to demonstrate dazzling physical feats than to provide character insights. The principal role required handsome athleticism, and Lee Majors was chosen from a sizable list of candidates. In 2003, UPN revisited this type of high-concept show with a younger lead who had superhuman powers; it even brought in Majors to guest star. But "Jake 2.0," although executed well, did not achieve the same level of success as its predecessor.

More recent examples of format-dominant shows include "Northern Exposure," "ER," "CSI," and "Cold Case." Under ideal circumstances, performers in these types of programs will add values that may not have been originally evident and make the series even more appealing, as was the case with the cast of "ER," where breakout performers such as George Clooney, Julianna Margulies, and Anthony Edwards were able to add just the right mix to the show. Sometimes a program will start format dominant but will become a star vehicle over time because a performer has shaped the show to his or her own designs, not always to the project's benefit. "Family Feud" began as a rigidly structured game show with the host serving as an affable traffic cop. But not long after the premiere, Richard Dawson changed the focus by kissing every lady contestant, reading his fan mail, displaying presents he had received, and generally favoring the audience with his view of world affairs. Many episodes required hours of editing to present a completed game.

The other type of show is one built around the skills and personality of a star. This is most clearly seen in talk and magazine programs such as "The Oprah Winfrey Show," "The Ellen DeGeneres Show," or "Dr. Phil." However, it also applies to fictional formats devised to display the performer's abilities—for example, "The Cosby Show," "Roseanne," all of Bob Newhart's series, "Everybody Loves Raymond" (built around the talents of Ray Romano), "Seinfeld," or "Whoopi."

Even though a star may be exceptionally talented and enjoy a large following, the development of an appropriate format can be elusive. Such illustrious names as Mickey Rooney, Frank Sinatra, James Stewart, Bette Midler, Dolly Parton, Geena Davis, Sally Field, and Tony Curtis have stumbled in their TV series either because they were not right for the medium or because the format was not right for them.

The strength of star-dominant programs is that they automatically define their appeal. If you know the performer, you pretty much know what to expect, and sampling time is greatly compressed. On the other hand, if a star-dominant show begins to slide (or the artist imposes impossible demands), there is no way to salvage it.

Although both format-dominant and star-dominant shows are capable of delivering big hits, buyers tend to favor the former. Their reasons are summarized in the experience of "You Bet Your Life" starring Bill Cosby. This syndicated series was bought by over 200 stations purely on the basis of Cosby's enormous success on the network sitcom, "The Cosby Show." "You Bet Your Life" had served as a creaky but workable format for the rapier wit of Groucho Marx in the 1950s, but when it was dusted off for Buddy Hackett in 1980, it was an instant failure. No matter. This was the 1990s and the host was Bill Cosby (Figure 6.5). How could it miss? It did, and badly. The series was canceled after one season. According to Greg Meidel, then president of Twentieth Television, there was a lesson to be learned: "Format first, star second. You can have a proven big star, but you really have to have a proven format. It was a great personality in the wrong vehicle."[9]

Figure 6.5
Bill Cosby and Carol Burnett at the Emmy Awards. (Courtesy the Academy of Television Arts & Sciences.)

Figure 6.6
"Friends" was a powerhouse for NBC, acquiring a loyal, almost fanatical fan base. (Courtesy the Academy of Television Arts & Sciences.)

Industry Professionals Weigh In

Industry professionals have many things to say about what contributes to successful programming.

Edgar Scherick, whose career in television and film spanned more than 6 decades, had a clear programming philosophy.

Scherick was head of programming at ABC. He created the "Wide World of Sports" concept, started the careers of many successful executives (e.g., Scott Rudin, Barbara Lieberman, Gary Hoffman, Brian Grazer, and Michael Barnathan), and produced many of television's signature programs, such as "The Kennedys of Massachusetts," "Raid on Entebbe," and "Little Gloria, Happy at Last." In 1965, Scherick developed a programming philosophy that continues to be applicable. Before going forward with a program, Scherick would ask, "Is this project touched with singularity?" Is there something unique or different in the concept and execution that will

attract viewers? If the answer was "no," then he did not go forward, a lesson many programmers might heed, even when more programming is needed to fill the floodgates.[10]

Alan Landsburg, one of television's more successful producers in all programmatic forms for more than 5 decades ("That's Incredible," "Unspeakable Acts," and "The Ryan White Story," among others) claims there are really only three themes that count in storytelling: sex, money, and power. These are the elements that compel people—the subjects that fascinate and motivate them. Any drama, or comedy, that explores these qualities is on solid footing.

Sex should be understood in the larger sense of love, romance, and the eternal, universal quest for the "right other person." Certain groups may object to the proliferation of sexual themes, for example in "Friends" (Figure 6.6) or in "Coupling," 2003's visible failure, but the topic of sex continues to

Figure 6.7
*"The Love Boat,"
whose cast is
prepared here for a
Christmas episode,
lasted 9 years on
ABC, another
testament to Aaron
Spelling's ability to
create shows with
wide viewer appeal.*
(Courtesy of
Bruce Bilson.)

— Sexy shows are now on where "family hour" programming used to be.

dominate, often even at 8:00 P.M., which used to be the **family hour.** Cable seemingly thrives on sexual content, and network reality shows such as "Temptation Island" and "Are You Hot?" offer sexual innuendo in every promo and every segment of a show.

Episodes about money touch all. The drive to get it or the fear of not having it are daily concerns. There is also the dream of sudden riches that makes people empathize with those who have come into prosperity. For example, Ralph Kramden, played by Jackie Gleason on early television's "The Honeymooners," was always after the quick buck that would make him rich. The plastic surgeons in cable's 2003–2004 success "Nip/Tuck" forgo making ethical decisions in favor of making the

kind of money that enables them to maintain their lavish lifestyles. Not to be forgotten are the TV game shows that have been trading on the money instinct for decades. The winners are news. Viewers want to see them and fantasize that they will be next.

"Power," according to Henry Kissinger, "is the ultimate aphrodisiac."[11] People strive for it, fight for it, lie for it, and kill for it. It has been the stuff of drama from Shakespeare to "Dynasty" to "The Apprentice" with Donald Trump. Pick up any weekly schedule of TV programs and read the capsule descriptions of dramatic episodes. You will find dozens that have a power struggle as their foundation.

Producer Aaron Spelling, who gave television "The Love Boat" (Figure 6.7),

Figure 6.8
The first-rate production values in "CSI" have helped it to develop into a No. 1 show. (Globe Photos, Inc.)

"Beverly Hills, 90210," "Melrose Place," and "7th Heaven," among others, believes that escapist entertainment is the key to success. Spelling perfected the art of casting attractive people in shows that do not contain too much realism. Realism can be depressing, and many people would agree with Spelling that after a hard day at work or attending to household chores escapist, entertaining television is what most people want.

Jerry Bruckheimer, whose shows "CSI" (Figure 6.8), "CSI: Miami," and "Without a Trace" provide CBS with a ratings edge, places great emphasis on first-rate production values, including a brilliant use of music on all of his shows.

For Susan Rovner, vice president of drama development at Warner Bros., quality is the key to success. She sees the drama series as a writer's medium, and she thinks that writers with distinctive voices are the key to successful shows. She said that shows have to be "about something" and that talented writers can make "contemporary variations on familiar themes" rise well above the mundane.

For some, such as producer Marcy Carsey, who with partners Tom Werner and Caryn Mandabach is responsible for many of television's signature successes including "The Cosby Show," "Roseanne," and "That '70s Show," a storytelling style that mixes the sweet and the sour leads to success.[12]

For Michael O'Hara, Emmy-nominated producer–writer of the blockbuster miniseries "Switched at Birth" and more than 30 television movies, "the key ingredient for a successful television show is striking a chord with a large segment of the audience. This can be a funny chord like 'Seinfeld,' a sad one like 'Roots,' or a silly one like 'Queer Eye for the Straight Guy.' The Holy Grail for any television executive is finding a show that people want to return to week after week."

Key Elements for Success

Some industry leaders, such as Judd Parkin, a former network executive at NBC and ABC and now a successful writer of television movies, believe successful shows are mostly a matter of luck. Despite the impossibility of predicting a hit, there are certain elements that winning programs or concepts possess. Their presence does not guarantee success, but their absence almost always assures failure. It is not as simple as going down the checklist and inserting each element into the mix. Skillful execution must be there regardless of the ingredients; however, success embodies some combination of the elements described in following sections.

— Key Elements
— Conflict   — trend awareness
— Durability   — Adequate Budget
— Likeability   — Salability
— Consistency   — Getting cross-over
*   Viewers.*
— Energy
— Professional Staffing   — 1 voice of authority
— Timing

Figure 6.9
The conflicts between the two brothers on "Frasier," whose cast is shown here, created strong comic moments. (Courtesy the Academy of Television Arts & Sciences.)

Conflict. Many regard conflict as the most important ingredient. Without the collision of interests or attitudes, there is little to hold the attention of viewers. This is true even where it is less obvious, for example, in talk and comedy. In situation comedies (sitcoms), core characters are placed in a primary arena where they respond to a story stimulus, usually a conflict. The genius of successful comedy creators is the ability to design characters so sharply that any stimulus immediately places them in conflict. The laughter results from the contrast in the attitudes. In "Cheers," Sam relentlessly searches for a night of romance. Rebecca abhors casual love-making. Any reference to sex automatically triggers a comedic conflict.

The two brothers on "Frasier" (Figure 6.9) may have some similar personality quirks, but they are in conflict about almost everything, creating comedic situations that enabled the show to remain at the top of the ratings for many years. Similarly, the two brothers on "Everybody Loves Raymond" clash on most issues, helping the show to enjoy its crown as CBS's top-rated comedy for several seasons.

The talk shows that produce the most interest are those with guests who have strong opinions that conflict with other panelists or members of the audience. Conflict is why talk shows such as "Jerry Springer" have **ambushes** in which one guest is pitted against another. In an ambush, each guest is charged up offstage to come out swinging, creating a staged conflict but a conflict nevertheless.

The goal of programmers is to construct shows that provide collisions. Even when mounting an information

— innovation & techniss

show, programmers should attempt to offer opposing or alternative attitudes. It is not only fair play; it is good television.

Durability. An idea intended to be a long-running success cannot be based on a premise that will flame out after brief exposure. Programmers must examine submissions carefully to be sure that the fundamental design of the show will sustain interest week after week.

One element that often helps create durability is the opportunity for many different characters to appear within particular episodes of a series. For example, in "Cheers," all types of characters can wander into the bar to interact with the regulars. Similarly, different individuals can come into the coffee shop in "Friends" to meet up with the series regulars and generate story complications.

Different individuals can enter the emergency room on "ER" as patients or doctors, and many politicians can gather in "The West Wing," providing story arcs. Even if outsiders are not used regularly, a large cast, such as the one on HBO's "The Sopranos," can allow the main story to revolve around different characters.

Even the most durable of episodic ideas eventually run their course. "M★A★S★H," "The Mary Tyler Moore Show," "Frasier," and "Friends" had the good grace to remove themselves from the airwaves voluntarily before their durability exhausted itself.

Syndication plays such an important role in the finances of network series that a show must be able to hold up for many years after its last episode has been shot. The success of "The Dick Van Dyke Show" in syndication, said the star, "is attributable to the wisdom of writer–director Carl Reiner, who had the foresight not to do any slang or idioms of the day or topical events."

The same avoidance of topical events in "Everybody Loves Raymond" made that particular show a syndication winner. Topical material rapidly becomes dated, hurting the long-term appeal of a show. All rules have exceptions, and the one about avoiding topical references does, too. "The Simpsons," for example, uses topical references liberally as a basis of its storytelling comedy; it has had a long run, both in first run and in syndication.

Whenever possible, programmers should think of specials and limited series as something more than single shots. This holds particularly true for reality shows. After a 6-week run, a successful reality show can spawn many offspring. For example, a "Survivor" show in one exotic locale can easily lead to another. "For Love or Money" did well enough for NBC in 2003–2004 to offer reality-obsessed fans a second installment, a reverse in which the woman who turned down an offer of love in favor of money in the first show became the one doing the selecting on the second show. And "The Bachelor" gave eager viewers "The Bachelorette." The phenomenal success of "Joe Millionaire" (Figure 6.10) in 2003 led to an international version, which, unfortunately for Fox, did not perform nearly as well as the first one with Evan Marriott.

In terms of durability in franchises, it is hard to beat "Who Wants to Be a Millionaire" (Figure 6.11). ABC may have overplayed its hand by putting the show starring Regis Philbin on too many times a week in 2001, effectively killing it on prime-time, but the show survives in syndication with Meredith Vieira and all over the world, where the "Millionaire" format has been adjusted to meet the needs of localism, (i.e., the questions have been adjusted to meet local needs).

No description of durability would be complete without a bow toward soap operas. "As the World Turns" has been on continuously since 1956 and "General Hospital" since 1963. "Another World" premiered in 1964, and "Days of Our Lives" came on a year later. But the all-time champion is "Guiding Light," which celebrated its 50th consecutive year on air in 2002. All of this longevity can be attributed to the remarkable abilities of such writers as Irna Phillips, Agnes Nixon, and Bill Bell, who mastered the art of intertwining stories about sex, money, and power.

Likeability. Viewers tune in to people they like and with whom they feel comfortable. It is a truism in Hollywood that viewers feel comfortable with familiar faces. Bill Cosby, Angela Lansbury, Michael J. Fox, Martin Sheen, Ted Danson, Kirstie Alley, and Whoopi Goldberg all exemplify the personalities who generally succeed in the medium. They are the kind of guests viewers are comfortable inviting into their living rooms.

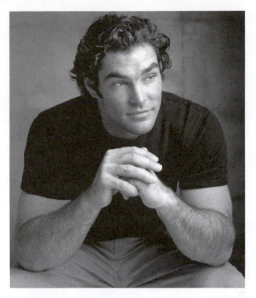

Figure 6.10
Evan Marriott of the reality dating show with a twist, "Joe Millionaire," which was a megahit in 2003. (Globe Photos, Inc.)

Figure 6.11
"Who Wants to Be a Millionaire" was a victim of overexposure. (Photo © ABC Photography Archives.)

Figure 6.12
"American Idol" found a good mix with its three judges, Simon Cowell, Paula Abdul, and Randy Jackson. (Courtesy the Academy of Television Arts & Sciences.)

Nowhere is the quality of friendliness more evident than with game show hosts. Some are more amusing, better looking, or more clear headed than others, but they all radiate cheer and goodwill. Audiences liked the nasty observations Simon Cowell made on "American Idol" (Figure 6.12), but he was one of three judges. Had he been by himself, his disparaging comments might not have been received so well. Indeed, it is difficult to imagine a successful emcee who, by himself, is downbeat, surly, and insulting to his contestants. Within a week viewers would run him out on a rail.

One might argue that Archie Bunker, J. R. of "Dallas," and Erica Kane of "All My Children" are hardly likable; nevertheless, they have developed enormous followings. However, it is important to understand they are playing the role of the burr under the saddle, the person you love to hate, to provide the conflict that makes the series work. Even Archie would occasionally let down his guard to allow some endearing humanity to slip through. When Alan Alda played a doctor who snapped nastily at people who questioned what he was doing with patients on "ER," this most likable television star's humanity allowed him to avoid being hated by viewers (Figure 6.13).

George Clooney's character in "ER" was a womanizer with serious problems, but his humanity made him intriguing and likable. Frasier, played by Kelsey Grammer, may be a pompous, self-obsessed individual, but he has nevertheless connected with audiences who appreciate his unique sense of humor and skewed view of the world. It also helps that the writing on the show is first rate.

The insult-tossing cast of "Married . . . With Children" also appears to be unlikable. But the audience seems to understand that underneath the family's surface of disrespect is a genuine affection. When the pilot program was tested, the 30 minutes of sarcasm ended with the couple walking up the staircase, the wife's hand gently patting the husband's behind. Viewer approval soared with the suspicion confirmed that deep down the spatters really loved each other. This was also the case with ABC's "Roseanne." Roseanne may have had a harsh tongue, but, according to Brett White, who was head of broadcast standards and practices at ABC for many years, viewers knew that deep down she cared deeply about her family.

Despite the trend toward "mean television" that coincided with the rise of reality television and the explosion of antagonistic talk show hosts such as Bill

Figure 6.13
When Alan Alda played a delusional doctor on "ER," he was able to maintain his humanity because of his likeability. (Courtesy the Academy of Television Arts & Sciences.)

O'Reilly and Rush Limbaugh, any programmer planning to launch a show with truly unlikable characters should be sure of two things: (1) the material is first rate and either very funny or very well executed, and (2) a backup program is readily available.

Consistency. All viewers bring a certain level of anticipation to every program. When they tune in to cable's "Queer Eye for the Straight Guy," they expect a variation on a makeover theme that contains helpful hints that reveal gays and straights can be supportive of each other. When they watch one of the

Figure 6.14
The "Law & Order" shows give audiences stories that reflect current events. (Courtesy the Academy of Television Arts & Sciences.)

Figure 6.15
"Murphy Brown," featuring Candice Bergen, achieved both consistency and topicality. (Courtesy the Academy of Television Arts & Sciences.)

"Law & Order" shows (Figure 6.14), they expect a well-crafted story that will reveal unexpected villains and determined, well-meaning detectives.

Deviations from these expectations disturb viewers and risk alienation. An occasional departure can be successful if the episode has a legitimate point to make. Comedies have tackled such serious themes as AIDS or the death of a parent and done them effectively. But these must be produced carefully and at great intervals. Too many laughless shows by a favorite comedy performer will in all likelihood send the audience searching for alternatives.

Diane English, creator and coproducer of the sitcom "Murphy Brown," understands the principle of consistency. In the winter of 1992 the show scheduled an episode based on the rights of journalists to protect their sources, an important constitutional issue (Figure 6.15). The story idea sprung from the televised Senate hearings of Anita Hill's allegation that Judge Clarence Thomas was not a suitable Supreme Court nominee because of his history of sexual harassment. The hearings would never have taken place if Hill's charges had not been leaked to Nina Totenberg of NPR, who reported the story but refused to identify the source. Totenberg was subsequently summoned to appear before a Senate special counsel. Said English, "As more of our freedoms dwindle, we need to use our freedom as writers to make people know what's going on. *And we also have to make it funny.*"(Emphasis added.)[13]

Writers, directors, and performers must be particularly mindful of "staying in character." Cast members must say and do things consistent with the roles they are playing. If Nick Fallin on "The Guardian" had suddenly become extremely verbal, ready to reveal his emotions about his love life, his relationship with his father, or his addictions, he would have broken character, violating the premise that creator David Hollander established for the show. A writer may occasionally get easy humor or pathos from a line, but if it is at the expense of the character's nature, it could be an expensive laugh or tear.

Sometimes broadcasters become too narrow in their interpretation of this point. There is the classic example of the executive who read a script of "My Favorite Martian," circled a line of dialogue and sent it back to the producer with the comment, "A Martian wouldn't say that."

One other element of consistency deserves mention: shows must remain true to their central intent. They cannot be all things to all people; there are limits to what programs can be and who they can reach. Broadcasters cannot insert 1-minute cooking tips inside Saturday morning cartoons in an attempt to attract adult women. Shows are what they are, and any effort to broaden the base with inappropriate elements not only fails to attract the desired new viewers but also alienates the core audience.

Energy. Energy is the quality that infuses a sense of pace and excitement into a show. It is not a synonym for frenzy. And it does not necessarily mean motion, which is often just movement without a point. Rather, it charges the screen with pictures that will not let the viewer turn away, whether it is a four-man shootout, a whisper, an intense love scene, or an upraised eyebrow. Actors contribute with their performances, the best ones making every scene riveting. Writers develop the dialogue and structure the acts in ways that produce rising tension and climactic endings. Directors stage the players and select the pictures that will generate the most satisfying viewer experience. Editors keep things moving, particularly as the attention span of audiences shortens. If any one of these elements weakens, thereby permitting the pace to flag and attention to wander, the loss of energy will quickly result in the loss of audience.

Maintaining energy is an essential for all talk show hosts. Too often interviewers allow their guests to dictate the tempo of the program. If the host is not alert, a low-key, deliberate-speaking guest can drag down the energy level, and the two can quickly find themselves in the quicksand of boredom. The producer and director should immediately cut to a commercial and go on stage to pump up the host—or give the guest an early dismissal.

Professional Staffing. Rarely, a show will succeed because of the novelty of its format or star even though the production is slipshod and the writing is poor. But the success will be brief. The novelty will wear off, the mediocrity will be exposed, and the show's decline will be assured.

Many a promising format has been squandered because of the insufficiencies of the staff and cast. And many an ordinary idea ("Malcolm in the Middle," "Becker," "Just Shoot Me," or "Miami Vice") has blossomed into enduring success because of the skills of the cast, writers, and production team.

Figure 6.16
"In the Line of Duty: Ambush at Waco" (1993), starring Tim Daly as Branch Davidian leader David Koresh, was an example of a successful telefilm ripped from the headlines and produced on a fast track by producer Ken Kaufman. (Courtesy Patchett Kaufman Entertainment.)

Figure 6.17
"A Woman Scorned: The Betty Broderick Story" (1992) hit the airwaves at just the right time. The film starred Meredith Baxter as a woman who seeks revenge when her husband, played by Stephen Collins of "7th Heaven," marries his young assistant. (Courtesy Patchett Kaufman Entertainment.)

Programmers must look beyond the concept of a show and closely examine the credentials of the executors before committing to its development. Of great importance to developers of programming, such as Susan Rovner at Warner Bros., is the participation of an experienced, successful showrunner, the person responsible for the day-to-day execution of a show. Without a showrunner who has a reputation for delivering quality shows on time and on budget, many concepts do not progress beyond a pitch. To some disgruntled observers whose projects do not have a viable showrunner attached, it can seem as if the showrunner is more important than the concept.

Unfortunately, sometimes fresh, young talent is ignored for established players who have been on the staff of several successful shows, but newcomers can and do work in by attaching to (and learning from) the recognized players. Many schools have mentor programs and internships to assist newcomers in becoming first-string players on the entertainment team.

Timing. For a program to work, it must be in harmony with the times. For a story to work, it must capture the attention of the times (Figure 6.16). Too far behind and the audience will dismiss it as outmoded; too far in front and viewers will rebel against it (Figure 6.17).

"Three's Company" is an example of a show that hit it just right and enjoyed a successful run from 1977 to 1984 (and for many years later in syndication). This sitcom dealt with a hot-blooded young man and two attractive young ladies who, for reasons of economy, shared an apartment. The man, Jack Tripper, played by John Ritter, pretended to be gay to avoid arousing the suspicions of the landlord. Although every episode was packed with sexual innuendo, the audience was encouraged to believe that nothing sexual ever happened between the three roommates. Tripper may have been hot blooded, but that did not mean sexual activity took place in a show the producers nevertheless tantalizingly saw as "French farce."

"Three's Company" was accepted because the time was right. The social upheavals that began in the 1960s and continued into the 1970s made cohabitation among unmarried people commonplace. The network surmised that the condition was sufficiently widespread to allow the national audience to accept the premise. They guessed right (Figure 6.18). The same format, if it had been introduced 10 years earlier, could have provoked a national outcry from media watchdog groups.

Some 20 years after "Three's Company," the 2002–2003 season saw an explosion of gay-themed shows such as "Queer Eye for the Straight Guy," "Boy Meets Boy," "Angels in America," and "It's All Relative." No innuendo here; no French farce needed. These shows contained characters who were clearly gay, not straight pretending to be gay as on "Three's Company."

Shows such as "Soap," with Billy Crystal playing the gay Jodie Dallas, which began its 4-year run in 1977; "Brothers," which premiered on Showtime in 1984; "Ellen," whose lead character came out in 1997; and "Will & Grace," which premiered in 1998, paved the way for the 2002–2003 emphasis on gays in television (Figure 6.19). For some, it seemed as if every show had to have gay characters, where just a season or two before sitcoms were thriving on single parents raising children as an inciting gimmick.

Figure 6.18
"Three's Company" found its place and time. (Courtesy DLT Entertainment.)

Figure 6.19
"Will & Grace" took gay characters mainstream on broadcast television. (Globe Photos, Inc.)

Figure 6.20
Jon Stewart's "The Daily Show" finds the right combination of humor and edge for topical comedy. (Courtesy the Academy of Television Arts & Sciences.)

Jon Stewart's "The Daily Show" (Figure 6.20), a fake news show on cable's Comedy Central, came into its own in 2001–2002, winning Emmy and Peabody awards and receiving excellent press coverage, including the cover of *Newsweek* for the January 5, 2004, issue. There are many reasons for the show's success, including first-rate writing that creates stories in the most unlikely venues; however, timing also played a major role.

In a country besieged by devastating news (9/11, the war in Iraq, a slumping economy, etc.), Stewart and "The Daily Show" found the right dose of humor that had an edge different from what was available on other shows. "The Daily Show" found the right approach for the times, an approach that eclipsed that of late-night legends Jay Leno and David Letterman. The headline of Frank Rich's April 10, 2003, article proclaimed Stewart's "perfect pitch."[14]

Trend Awareness. A capable programmer must also be aware of trends that might generate a hit or guarantee a failure. Riding a trend wave is not an essential element of a successful program. But it can be a way to tap into a prevailing audience preference that will enable a show to deliver strong ratings. Similarly, an awareness of a trend that is over can help a programmer to avoid a concept whose time has passed.

A programming trend occurs when producers develop shows or concepts similar in theme, format, or content. In network prime-time television in the 1950s, there was a strong trend toward live, dramatic productions; in the 1960s, the favored form was westerns; in the 1970s, it was sitcoms with sharp social commentary; and in the 1980s, dramatic serials were prominent. In the 1990s, comedies and prime-time news shows dominated, and starting in 2000, the

The gay-themed explosion could not have happened at the time of "Three's Company," just as "Three's Company" would have been found behind the times had it premiered in 2002–2003. It is all a question of timing, and the savvy programmer has to understand this important dynamic.

The idea of a network devoted to documentaries may have been discussed for years, but it did not become a reality until John Hendrink, a history professor, felt the timing was right for founding the Discovery Channel in 1985. Niche channels such as the Discovery Channel, The Outdoor Channel, Home & Garden Television, and Court TV, have successfully challenged the previous dominance of the conventional networks. *Broad*casting targeting the broadest possible audience has given way to specialized niche programming that seeks a particular audience, and the Discovery Channel and the niche networks that followed succeeded mostly because of timing.

trend was clearly toward so-called reality television.

TV syndication has seen similar runs. In 1982, Group W Productions introduced a first-run daily cartoon series, "He-Man and the Masters of the Universe." Never before had daily, animated programming been made expressly for the syndicated marketplace. Within 2 years there were 28 first-run animated series offered for syndication. It is another truism in Hollywood that imitation is the sincerest form of flattery.

Trends develop in two ways: economic or technological necessity and phenomenal success of a program, which suggests that variations on the form can enjoy similar rewards. In television, as opposed to film, the first copy of a successful program usually delivers, or so goes the conventional wisdom.

The tendency to program live, dramatic fare in the 1950s was primarily the result of technological limitations. The new medium was centered in New York City; tape had not yet been invented, the Hollywood film industry disdained the new industry, and film production facilities in New York were scarce. But there were excellent actors, producers, and writers available in New York theater, and they immediately gravitated to the live dramatic form.

When prime-time network scheduling turned strongly toward news-oriented programs in the 1990s, the reason was economics. Economics also supported the development of the reality trend. The economics of reality programming plus its attraction of the desirable younger demographic made reality desirable to programmers. As audiences continue to dwindle and costs continue to rise, programmers have to be mindful of what the trends are and what audiences will watch at what costs. Sometimes embracing the live or live-on-tape news presentations or reality shows makes the most sense. Even a modest rating performance can deliver a profitable return because of the low cost of production.

Even more extreme is the trend toward infomercials—30-minute programs that masquerade as talk or interview shows but are devoted to extolling the virtues of some commercial product such as a diet, baldness treatment, or brand of sunglasses. Stations that might not program this material when times are good will do so in lean periods because the producers provide the programs for free and even pay the stations for the airtime.

Often trends are started by the emergence of an enormous hit. The industry studies the soaring ratings and wonders whether other versions of the theme can be developed. Frequently they can. The originator may have fed an audience appetite that is not satisfied with just one dish. The industry will immediately offer variations, and the process will continue until viewers are sated. In many instances, the show that began the trend will outlast all the imitators.

"Gunsmoke" triggered the western frenzy in 1955. By 1961, there were 12 series slappin' leather each week. In 1975 only one remained—"Gunsmoke," which holds the record as the longest-running series with 635 episodes. The same pattern held true for prime-time serials. The form was introduced by "Dallas" in 1978 and was an instant hit. By 1981, the number of serials had mushroomed to five. Ten years later it had receded to two, one of which was "Dallas," with a run of 357 episodes.

All trends run their course. Viewers become saturated, the original idea becomes jaded and stale, ratings decline, and the search for a new appeal begins. Judging when a trend has crested is one of the programmer's more difficult decisions. One clue is a rising demographic. If the younger viewers, the most volatile and easily sated segment of the audience, are drifting away, the chances are good that the show has seen its best days. Even if the audience size remains satisfactory, the older skew will herald a falloff in revenue. Any new projects in the same genre are probably ill advised.

Adequate Budget. Programmers must allocate sufficient funds for producers to make their shows. It is true that most producers will strive to obtain the largest possible budget, especially if they retain the difference between the package price and the actual cost of production. But they mostly just want to be sure they have enough resources to mount the product they are committed to delivering.

The cost of first-rate special effects has decreased significantly over the last few years. Companies such as Stargate Digital have perfected the art of special effects in shows such as "ER" and "Las Vegas" at affordable costs, enabling producers to deliver the promised product even if production costs are not increased. Exteriors on these shows look real, using the Stargate technology, instead of cheap and unrealistic. This is important to an increasingly savvy and demanding audience, and it is important to cost-conscious producers.

Distributors such as networks and syndicators are paid to keep costs down. Therefore, establishing a mutually acceptable budget frequently triggers a lively dispute. The debate is worthwhile if the result is a figure that allows the creative vision to be realized. When viewers reject a program because "it looks chintzy," everyone loses. It is important to find the money to do it right.

Salability. In the world of commercial television, the greatest idea in the world is worthless if no one will buy it. As Art Astor of Astor Broadcasting, whose career spans more than 40 years, said to a group of students at California State University, Fullerton, in 2003, "Sales is where it's at. If a good salesperson can't sell a show to stations and advertisers, it simply doesn't belong."

Salability must be effective at three stages: when the creator is trying to find a distributor; when the distributor is trying to find advertisers; and when both the creator and the distributor are trying to find an audience. If there is a failure at any stage, the program either will never reach the air or will be off after a brief stay because of lack of revenue.

Surprisingly, the selling approach is not always the same at all three levels. Buyers of programs—networks, syndication companies, and station executives—tend to have fast-paced business days. The phone rings incessantly; associates pop in and out; and meetings are forever backed up. They also regard themselves as quick studies, their experience and natural gifts allowing them to cut through rhetoric and pierce to the heart of the show. Consequently, sellers keep their pitches short and concentrate on the "catchiest" elements.

In syndication, for example, program concepts are usually presented in tapes that proceed at a breakneck pace. If possible, they are enlivened with quick cuts of spicy or sensational material to maintain the buyer's interest and present an image of cutting-edge sharpness. But the program may be successful with the audience only if it is produced in a deliberate, thorough style.

"When Group W launched 'Hour Magazine'" (an hour-long syndicated woman's service show that ran from 1980–1989), said George Resing, then senior vice president of the production company, "we made a zippy bells-and-

(a)

(b)

whistles 15-minute demonstrator that made the show seem paced like 'America's Funniest Home Videos.' It was the only way we could keep the attention of station buyers. But we knew from research that viewers wanted each topic dealt with fully and responsibly. Subjects that appeared to be done once over lightly caused deep viewer resentment. But when selling advertisers, we used a completely different approach. We emphasized the wholesomeness and reliability of the program to indicate their commercials would be placed in a very favorable environment. Pace was never mentioned. This two-step strategy seemed to work. The show was profitable for 10 years."

Getting Crossover Viewers. If a show can reach its target audience and connect with a subsidiary audience, the show's chances for success increase dramatically. For example, as Sean M. Smith reported in the June 23, 2003, issue of

Newsweek, "'Queer as Folk,' a series on Showtime about the life of gay men in Pittsburgh, which is an adaptation of a successful British series with the same name, has a 50% audience of women. Similarly, HBO's phenomenal success, 'Sex and the City,' a show about the lives and loves of four heterosexual women, has a large male following: About 40% of its audience in the 18 to 34 demographic is male"[15] (Figure 6.21).

Inventive scheduling can also help a network to gain crossover viewers. For example, the reality phenomenon "American Idol" on Fox greatly boosted the ratings of "24," the critically acclaimed series that began in 2001. Viewers who were fans of "American Idol" may not have been planning to stay tuned for "24," but the flow from one show to the next brought new viewers to "24," many of whom found "24" to their liking. Any program that attains crossover status has a good chance of survival.

Figure 6.21
(a) "The L Word" and (b) "Queer as Folk" on Showtime appeal to a large audience base, not just gays and lesbians. (Globe Photos, Inc.)

Figure 6.22
The PBS series "The Civil War," which featured photographs such as this one of Camp Griffin at the beginning of the war, had one basic authority—Ken Burns. It was also high in prestige, awards, and units of good. (Courtesy Florentine Films.)

One Voice of Authority. Committees rarely design anything worthwhile. The compromises required to keep peace in the conference room usually demolish the original concept. An adjustment here, a new element there, and suddenly the magic is gone. With deregulation, significant disagreements between new corporate owners, often viewed as "the suits" or "bean counters," and the production team often take place, resulting in too many opinions and approaches that threaten the integrity of a project.

To be sure, constructive suggestions should be offered and welcomed. But it should be clear from the first meeting that one person will make all creative decisions. The alternative leads to chaos.

The single-authority requirement is becoming more important in broadcasting. As costs rise and risks grow, there has been a developing trend toward funding by consortium with many contributors sharing in the costs of a project. However, each investor is inclined to believe he or she is entitled to give creative input. It is best to address that before the papers are signed and to have the authority figure identified in the contract.

Although some creators can be labeled as micromanaging egotists, too many cooks spoil the broth. There is a reason that people such as Aaron Sorkin, David E. Kelley, David Chase, Diane English, Alan Ball, and Steven Bochco represent the best that television has to offer. Their shows bear their stamps as the individuals in charge.

The one voice of authority, however, is not predominant in public broadcasting and in educationally oriented institutions such as universities. Public broadcasting has committees and advisors and sometimes advisors to committees. Although some public broadcasting concepts are conceived and executed primarily by one person (e.g., Ken Burns's "The Civil War"; Figure 6.22), many others are the work of committees. Content experts, educational evaluators, community leaders—all are brought in to give opinions. Usually they are not window dressing. They are leaders in their respective fields who are used to having their ideas taken seriously. If ignored, they can cause trouble.

One college-credit science course was undermined by a university professor who felt his ideas had been neglected. This professor, whom we will call Dr. X for anonymity, was one of a committee of professors called in to advise on content. He tried to dominate all the meetings to the extent that the other professors asked the producer to remove him from the committee. Upon hearing rumors of this, Dr. X listed all the problems he saw with the design of the series and then resigned from the committee. When the series aired, he nitpicked the content and presentation, called the press, and "proved" that the course was basically ill conceived. Although some of his accusations were false, the publicity that he stirred up kept the course from ever airing again.

Despite negative incidents of this type, public broadcasting does not seem to want to drift toward one voice of authority. Some that fund public broadcasting require in their applications the names of people who will be consulting on program concepts. The longer the list (especially if the names are prestigious), the better the chances it will be funded.

Although the loss of one voice of authority often results in chaos, chaos seems to be more acceptable within public broadcasting than within the commercial broadcasting realm. There are even those who profess that chaos leads to art, but this is a dangerous position that beginning programmers should avoid.

Innovation and Freshness. More than 50 years ago, a man named Ted Bates built an advertising empire out of a single notion. Every ad prepared by his agency had to have a **unique selling proposition.** By that he meant the ad had to find one quality that could only be found in, or said about, the product. That uniqueness distinguished the product from all others and thus stimulated a buying appetite in the consumer.

The same is true for programs. If there is nothing unusual, fresh, or different about a show, why should anybody watch it? The kiss of death for any show is when the viewer says, "I get the feeling I've seen it a thousand times." A distinct voice can make a

familiar theme fresh, but that voice has to provide something new.

Points of differentiation do not have to be major departures from all other forms on the air. A single inventive difference is frequently sufficient. It can be as simple as producing a conventional form in an unconventional way.

Programmers should be cautious about the following:

1. Every buyer of network programs has a file full of "breakthrough" program submissions that "can't miss because they're so different," such as the one-armed detective who lives in a state-of-the-art tree house or the female Siamese twins who are defense attorneys (casting was seen as a problem on this one). In the early 1990s, the celebrated producer Steven Bochco attempted a weekly hour-long musical drama, "Cop Rock." It sank like one. The idea was bold and inventive, but the innovation failed to address a need.

   Interestingly, ABC at the start of the 2002–2003 season announced that it was not going to be introducing any "breakthrough" shows, relying instead on more traditional programming. This angered members of the press quick to find fault with any programming announcement, reinforcing the notion of television as a "vast wasteland," but ABC's strategy revealed that many programmers are aware of the pitfalls of "breakthrough" programming.

2. The acceptability of innovation by buyers is in direct proportion to the economic health of the industry. In hard times, buyers tilt toward conservatism. Innovation means risk, and risk can mean the loss of scarce dollars. In tough economic times, station owners are loathe to cancel even marginally profitable shows for fear their replacements might do worse. Better to stay

with something that is not losing than take a chance on a big hit and miss.

Real success in programming can only be obtained by invention, finding new ways and new people to inform and entertain. In the first 50+ years of television's history, only two animated programs had ever been successful on prime-time network schedules—"The Jetsons" and the "Flintstones." No other animated program had survived in prime time since "Flintstones" bowed out in 1966. The gambling, innovative Fox network introduced "The Simpsons," a weekly half-hour animated series in 1990. The show quickly zoomed into Top 20 status and became a marketing phenomenon. Such success stories never happen to "safe" derivative programs. They only occur when a dreamer has an inspiration and a programmer decides to accept the risks.

RADIO PROGRAMMING

Commercial radio is different from television in its program objectives. Despite this, the qualities that make programming successful are similar.

Programming Objectives

Rarely is a radio audience a large one. Because people have such a wide divergence of musical tastes, a radio station that tries to program to reach everyone will probably attract no one. Radio stations target a specific audience—teenage males who like hard rock, older women who enjoy listening to talk, people who want 10 minutes of capsulated news. Because radio is relatively inexpensive, stations can make a profit even though they do not have a large audience.

Prestige and awards are not major radio objectives, although stations certainly tout awards when they win them. The few remaining commercial stations

that program classical music consider prestige. These stations do not expect large audiences or large amounts of advertising, but the owners are willing to continue the format because the prestigious nature of the audience attracts enough specialized advertisers to generate a profit. Public radio networks and stations also court prestige, especially in their news departments. A track record of honors can help in garnering financial support from the government and the public, especially if the awards are from avowed apolitical organizations such as the Peabody Awards and the National Association of Broadcasters.

Two programming objectives deserve special consideration. One, fulfilling a particular local purpose, is more dominant in radio than in TV. The other, creating a particular mood, is peculiar to radio.

A Particular Local Purpose. Radio is more likely than television to attempt to fulfill a local purpose. Interacting with the community helps license renewal, but it is also an essential element of station operations because radio (satellite radio aside) is primarily a local medium. Radio stations often engage in activities that are part promotion and part local public service.

For example, KIZN in Boise, Idaho, sponsors an annual "Keep Kids Warm" clothing drive and auction. As its website states, the event initially sprouted from an on-air contest that had no community service tie-in: "Keep Kids Warm started in December of 1996 with a single phone call from a young girl that was trying to win money from KIZN so she could order some heating oil for her family. The morning show at the time (Mark Rivers and Rich Summers), had been giving away cash with a 'song of the day' contest the previous few weeks. The contest had come to an end but Kissin' listeners were still calling Mark &

Rich, asking about the 'song of the day.' When they explained on the air that the contest was over, the studio phone rang, and there was Christian, a young girl who asked Mark & Rich this question, 'If I can't win the money, can I win some heating oil for my family? . . . our house is cold, and we just want to be warm for Christmas . . .'" The annual drive brings in about $40,000 per year and has numerous sponsors, including country artists, NASCAR teams, sports greats, and entertainment celebrities, who contribute on-air auction items.[16]

Many stations program short segments that describe upcoming weekend happenings. The Beat, 95.5 FM in Atlanta, Georgia, along with making on-air announcements, heavily promotes its online events calendar, where listeners can find an exhaustive listing of local events broken down by location, date, and type.

In addition, call-in shows concerned with local issues are often top rated on stations with all-talk formats or even stations that only do occasional talk shows. Talk show hosts and disc jockeys appear at many charitable functions in the community, partly to add allure to the community event and partly to build awareness (and ratings) for the station. Even the numerous contests where listeners can win money, tickets, or CDs often have local tie-ins. For example, the tickets may be for a concert by a local music group. Hometown involvement makes good, sound business sense for most commercial radio stations. Even with voice tracking, disc jockeys recording shows in San Diego to be broadcast in Albuquerque go to great lengths to add segments that specifically reference local events because the feel of localism is so important to local audiences.

A Particular Mood. One of the main programming objectives of radio, which is not really apropos to television, is that

it strives to create a particular mood. Although individual TV programs may make a person sad or angry, the moods do not usually affect what a person is doing other than watching TV. For a TV program to put you in a certain mood, you must give it your attention. But such is not the case with radio, which encourages inattention. Music is background oriented and can influence how people feel about other activities. Radio programmers try to select music that will fit the predominant moods of their target audience.

Rhythm, pitch, loudness, instrumentation, melody—all of these aspects of music can affect mood. For example, high-pitched music is more pleasant and playful than low-pitched music, which tends to be serious or sorrowful. Saxophones are more romance inducing than trumpets. Loud music is more capable than soft of providing isolation—a sound wall to keep out other people. Programmers must think of the music they select in terms of its general appropriateness for the target group and the specific activities that the audience might be engaged in at various times of the day. For example, young men like fast, hard music and older women prefer something slower and softer. But early in the morning, when everyone must move rather rapidly, the music played on a station appealing to older women should be more sprightly than it is late at night, when audience members are more likely to be relaxing or winding down.

Overall, the primary objectives that radio programmers deal with are those of attracting a demographically specific audience, fulfilling local needs, and establishing a mood.

Fundamental Appeals to an Audience

Although television serves a smorgasbord of appeals to audiences, radio, after

Figure 6.23
Country superstar Tim McGraw's "Red Rag Top" proved challenging for programming directors in some localities in 2002. (Globe Photos, Inc.)

6.23) was pulled from many stations after initial negative feedback from listeners who were uncomfortable with the song's references to the hot-button issue of abortion. WSM-FM (Live 95) Nashville's programming director, Kevin O'Neal, pulled the song, "just to be safe," after a handful of spins because of listener complaints. He later reversed that decision, saying, "I think the song is reality . . . We are not in the censor business."

But if O'Neal's station were more squarely in the nation's Bible Belt, he might sing a different tune, as did Operating Manager/Programming Director Ron Brooks of WCOS Columbia, South Carolina. Brooks said his station "played 'Red Rag Top' on a Friday afternoon and took calls for about 45 minutes. We did not say what the song was about; (we) just asked the audience to listen closely and give us their opinion. Approximately half of the calls were strongly against the song due to the characters' choice of abortion. Many folks also felt that that song did not reflect nearly enough remorse over the decision, regardless of their personal stance on abortion. Abortion is the most divisive issue in our nation, and it is a very hot topic in this part of the country."

Brooks added, with some frustration, that local listeners do not kowtow to stardom when it runs up against or even seems to challenge their beliefs. "It's frustrating to me to go in to the fall (ratings) book anticipating new music from one of our current superstars and we get something this dangerous. Our superstars can get away with a lot, but there are also limits. The country audience in Columbia expects WCOS to be a radio station where they don't have to worry about their kids being exposed to what they would consider dangerous content."[17]

the advent of television, has thinned its menu and purpose, sidestepping comedy and drama for the aural comfort foods of music, talk, and news, much of which serves as background for listeners' other activities.

Music. There is no question about the audience for radio music. It is just a matter of selecting the right sound for the right group. This is easier for stations than for networks or syndicators because stations can take into account the moral attitudes of the local community. Networks and syndicators that program rock and hip-hop music, in particular, have trouble because stations in certain parts of the country do not want to broadcast profane or sexually oriented lyrics. But other formats can run into this problem, too. In 2002, a new song, "Red Rag Top," by country music superstar Tim McGraw (Figure

Hard News. Radio is a vital factor in many people's lives for obtaining information. Waking up to radio news is common. People want to learn what has happened during the night—or sometimes they just want assurance that a major disaster has *not* happened. Once they are convinced that life is going on as usual, they are willing to switch to another appeal, such as music. Often the main elements of news broadcasts that attract audience members are the ones that affect them most personally— weather, traffic, or both. All-news stations provide hard news throughout the day so that people can know about the latest happenings at any time.

When radio was deregulated in the 1980s, stations were no longer required to broadcast news. Although some have dropped all newscasts, many others have continued to bring listeners news at least once an hour because people want to know what is going on in the world.

Soft News. Talk shows are the most profuse supplier of soft news. Call-in shows on which people discuss their problems, their questions regarding sports, or their opinions on current events cater to curiosity. Soft news is also programmed from features supplied by syndicators and networks, such as commentaries on controversial subjects, background information on stories in the news, and interviews with celebrities.

Qualities Tied to Success

Although radio is an exclusively aural medium and TV relies greatly on the visual, the qualities that make programming successful are the same. For example, conflict is often an important element in talk radio. These programs come alive when the caller takes issue with the host or other callers. Likewise, radio stations need adequate budget and professional staffing. The latter often translates into a need to have people who really understand the type of music the station plays. A professional, high-minded person who really knows jazz will be of little use to an easy listening station.

Formats need both durability and consistency. If a format is too narrow in scope, it will not endure. For example, one radio station decided to try an all-Elvis format. It did not last long. Disco music was also short lived because the music was not varied enough—all of it was high energy and glittery. However, if a particular station's sound is not consistent, listeners will change the dial. Imagine the result if a classical music disc jockey, bored with Beethoven, decides to send out to the listeners Dave Matthews' latest hit. Or vice versa. Similarly, people who have put a rock station in their car radio settings will tune out quickly if they hear a cooking show when they push the button.

Timing and trends can help bring a radio station success. A station that switches to an all-news format just before a major international or national crisis has the fortune of good timing. One that latches on to a new sound in music that becomes big has cashed in on a trend.

But of all the qualities tied to success, the two that are probably most important for radio are likeability and innovation.

Likeability. Likeability is important for disc jockeys. They are the single-most distinctive element in radio programming and are largely responsible for attracting the audience, especially if several stations in one market program the same type of music. One of the major elements that makes a disc jockey likeable is energy. This is especially true for radio formats that feature music with high energy.

Figure 6.24
The band Nirvana tapped into an unexpected audience in 1991. (Globe Photos, Inc.)

and antipathy toward Stern himself, or perhaps he fulfills a deep vicarious need for his audience. Stern says things and asks questions the audience may be thinking themselves but would not dare say—certainly not in public.

More traditional talk show hosts, such as Neal Conan of NPR's "Talk of the Nation," stand in for the audience in a more conventional way—asking some questions audience members might ask were they in the room. Conan limits his comments to neutral questions; other hosts express strong opinions, such as the uncompromised moralizing of Dr. Laura and the political commentaries by the likes of Bill O'Reilly and Al Franken, some of whom claim that their opinions are not just opinions but the truth. Listeners are drawn to the material, whether they agree with it or not, simply because it provides addictive conflict and drama.

Several program directors were asked what they looked for in a disc jockey. Most of the answers related to likeability—"upbeat people who don't feel they have to talk a lot," "someone who sounds natural and not like a radio personality," "the ability to relate locally and know the town," "a sense of humor," and "energy and a knowledge of music."

Talk show hosts must be either people you like or people you love to hate—although sometimes they are a combination of the two. So-called shock jock Howard Stern has received much flack for his caustic talk show but has remained an unflappable force in radio for years. His insulting and no-holds-barred approach to callers and in-studio guests is instrumental in creating attention-sustaining conflict. Perhaps some of the secret to his success is that his style engenders sympathy for interviewees

Innovation. Innovation is supplied primarily by changes in musical tastes. Each generation tends to develop its own style of music. A radio programmer must be attuned to the changes and be aware of when a music format is reaching a midlife crisis and needs a change. The world moves on and what works in radio today may be out of date tomorrow. Often the changes in musical taste are dramatic—almost unbelievably so. The early 1990s saw, perhaps, one of the most shocking and swift changes in musical taste. Pop audiences had been consuming a diet of sugary, featherweight fare, such as Milli Vanilli's "Girl You Know It's True," which highlighted the emphasis of late-1980s music on image rather than substance when it was disclosed that the band members, after receiving a Grammy for best new artist, had not even sung on their own album. But in 1991, a band out of Seattle, Nirvana (Figure 6.24), whose first album had come and gone without notice, released its follow-up, *Nevermind*. Almost overnight, the pop airwaves, which had been lightly sprinkled with electronic keyboards and purple prose, were being assaulted by guitars, drums, and unadulterated rage. The audience's unexpected appetite for this new music left programming directors scrambling to try other previously "underground" bands on their stations. Playing Nirvana's "Smells Like Teen Spirit" beside a new release from Michael Jackson's 1991 *Dangerous* album presented a consistency problem for stations whose expectations about the future of music were blindsided.

Other less dramatic and more graduated changes have occurred since 1991. Each marked a change program directors have had to track and, in the best case, stay ahead of to keep their innovative edge: the arrival of the so-called boy bands in the mid-1990s and the steady ascendancy of hip-hop in the new millennium.

Usually a programmer has more free rein to be innovative in good economic times than in bad. If enough money is available to cover a bad guess concerning the fickleness of the public, a programmer is more likely to be given the go-ahead to try something new. When economic times are rough, radio, like many other endeavors, tends to be conservative. As Joe Garner, senior national affiliate relations manager of the Westwood One network, said during one of the down periods, "Radio is now the playground for the proven rather than the playground for innovation. Programs do not have a chance to grow and find an audience; programmers go with the proven rather than experiment."[18] This should not become the standard operating procedure for radio. Innovation is needed to keep the medium healthy—and wealthy.

INTERNET PROGRAMMING

The Internet, allowing a convergence of all media, relies upon many of the same elements for success as television and radio. Problems arise in Internet programming when programmers do not adhere to these elements. The Internet, unlike radio and television, is not a temporal medium in that much Internet content is not broadcast in real time but instead waits for viewers to happen upon it. It is easier, then, for Internet developers to simply put up content and leave it there, unchanged, until web surfers chance upon it.

In some cases, this strategy is appropriate, but it does not encourage return visits or brand loyalty.

Freshness

One of the most important strategies to keep in mind when developing web content is to keep it fresh. If a radio or television station simply played the same content over and over, viewers would have little reason to return to it. A **blogger** (essentially a person who keeps an online diary, open for others to see) whose latest entry is 2 months stale will likely lose her or his audience. Likewise, an Internet store that does not seem to be introducing products and services or a web portfolio that does not seem to contain new material will not beckon a visitor to return.

The operative word here is "seem." An Internet site must seem, to a first-time visitor, as if it will be updated with new content in the foreseeable future if not immediately. The easiest and most surefire way to give this impression to visitors is make it a fact—and to tout that fact. In the early days of the Internet, a craze developed wherein web designers inserted dynamic code that displayed the current date in a prominent place on their sites. The idea was that visitors to the site would see the current date and think that the content of the site was current. Visitors who, based upon this assumption, returned later to find that the only thing changed on the site was the date soon became wary of such transparent ploys. They wanted the real thing—real change.

Displaying the date new material is added can give visitors a sense for how often the site is updated and can, therefore, encourage them to return. Making promises or teasing upcoming material is also a good ploy—provided the promises are fulfilled. Nothing will so quickly turn off a visitor as a flashy promo for new content that will be added June 1 when the date is already August 17. With the millions of websites on the Internet, most sites only get one chance to connect—or disconnect—with a visitor.

It is possible, however, to get websites to change themselves each time they are visited, using computer programming. Many sites, such as those that display news headlines, automatically swap out old news stories, replacing them with the latest stories as those stories are added to the queue. Websites for television and radio stations are often programmed to automatically adjust their content to match the program currently broadcasting on the station. Some web developers, to give visitors different experiences each time they visit, simply create a section of their home page where random content can be added each time the site is visited. For example, a site for a university might have a "spotlight" section on the home page that has space for a picture and some text. Each time the site is visited, computer programming in the home page generates a random number that corresponds to one of many different pictures and text available. When you first visit the site, a picture and text spot-

lighting the chemistry department may show; the next time, a picture and text spotlighting the theatre department will take the chemistry department's place. The site is not actually updated; it is just randomly cycling through a finite number of choices.

Targeting Content

Another way to keep a site seemingly fresh is to target the content in it specifically to each visitor based upon information gleaned from previous experience with the visitor. In this way, websites, such as Amazon.com, which feature an inventory of hundreds of thousands of products and services for sale, can offer suggestions to browse through based on previous purchases by a specific visitor. If you bought an electric drill last time you visited, maybe you would be interested in an electric saw.

Browsing, whether in a store, with the radio dial, or through a television remote control, is an important commercial activity, resulting in the germination of new interests for consumers and countless impulse buys. In grocery stores, featured products are placed at eye level (both for adults and for little ones straggling along—begging for attractive products strategically slated for lower shelves). The Internet pursues similar strategies but with distinct advantages in information collection and dynamic delivery.

To carry the supermarket analog further—if you sign up for a supermarket member card that gives you special member rebates when you use the card at the check stand, you may be unknowingly getting more than you bargained for. Without using the card, you are just an anonymous buyer to the supermarket; when you use the card, the supermarket is able to track your purchases—how often you buy alcohol, frozen peas, low-carbohydrate frozen entrees, etc. If you are a regular customer at the supermarket, this information can help the store to adjust its inventory to better suit your buying habits along with the rest of its card- and non-card-using customers. Although many worry that this information collection is an invasion of privacy, it undeniably can help businesses to streamline their offerings and consumers to get what they commonly want when and where they want it.

The Internet allows a similar but far more advanced system of tracking and responding to customer habits. Imagine if you walked into a supermarket, slid your member card through a card reader at the front door, and the entire store rearranged itself to favor your pattern of shopping and suggested products that, based on your past shopping preferences, you might be interested in purchasing.

The 2002 Tom Cruise/Steven Spielberg movie "Minority Report" imagined a future much like this—where advertising spaces recognized consumers as they walked by, scanning the unique signatures in their retinas, and delivered advertisements that spoke personally to them and their recorded tastes. Although "Minority Report" was set in the year 2054, in a way the future the movie envisages is already here. Unless consumers set up their computers to block them, many websites drop identifiers, called **cookies**, into visitors' computers to help the website individually adjust its web content to repeat customers' on subsequent visits. In this way, if you placed products into your shopping cart on a website on a previous visit but did not complete the transaction, the site will be able to remind you of your incomplete purchases on your next visit. Or, if you viewed a music video by Christina Aguilera or Rob Zombie on a previous visit, the site could, by accessing the cookie it left in your computer on your last visit, place an advertisement for that artist's latest album or song download that might entice you to buy.

Some web companies, such as Doubleclick.com, make it their sole business to collect information and preferences of web surfers and provide that information to their subscribers so that those subscribers can more effectively target content to surfers that come to their sites. Of course, Doubleclick.com aims to make a good profit at it.

Because the Internet consists of a growing roster of millions upon millions of sites and options, content targeting can be valuable for both the creators and the viewers of Internet content. Nevertheless, it raises privacy concerns, some of which will be addressed in Chapter 8.

Consistency

Another important strategy for success in web content is consistency. If a radio or television station played children's shows one afternoon and a sex advice program the next, viewers would see the station as a crapshoot and might not like their odds of tuning in to something they enjoy. An e-commerce site that sells women's scarves one day and power tools the next will obviously have trouble keeping its buyers unless it is implementing targeted content strategies as described previously. A blogger who switches from describing the difficulties of being a teenager to obscure musings on quantum physics, even if genuinely interested in these two subjects, risks losing the audience. Even if the audience shares this mix of interests, *when* these interests surface may not coincide between the content creator and the consumer. Although you may like, at different times, romantic and horror films, imagine being in the mood for and going to see a movie you thought was a horror film only to find that it is a romantic comedy.

Another important issue in this area is consistency of quality. Unlike with television and radio, there are not necessarily the same bureaucracies and testing strategies in place to safeguard the quality of what goes online. For some, the answer to "Why did you put this on a website?" is "Because I can." That answer is fine if all that you want to do is have a website—but if you want your website to have an effect or to garner loyal visitors, more thought has to be put into it. Thought has to be put into every page and every element of the site. One lousy or inconsistent page can turn off a visitor, especially if that is the first page your visitor sees. But even if it is the 3rd or 20th, it can foul a visitor's impression of the entire site.

Innovation

The Internet is nothing if not a fertile ground for innovation. New applications and technologies are always being developed. The technology bubble of the late 1990s saw companies and investors alike taking great leaps of faith into "revolutionary" Internet technologies and uses. Some of these technologies may have been revolutionary—but any revolution must, to take hold, catch fire with the general population and not just with the innovators who envision it. Many consumers are drawn to the leading edge; others cannot tolerate being guinea pigs for buggy adventures along the edge of the horizon.

Because Internet sites may target small niches of visitors, some more or less tolerant of the inevitable glitches that come with new technology, there is no rule about how far out on the edge is too far. One thing is certain, however —the main innovation that Internet programmers are trying to develop is a way to make use of the Internet's inter-

activity in a way that will engage audiences without taxing their attention spans to the breaking point. Programmers who are able to successfully find a balancing point between innovation and user friendliness may strike Internet gold—siphoning off viewers and advertising dollars from traditional mediums such as radio, television, and film.

Many attempts have been made to make television viewing interactive by adding Internet-like elements or layering Internet content and pages onto television broadcasts, but any success these ventures have had has been more in the hype leading up to their launch than in actual sustained usage by pioneering television viewers. Developers will no doubt continue their search— more in enterprising, good economic times than when belts are drawn tight.

Branding

Once an Internet programmer has chanced upon a winning Internet product, has developed strategies to keep it fresh and consistent, and has navigated the balance between innovation and comfort, it is important to the success of the site to develop brand recognition. A perfect example of **branding** can be found in the granddaddy of Internet sites, Amazon.com. The site began in 1995, primarily as an online bookseller. Many other sites came along to sell books— some, like Barnesandnoble.com, with tie-ins to brick-and-mortar stores that may have made them seem more reliable, especially to a public just beginning to wade into cyberspace. Amazon.com launched an aggressive marketing campaign and, possibly because it did not have a confusing tie-in to a known quantity in the "real" world, captured the attention of web surfers. Thus, instead of going to a search engine website to seek a book they may be looking for, shoppers started going straight to Amazon.com.

The prices on Amazon.com may not have been lower than those on other sites, but brand recognition won.

Later, when Amazon.com began to branch into selling other products and services, its lack of a tie-in to a known brick-and-mortar entity became a real asset. Barnesandnoble.com, a known bookseller, could not easily branch into children's toys and small kitchen appliances, but Amazon.com could. The brand recognition that Amazon.com had developed continued to draw visitors to its ever-growing offerings, thus highlighting the usefulness of developing brand recognition, especially in the malleable and scalable world of the Internet (Figure 6.25).

Programmers labor mightily to put their shows together. Juggling the creative elements is a time-consuming and at times an exhausting task. But the job is further complicated by the need to accommodate a host of other considerations, enumerated in Chapters 7 and 8.

Figure 6.25
Amazon.com, without a tie to a bricks-and-mortar entity, is able to expand its offerings using the Internet's flexibility and its brand. (Photo © 2004 Amazon.com.)

EXERCISES

1. Select a show on television that you feel lacks an adequate budget. What about the show looks "cheap," and how does this affect your evaluation of the show?

2. Select a program currently on the air and examine elements the show has that define its success or failure. If the show is a failure in your opinion, what elements is it lacking?

3. Identify what you think will be the next trend on television. Why did you select this trend?

4. Describe a show in which you think viewer expectations have not been met. What specifically did the show promise and not deliver? Did a particular character act in a way that was not true to his or her personality?

5. What changes, if any, do you see in format-dominant shows?

6. Watch some classic television shows on TV Land. Why were these shows successful when they aired? In your opinion, why are people still watching them today?

7. What qualities do you think a niche network should have to succeed?

8. Come up with a list of potential activities a local radio station might be able to sponsor, organize, or be involved in pertaining to an upcoming event, holiday, or underserved local need.

9. Analyze a program by a well-known radio talk show host. Examine each segment to plot the drama and conflict inherent in the segment and evaluate its effectiveness in maintaining audience attention.

10. Examine a well-known website. How does it convey (or not) to new visitors that its content is fresh and will be updated?

11. Examine a well-known website. In what ways could it use its brand recognition to venture into offering other goods or services to its visitors?

REFERENCES/NOTES

1. Sallie Hofmeister. "Fuzzy Picture for NBC's Newest Cable Property," *Los Angeles Times,* October 12, 2003, p. C-1.

2. Rick Du Brow. "The Goldenson Years," *Los Angeles Times Calendar,* February 3, 1991, p. 78.

3. Bill Carter. "TV for the ARP Set," *The New York Times,* November 3, 2003, p. C-10.

4. Stuart Elliott. "Advertising," *The New York Times,* April 21, 2003, p. C-12.

5. Allison Romano. "Chris Albrecht's Goombas," *Broadcasting and Cable,* September 9, 2002, pp. 12–13.

6. Paul Brownfield. "TV's Big Noise-maker—and Proud of It," *Los Angeles Times,* November 20, 2002, pp. E-1 and E-13.

7. John Leverence. Awards Director. Academy of Television Arts & Sciences. Interview, January 14, 1992.

8. Ken Auletta. *Three Blind Mice: How the Networks Lost Their Way* (New York: Random House, 1991), p. 114.

9. Greg Braxton. "TV Convention Draws Record Crowd," *Los Angeles Times,* January 28, 1993, p. F-4.

10. Goldenson, p. 243.

11. *Bartlett's Familiar Quotations,* 15th edition (Boston: Little Brown, 1980), p. 902.

12. Emily Nussbaum. "The First Time Around, She Blew It. Or Did She?" *Los Angeles Times,* July 27, 2003, p. E-1.

13. Diane English. "NPR's Totenberg: Pushed into the Limelight," *Broadcasting,* November 4, 1991, pp. 58–60.

14. Frank Rich. "Jon Stewart's Perfect Pitch," *The New York Times,* April 20, 2003, Section 2, p.1.

15. Sean M. Smith. "Fan Swapping: Gay, Straight, Up Late," *Newsweek,* June 23, 2003, p. 65.

16. KIZN 92.3 FM. "Keep Kids Warm On-Air Auction," http://www.kizn.com/keep_kids_warm.php. Accessed January 17, 2004.

17. Billboard Country Monitor, September 27, 2002, http://www.kathyhussey.com/redragtop.html. Accessed October 13, 2004.

18. Joe Garner. "Marketing Programming in the 1990s," *College Broadcaster,* November/December, 1990, p. 5.

7 Influences on Television Programming

In this chapter you will learn about the following:

- The external and internal forces that influence programming
- How pressure groups operate
- The role the government plays in television programming
- How and why advertisers and pressure groups target specific programs
- How different internal departments affect programming decisions
- The various functions of internal departments and how these functions influence what audiences experience
- How different departments jockey to ensure their influence will be recognized
- The areas that censors monitor

In this chapter, we examine both the external and the internal forces that exercise considerable power over television programming. External forces are those entities not directly involved in the creation and production of a product. We look at outside forces that include stations, advertisers, pressure groups, the media, academic and nonprofit studies, and various branches of the government. Internal forces are those departments or divisions that have a say about the programming content. We look at the sales department; the

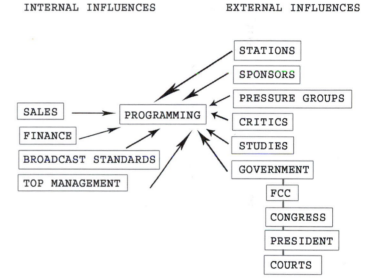

Figure 7.1
Influences that affect programming.

finance department; the broadcast standards and practices department, most often aligned with the legal department; the promotion and marketing departments; and research departments. We also examine the influence of top management, and, as more companies merge, the influence of the parent company (Figure 7.1).

EXTERNAL INFLUENCES ON TELEVISION

Commercial television, with its reliance on advertising, its obligation to maintain broadcast **licenses,** and its importance

161

as a cultural phenomenon, is susceptible to several outside influences. Also, its visibility in the entertainment landscape seemingly invites close scrutiny from many quarters.

Cable TV programming, on the other hand, is subject to much less outside influence. One reason for this stems from cable's narrowcasting philosophy. Pressure groups that want specific types of programming have difficulty pushing their demands on a network that is not trying to capture a broad audience.

In addition, cable came to fruition during the deregulatory era of the 1980s. When the government was rescinding regulations regarding broadcasting, it was not about to create them for cable. Also, the FCC was reluctant to regulate cable because the signals went through wires, not through the public airwaves. Nevertheless, the FCC made some rulings that affected cable in areas where cable and broadcasting overlapped, such as the **must–carry rule.** These regulations mostly were an attempt to protect broadcasting interests from competition that might be created by cable.

In many ways, the appearance of cable helped commercial broadcasters throw off some government shackles. Regulation of broadcasting was based largely on the **scarcity theory.** Because the airwaves only allowed four or five channels in most cities, few people could own commercial stations. Therefore, the government felt obligated to protect this rare commodity and ensure it was operated in the public interest. But when cable came along, just about anyone could start a network, so scarcity was no longer a viable idea. The fractionalization of programming and audience, with the philosophy of deregulation, led to a limiting of controls on cable programming and a lessening of controls on broadcasters.

Station Influence

Although there is a close connection between the commercial networks and the stations that carry the networks' programming, almost as if they were part of the same family, we consider stations as outside entities. There is clearly a symbiotic relationship between stations and networks. As outside forces, stations exercise control on program content. The network may generate the program, but the stations command the distribution base. For example, in 2003, two CBS affiliates in Texas, KZTV and KVTV, refused to carry the Hitler miniseries, "Hitler: The Rise of Evil," for fear the program might cause young people to view Hitler in too sympathetic a light.

If many stations refuse to present a network program, the audience will be dramatically reduced and a huge financial payback to the advertisers will be required. Therefore, network programmers are sensitive to the program evaluations of station programmers and managers.

Making decisions in this area is a difficult juggling act because of the enormous range of tastes across the country. A program acceptable in San Francisco may be boycotted in Little Rock. When a network is developing a potentially controversial movie, series episode, or documentary, it will frequently contact a committee of key affiliate managers to take a temperature reading. Many times, this advance notice will produce some script adjustments that will avoid a wholesale bailout and an unseemly dispute.

The relationship between syndicators and stations is not nearly as close. Networks and affiliates are joined at the hip throughout the broadcast day, every day, week in and week out. Because stations and syndicators come together just for particular shows, their association is a lot less familiar. There is no mechanism set up to notify stations about controversial material, nor are there subcommittees among the stations to monitor and protest content. However, if a production company consistently supplies programs that cause trouble in local markets, the station managers are not shy about voicing their displeasure, and they hold the ultimate weapon, a cancellation.

In the world of cable, cable systems decide which cable channels they will offer subscribers. Complicated financial negotiations and the demands of the public tend to determine which channels are carried. This also holds true for satellite television such as Direct TV, where customer service representatives solicit callers regarding channels that might be added to the service.

For public television, the influence and interrelationships between public stations and the central PBS network are strong. Stations pay the network for programs. They are the network's primary customers, and stations are quick to tell PBS what they do not like or what is not working for them.

Advertisers

One of the strongest influences on programming is the advertiser. Shows unable to attract sponsors, or hold the ones they have, will lead short, unhappy lives. Advertisers are extremely sensitive to program content that may alienate or infuriate potential customers. Their goal is to expand gross sales, not extend artistic boundaries. Although some are genuinely concerned about free expression, their primary obligation is to stockholders, and this imposes severe limits to their programming boldness.

ABC reported that it lost more than $1 million in revenue in 1990 when advertisers pulled out of an episode of "thirtysomething," which featured two guest-starring men talking in bed, apparently after having sex. To avoid further financial setbacks, the network decided not to rerun the episode. In the following season, the network said it lost $500,000 in another "thirtysomething" episode that depicted the two men accidentally meeting for the first time since the one-night stand.

The dilemma of the broadcaster who must attempt to reflect the realities of contemporary society within the confines of advertiser acceptability was eloquently addressed by Robert Iger when he was president of ABC Entertainment: "The danger of having to impose some form of content standards because of advertiser pressure is one of the more disturbing parts of my job. I am running a division that has a fiscal as well as a creative and social responsibility, and to maintain a balance between them is sometimes very difficult."

Not every wish of an advertiser is honored. When the sponsor's requirements conflict with the integrity of a production, the demands are frequently rejected. A classic example occurred with "Missiles of October," ABC's 1974 3-hour special that recreated the events of the Cuban missile crisis, which began when the United States discovered that the Soviet Union was installing offensive nuclear weapons 90 miles off Florida's shore. President John F. Kennedy demanded that Soviet President Nikita Khrushchev remove the launch sites without delay. Khrushchev refused, and for 13 days the world stood poised for a nuclear holocaust.

A Japanese automaker was impressed by Stanley Greenberg's teleplay and offered to sponsor half the program, a purchase worth slightly more than $1 million. However, the deal was contingent upon the deletion of two lines in

Figure 7.2
"Gilmore Girls" is one of the shows that has taken advantage of Family Friendly Programming Forum funding. (Globe Photos, Inc.)

the script. Both were references to Japan's participation in World War II, the most important of which was a statement by Attorney General Robert F. Kennedy that the president had insisted that the U.S. Air Force immediately disperse American bombers and fighter planes. "My brother doesn't want them lined up wing tip to wing tip the way they were at Pearl Harbor when the Japanese nearly wiped out our Air Force."[1] Greenberg and producer Herbert Brodkin objected to the change, pointing out that it was a major concern of the president and that its omission would make Kennedy look naive and inattentive to the lessons of history. The network agreed, the lines stayed in; the automaker withdrew its sponsorship. The sales department sold the time to a scattering of clients, and the network lost in excess of $500,000 in billings. But the show, available on DVD, aired exactly the way the author intended.

Public broadcasting was designed to be free of commercials so that advertisers could not influence program content. But as government funding has decreased, public broadcasting has had to rely more on corporate underwriting. In 2003, the PBS board of directors voted to increase its underwriting messages

from 15 to 30 seconds to entice more underwriters to come on board. These longer spots cannot engage in direct selling, in keeping with public broadcasting's guidelines, but many think the messages on public television are becoming more like ads on commercial television.

The Family Friendly Programming Forum

Perhaps lamenting the early days of television when advertisers controlled programming, some advertisers crave direct control over programming. Not content to wait to see what will be produced and available, these advertisers want to be fully involved. For example, the Family Friendly Programming Forum, formed in 1999, consists of a group of major national advertisers who provide the networks with seed money to develop "family friendly" series. Some of the advertisers who comprise the council include Procter & Gamble, FedEx, Ford, General Motors, and Johnson & Johnson.

This is the way the forum works: The networks submit scripts they think support the forum's objectives. If the forum agrees, seed money is provided to bring the projects to fruition. If the network puts the series into production, the networks return the seed money to the script development fund of the forum. If the series go on air, the networks are assured that the participating advertisers will willingly buy spots in the shows.

The WB in particular has taken advantage of the opportunity provided by Family Friendly Programming Forum funding, with such shows as "Gilmore Girls" (Figure 7.2) and "Family Affair." NBC's "American Dreams" and ABC's "8 Simple Rules" have also participated.

Achieving a balance between controversy and comfort is difficult for advertisers that are, generally, an extremely cautious group. Viewers, in particular the younger viewers that advertisers seek, want a sense of excitement or controversy. More viewers mean more people are exposed to an advertiser's spots. Yet, as a rule, advertisers steadfastly avoid controversy. Controversial shows therefore end up more often on cable, such as Showtime's frank "Queer As Folk" and HBO's "Sex and the City" and "Six Feet Under," all of which sport characters and situations far past the line at which most advertisers are comfortable—even if such shows have become award-night powerhouses. Nevertheless, gone are the days when Ricky and Lucy Arnaz had to sleep in separate twin beds and avoid the mention of Lucy being "pregnant"—even if Little Ricky did eventually appear, surreptitiously, in one of the most-watched episodes in television history. Shows such as "Will & Grace" and even "Friends" have featured ample racy situations but continued to garner top dollars from advertisers.

Pressure Groups

Several organizations have been set up specifically to monitor television programming. Their mission is to encourage programming that conforms to their standards of taste, political correctness, and morality and to eliminate programming they find offensive. Pressure groups run the gamut from very conservative to very liberal. Although they are frequently maligned by producers and broadcasters, they serve a valuable function, providing a variety of perspectives.

ACT was one of the most durable of such groups. It was formed in Boston in the 1960s by a group of parents who wanted networks and stations to improve the quality of children's programming, which at the time consisted mainly of cartoons, many of them violent. The organization, led by Peggy Charren, succeeded in convincing the FCC that it should develop guidelines for children's programs that broadcasters were to adhere to.

These guidelines, issued in 1974, stated, among other things, that stations would be expected to present a reasonable number of programs designed specifically for children and that they were to use imaginative and exciting methods to further children's understanding of such areas as literature, fine arts, history, science, the environment, human relations, reading, and math. For several years, these strictures were observed and both stations and networks developed programs such as after-school dramas, science shows, and news programs for young people.

Although these efforts were meritorious, they attracted smaller audiences than traditional cartoon fare and the broadcasters' bottom line was adversely affected. When deregulation came into vogue in the 1980s, the FCC stopped enforcing the 1974 regulations and fast-paced adventure cartoons returned to dominate the schedule. ACT sprang into action again. Through its lobbying efforts, it succeeded in convincing Congress to pass the Children's Television Act in 1990, which increased the amount of educational and informational programming to serve the needs of children. After this success, Charren declared her mission achieved and disbanded the organization, although she remains active as a spokesperson for quality television.

Another pressure group is Media Research Center, whose principal concern is the invasion of leftist doctrine in TV programs. Headed by

10 Best Shows
1. "Touched by an Angel"
2. "Doc"
3. "Sue Thomas F.B. Eye"
4. "7th Heaven"
5. "Life with Bonnie"
6. "Smallville"
7. "Reba"
8. "Star Search"
9. "George Lopez"
10. "8 Simple Rules for Dating My Teenage Daughter"

10 Worst Shows
1. "CSI: Crime Scene Investigation"
2. "Kingpin"
3. "Fastlane"
4. "NYPD Blue"
5. "Fear Factor"
6. "Angel"
7. "Girlfriends"
8. "Will & Grace"
9. "Friends"
10. "Big Brother"

Figure 7.3
The Parents Television Council's Top 10 best and worst shows for families in the 2002–2003 season. (Parents Television Council, a nonsectarian watchdog group that advocates family-friendly TV programming.)

L. Brent Bozell, the center reports on the left-wing bias it observes on television.

The Parents Television Council, also headed by Bozell, analyzes the appropriateness of programs for family viewing. Every year it publishes its list of the 10 best and 10 worst shows on the seven broadcast networks (Figure 7.3). The list includes "a quantitative analysis of the frequency of foul language, sexual content, and violence on each series, as well as the time slot, target audience, themes, and plotlines of the programs."[2] The Parents Television Council proudly announces successes it has in getting advertisers to pull their ads from shows, as was the case when "Nip/Tuck," FX's controversial series, lost some of its advertisers over controversial content about suicide.

Probably the most prominent conservative activist is the Reverend Donald Wildmon, founder of the American Family Association in 1977. A Methodist minister from Tupelo, Mississippi, Wildmon has attempted to influence program decisions primarily through pressure on advertisers. He blames the entertainment industry for abandoning traditional values; for example, objecting strongly to what he calls the "normalization" of premarital sex.

Over the years, Wildmon has targeted such shows as "LA Law" ("perverse and illicit sex"), "Growing Pains" ("perverted family entertainment"), "48 Hours" ("subtle swipes at Christianity"), and "thirtysomething" ("homosexual scene"). He numbers among his boycott successes NBC's "Roe vs. Wade," an Emmy Award–winning 1989 TV movie from which advertisers withdrew more than $1 million in advertising when it did not support his views against abortion. He also persuaded Pepsi Cola to abandon a $5 million advertising campaign featuring Madonna because of the entertainer's alleged "anti-Christian symbolism in her songs and videos."[3] He includes among his victories the cancellation of "Ellen" in 1998, the show that starred Ellen DeGeneres as an openly gay character.

Wildmon does not support the V-chip, a device parents can use to block programs they think are not suitable for their children and one of the provisions of the 1996 Telecommunications Act. He thinks the V-chip absolves the entertainment industry of its responsibilities. Instead, he supports a device called TVGuardian, a foul-language filter that automatically filters out offensive language for television, videos, and DVDs.

Resisting the efforts of conservative organizations is People for the American

Way, a liberal group that encourages the media's freedom of expression. Founded by TV producer Norman Lear, the group carries on a relentless struggle against the "religious right" in courts, Washington, and the nation's press.

Added to all these formal organizations are ad hoc groups or individuals who protest only when a program offends their particular interest. For example, Terry Rakolta, a Michigan homemaker, did not like a "Married . . . With Children" episode in which Peg Bundy shopped for a bra. She tried to incite a boycott of the sponsor's products. The movement backfired when many new viewers tuned in to see what all the hollering was about. Undeterred, Rakolta formed Americans for Responsible Television, a group dedicated to the restoration of family values in television programs.

Despite periodic attacks on the "liberal slant" of public broadcasting, pressure groups generally tend to pay less attention to cable and public television, partly because their audiences tend to be smaller and more fragmented than those for commercial television. Commercial television, which does not require viewers to pay a fee (ostensibly to get what they are paying for), remains the main focus of most pressure groups. Grumbles about cable pushing the envelope may result in a lot more attention for cable.

Shows that touch on sensitive themes remain likely to draw fire. One day it may be the National Association for Advancement of Colored People; the next day it might be the Veterans of Foreign Wars followed by the National Organization of Women, the Anti-Defamation League, or the Knights of Columbus. What is a poor programmer to do? "Show some courage," said Steve Mills, for many years CBS's vice president of movies made for television. "Every program will step on somebody's toes. All you can do is make it honest, make it fair, and make it good. And when the heat comes, tell the complainers why you think it's a picture that should be seen and hold firm to your convictions."

The Religious Right

The religious right has a large following, one vocal about its displeasure with programming that presents conflicting values. Many such people complained about the inadequate supply of family-friendly programming. Their complaints did not go unnoticed, particularly when it became clear that there were dollars to be made by providing entertainment the religious right would find appealing, possibly starting with the premiere of "Touched by an Angel" on CBS in 1994 or the successful theatrical release of *The Omega Code* in 1999, followed by the phenomenal success of *The Passion of the Christ* in 2004.

Publications such as *Christianity Today* and numerous websites direct the public to fare that contains positive, wholesome values. Cleanflicks edits videos to remove objectionable elements from violent, sexually explicit films. Sensitive to this trend, Jonathan Bock formed a company called Grace Hill Media in 2000. This company markets entertainment product to religious groups, groups that Hollywood tended to ignore. He consults on films and television programs alike.

For Bock, "On any given weekend, the number of people who attend religious services—roughly 122 million—is vastly greater than the number who go to the movies—and that kind of ticket-purchasing power can be tapped."[4]

If Bock or others cannot convince religious groups that a particular work contains a strong moral message, then fundamental religious groups are quick to call for bans, advertiser boycotts, FCC fines, or legislative action.

Timing

A group or advertiser's timing in applying pressure can vary. An advertiser, for example, may decide to embrace or avoid a program at the conceptual stage. Although most programmers advocate making shows without the advertisers in mind, some cautious executives will avoid developing shows they do not think the ad buyers will want. Before venturing into development, some may even check with the sales force that may, in turn, "pass the idea by" a major advertiser.

Sometimes an advertiser will protest the making of a show, blocking it from getting made. For example, in 2000, producer Ilene Amy Berg got a green light from the USA cable network to make a telefilm called "Who Killed Sue Snow?" It was the story of a woman, Stella Nickell, who in 1986 in Seattle killed her husband by lacing Excedrin capsules with cyanide. To draw suspicion from herself and to make it look like a copycat killing, Nickell put cyanide in other containers of Excedrin.

Five days before the start of shooting, USA pulled the plug on the movie under pressure from Johnson & Johnson, the maker of Tylenol. Johnson & Johnson does not make Excedrin, but it objected to any portrayal of drug tampering. It figured that a movie that drew attention to drug tampering would be harmful to the company. Johnson & Johnson threatened to pull all its advertising from USA, revealing "the growing clout of major advertisers in the competitive television market."[5]

Drug companies are the nation's fifth largest advertisers.[6] Even though "Who Killed Sue Snow?" had been carefully reviewed by USA's legal department before it received a green light, the threat of an ad boycott for the entire network for a single film was not worth the risk for USA, regardless of how responsibly the script handled the topic of drug tampering.

The last-minute pressure exercised on "Who Killed Sue Snow?" was unusual. Most often, ad buyers will decide where they want to place their ad dollars at the "up fronts" in May, when the schedules are announced. Buyers will purchase "blocks" of advertising times at the start of the season, although they may select to buy time in individual shows during the year, known as "scatter buys."

Advertisers have the opportunity to screen advance copies of shows to see whether they want to keep the spots they have purchased or to pull out. For example, if an automobile manufacturer has bought blocks of time in a series and one of the episodes deals with SUVs' poor safety performance, that advertiser will have the opportunity to withdraw the spot. The salesperson at the network will try to convince the ad buyer to stay in, perhaps stressing that the driver of the SUV in the show was shown to be negligent, but the advertiser still has the opportunity to withdraw.

Many times, salespeople will contact the programming executive to get the right **spin** to describe a show, one that can be used to assuage an anxious buyer. ("Yes, the show does portray life on the streets as dirty and depressing, but the show's message is really about the redemptive power of forgiveness.")

If you are watching a prime-time show that contains numerous public service announcements, a lot of local ads, and few national ads, chances are good that an advertiser pulled out, maybe even at the last minute, feeling the particular program was not an appropriate venue for its product.

In 2003, a major controversy took place when CBS opted to cancel its $10 million miniseries "The Reagans" 2 weeks before it was scheduled to air during the November sweeps. The pressure was applied *after* the film was made, *after* an airdate had been assigned, and *after* the publicity had begun. In announcing his decision to pull the plug, CBS President Les Moonves said the film was not the one he had ordered, that it was advocacy instead of entertainment,[7] and that he was making a moral decision not to air it,[8] offering it instead to Showtime, owned by Viacom, CBS's parent company.

At play in the timing of the decision about "The Reagans" was a strong objection from conservative groups to the project as a hatchet job, unfair to Nancy Reagan and to former President Ronald Reagan, whose Alzheimer's condition prevented him from defending himself. Conservatives (who had not seen the finished film) labeled it unfair and inaccurate, urging CBS not to air it.

A groundswell of conservative protests ensued. The Media Research Center sent a letter to 100 television sponsors encouraging them not to advertise their products on the show.[9] Former Republican congressional staff member Michael Paranzino started a website called BoycottCBS.com.[10]

Was the cancellation of "The Reagans" a victory for the conservative right, getting a finished film pulled after it had already been announced in the press? Was pulling it at the last minute a valid moral decision by a man who found the film unbalanced? Was it further evidence of the cowardly nature of the networks? These and many other points of view were expressed about this hot-button telefilm. As Meg James, Greg Braxton, and Bob Baker noted in the *Los Angeles Times,* "Never before had a network pulled a major, completed production off the air amid such pressure."[11]

The Media

Television reporting is news—big news. "Entertainment Tonight," "Access Hollywood," "Entertainment Weekly," and countless other outlets keep an eager audience informed about what is going on in the television industry. Television shows are reviewed and dissected daily. Cast changes, cancellations, station defections, and ratings are breathlessly reported to a seemingly insatiable public. The buzz about television can be deafening, but what effect does the media attention have on programming?

When *TV Guide* publishes an article about good shows that viewers are not watching, do ratings improve? Most often, no. Does a coveted *TV Guide* cover guarantee ratings? No. If media observer Mark Andrejevic notes that reality shows "glamorize surveillance" and that living under "Big Brother" on reality shows is now cool, because twice as many people apply to be on MTV's

Figure 7.4
"The Real World" has connected with teen viewers for more than 10 years. (Globe Photos, Inc.)

Figure 7.5
"According to Jim" has found an appreciative audience despite lukewarm reviews. (Photo © ABC Photography Archives.)

"The Real World" (Figure 7.4) than to attend Harvard University,[12] will these insights alter people's viewing habits? Again, probably not.

John McMahon and Karen Moore produced many telefilms for USA under the Wilshire Court banner. They used to joke that they wanted bad reviews for their movies, bad reviews that suggested the movies might be fun to watch—"guilty pleasures," in other words. For them, a review that said a program was good for you, one that elevated the genre, or one that would teach viewers a meaningful lesson was a ratings kiss of death. It might be necessary to take medicine if you are ill, but there is no appeal in a television program designed to make you feel better.

Many programmers similarly dismiss poor reviews, insisting that when it comes to commercial television, good reviews do not mean ratings. These programmers think that many media critics are too lofty in their expectations and that they do not understand the business. A programming executive might thus use ABC's "According to Jim," starring Jim Belushi (Figure 7.5), as an example of a show that would never make any critic's Top 10 list even though it is a show that viewers have embraced, to highlight how critics have no insight into viewer tastes.

However, most programming executives do not like to see their shows constantly pilloried in the press. A string of negative reviews could make them more receptive to a quality submission just to relieve the heat.

Good reviews have a more significant effect on cable and a much more significant effect on public television. There are so many options on cable that a show singled out for praise can break from the pack. "The Sopranos" on HBO more than likely owes its phenomenal success to the reviews that praised the quality of the writing.

Although public television does not rely on advertisers and is not driven by ratings, it wants to program quality-driven shows. Public television also wants its shows to receive attention, partly to keep underwriters committed to sponsorship. Good reviews are thus important for public television stations. Over the years, the press has been generally responsive to public television offerings, giving public TV programs positive reviews and covers of Sunday television-magazine supplements—to the great frustration of commercial and cable programmers that would like the exposure. But again, it is uncertain whether the supplement covers significantly affect what the average viewer watches.

Academic and Nonprofit Studies

Universities and foundations frequently examine aspects of television and publish their findings. Although programmers rarely make decisions based on these reports, the studies can create an environment that will eventually influence program content. The National Coalition of Television Violence, a nonprofit organization of mental health specialists and media researchers, periodically reviews the nation of trends in television violence. For several decades, Dr. George Gerbner of the University of Pennsylvania has had a staff counting incidents of violence on television programs and conducting various research studies about violence. His studies have helped to create an awareness of the daily mayhem, but whether these studies have caused any reduction is questionable.

One group of studies that probably affected programming was solicited in 1969 by the U.S. Surgeon General to explore the effects of violence on children.[13] These studies, supervised by 12 prestigious researchers, concluded that a modest relationship exists between violence viewed on TV and aggressive tendencies in children. These studies were undertaken while ACT was promoting reforms in children's television. The reforms that came were the result of various factors; these research studies were among them.

In 2002 and 2003, commentary about the state of television frequently included observations by Robert J. Thompson, professor and director of the Center for the Study of Popular Television at Syracuse University. The author of several studies, including *Television's Second Golden Age* (1996) and *Prime Time, Prime Movers* (1992), Thompson presents a unique approach to the medium by refusing to undermine "popular" television and refusing to adopt the loftier-than-thou approach many commentators cling to. By taking a friendlier approach to television, Thompson has brought a refreshing perspective to academic studies.

The Government

Commercial television transmits its product using signals that pass through the nation's airwaves. These airwaves belong to the public and are, therefore, subject to the supervision of government. In 1934, Congress passed the Communications Act that delineated the rights and limitations of broadcasters and established the FCC to carry out the regulations prescribed in the act. The FCC is still the broadcasters' main interface with government.

The Federal Communications Commission. The FCC is an independent executive agency comprising five com-

missioners, no more than three of whom may be members of the same political party, appointed by the president with the consent of the Senate for 5-year terms. Among its powers are the ability to grant, renew, revoke, or modify broadcast station licenses.

Although networks are not licensed, all stations are. Because all of the networks own and operate several stations, the government can influence their performance by threatening them with the loss of one or more of their owned and operated stations. In addition, networks do not want to cause problems for their affiliated stations by sending them programming that might give them difficulties at license renewal time. Syndicators, too, are aware that the stations would not be happy with syndicated material that placed their licenses in jeopardy.

License renewal depends on many factors, such as fulfilling equal employment obligations and broadcasting on the right frequency with the right power. The quality of a station's programming is also a factor in licensing decisions. The FCC does not proscribe any programming ahead of time—a clause in the 1934 Communications Act prevents such **prior censorship.** But another clause in the Communications Act states that "The Commission, if public convenience, interest, or necessity will be served thereby, subject to the limitations of this Act, shall grant to any applicant therefore a station license provided for by this Act."[14] This "public convenience, interest, or necessity" clause has become the keystone for license renewal. Its definition is sufficiently broad for any administration to make life uncomfortable for any station that, in the FCC's judgment, is misbehaving.

Few TV stations have lost their licenses because of their programming,

but it has happened. For example, in 1990, a Chicago station was denied license renewal partly because the station at one time aired pornographic movies. In 1964, the FCC issued a short-term license to WLBT in Jackson, Mississippi, because of the manner in which it presented racial issues. This station's license was later revoked because of a court ruling.

If the FCC thinks a station is doing something improper, at license renewal time or at some other time, it can take actions other than revoking a license. It can fine a station, or it can issue a cease and desist order that notifies the station that it is to stop a certain action or it may receive further punishment.

Many think that the fines levied are simply gentle rebukes because the fine amounts are too low to cause the broadcasting stations real discomfort. In 2003, the maximum single fine was $27,500; the amount has since increased significantly, as there is a concerted effort in Washington to increase fines and levy more of them. This is evidenced by the 2004 fines stations owned and operated by CBS received for the Janet Jackson "wardrobe malfunction" and the fines Fox stations received for "Married by America." For example, the repeated fines levied on "The Howard Stern Show" over the years are easily offset by the show's considerable profits.

Many also think that the FCC is too lenient. For example, in 2003, when Bono used f—during the broadcast of "The Golden Globes" on NBC, the FCC responded to complaints by determining that Bono's use of the term was not obscene because it was not used in a sexual context. This ruling, which the FCC subsequently reversed, infuriated many who want to FCC to be tougher—possibly the same people who were surprised earlier when the FCC ruled that a broadcast of a "Victoria's Secret Special" with women in sexy lingerie did not constitute **indecency.**

Although the FCC is the main government body that broadcasters deal with, various facets of the executive, legislative, and judicial branches of government can affect programming policies. For example, after the FCC allowed companies to own TV stations that collectively reach 45% of the nation's viewers, Congress voted to set the cap at 39%.

Congress. Congress, as already mentioned, approves FCC commissioners and passes laws that govern or affect broadcasting. In addition, various congressional committees occasionally investigate aspects of broadcast programming.

One subject investigated at least once a decade is violence on TV. As far back as 1950, Senator Estes Kefauver mused on the Senate floor that perhaps there was too much violence on TV. An investigation into violence that occurred in the 1961–1962 season was mainly the result of ABC's attempt to reach its target audience of 18 to 34 year olds by cranking up sex and violence in action–adventure shows, which became known as "jiggle television." As the mayhem and heavy breathing increased, so did the audience.

In response, the other networks went up a few decibels and the nightly din was deafening. Viewers contacted their Congress members, and network leaders were summoned to Washington to be grilled before Senator Thomas J. Dodd and his committee members. The ABC president, Oliver Treyz, was a target. His series, "Bus Stop," had presented an episode in which rock singer Fabian portrayed a psychopath who lived to kill and torture. When a senator asked the beleaguered executive if he allowed his own children to see such a show, the

answer was a stammered, "no." Shortly thereafter, "Bus Stop" was canceled and so was Treyz.

In 1993, intense congressional heat was once again being applied to the industry, this time by Senator Paul Simon, author of the 1990 Television Violence Act. The agreement by the four networks earlier in the year to affix viewer advisories to self-evaluated violent programs apparently was not satisfactory to the legislator. Broadcasters insisted that government interference was not needed, and Simon insisted that the broadcasters were not doing enough to curb violence on television.

After the exposure of Janet Jackson's breast at the Super Bowl half-time show in 2004, a storm of protests gathered. That children were in the audience fueled the outcry, although no one seemed to object that these children saw many ads for erectile dysfunction products during the game. Shortly after the Super Bowl, Viacom President and Chief Operating Officer Mel Karmazin, representing CBS, which broadcast the Super Bowl, and National Football League Commissioner Paul Tagliabue were urgently summoned to testify before the Senate Commerce Committee and a subcommittee of the House Committee on Energy and Commerce.

Congressional hearings have covered many other programming-related subjects. During a 1950s House subcommittee hearing, Charles Van Doren, the most famous of the "Twenty-One" quiz show winners, confessed that he had been helped with answers to defeat contestants who were less appealing to the public. At the time, there was no law that prohibited this practice, but it was unfair to other contestants and unfair to the audience that believed the competitions were genuine. As a result of its hearings, Congress amended the Communications Act, making it unlawful to give such help to a contestant.

The President. The president and other members of the executive branch do not have as much formal power to influence programming as Congress. Presidents can veto bills related to broadcasting, just as they can any other bills, and they appoint the members of the FCC. However, the power wielded over programming by the executive branch tends to be informal. For example, in the late 1960s and early 1970s when anti-Vietnam War and civil rights demonstrations dominated the evening news, the Richard Nixon administration applied considerable pressure to the networks and stations to present "a more balanced" perspective of the national mood. In the administration's judgment, the "silent majority" of Americans supported the president's policies, but the dissidents were receiving a disproportionate amount of attention because their demonstrations supplied the media with interesting pictures. Although the government never initiated any formal action against the networks, the capacity (some said "implied threat") to do so caused industry executives to monitor carefully all footage with political implications to avoid accusations of bias.

Theoretically, the CPB was set up to insulate public broadcasting from the government. The money allocated by Congress is forwarded to the CPB, which then distributes it to stations and networks. The CPB's role is to make sure that the government does not pass along its politics as it passes along its money. This has not always been the case; less money can be allocated if the administration is not pleased with what is being broadcast. This occurred when

President Nixon vetoed public broadcasting's 1972–1974 budget.

More recently, in 2001, Karl Rove, President George W. Bush's senior adviser, met with some 47 top Hollywood executives to encourage them to make more patriotic, antiterrorist entertainment in the wake of the attacks on the World Trade Center on September 11, 2001. Although Rove and his colleagues said they were not asking Hollywood to make propaganda films, it was nevertheless clear that they were interested in having traditionally liberal Hollywood embrace the President's policies.

The Military. The military can similarly exercise significant influence over programming—especially any programming that may wish to use images or assets from the military in production. By cooperating or not cooperating with a particular production, the military can substantially decrease or increase production costs. Although these costs primarily affect theatrical films, the military's stamp of approval of a particular television program not only can lower costs but also can provide much-valued realism.

In this regard, George Washington University law professor Jonathan Turley noted, "Most Americans are unaware that the U.S. military routinely reviews scripts that might require Defense Department cooperation and that the Pentagon compels changes for television and movies to convey the government's message."[15] He added that a team of military advisers embedded in Hollywood worked on a "JAG" script "to present its controversial military tribunals as something of an ACLU [American Civil Liberties Union] lawyer's dream."[16] If the military does not like a particular portrayal, access to military equipment, locations, and stock footage is readily denied.

The Courts. The judicial system becomes involved with broadcasting when cases are brought to it. These cases can be brought by individuals or companies that think they have been wronged by some aspect of commercial broadcasting, or they can be brought by one media organization against another. In addition, if a broadcaster does not like an FCC decision, that broadcaster can appeal through the U.S. Court of Appeals.

When cases related to programming are tried in court, they are handled by lawyers rather than programmers. But programmers are sometimes called as witnesses or are asked to give background information to the lawyers.

Often, the various branches of government interrelate. Congress may pass a general law interpreted by the FCC in a manner unfavorable to broadcasters. The broadcasters can take the FCC ruling through the courts and, if the ruling is still unfavorable, they can go back to Congress to attempt to have the basic law changed. The interrelationship, involvement, and influence of the various branches of government can be seen by taking a close look at **equal time** provisions.

Equal Time. During political campaigns, broadcasters are required to make time available in their programming schedules to all candidates running for federal office. They are also strongly encouraged to allow time for state and local candidates. When time is made available to one candidate for a particular office, equal time must be allowed for all other candidates running for the same office. This applies to political commercials and to programs. If one candidate buys $100,000 worth of time

to run political ads, all other candidates must have the opportunity to buy an equivalent amount of time at the same ad rate. A station cannot charge one candidate more money to place an ad than it has charged another.

The equal time provision comes from Section 315 of the 1934 Communications Act. Section 315 states that broadcasters "shall afford equal opportunities to all other such candidates for that office,"[17] but over the years this section has been commonly referred to as the equal time provision.

Now that several actors have made their way into politics, a similar problem arises with entertainment programming. When Reagan ran for president, stations were legally obligated to give equal time to opponent Jimmy Carter anytime they ran an old movie with Reagan in it. Most stations avoided the problem by making sure they did not run Reagan movies for the duration of the campaign, but Carter also made light of the situation, joking that Reagan would probably lose votes if his old movies were shown. A similar situation occurred in 2003 when actor Arnold Schwarzenegger ran successfully for the governorship of California not long after his movie "Terminator 3" hit theaters with its accompanying broadcast media marketing blitz, which featured Schwarzenegger prominently and often. Programmers who had previously scheduled movies featuring Schwarzenegger to air on their stations had to shuffle their offerings.

But not all broadcast programming is subject to equal time provisions. News programs are exempted. The FCC determines which programs are classified as news. For example, the FCC classified Howard Stern's program as a news show, so his program was not required to have all the presidential candidates if he had one or two of them as guests. As reporter Sharon Waxman notes, the FCC considers interviews on shows such as "The Tonight Show with Jay Leno" news, similarly not subject to equal time requirements.[18] So when Arnold Schwarzenegger used "The Tonight Show" to announce his candidacy for the governorship in 2003, Leno was not obligated to allow all 135 other candidates do the same. Leno neverthe-less opted to make offers to the other candidates to appear en masse on his show, although he was not required to do so.

Now that the **fairness doctrine** is no longer in effect, programmers clearly should be well versed in the provisions, exclusions, and aberrations of the "equal time provision," and they should keep legal counsel handy during election times.

THE ISSUE OF "STOP THE CHURCH"

"P.O.V." ("Point of View") is one of PBS's long-running series. Each episode consists of a short film on a matter of social or political conse-quence. The shows are designed to raise consciousness on subjects the producers think are underexposed, misunderstood, or both.

In July 1991, one of the productions ran into a firestorm of criticism. The show, "Tongues Untied," dealt with black male homosexuality and included frank language and some nudity. Hundreds of PBS stations refused to air the program, and others ran it at off hours to minimize its audience.

On August 12, PBS announced the cancellation of the next scheduled "P.O.V." episode, "Stop the Church." Produced by the AIDS Coalition to Unleash Power (ACT UP), a gay activist organization, the film depicted the preparation for and execution of a 1989 demonstration at St. Patrick's Cathedral in New York City against the Catholic Church's stance on AIDS. The satirical song, "The Vatican Rag," was played as background music to scenes of Catholic worship, and ACT UP members were shown disrupting a mass conducted by Cardinal John O'Connor. During the services, activists were heard yelling at O'Connor, "Stop killing us, stop killing us," presumably because of the Church's objection to the promotion and distribution of condoms.

David Davis, president of P.O.V., acknowledged the earlier disturbance over "Tongues Untied" and explained that he was pulling "Stop the Church" because "I felt another controversy at this time would break (stations) backs and undermine their confidence in 'P.O.V.'"[19] But PBS spokesperson Mary Jane McKinven denied the linkage with the earlier show. She stated that the "Stop the Church" program, on its own merits, had "a per-vasive tone of ridicule which rather overwhelms its critique of church policy."[20] Her comment was supported by John Grant, PBS's vice president for scheduling: "Our decision has nothing to do with the attack on the church . . . , it has nothing to do with the fact that it was made by an AIDS activist group. It was the tone and the ridicule that we found inappropriate for broadcast."[21]

Although PBS officially removed the program from its schedule, individual stations were still free to obtain a print and play it. Three chose to do so: KCET in Los Angeles, WGBH in Boston, and KQED in San Francisco.

KCET's decision to run the program caused a brouhaha in Los Angeles. Cardinal Roger M. Mahony accused the station of surrendering to "black-

7 **Influences on Television Programming**   177

mail" by gay activists and called on Southern Californians to consider withholding contributions from KCET. According to Mahony, gays and AIDS activists had pressured the Los Angeles station to run the controversial program by threatening to withdraw their financial support of the station and to jam the switchboard during the station's August pledge drive to make it impossible for other donors to register their contributions.

At his press conference September 5, two days before the scheduled broadcast, the Cardinal said, "This absence of responsible leadership at KCET leads me to believe that we should hold the station morally, and possible legally, responsible for every future act of terrorism against churches, temples, and synagogues because KCET has told potential perpetrators of such hate crimes that not only is such activity acceptable, it is worthy of televised documentaries celebrating and glorifying it."[22]

Despite this blistering attack, KCET held to its decision to air the show. At his own news conference held later the same day, then KCET President William Kobin said that he was "distressed by Mahony's actions. KCET believes strongly that its viewers deserve the same opportunity as Cardinal Mahony to view this film and make up their own mind regarding this controversy."[23]

A surface solution would be to honor the judgment of the network officials and withhold the program. However, activist organizations are well aware that individual PBS stations operate with considerable autonomy and are capable of broadcasting shows disapproved of, or discouraged, by the network. What to do? Either way the station would alienate a broad constituency and run the risk of revenue loss. KCET chose to schedule the program and attempted to moderate Catholic fury by scheduling an aftershow panel session in which church advocates had an opportunity to rebut the charges.

Airing the program did have direct adverse financial consequences. KCET estimated it lost $55,000, most of it because one local businessman pulled back a large pledge. Compounding the problem, the controversy came during a recession, when contributions were hard to come by. But the station claimed this experience would not change its programming philosophy. Barbara Goen, KCET's vice president for public information, said, "Any attempt at curtailing our income source, or threatening it, is very serious. It probably has greater significance in hard times than in flush times. But does it mean we change the way we make program decisions? No, it doesn't."[24] Despite the idealistic tone, it is also possible the station was bowing to pressure from the activists, who could have caused the station to lose much more income had the station not aired the program.

It is interesting to speculate what advice a TV program consultant, had one been retained, might have offered the cardinal. "Stop the Church" registered a 4.5 rating and a 9.0 share. For the five preceding weeks, the time period averaged a 1.7 rating and a 3.5 share; for the five weeks following, the figures were 1.2 and 2.3. In short, the heated controversy over the show generated an audience approximately three times greater than normal. Perhaps the cardinal felt that no matter what the audience results were, he could hardly let the broadcast take place without protest. But on a purely statistical basis, an airing without any controversy would surely have resulted in a smaller audience, an outcome he would have preferred.

Again, the question of whether controversy helps or hurts ratings comes into play. In this instance from television's past, controversy raised awareness and ratings. Whether ratings are helped or hurt by controversy and the actions of pressure groups remains a constant. Many external corporations, groups, and individuals work hard to promote programs that support their points of view and concerns and work equally hard against programs that cross or question their values.

INTERNAL INFLUENCES ON TELEVISION

Internal influences also play a significant role. Different departments or divisions offer input that determines what types of programming viewers experience. Every department in an organization engaged in making or distributing programming wants to ensure that its influence is duly appreciated. All divisions are eager to make sure that they are not left out of success, and they are quick to lay blame elsewhere in failure.

The programming departments may be more visible than other television divisions, but they do not function in isolation. No programming department stands alone. Occasionally an adventurous programming executive will want to make a decision on his or her own, choosing not to consult anyone, but such rash decisions often backfire. Producers often try to force executives to make instant decisions in their favor, but even high-level programming executives are better off not committing to any final actions without "consulting" with other departments.

In support of this view, programmers like to tell the story of a young development executive, a so-called baby mogul, who was so sure everybody would love a particular project that he, on his own, committed to a production order. To his surprise, the network did not agree. Not one department agreed with his choice, and he had to "eat crow," taking back his commitment. Had he said he needed to check with his and other departments, he would have looked more like his own man than he did making promises he was unable to keep.

The Sales Department

Many industry professionals have a sales background, and there is a good reason for this. Simply put, salespeople understand what sells. Although students may feel that the sales division is less glamorous than development or production, sales executives have a real pulse on what the all-important advertisers are going to respond to. They also know from experience what the viewing public will want to see.

Because of their antennas, salespeople are often consulted before final programming decisions are made. If the salespeople screening pilots at a commercial or cable television network feel strongly that a particular program will not appeal to advertisers or to the public, that is important information for the network to factor into the mix. Programmers may publicly claim that the concerns of sales do not figure in programming decisions, but this is not always the case—nor should it be. It would be foolish to forge ahead with a program that sales cannot sell, as was the case in 2000 when ABC put on "Wonderland," a gritty series about life at a New York psychiatric hospital. In the first episode, a pregnant woman was jabbed in the stomach with a dirty drug needle, causing viewers to flee. "Wonderland" premiered March 30 and had its last airing a week later on April 6, proving that the salespeople had been right.

Salespeople also have knowledge about what will sell abroad. For example, suppose that a telefilm needs $700,000 from the foreign market to be financially viable and the sales team says that the most that can be counted on is $200,000. That is a $500,000 deficit, no small matter. If the production of the film goes ahead and the salespeople were correct about their predictions, they will make sure everyone knows, both to bolster their division and to prevent similar mistakes.

In previous chapters, we mentioned the adage that "sex sells." There is ample evidence that sexual content is prolific in many programs, but many savvy sales executives know that sex does not always sell (Figure 7.6). A 2003 study at the University of Michigan supports this position, finding that viewers remember ads in programs that do not include sexual content.[25] Thus salespeople might speak for programming that favors advertisers by avoiding overt sexual content to keep advertisers happy and rates high.

In syndication, two sales voices must be heard: the one in charge of clearances and the one in charge of **barter.** If either states that the program is unsalable, the project likely will be abandoned. But the ultimate decision maker, presumably the president of the production company (or distributor), must be alert. Many salespeople tend to evaluate programs on the anticipated degree of difficulty in selling the show. A program that will sell easily will be supported enthusiastically; one that looms as a tough sell will be received coolly. None of this may relate to the inherent strength of the show.

The Finance Department

No projects see the light of day without the finance department, sometimes called business affairs. As noted in Chapter 4, no project goes into development until the finance department has closed a deal. Many programs are never made because money matters cannot be resolved. Showtime, for example, under Jerry Offsay's leadership, would not put a project into development if the finance department was not convinced it was financially feasible. Thus, programming executives had to get internal approval that the project being proposed could be produced within Showtime's financial guidelines.

In general, when a given project is selected for production, a license fee

Figure 7.6
Sex does not always sell, as the failure of NBC's "Coupling" demonstrated in 2003. (Globe Photos, Inc.)

needs to be negotiated by the financial department. The amount of the license fee will, to a great extent, determine how a project turns out: Cheap? Well produced? Somewhere between these extremes?

Most programmers are respectful of the influence of the finance department, careful to maintain a cordial relationship; however, friction can develop when it appears that the finance department, always seeking to contain costs, is standing in the way of the programming department's agenda. For example, when Susan Lyne was head of TV movies at ABC in 2000, she was upset that a low offer had been made to an established star. The star flatly rejected the offer. Lyne felt that a higher offer would have secured the star's services, giving the telefilm what all television executives want—a star who never does television. Generally, programming and finance work well together, but when costs are cut arbitrarily and quality begins to suffer, programmers should challenge financial dictates. Low-quality programs lead to lower audiences, which lead to reduced sales that lead to a devastating bottom line. There is no such thing as a cheap disaster.

Martin Carlson, vice president of business affairs at the Fox network, is a

Figure 7.7
"NYPD Blue," starring Dennis Franz and Mark-Paul Gosselaar, carries advisories for language and partial nudity. (Photo © ABC Photography Archives.)

tices department to catch an offensive word or scene before it causes trouble (Figure 7.7).

Networks cannot air entertainment programming unless it has been cleared by the broadcast standards and practices department (this department does not cover news or sports, though that may change post–Janet Jackson and the Super Bowl), which gives these "censors," as they are frequently called, a great deal of influence. This creates many heated discussions when the programming department wants something included in a program and the censors do not agree, particularly if the broadcast standards and practices executives feel a need to inflate their importance. For example, Alfred Schneider, whose book *The Gatekeeper* describes his 30 years as a network censor, would ask his staff, "Why are we making this?" as if the broadcast standards and practices department, not the programming department, was deciding what to put on the air.

Broadcast standards and practices editors need to be adept at the art of negotiation to guide producers and programming executives to accept their rulings without appearing to be dictatorial. Often, waiting for all of the participants to speak before requesting changes can assist a censor in achieving the desired goal.

Although many people believe that broadcast standards and practices departments have official lists of acceptable and unacceptable content, there are no fixed rules. Being a network censor involves making informed judgment calls, not following set rules.

Because judgments about program substance are largely subjective, programmers and producers frequently view broadcast standards and practices representatives as the enemy and accuse them of being arbitrary and destructive. "Not so," says Ted Cordes, former head

full-service finance executive who defines his role as a facilitator, bringing parties together to make television. He negotiates a variety of contracts (for actors, producers, directors, etc.) and is intimately involved in all aspects of production. What viewers see on Fox would not make it to air without executives who take charge of the finances.

The Broadcast Standards and Practices Department

To operate profitably, a network must avoid offending any of its many constituencies: government, advertisers, affiliated stations, and the scores of groups that make up the general public. The wrath of any one of these can inflict heavy losses on the broadcaster. It is the job of the broadcast standards and prac-

censor at NBC, whose career spanned 4 decades. "We always try to work with the program people to find another way to make the scene effective." Brett White, former head censor at ABC, also found that many times producers and programmers told him that the requested edits improved scenes. After all, how creative is it to simply repeat swear words?

A SAMPLE STANDARDS REPORT

The following representative standards report for a fictional program on commercial television reveals the kinds of areas the broadcast standards and practices department addresses. This is the type of report that would be sent to a producer before filming.

- Reduce the number of "hells" and "damns."
- Substitute another word for "goddamn."
- Please make an effort to hire minorities in leading and supporting roles.
- Please avoid racial stereotypes. The dialogue "Muslims are all terrorists" must be deleted.
- Significantly reduce the number of hits during the fight sequence.
- Do not point guns directly at the camera.
- Please ensure that all medical information presented is accurate and provide us with the supporting documentation.
- Please have the driver and passenger fasten their seat belts when they are driving.
- One use of "bastard" is approved. Lose the other instances.
- Men in the locker room should be wearing boxer shorts, not briefs. No nudity is allowed.
- Avoid thong bikinis for the women in the sequence at the beach.
- Do not use blood squids in the fight sequence. The scripted throat slashing should take place off-camera, and no slashing sound effects should be included.
- Regarding the scripted discussion of the controversial topic of abortion, please ensure that different points of view are presented; we want to avoid advocacy programming. The abortion discussion is not approved until we have seen revised pages.
- Please secure appropriate clearances for the use of the sports photographs in the office of the PR agency.
- Avoid characters smoking.
- In the bedroom scene, please make sure there is no nudity. Head movement cannot suggest that oral sex is taking place. There can be no grinding activity. Be sure to provide ample coverage for this scene to avoid problems with the rough cut. Use discretion in staging this scene to avoid having the program carry an advisory.
- Use generic labels for the sodas in the kitchen.
- Substitute other words for the dialogue that all teenage boys have tried pot by the age of 14; this type of generalization is misleading to viewers.

In the late 1980s, there was a movement at the networks to reduce the size of broadcast standards and practices departments. For example, in 1988, the new management at NBC decided that an extensive broadcast standards and practices department was unnecessary, and the unit was drastically downsized. The theory was that the executives of the programming department, working cooperatively with the producer, would exercise the required taste and judgment to air suitable material. It was an egregious miscalculation. It ignored that both the programmer and the producer were primarily rewarded for attracting large audiences. Whenever they had to choose between a juicy scene with a high rating potential and a softer scene with the probability of lower ratings, they tilted toward the former. During the first 12 months of this new joint "supervision," the network was forced to forfeit $12 million in lost revenue because of defections by sponsors, affiliates, or both. The broadcast standards and practices departments at NBC and other networks were substantially increased the following year.

Following the failed downsizing experiment, broadcast standards and practices departments, which most often function with the legal departments, again became powerful members of internal teams.

Most censors are aware of their role as part of the system and aware of their responsibility to protect the interests of the networks. In so doing, they significantly affect what audiences see on television.

Olivia Cohen–Cutler, senior vice president of broadcast standards and practices at ABC, sums up her role as the head censor as ensuring that viewers are not surprised or caught off guard when they turn to her network.

WHAT CENSORS DO

According to ABC's Olivia Cohen-Cutler, censors review all entertainment programming for acceptability; their responsibilities include the following:

- Monitoring violence, sexual content, and language
- Ensuring that children's programming meets governmental guidelines
- Editing theatrical films for broadcast on television. (Interestingly, in 2001 and 2002 ABC aired the theatrical film *Saving Private Ryan* without edits. This included 32 usages of f—. Cohen-Cutler determined that the audience would accept the honored film about WWII without edits. The decision proved to be the right one; the FCC received only one complaint, a complaint it dismissed. In 2004, however, a large number of stations refused to carry the unedited film for fear of FCC reprisals following the Janet Jackson Super Bowl wardrobe malfunction.)
- Deciding which programs require advisories
- Informing viewers about controversial content
- In association with the legal department, determining whether docudra-

mas (fact-based stories) have enough of a factual basis to be broadcast as "based on a true story" and are legally free of problems
- Avoiding racial or sexual stereotypes
- Clearing all the promotional spots that air on the network and determining whether any spots need to be restricted to certain times (e.g., determining that some spots should only air after 9:00 P.M.)
- Clearing all commercials and making certain that all claims on commercials can be verified
- Making sure that any medical information in shows is correct, for example, modifying a line containing faulty information that would alarm individuals suffering from cancer
- Monitoring to see whether current events (such as 9/11) require changes in programming content
- Answering viewer questions and complaints
- Establishing rules for reality programs and making sure that the rules are adhered to
- Monitoring live programs to determine whether edits are needed for the broadcasts in different time zones

Broadcast standards and practices executives must also testify before Congress and the FCC, often on their own

and sometimes with other key executives. They need to prepare reports describing how the network has dealt with issues that concern the people in Washington, DC. Because the networks do not want to risk censure, broadcast standards and practices executives tend to carefully monitor content for **obscenity** and indecency.

The present definition of obscenity stems from a 1973 court case, *Miller v. California*. According to this decision, for a program to be obscene it must contain the depiction of sexual acts in an offensive manner; must appeal to prurient interests of the average person; and must lack serious literary, artistic, political, or scientific value (known as the **SLAPS test**). The difficulty is that material is perceived differently by various individuals. One person's art is another's obscenity. Perceptions also change over time. What was offensive in one decade may be acceptable in the next.

Another problem is that obscenity and indecency are often confused. Obscenity is never allowed; indecency is allowed at certain times, specifically from 10:00 P.M. to 6:00 A.M. This is known as the **safe harbor** for adult programming, the assumption being that this is not a time when children are likely to be watching. The family hour no longer exists, but the safe harbor remains. Indecency is not as serious as obscenity and is generally considered to occur when something is broadcast that is offensive in relation to the standards of a particular community.

Thus it is important for censors to review all programming to evaluate what is and is not acceptable, sometimes preempting a show for another program that will be more in line with community standards. Local stations sometimes even check in with the network (national) broadcast standards and practices departments for guidance when they are concerned about the acceptability of a show in their particular area. Clearly, no one wants to incur the wrath of the FCC.

Working with the legal department, the broadcast standards and practices department also deals with matters of **libel** and **invasion of privacy.** Libel involves defaming someone's character in a way that affects that person's reputation or livelihood. Generally, the people who believe they have been libeled take the broadcaster to court. One of the idiosyncrasies of libel is that people who are considered public figures have to prove that the disparager was malicious. In other words, famous people have to prove that the broadcaster was out to get them and purposely broadcast false information.

Invasion of privacy is related to libel in that it often leads to information that is damaging to a person. But the thrust here is on how the information is gathered. Invasion of privacy laws are the province of individual states. In most states, invasion of privacy means that a person has a right to be left alone. In terms of entertainment programming, libel and invasion of privacy are serious concerns, primarily in connection with docudramas and other fact-based programming.

Broadcast standards and practices departments and legal departments also work together to protect the network in matters involving **copyright,** that is, who controls the rights to a certain property. If the rights are unclear, chances are that property will not be found on television screens across the country. As Mark Twain noted many years ago, copyright is so complicated that even God cannot figure it out—so many hours are spent determining the rights situation. For example, in 2003, Disney expended considerable effort trying, unsuccessfully, to claim it had the rights to the lucrative Winnie-the-Pooh merchandizing empire, trying to bar the heirs of the writer and creator of Winnie-the-Pooh, A.A. Milne, from producing and selling their own Pooh merchandise.

In premium and basic cable and in public broadcasting, broadcast standards and practices departments, if they exist, do not function in the same way as in commercial television. Basic cable has advertisers to worry about, but premium cable does not; it just has subscribers. Premium cable proudly proclaims that it has no restrictions regarding sex and violence. It has, as Showtime, declares, "No limits." However, premium cable has extensive legal and research divisions to ensure that fact-based programming in particular is free of factual inaccuracies and legal problems. Specifically, HBO would not want its fact-based movies to be the subject of attacks by the press for factual errors. Such criticism would clash with HBO's brand.

Similarly, public television wants to maintain viewer, government, and underwriter support and to avoid censure in the press. Thus, its overseers will voice concerns about projects, requesting any changes they think are needed. Factual accuracy, equated with responsible broadcasting, helps to keep public television's brand positive.

The Top Management

Programmers have bosses. They usually report to station managers, general managers, presidents, or chief executive officers. Often the person the programming head reports to has to go further up the organization chart. For example, the network president may report to the chief operating officer of a parent company (NBC to General Electric, ABC to Disney).

At the station level, the general manager may be responsible to someone at the group owner (Cox, Hearst, Gannett, or Tribune). These top executives can overrule the decisions made by the programming department. Sometimes they do. Occasionally, a group owner will dictate what syndicated programming a station must play because it has purchased the programs, at a discounted rate, for all its stations.

Influence from top management is not necessarily bad. Programmers can get so bogged down in stress and minutiae that they lose perspective. A good top manager can point out new directions or keep the programmer's eye on the target. But if everyone under the top manager is afraid to speak up for fear of losing a job, then the head person's usefulness in terms of making the right programming decisions may be severely compromised. "Whatever you say, chief," does not lead to first-rate programming.

But members of top management who micromanage the programming department or constantly play "Monday-morning quarterback" against the head of programming can also be destructive, as can top managers who are timid and unwilling to take risks with new programming concepts.

The main external influence on cable programming comes from within the cable structure—the MSOs. Cable TV has a great deal of vertical integration wherein large companies have ownership roles in organizations that produce programs, networks that distribute programs to systems, and systems that exhibit networks to the consumer. For example, Time Warner is a producer of programs, a distributor of programs, and an owner of cable systems.

MSOs frequently have a great deal of say as to which cable networks their cable systems carry. They naturally want their cable systems to offer all those networks in which they have a financial interest. Doing so fills the MSO's coffers. Therefore, some cable networks seek financial ownership by an MSO; in that way, they can be included in the "family" of channels chosen by the MSO. The downside is that "he who pays the piper calls the tune." These MSOs will want some say in programming philosophy.

Some MSOs like to select virtually all the network services their systems should carry—even ones they do not own. The degree of MSO control depends primarily on the philosophy of top management.

Arguments can be made for both approaches. Centralization produces economies of scale. If the MSO is buying for all its systems, it can sometimes negotiate better deals from the networks than individual systems can. This centralized approach also cuts down on the need for local system programmers, a plus on the balance sheet (but not for those who want jobs in programming). On the other hand, such a policy is not likely to be responsive to local needs. Not all communities are demographically similar. Some skew older or more rural than others. Because so many cable channels narrowcast, the services desired by the citizens of one community might be different from those of another. It would be a disservice to the subscribers if a system loaded up on all the children's services available in a community consisting almost totally of senior citizens.

With satellite television, the top management similarly will exercise a great deal of control. Rupert Murdoch, head of Direct TV, is not a man afraid to take a position. The voice of top management will clearly be heard.

The Promotion, Marketing, and Research Divisions

The promotion and marketing departments significantly affect programming. For example, promotion departments make up weekly schedules indicating where they have slotted on-air promotional spots for shows (5, 10, 15, or 30 seconds in length). Once a promo has been slotted, it is up to someone such as Doreen Hughes at ABC to integrate the promo into the schedule. Hughes reports that there is a lot of jockeying for slots and that there are many last-minute changes as different voices seek particular placement. If a show is given few spots or if the spots are not placed where they will be seen by the targeted viewers, a show is likely to suffer, leading to programming changes. Thus, the battle for slots is often intense.

Similarly, if the marketing department does not position a program correctly, that program will suffer. For example, if the marketing brochures take the wrong tactic, the program will not connect with the intended audience, possibly losing a place on the schedule. Not all television marketing chiefs are as savvy as the film industry's Harvey and Bob Weinstein at Miramax, who have the skill and the financial resources to enable such arguably mediocre films as *Chicago* and *Gangs of New York* to become commercial and critical successes, but their television counterparts have to do their best to market their slate of programs.

The conventional wisdom, as expressed by Howard Schneider, former head of on-air promos at Fox, is that good, well-placed promos can launch a show by creating awareness and a desire by viewers to sample a show, but that promos alone cannot keep a show on the air if the audience loses interest. Noting the complex dynamics that exist among different departments, Stu Brower, long-time promo head at ABC, observed, "If a show fails, the failure is blamed on the promo department; if a show succeeds, all the other departments take the credit."

If a show cannot be promoted on air or if extensive media coverage cannot be secured, shows will find it harder to succeed, often being replaced by other programming that executives think might better succeed. If the promotion and publicity machine fails, the programming department quickly moves on to the next option.

Press coverage can easily get out of control. Writer–producer Michael O'Hara refers to **blowbacks,** which happen when a network or individual takes an approach that produces a totally different result. A blowback may have occurred, for example, when someone slipped a script of the CBS miniseries "The Reagans" to the press in 2003, hoping to start a groundswell of support for the show. Instead, the controversy resulted in the shunting of the program from CBS to Showtime. Clearly, the Janet Jackson and Justin Timberlake stunt resulting in the exposure of one of Jackson's breasts during the 2004 Super Bowl backfired on them, getting the attention but not the response they wanted. The stunt prompted a backlash that caused the FCC and others to reexamine what is and is not acceptable for television. The stunt also instigated a serious discussion about fining performers as well as stations for indecency violations.

In terms of the research department, if the research findings on a potential new program prove weak and there is no strong advocate in favor of the program to counter the research findings, that program likely will not go farther. If research does not support the next step, viewers are often not given the chance to tune it in. This holds true across the board—in commercial, cable, and public television.

External and internal influences have their downsides for those charged with developing programming. Rules, regulations, and opinions often obscure what appears to be logical programming and scheduling. But there are many positive points to be made for the existence of these inside and outside forces. Programmers with the power to influence the minds of millions of listeners and viewers should not work unchecked. "Power corrupts, and absolute power corrupts absolutely." The necessity of thinking how others may react often leads to more responsible actions.

In Chapter 8, we examine the forces that influence radio and the Internet.

EXERCISES

1. Explore why the miniseries "The Reagans" did not generate as much controversy when it aired on the Showtime cable network as it did when it was scheduled to air on CBS during the November sweeps in 2003.

2. Count the number of pharmaceutical ads during a news show. Then watch an entertainment program and count the number of pharmaceutical ads in that show. What are the differences? Analyze why pharmaceutical ads tend to be more prevalent in news programming.

3. Determine which shows have had last-minute advertiser dropouts. What makes you think the advertiser dropped out?

4. Agree or disagree with the former head of television movies at CBS, Steve Mills, who said programmers should make the programs they think are good, and if someone complains, the programmer should stand fast in his or her convictions. What else might be at stake?

5. Go to the FCC website (http://www .fcc.gov/cgb) and look at some of the FCC's

recent decisions. In your opinion, did the FCC make the right rulings? Were they perhaps too lax or too strict?

6. Describe any show you think advertisers should not sponsor. What about the show makes you think this?

7. When you are watching a show, ask yourself what made you watch that program. Was it because the program was controversial? What is a "good" review?

8. Research docudramas criticized for commingling fact with fiction. Why do you think a mixture of fact and fiction presents a problem for a network? For the press? For viewers?

9. Some people think that television reflects society and that it is the responsibility of the broadcast standards and practices department to make edits that reflect current trends in society. Do you agree or disagree with this way of determining what is acceptable on television?

10. Identify some edits in television programming that you think were requested by the broadcast standards and practices or sales departments. Why do you think the edits or changes were made?

11. Examine several key on-air promotional spots on television. Do the spots sell the shows correctly? Are the spots placed in the right shows?

12. Analyze why a show that started out well in the ratings failed to maintain its viewership. What happened to the show's momentum?

13. Analyze a successful or unsuccessful television marketing campaign. What was right or wrong?

REFERENCES/NOTES

1. Stanley R. Greenberg. "Missiles of October" script, ABC Television Network, January, 1974.

2. Parents Television Council. "The PTC Presents the 2002–2003 Top 10 Best and Worst Shows on Primetime Broadcast TV," http://www.parentstv.org/PTC/publications/reports/top10bestandworst/2003/main.asp. Accessed January 16, 2004.

3. "Viewpoint: Censorship Today," Forum, Spring/Summer, 1991, p. 2.

4. William Lobdell. "A Shepherd of Movies into the Religious Flock," Los Angeles Times, November 24, 2001, p. F-10.

5. Claudia Eller and Sallie Hofmeister. "USA Network Cancels Film After Advertiser Protest," Los Angeles Times, December 6, 2000, p. A-1, A-32, A-33.

6. Ibid., p. A-33.

7. J. Max Robins. "Why CBS Blinked," TV Guide, November 15, 2003, p. 63.

8. Bill Carter with Jim Rutenberg and Bernard Weintraub. "Shifting 'Reagans' To Cable Has CBS Facing New Critics," The New York Times, November 5, 2003, p. C-1.

9. Ibid., p. C-2.

10. Ibid.

11. Meg James, Greg Braxton, and Bob Baker. "The Vetoing of 'Reagans,'" Los Angeles Times, November 10, 2003, p. E-12.

12. Emily Eakin. "Greeting Big Brother with Open Arms," The New York Times, January 17, 2004, p. E-12.

13. George Comstock et al. Television and Social Behavior: A Technical Report to the Surgeon General's Scientific Advisory Committee on Television and Social Behavior (Washington, DC: Government Printing Office, 1972).

14. 73rd Congress. Public Law No. 416, June 19, 1934 (Washington, DC: Government Printing Office, 1934), Section 307 (a).

15. Johnathan Turley. "Hollywood Isn't Holding Its Lines Against the Pentagon," Los Angeles Times, August 19, 2003, p. B-13.

16. Ibid.

17. 73rd Congress. Public Law No. 416, June 19, 1934 (Washington, DC: Government Printing Office, 1934), Section 315.

18. Sharon Waxman. "The Recall Show with Jay Leno," The Washington Post, October 9, 2003, p. C-1.

19. Sharon Bernstein. "PBS Network Hit by Charges of Censorship," *Los Angeles Times,* August 14, 1991, p. F-1.

20. Ibid.

21. Ibid.

22. Sharon Bernstein. "KCET Unworthy of Public Support, Mahony Declares," *Los Angeles Times,* September 6, 1991, p. F-1.

23. Ibid.

24. Sharon Bernstein. "KCET Pays Price in Flap with Church," *Los Angeles Times,* October 10, 1991, p. F-1.

25. Kevin Downey. "Want Ad Recall? Avoid Sex and Violence," http://www.medialifemagazine.com/news2003/aug03/aug11/1_mon/news3monday.html. Accessed August 13, 2003.

8 Influences on Radio and Internet Programming

In this chapter you will learn about the following:

- The limited scope of internal pressures on local radio station programming
- How pressure groups and advertisers can flex economic muscle to affect radio programming
- Government's considerations and problems with controlling obscenity and indecency on radio as it pertains to both show hosts and music lyrics
- Government regulations to control payola in radio
- Issues that corporate and personal website developers should consider before putting content on the web
- Government's trouble regulating content within the unique global and on-demand qualities of the Internet
- How pressure groups may succeed in influencing web content where government cannot
- The dream and reality of a democratic, noncommercial Internet commons
- Privacy concerns related to collecting information about web surfers
- Entertainment-industry attempts to control illegal file-sharing online
- How easy user access to international websites creates new competition for local programmers and thus influences programming

INFLUENCES ON RADIO PROGRAMMING

The influences on radio are more similar in form and intensity than those of cable TV are to commercial television. But they are not as intense as those exerted against TV, mainly because radio is more fragmented and less visible (no pun intended) than TV.

Internal Influences on Radio

Stations, networks, and syndicators have to work together, but they do not influence each other a great deal. Local stations do not live or die by their network or syndicated programming. Networks affiliate with so many stations that the ties to any one station are not that strong. The situation is similar for syndicators. In some instances, this loose relationship has tightened after the consolidation of ownership that resulted from the 1996 Telecommunications Act. Megastation owners, such as Clear Channel, have stepped up efforts to create national brands, such as Clear Channel's KISS stations that dot the nation. With voice tracking of star deejays, these stations rely more on network-arranged programming, even if that programming is cleverly customized to make it seem as if it originates locally.

Also, with the merger of radio ownership, directives and "suggestions" for programming choices have the opportunity to come from corporate entities to many stations at once. After the 9/11 terrorist attacks in 2001, for example, Clear Channel released a list to all of its stations of more than 150 songs it deemed to have questionable or difficult lyrics in light of the terrorist event (Figure 8.1). It did not, however, require any of its stations to remove these songs from their playlists.

The circulation of this list received much attention in the media, and rumors flew that individual stations were "banned" from playing any of the songs. A program director at Clear Channel explained that "after and during what was happening in New York and Washington and outside of Pittsburgh, some of our program directors began emailing each other about songs and questionable song titles . . . A Clear Channel program director took it upon himself to identify several songs that certain markets or individuals may find insensitive today. This was not a mandate, nor was the list generated out of the corporate radio offices. It was a grassroots effort that was apparently circulated among program directors."

Figure 8.1
Some of the songs Clear Channel placed on its questionable lyrics list.
(http://ericnuzum.com/banned/incidents/2001_clearchannel.html, accessed February 24, 2004.)

Artist	Song
3 Doors Down	"Duck and Run"
311	"Down"
AC/DC	"Dirty Deeds," "Hell's Bells," "Highway to Hell," "Safe in New York City," "Shoot to Thrill," "Shot Down in Flames," "TNT"
Ad Libs	"The Boy from New York City"
Alanis Morissette	"Ironic"
Alice in Chains	"Down in a Hole," "Rooster," "Sea of Sorrow," "Them Bone"
Alien Ant Farm	"Smooth Criminal"
Animals	"We Gotta Get Out of This Place"
Arthur Brown	"Fire"
Bangles	"Walk Like an Egyptian"
Barenaked Ladies	"Falling for the First Time"
Barry McGuire	"Eve of Destruction"
Beastie Boys	"Sabotage," "Sure Shot"
Billy Joel	"Only the Good Die Young"
Black Sabbath	"Sabbath Bloody Sabbath," "Suicide Solution," "War Pigs"
Blood, Sweat & Tears	"And When I Die"
Blue Oyster Cult	"Burnin' For You"
Bob Dylan/Guns N Roses	"Knockin' on Heaven's Door"
Bobby Darin	"Mack the Knife"
Boston	"Smokin'"
Brooklyn Bridge	"Worst That Could Happen"
Bruce Springsteen	"Goin' Down," "I'm On Fire"
Buddy Holly and the Crickets	"That'll Be the Day"
Bush	"Speed Kills"
Carole King	"I Feel the Earth Move"
Cat Stevens	"Morning Has Broken," "Peace Train"
Chi-Lites	"Have You Seen Her"
Creedence Clearwater Revival	"Travelin' Band"
Dave Clark Five	"Bits and Pieces"
Dave Matthews Band	"Crash Into Me"
Dio	"Holy Diver"
Don McLean	"American Pie"
Drifters	"On Broadway"

Artist	Song
Drowning Pool	"Bodies"
Edwin Starr/Bruce Springsteen	"War"
Elton John	"Bennie and The Jets," "Daniel," "Rocket Man"
Elvis Presley	"(You're the) Devil in Disguise"
Everclear	"Santa Monica"
Filter	"Hey Man, Nice Shot"
Fontella Bass	"Rescue Me"
Foo Fighters	"Learn to Fly"
Frank Sinatra	"New York, New York"
Fuel	"Bad Day"
Godsmack	"Bad Religion"
Green Day	"Brain Stew"
Happenings	"See You in September"
Hollies	"He Ain't Heavy, He's My Brother"
J. Frank Wilson	"Last Kiss"
Jackson Brown	"Doctor My Eyes"
James Taylor	"Fire and Rain"
Jan and Dean	"Dead Man's Curve"
Jerry Lee Lewis	"Great Balls of Fire"
Jimi Hendrix	"Hey Joe"
John Lennon	"Imagine"
John Cougar Mellencamp	"Crumbling Down," "I'm On Fire"
John Parr	"St. Elmo's Fire"
Judas Priest	"Some Heads Are Gonna Roll"
Kansas	"Dust in the Wind"
Korn	"Falling Away From Me"
Led Zeppelin	"Stairway to Heaven"
Lenny Kravitz	"Fly Away"
Limp Bizkit	"Break Stuff"
Local H	"Bound for the Floor"
Los Bravos	"Black is Black"
Louis Armstrong	"What A Wonderful World"
Lynyrd Skynyrd	"Tuesday's Gone"
Martha & the Vandellas	"Nowhere to Run"
Martha & the Vandellas/Van Halen	"Dancing in the Streets"
Megadeth	"Dread and the Fugitive," "Sweating Bullets"
Metallica	"Enter Sandman," "Fade to Black," "Harvester of Sorrow," "Seek and Destroy"
Mitch Ryder and the Detroit Wheels	"Devil with the Blue Dress"
Mudvayne	"Death Blooms"
Neil Diamond	"America"
Nena	"99 Luftballons," "99 Red Balloons"
Nine Inch Nails	"Head Like a Hole"
Norman Greenbaum	"Spirit in the Sky"
Oingo Boingo	"Dead Man's Party"
P.O.D.	"Boom"
Paper Lace	"The Night Chicago Died"
Pat Benatar	"Hit Me with Your Best Shot," "Love is a Battlefield"
Paul McCartney and Wings	"Live and Let Die"
Peter and Gordon	"A World Without Love," "I Go To Pieces"
Peter Gabriel	"When You're Falling"
Peter, Paul and Mary	"Blowin' in the Wind," "Leavin' on a Jet Plane"
Petula Clark	"A Sign of the Times"
Phil Collins	"In the Air Tonight"
Pink Floyd	"Mother," "Run Like Hell"
Pretenders	"My City Was Gone"
Queen	"Another One Bites the Dust," "Killer Queen"
Rage Against The Machine	All songs
Red Hot Chili Peppers	"Aeroplane," "Under the Bridge"

Figure 8.1
Continued

Artist	Song
REM	"It's the End of the World as We Know It"
Ricky Nelson	"Travelin' Man"
Rolling Stones	"Ruby Tuesday"
Saliva	"Click Click Boom"
Sam Cooke/Herman Hermits	"Wonder World"
Santana	"Evil Ways"
Savage Garden	"Crash and Burn"
Shelly Fabares	"Johnny Angel"
Simon and Garfunkel	"Bridge Over Troubled Water"
Skeeter Davis	"End of the World"
Slipknot	"Left Behind," "Wait and Bleed"
Smashing Pumpkins	"Bullet With Butterfly Wings"
Soundgarden	"Black Hole Sun," "Blow Up the Outside World," "Fell on Black Days"
Steam	"Na Na Na Na Hey Hey"
Steve Miller	"Jet Airliner"
Stone Temple Pilots	"Big Bang Baby," "Dead and Bloated"
Sugar Ray	"Fly"
Surfaris	"Wipeout"
System of a Down	"Chop Suey!"
Talking Heads	"Burning Down the House"
Temple of the Dog	"Say Hello to Heaven"
The Beatles	"A Day in the Life," "Lucy in the Sky with Diamonds," "Obla Di, Obla Da," "Ticket to Ride"
The Clash	"Rock the Casbah"
The Cult	"Fire Woman"
The Doors	"The End"
The Gap Band	"You Dropped a Bomb On Me"
Third Eye Blind	"Jumper"
Three Degrees	"When Will I See You Again"
Tom Petty	"Free Fallin'"
Tool	"Intolerance"
Trammps	"Disco Inferno"
U2	"Sunday Bloody Sunday"
Van Halen	"Jump"
Yager and Evans	"In the Year 2525"
Youngbloods	"Get Together"
Zombies	"She's Not There"

Figure 8.1
Continued

The New York Times reported the following:

Compliance with the list varied from station to station. Angela Perelli, the vice president for operations at KYSR 98.7 FM in Los Angeles, said the station was not playing any of the listed songs and had previously pulled a couple of the cited songs, "Jumper" by Third Eye Blind and "Fly" by Sugar Ray, on its own accord. On the other hand, Bob Buchmann, the program director and an on-air personality at WAXQ 104.3 FM in Manhattan, said that some songs on the list ("American Pie" by Don McLean, "Imagine" and others) happened to be among the most-played songs on his station. In the meantime, the station decided not to broadcast some songs even though they did not make the list, such as "When You're Falling," a collaboration between Peter Gabriel and Afro-Celt Sound System that had fictional lyrics too eerily similar to the truth.[1]

When a radio station is selecting or changing a format, it is influenced by owners, station representatives, the sales department, and others who have something to gain (or lose) from the station's overall prosperity.

But salespeople, accountants, group owners, and the like rarely express opinions about individual aspects of programming. If a controversial disc jockey is making it hard for the salespeople to sell time, they might complain, but so much of radio involves selling spots that appear within numerous time segments that advertisers do not usually react to having their ads near certain musical selections—which come and go quickly.

No broadcast standards department breathes down the neck of radio programmers, but the program directors are expected to police what is aired and keep it in line with community standards. Songs are reviewed by critics, but radio programming is not subjected to much critical review.

External Influences on Radio

External influences on radio are, again, similar to those of television, but the low visibility of radio makes it less susceptible to the overwhelming outcries that television can experience when it oversteps a community's moral boundaries.

Although there are academic studies on the effects of radio programming, they are not as profuse as those related to TV. The National Association of Broadcasters has a grant program designed to encourage people to undertake research studies involving radio; it has few takers.

Pressure Groups and Advertisers. Many radio talk shows are simply a forum for public opinion—they do not espouse or promote controversial opinions, although they allow callers or community members to voice their own opinions. Therefore, they are rarely the target of pressure groups, who, instead of trying to shut down discussion that runs contrary to their beliefs, can simply contest it on air. Unless pressure groups become bothersome by tying up the lines, they are welcomed.

Other talk shows, however, feature hosts who, instead of simply mediating listener opinions, express their own. Many of these shows rank at the top of the ratings because of their inherent drama. They can become the target of activist groups or individuals who have an ax to grind about the topics discussed. Many such cases have led to firings of controversial hosts who, on principal, have refused to back down. When this happens, both sides cry foul. Hosts protest that they are being censored and that the fundamental American principal of free speech is being violated. Managers say flatly that any decision they make takes no ideological stance; it is a simple case of economic fundamentals—if advertisers pull out, there will be no station on which to express any opinions, controversial or not. (See sidebar.)

CENSORSHIP OR ECONOMIC REALITY? IRA HANSON AND U.S.-ISRAELI POLICIES

The rhetoric and conspiracy theories can become thick in the debates over why a controversial talk show host was fired, even if there is little possibility of verifying many of the charges tossed about. As an example, in 2002, radio talk show host Ira Hansen at KKOH 780 AM in Reno, Nevada, was fired, according to Hansen, when powerful pro-Israel supporters forced the owners of his radio station to eject him over his criticism of U.S. policy toward Israel.

continued

In 2000, after a new round of Israeli–Palestinian hostilities began, Hansen says he did some research on the conflict's origins and, based upon this research, said on air, "Look, the majority of these problems, if not all of it, can be blamed on Israel and its behavior toward the Palestinian people." Almost immediately, Hansen said, "I was attacked as 'anti-Semitic' and called names. They started calling my boss at the radio station, behind my back, and threatening to boycott the station. By 'they' I mean some local Jewish people."

According to Hansen, his boss called him in and told him, "We're getting all kinds of heat from people over this. Knock off talking about Israel."

"Well," said Hansen, "because it was pretty much the sword hanging over my head there, I stopped talking about Israel." But world events, specifically the terrorist attacks of 9/11, brought the issue of Israel back into Hansen's consciousness. He heard most media outlets in the United States scratching their heads over the hostility that large portions of Muslim and Arab society seemed to have for the United States. To him, there was no mystery, and he started saying so on air. "[The hostility] is not," Hansen asserted, "necessarily even about 'anti-Westernism,' however you define it. It is about the absolute blind allegiance of the United States to Israel and how we give Israel *carte blanche* treatment. That is the root cause of the entire hatred of the Muslim world toward the United States."

Hansen's return to the sore subject of Israel landed him again in his boss's office. "I was sitting there in my boss's office," Hansen said, "when [the owner of a major gambling casino in Reno, the Atlantis Casino, John] Farahi called and my boss was actually holding the phone six inches from his ear, because Farahi was screaming at him. Farahi demanded a right to defend Israel and said how he was pulling off all of his advertising." Hansen was fired.

Though Hansen was off the air, he still had his job as a columnist for a local paper, where he continued to press the issue and question the motives behind his firing from the radio station. "It's kind of ironic," Hansen said, "because I told [Farahi] through a newspaper column that I would have gladly had him as a guest on my radio show and we could have discussed the issue. But instead he got me kicked off the air . . . I have had zero response from the local Jewish people who are willing to go behind my back and boycott my radio station but don't have the guts to debate me in public."

Hansen goes even further, implicating the entire radio industry: "I found, after studying this and looking at who owns what—even Citadel Communications, which owns my former station, was recently purchased (after I got fired) by billionaire investor Ted Forstmann, a Jewish-American who is a strong supporter of Israel. So there's a definite dominance there. Critics say that pointing this out is 'bigotry,' but it's an absolute fact. If you look at who owns all the national media outlets, it's no surprise that the media is totally in favor of Israel and totally biased against the Arabs."[2]

Whether the claims of bias are true or not, managers have an indisputable point when they argue in favor of the purse strings. They do not have to discuss the political implications of their hiring and firing choices, only the economic ones. If they cannot make advertising money from programming, they have no room for that programming in their lineup. Even if media companies have been purchased by owners with specific political agendas, with the flourishing of the Internet, owners can point out that they have neither the capacity nor the desire to silence dissident voices. Anyone with an Internet connection can start a blog and share opinions and points of view democratically with whomever will listen. Why should a business venture be burdened with broadcasting unpopular or controversial opinions that might be bad for the bottom line—to say nothing of being bad for an owner's political aims?

Because the frequencies on which radio broadcasts are owned by the federal government and only licensed to broadcasters, a case can be made that broadcasts should serve the greater good of the community, not just the greater good of the station owner's pocketbook. But "greater good" is difficult, if not impossible, to define objectively. Nonetheless, the government intervenes in some instances.

The Federal Communications Commission. During the early years of radio when the Federal Radio Commission (FRC, the forerunner of the FCC) oversaw radio, several licenses were revoked because of improper programming. One of these was for a station run by Dr. J.R. Brinkley, who prescribed medical treatments over the radio. Usually his listeners' health problems could be cured only by special prescriptions obtainable from druggists who belonged to a pharmaceutical association that Brinkley owned. One of his most creative cures involved goat gland treatments to improve male virility. The FRC took a jaundiced view of most of these medical treatments, but Brinkley was crafty, so it took some fancy legal maneuvers to remove him from the airwaves.

A few other early stations had licenses revoked for programming policies, mainly those of engaging in bitter attacks against individuals or groups—politicians, Jews, prostitutes, or judges. But overall, the number of station revocations was small.

In 1946, the FCC issued an 80-page document detailing what stations should do to have their licenses renewed. This included numerous details about airing local public affairs programs, keeping commercials limited, and maintaining a well-balanced programming schedule. Radio broadcasters immediately dubbed this document the "Blue Book," partly because of its blue cover but mostly because blue penciling is associated with censorship. The reaction to the Blue Book was so negative that the FCC never really implemented its provisions.

In the 1960s and 1970s, radio stations, and their TV counterparts, underwent elaborate license renewal that involved a process called **ascertainment.** Station personnel had to interview community leaders about problems in the community and then propose program ideas to deal with these problems. They would make promises concerning airing these programs in documents submitted to the FCC for their license renewal. When their next renewal came up (at that time, station licenses were up for renewal every 3 years), they had to prove that they had aired the programs on community problems as promised in their last renewal. This process was called **promise vs. performance.** Pressure groups of local citizens were also involved in license renewal during this period. They would demand that stations air certain types of programs (more children's programs, more Chicano programs, more programs about community organizations, etc.). If the stations did not respond to their liking, they would write nasty letters to be included in the stations' file at the FCC, submit formal petitions to deny the station its license renewal, or even ask to take over the station.

In general, license renewal during this period was a complicated, paper-intensive process. Stations usually sent large boxes of documents to Washington, where they were supposedly read by FCC staffers. The license renewal process placed great burdens on the programming departments in terms of interviewing community leaders about problems, dealing with pressure groups, and preparing much of the mass of paper that was submitted.

Then came deregulation. Today, radio station licenses only are looked at every 8 years. Ascertainment is gone, as is promise vs. performance. Radio stations do not even have to program news or public affairs. And license renewal can be obtained by filling out a perfunctory 4–page application (Figure 8.2). The programming department is hardly involved.

Federal Communications Commission
Washington, D. C. 20554

OMB 3060-0110
October 2003

FOR FCC USE ONLY

FCC 303-S

APPLICATION FOR RENEWAL OF BROADCAST STATION LICENSE

FOR COMMISSION USE ONLY
FILE NO.

Section I - General Information- TO BE COMPLETED BY ALL APPLICANTS

1. Legal Name of Licensee

   Mailing Address

   City | State or Country (if foreign address) | ZIP Code

   Telephone Number (include area code) | E-Mail Address (if available)

   FCC Registration Number | Call Sign | Facility Identifier

2. Contact Representative | Firm or Company Name

   Mailing Address

   City | State or Country (if foreign address) | ZIP Code

   Telephone Number (include area code) | E-Mail Address (if available)

3. If this application has been submitted without a fee, indicate reason for fee exemption (see 47 C.F.R. Section 1.1114):

   ☐ Governmental Entity   ☐ Noncommercial Educational Licensee   ☐ Other _____

Figure 8.2
Application for renewal of radio station license.

FCC 303-S
October 2003

4. **Purpose of Application.**

☐ Renewal of license

☐ Amendment to pending renewal application
If an amendment, submit as an exhibit a listing by Section and Item Number the portions of the pending application that are being revised.

Exhibit

5. **Facility Information**: ☐ Commercial ☐ Noncommercial Educational

6. **Service and Community of License**

a. ☐ AM ☐ FM ☐ TV ☐ FM Translator ☐ LPFM
☐ TV Translator ☐ Low Power TV ☐ Class A TV

Community of License/Area to be Served	
City	State

b. Does this application include one or more FM translator station(s), or TV translator station(s), LPTV station(s), in addition to the station listed in Section I, Question 1? (The callsign(s) of any associated FM translators, TV translators or LPTVs will be requested in Section V).
☐ Yes ☐ No

7. **Other Authorizations.** List call signs, facility identifiers and location(s) of any FM booster or TV booster station(s) for which renewal of license is also requested.

Exhibit No.

☐ N/A

FCC 303-S (Page 2)
October 2003

Figure 8.2
Continued

NOTE: In addition to the information called for in Sections II, III, IV and V, an explanatory exhibit providing full particulars must be submitted for each item for which a "No" response is provided.

Section II - Legal -TO BE COMPLETED BY ALL APPLICANTS

1. **Certification.** Licensee certifies that it has answered each question in this application based on its review of the application instructions and worksheets. Licensee further certifies that where it has made an affirmative certification below, this certification constitutes its representation that the application satisfies each of the pertinent standards and criteria set forth in the application, instructions, and worksheets.

   ☐ Yes ☐ No

2. **Character Issues.** Licensee certifies that neither the licensee nor any party to the application has or has had any interest in, or connection with:

   a. any broadcast application in any proceeding where character issues were left unresolved or were resolved adversely against the applicant or any party to the application; or

   ☐ Yes ☐ No   See Explanation in Exhibit No.

   b. any pending broadcast application in which character issues have been raised.

   ☐ Yes ☐ No   See Explanation in Exhibit No.

3. **Adverse Findings.** Licensee certifies that, with respect to the licensee and each party to the application, no adverse finding has been made, nor has an adverse final action been taken by any court or administrative body in a civil or criminal proceeding brought under the provisions of any laws related to the following: any felony; mass media-related antitrust or unfair competition; fraudulent statements to another governmental unit; or discrimination.

   ☐ Yes ☐ No   See Explanation in Exhibit No.

4. **FCC Violations during the Preceding License Term.** Licensee certifies that, with respect to the station(s) for which renewal is requested, there have been no violations by the licensee of the Communications Act of 1934, as amended, or the rules or regulations of the Commission during the preceding license term. If No, the licensee must submit an explanatory exhibit providing complete descriptions of all violations.

   ☐ Yes ☐ No   See Explanation in Exhibit No.

5. **Alien Ownership and Control.** Licensee certifies that it complies with the provisions of Section 310 of the Communications Act of 1934, as amended, relating to interests of aliens and foreign governments.

   ☐ Yes ☐ No   See Explanation in Exhibit No.

6. **Anti-Drug Abuse Act Certification.** Licensee certifies that neither licensee nor any party to the application is subject to denial of federal benefits pursuant to Section 5301 of the Anti-Drug Abuse Act of 1988, 21 U.S.C. Section 862.

   ☐ Yes ☐ No

I certify that the statements in this application are true, complete, and correct to the best of my knowledge and belief, and are made in good faith. I acknowledge that all certifications and attached Exhibits are considered material representations. I hereby waive any claim to the use of any particular frequency as against the regulatory power of the United States because of the previous use of the same, whether by license or otherwise, and request an authorization in accordance with this application. (See Section 304 of the Communications Act of 1934, as amended.)

Typed or Printed Name of Person Signing	Typed or Printed Title of Person Signing
Signature	Date

WILLFUL FALSE STATEMENTS ON THIS FORM ARE PUNISHABLE BY FINE AND/OR IMPRISONMENT (U.S. CODE, TITLE 18, SECTION 1001), AND/OR REVOCATION OF ANY STATION LICENSE OR CONSTRUCTION PERMIT (U.S. CODE, TITLE 47, SECTION 312(a)(1)), AND/OR FORFEITURE (U.S. CODE, TITLE 47, SECTION 503).

Figure 8.2
Continued

FCC 303-S (Page 3)
October 2003

Section III - TO BE COMPLETED BY AM and FM LICENSEES ONLY

1. **Biennial Ownership Report:** Licensee certifies that the station's Biennial Ownership Report (FCC Form 323 or 323-E) has been filed with the Commission as required by 47 C.F.R. Section 73.3615.

☐ Yes ☐ No | See Explanation in Exhibit No. |

2. **EEO Program:** Licensee certifies that:
   a. The station's Broadcast EEO Program Report (FCC Form 396) has been filed with the Commission, as required by 47 C.F.R. Section 73.2080(f)(1).

☐ Yes ☐ No | See Explanation in Exhibit No. |

   Specify FCC Form 396 File Number [   ]

   b. The station has posted its most recent Broadcast EEO Public File Report on the station's website, as required by 47 C.F.R. Section 73.2080(c)(6).

☐ Yes ☐ No ☐ N/A | See Explanation in Exhibit No. |

3. **Local Public File.** Licensee certifies that the documentation, required by 47 C.F.R. Sections 73.3526 or 73.3527, as applicable, has been placed in the station's public inspection file at the appropriate times.

☐ Yes ☐ No | See Explanation in Exhibit No. |

4. **Discontinued Operations.** Licensee certifies that during the preceding license term the station has not been silent for any consecutive 12-month period.

☐ Yes ☐ No | See Explanation in Exhibit No. |

5. **Silent Station.** Licensee certifies that the station is currently on the air broadcasting programming intended to be received by the public.

☐ Yes ☐ No

6. **Environmental Effects.** Licensee certifies that the specified facility complies with the maximum permissible radiofrequency electromagnetic exposure limits for controlled and uncontrolled environments. Unless the licensee can determine compliance through the use of the RF worksheets in the Instructions to this Form, **an Exhibit is required.**

☐ Yes ☐ No | See Explanation in Exhibit No. |

By checking "Yes" above, the licensee also certifies that it, in coordination with other users of the site, will reduce power or cease operation as necessary to protect persons having access to the site, tower, or antenna from radiofrequency electromagnetic exposure in excess of FCC guidelines.

FCC 303-S (Page 4)
October 2003

Figure 8.2
Continued

Obscenity and Indecency Laws. The U.S. Supreme Court has carefully, if vaguely, defined obscenity and indecency in several cases over its history.

As described earlier, obscene material may never be legally broadcast on radio and elsewhere. The standards for defining obscenity, laid out in *Miller v. California,* are as follows:

1. The average person, applying contemporary community standards, would find that the work, taken as a whole, appeals to the prurient interest

2. The work depicts or describes in a patently offensive way, as measured by contemporary community standards, sexual conduct specifically defined by the applicable law

3. A reasonable person would find that the work, taken as a whole, lacks serious literary, artistic, political, and scientific value

Indecent material is defined by the FCC as "language or material that, in context, depicts or describes, in terms patently offensive as measured by contemporary community standards in the broadcast medium, sexual or excretory activities or organs." Indecent material may not be broadcast if the conditions of its broadcast are such that the following are true:

1. It has a pervasive presence in the lives of "all Americans," and indecent material confronts citizens not only in public but also in the privacy of the home, "where the individual's right to be left alone plainly outweighs the First Amendment rights of an intruder"
2. The "broadcasting [of the material] is uniquely accessible to children, even those too young to read"[3]

Reining in Radio Hosts. Obscenity and indecency charges arise most often about talk show topics and music lyrics. During the 1980s, a phenomenon known as **topless radio** spread around the country. People would call in and recount to a talk show host (and the listening audience) their explicit sexual experiences. After the FCC fined one station for this and the fine was upheld in the courts, topless radio stopped. People still call radio talk shows and talk about sexual experiences, but not as explicitly as they were encouraged to do for the brief era of topless radio. **Call screeners,** station employees who talk to callers before they are allowed on the air, have been instructed to screen out anyone who might talk too explicitly.

Stations may be fined by the FCC for airing indecent material. The maximum fine per incident has stayed a steady $27,500, but in recent years there has been a drive to increase the fine. With the large amounts of revenue possible with syndication and megamergers, many, including FCC Chairman Michael Powell, have argued that a $27,500 fine is "peanuts" to big media companies. Rather than adjusting their broadcast practices to avoid fines, many believe that media companies have simply factored in fines as part of their "cost of doing business."[4]

Several high-profile indecency charges were filed against shock jock Howard Stern in the 1980s and 1990s. Infinity Broadcasting, which airs Stern's show, fought the charges in courts for several years then finally agreed to settle for a lump $1.7 million payment in 1995.

The fine Infinity paid for Stern was for a series of indecency infractions, but fines have been growing, despite the $27,500 cap. In 2001 WXTB/Tampa morning host "Bubba the Love Sponge" aired the live castration and mutilation of a wild boar in the station's parking lot. The host of the show was suspended for several weeks and the state attorney, Mark Ober, filed animal-cruelty charges against the host, the show's producer, and two listeners who carried out the on-air slaughter. Although all were found not guilty by a Tampa jury, in 2004, the FCC levied a belated fine of $755,000 against WXTB owner Clear Channel. To get around the cap, the FCC apparently lumped various other technical infractions with the indecency charge; nevertheless, the fines will undoubtedly have to wind their way through the courts.[5]

The U.S. Congress, however, has made some steps toward codifying higher fines into law. As of July 2004, there was pending legislation to boost the penalties for indecency almost tenfold, from $27,500 to $275,000, and to as much as $3 million a day for repeat violations.

Dealing with Music Lyrics. Problems arise with music lyrics when they contain words used to describe sexual or excretory acts. Again, this is a gray area in terms of what is appropriate from one time to another and from one community to another.

The practice of banning "objectionable" songs from radio play goes back nearly as far as music radio. In 1956, for example, ABC radio banned the Cole Porter-penned Billie Holiday song "Love For Sale" from all of its stations because of its seemingly overt references to prostitution. ABC also arranged a lyric change for Porter's "I Get a Kick out of You"—from "I get no kick from cocaine" to "I get perfume from Spain." Also in 1956, all three of the major radio networks banned the novelty hit by Dot and Diamond called "Transfusion" because, according to an NBC executive, "there's nothing funny about a blood transfusion."

In the 1960s, some stations banned artists simply because some of their lyrics might be offensive. An El Paso, Texas, station, for example, banned all songs performed by Bob Dylan because many of the lyrics were garbled in Dylan's delivery. The station's ban did not include songs written by Dylan and performed by other artists who delivered the lyrics with better diction.

During the 1980s, a group of wives of congressmen made a strong case against sexually oriented lyrics, suggesting that records with such lyrics should be labeled and that such material should be kept off radio. About all they succeeded in doing, as far as radio was concerned, was taming things down for a while.

Station programmers mostly make individual decisions about what their station should or should not air. Sometimes radio station program directors make decisions about whether to play a song based on how understandable the lyrics are. A rock station deejay noted about one such track: "Unless you read the lyric sheet or are an incredibly huge fan of the band, it's hard to discern what they're saying."[6] Then, too, if music groups fear their music might not be played because of certain offensive words, they will change, bleep, or muffle the words on a recording sent to radio stations but leave the original words on CDs sold in stores.

Muffled offensive lyrics, however, are not a guarantee against censorship and fines. In 2001, the FCC fined two radio stations for playing Eminem's "The Real Slim Shady." Wisconsin's WZEE was fined for airing the original (unedited) version, but KKMG in Colorado was fined for playing a profanity-free radio edit that other stations across the nation had played without incident. Although the fine was reversed in 2002, it still illustrates that perceived local norms form the basis for government intercession in radio indecency cases.[7]

Other Laws and Regulations. Government regulations other than those related to license renewal and obscenity affect radio programmers. In the 1950s, Congress held hearings on payola (accepting gifts in exchange for playing a record on the air) and amended the 1934 Communications Act to prevent this practice. Payola still occurs, but it is patently illegal. **Plugola** (promoting a certain restaurant, concert, music store, etc., in exchange for favors) is also a station no-no.

The U.S. Criminal Code says radio and TV stations cannot hold **lotteries.** A contest is deemed a lottery if people have to pay to enter, if chance is involved, and if a prize is given. Radio stations usually avoid lotteries by ensuring that people do not have to pay to enter their contests.

Radio stations, like TV stations, are subject to equal time, libel, invasion of privacy, and other government laws and regulations. Issues related to these are more likely to come up for networks than for stations because decisions are likely to involve news. Except for all-news stations, radio stations do not concentrate on gathering news—they obtain it from networks.

INFLUENCES ON INTERNET PROGRAMMING

Internet content must, in theory, adhere to the same codes and laws as radio and television. It is, also in theory, susceptible to the same internal and external influences as its broadcast cousins. But the sheer volume of content available on the Internet makes policing it difficult. Sites can go up and come down in an instant, the identities of those who put up content can be erroneous or difficult to ascertain, and standard conventions easy to define and apply to television and radio become exceedingly slippery in the timeless, formless, locationless, ever-**hyperlinking** environment of cyberspace.

Internal Influences on Internet Content

Websites can be developed and placed on the Internet by anyone—from individuals to multinational corporations to educational institutions and governments. Thus the internal influences vary greatly—from one person's conscience to multiple departments in a sprawling bureaucracy. Oversight, where there is oversight, of Internet content mostly falls to entities similar to those mentioned in Chapter 7. Issues that go into and influence the development of Internet content can involve financing, advertisements, and standards and practices (censorship). Sometimes the web hosting service on which a site is stored will also have rules for content that must be adhered to or the site will risk being taken down (see the sidebar on Yahoo GeoCities membership).

PART OF THE YAHOO GEOCITIES MEMBERSHIP AGREEMENT FOR HOSTING SITES ON YAHOO'S SERVERS

MEMBER CONDUCT

You understand that all information, data, text, software, music, sound, photographs, graphics, video, messages or other materials ("Content"), whether publicly posted or privately transmitted, are the sole responsibility of the person from which such Content originated. This means that you, and not Yahoo, are entirely responsible for all Content that you upload, post or otherwise transmit via the Service. Yahoo does not control the Content posted via the Service and, as such, does not guarantee the accuracy, integrity or quality of such Content. You understand that by using the Service, you may be exposed to Content that is offensive, indecent or objectionable.

You agree to not use the Service to:

(a) upload, post or otherwise transmit any Content that is unlawful, harmful, threatening, abusive, harassing, tortious, defamatory, vulgar, obscene, libelous, invasive of another's privacy, hateful, or racially, ethnically or otherwise objectionable;

(b) harm minors in any way;

(c) impersonate any person or entity, including, but not limited to, a Yahoo official, forum leader, guide or host, or

Influences on Radio and Internet Programming

falsely state or otherwise misrepresent your affiliation with a person or entity;

(d) forge headers or otherwise manipulate identifiers in order to disguise the origin of any Content transmitted through the Service or develop restricted or password-only access pages, or hidden pages or images (those not linked to from another accessible page);

(e) upload, post or otherwise transmit any Content that you do not have a right to transmit under any law or under contractual or fiduciary relationships (such as inside information, proprietary and confidential information learned or disclosed as part of employment relationships or under nondisclosure agreements);

(f) upload, post or otherwise transmit any Content that infringes any patent, trademark, trade secret, copyright or other proprietary rights of any party;

(g) upload, post or otherwise transmit any unsolicited or unauthorized advertising, promotional materials, "junk mail," "spam," "chain letters," "pyramid schemes," or any other form of solicitation, except in those areas of the Service that are designated for such purpose;

(h) upload, post or otherwise transmit any material that contains software viruses or any other computer code, files or programs designed to interrupt, destroy or limit the functionality of any computer software or hardware or telecommunications equipment;

(i) disrupt the normal flow of dialogue, cause a screen to "scroll" faster than other users of the Service are able to type, or otherwise act in a manner that negatively affects other users' ability to engage in real time exchanges;

(j) interfere with or disrupt the Service or servers or networks connected to the Service, or disobey any requirements, procedures, policies or regulations of networks connected to the Service;

(k) intentionally or unintentionally violate any applicable local, state, national or international law, including, but not limited to, regulations promulgated by the U.S. Securities and Exchange Commission, any rules of any national or other securities exchange, including, without limitation, the New York Stock Exchange, the American Stock Exchange or the NASDAQ, and any regulations having the force of law;

(l) "stalk" or otherwise harass another;

(m) collect or store personal data about other users;

(n) promote or provide instructional information about illegal activities, promote physical harm or injury against any group or individual, or promote any act of cruelty to animals. This may include, but is not limited to, providing instructions on how to assemble bombs, grenades and other weapons, and creating "Crush" sites;

(o) use your home page (or directory) as storage for remote loading or as a door or signpost to another home page, whether inside or beyond Yahoo GeoCities;

(p) have multiple Yahoo GeoCities addresses that are within the same Yahoo GeoCities neighborhood or that have the same theme; or

(q) engage in commercial activities without enrolling in Yahoo-approved affiliate programs. This includes, but is not limited to, the following activities:

- offering for sale any products or services;
- soliciting for advertisers or sponsors;
- conducting raffles or contests that require any type of entry fee;
- displaying a sponsorship banner of any kind, including those that are generated by banner or link exchange services, with the sole exceptions of the GeoGuide Banner Exchange program and the Internet Link Exchange; and
- displaying banners for services that provide cash or cash-equivalent prizes to users in exchange for hyperlinks to their websites.

(http://docs.yahoo.com/info/terms. Accessed July 20, 2004.)

Issues for Major Public Sites. Obviously brick-and-mortar and highly public entities will want to carefully control the content of their websites because anything put on the site will reflect upon their company or organization and could become fodder for public or legal action. In 2004, for example, the well-known liberal political activist website MoveOn.org landed in hot water when it sponsored a competition, "Bush in 30 Seconds." The competition publicly solicited 30-second television commercials critical of President George W. Bush's administration, which it then put on its website for visitors to view and comment on. The winning entry was slated to be aired during the Super Bowl. The controversy occurred when two of the entries that MoveOn.org posted on their website compared George W. Bush to Nazi leader Adolph Hitler. One entry even showed the face of Hitler morphing into Bush's face.

A great outcry came from the public, especially Jewish and Republican leaders. Jack Rosen, president of the American Jewish Congress, writing in the *Wall Street Journal,* said the comparison is "not only historically specious, it is morally outrageous." The ads were quickly removed from Moveon.org's website, but the maelstrom lingered for weeks in the press. The Republican National Committee made copies of the controversial ads available on its website, allowing its visitors to view the "outrageous" ads for themselves, adding fuel to the flames. Wes Boyd, president of MoveOn.org Voter Fund, said in a statement, "None of these was our ad, nor did their appearance constitute endorsement or sponsorship by MoveOn.org Voter Fund."[8]

Despite Boyd's denial, the organization had to shoulder all the blame and a public relations nightmare. The winner of the contest, a more benign commercial that showed children working in factories and other blue-collar jobs, then asked the question, "Guess who is going to pay off President Bush's $1 trillion deficit?" was later rejected by CBS as unsuitable to air during the Super Bowl, although there is considerable controversy over how CBS defined "unsuitable."

Issues for Personal Sites. Although millions of websites get little or no traffic, the more traffic a site gets, the more it will become susceptible to influence. In many cases, web developers, especially individuals, have no desire for mass traffic to their sites. A person who puts up a website with a photo album of a summer trip to Mexico so that friends and family can see it usually intends the site to be seen only by a select few. Nonetheless, if that person wants the site to be effective, he or she has to take into account the audience. If grandpa is a web neophyte, a straightforward design might be in order. If Aunt Mabel is using a dial-up connection with a slow modem, small picture files will help her. But just because a web developer may not want outsiders to view a site, this does not mean others will not chance upon it.

Developers should keep in mind that this technology that allows them to so effortlessly exchange information with friends and family also makes it easily available to interlopers. This fact does, and should, influence developers' choices about what to put on the web. Chris Bryant, a member of the British Parliament with aspirations to become a leader of the Labor Party, learned this lesson the hard way when a photo of him scantily clad was discovered by a journalist on an Internet chat site and was subsequently published in a British daily paper in 2003. Although Bryant's status as a public figure made the publishing of his picture legal—if ethically suspect—a heavy toll can be paid for a moment's indiscretion.[9]

External Influences on Internet Content

The Internet is not a one-way medium like radio and television. So, there are more issues to deal with, champion, condemn, and regulate—or at least try to. Many different activities occur on the Internet, including the following:

- Websites deliver content.
- Websites collect information about those that visit them.
- Users communicate and exchange information and data directly in **peer-to-peer** networks or using email.

All activities that take place on the Internet have and will doubtlessly continue to inspire great controversy—in the halls of government, in courtrooms, and in the court of public opinion.

The Delivery of Content. As mentioned previously, content delivered using the Internet is, in theory, susceptible to the same influences and regulations as all other broadcast material. However, many unique attributes of the Internet have altered or confounded the application of these influences and regulations.

The Government. The greatest difference between the radio and television and the Internet is that the radio and television are localized and, in the case of aerial broadcasts, the frequencies for broadcasting are "owned" by the federal government and licensed to broadcasters. This fact alone gives the federal government significant leverage over broadcasters that violate indecency and obscenity standards. This is not the case with sites on the Internet, which can originate from and be distributed to any location worldwide.

Although the United States arguably has the strongest free speech and expression protections in the world, some forms of expression outlawed in the United States (such as child pornography) are not outlawed or are defined differently in other countries. Likewise, certain kinds of speech allowed in the United States are illegal in other countries (such as hate speech associated with racism or neo-Nazism, which is illegal in Germany). Can the United States prosecute foreign distributors of materials illegal in the United States but not in their home countries? Questions such as these will take years to iron out in courts around the world.

Another similar concern takes place in the United States, where definitions of indecency and obscenity, at least partly, depend on the social boundaries of local communities. What is considered indecent in one locality may be viewed differently in another locality. Because access to sites on the Internet is not limited by locality, whose social boundaries should be applied to make a determination of indecency? Again, this issue is still being tackled by local, state, and federal governments across the United States and around the world. In addition, indecent material is often legal to broadcast at night because the law assumes that children will not be awake to experience it. But the delivery time of much content on the Internet is determined not by the deliverer but by the consumer, who can click on content to view it anytime. Even if on-demand indecent content were disabled during daylight hours, the question would then become, during whose daylight hours? The United States and its territories alone stretch across 11 of the 24 world time zones.

Because of concern that indecent material on the Internet would be too accessible to children, the 1996 Telecommunications Act included a section called the Communications Decency Act. Although all obscene material is illegal according to U.S. law already, the Communications Decency Act sought to criminalize all indecent material as well. But in June 1997 the U.S. Supreme Court ruled that most of the act was unconstitutional, protecting, at least for now, indecent content on the Internet.

With all of the pitfalls in regulating indecency on the Internet, prosecutors have tried to play the obscenity card instead, charging that objectionable material "lacks serious literary, artistic, political, and scientific value" and is therefore not protected by the First Amendment. But here another wrinkle unique to the Internet is encountered. The full wording of the third definition of obscenity set by the U.S. Supreme Court in *Miller v. California* is as follows: "That a reasonable person would find that the work, taken as a whole, lacks serious literary, artistic, political, and scientific value." What, on the Internet, is the *whole* work? A court cannot rule that *one page* of a printed book is obscene—it must make its determination based upon the book *as a whole*. If an Internet page has links on it to other pages, are those pages considered part of the *whole* of the work? Those subsequent pages may link to still other pages—are those part of the work in question as well? At this writing, the courts are still tackling this issue.

One provision of Internet regulation has seen success in the U.S. Supreme Court. In 2000, the Children's Internet Protection Act was signed into law. The law denies federal funding to libraries that do not install content filters on computers that allow library patrons to access the Internet. Opponents of the act argued that Internet filters would unduly restrict library patrons' rights to access free speech. They suggested, for example, that filtering software might block Internet resources for breast cancer because the word "breast" might be flagged by the filtering software as potentially indecent. Nonetheless, in a 6–3 ruling, the Supreme Court upheld the constitutionality of the law.[10]

One problem that some web developers have encountered as a result of all of these ill-defined legal concerns is that nearly anyone who places content on the Internet that could be construed as indecent or obscene in any locality runs the risk of being prosecuted and, some might say, harassed or intimidated by government authorities. Many developers of web content are individuals or small entities that do not have the resources to fight off the dizzying onslaught of charges that can be foisted upon them by an eager prosecutor. Rather than fighting, they often choose to close shop under the pressure. Those that do fight charges on the basis of First Amendment rights often find that civil liberties legal watchdog groups are sympathetic to their plight and the wider implications of the outcome of their case. The ACLU has stepped up to bat in many instances, but this support does not keep defendants' names and reputations from being dragged through the media in a way that they might not like to have advertised.

In most cases in which defendants do not immediately fold, charges have eventually been dismissed. Prosecutors are wary to let courts have the cases, many argue, because they are afraid that judges might find against them, which would make them less able to bring the same charges (scaring many into desisting without a fight) in similar cases.

Pressure Groups. Although the hands of the government may be legally bound, for better or worse, when it comes to influencing web content through legal channels, pressure groups and public outcry has seen some success. In 2003, during the war in Iraq, Arabic news organization Al-Jazeera broadcast graphic videos of American prisoners of war and war casualties. Although all major U.S. news outlets decided not to rebroadcast the videos, an Internet news site, YellowTimes.org, captured stills of dead American soldiers from the broadcast and placed them on their site. Vortech Hosting, YellowTimes' hosting service, began receiving complaints about the photos and suspended the YellowTimes account for "inappropriate graphic content." Later, photos that included images of dead American soldiers were posted on the conservative-leaning website DrudgeReport.com, but that site was not shut down.

YellowTimes' Editor Erich Marquardt sees a troubling contradiction because his site was shut down and the Drudge Report was not, even though the complaints cited by the hosting company when it shut down YellowTimes could be made about the Drudge Report images: "No mother, brother, sister, wife or child should see their love (sic) one plastered all over the Net wounded or dead." Marquardt contends that the photos on the Drudge Report site, which included a grinning Iraqi standing over dead American soldiers, were chosen to enflame Americans into supporting the war, whereas Marquardt says his site posted casualties on both sides of the war in a nonsensationalistic manner.[11]

The remedy that most pressure groups have for their displeasure with web content is to contact the hosting service to complain, as was done in the YellowTimes case. Hosting services, like restaurants with their signs stating, "We reserve the right to refuse service to anyone," have no legal obligation to continue to host a site that they find objectionable, just as any other business can refuse to take a job or provide a service that someone asks of them. A web developer is free to look elsewhere for a hosting service that will agree to host a site turned down by another hosting service. Anyone with an Internet connection and the right hardware and software can become a hosting service—but they may receive public complaints if they host controversial material, even if that material is protected by the free speech clause of the First Amendment.

In 2002, complaints and news reports surfaced about a website glorifying the Palestinian group Hamas's "martyr brigade" of suicide bombers. U.S. Department of Justice spokeswoman Jill Stillman indicated that the department was aware of the site but that it would do nothing about the site, even amid the U.S. government's "war on terrorism." Hamas was classified as a terrorist organization by federal officials and was therefore subject to stricter controls. But, Stillman said, because the site did not solicit funds for Hamas, the site's support, in speech only, was protected by U.S. law.

It was, however, found that the site was hosted by a U.S. hosting company, and the name of the company, Connecticut-based OLM, was publicized in the media. The site, without explanation, was soon out of commission.[12]

The Move for an Internet Commons. When the Internet was first envisioned as a worldwide tool for the dissemination of information and communication, there was great excitement about its potential to allow a democratic, balanced environment where everyone's

Figure 8.3

After his home was raided, his computer equipment was confiscated, and Sherman Austin was sent to jail, his website, Raisethefist.com, was taken down.

views and experiences could be expressed and weighted equally. Web "surfing," it was imagined, would be an experience of organized anarchy, like a public sidewalk in a metropolitan city bustling with diverse pedestrian traffic. With the Internet's easy ability to hyperlink, users of the Internet would have unanticipated encounters with the thoughts, ideas, opinions, and experiences of others.

Although the mechanical structure of the Internet allows the promiscuous panoply of information of which Internet pioneers dreamed, many have been dismayed at the way commercial entities have co-opted, twisted, and reined in the Internet's democratic potential. Cultural critics had plenty of complaints about America Online's dominance as an Internet service provider in the late 1990s and early 2000s—not just because it drove up the cost of Internet access but also because it, to an extent, privatized the promise of the Internet by offering "premium" services and content only to its subscribers.

Proponents of true Internet democracy, such as University of Chicago law professor Cass Sunstein, would like to see websites "designed to ensure more exposure to substantive questions." Websites containing commentary or opinion about controversial issues, Sunstein thinks, should have hyperlinks to websites that feature differing and opposing opinions. Sunstein suggests that government could even regulate this kind of open and multifaceted Internet debate by enforcing compliance upon websites guilty of "failure to attend to public issues." Sunstein therefore suggests that the definition of free speech on the Internet should be broadened from the standard definition of people being *able* to say what they want to providing a platform for this free speech, where what people say can be given a good chance of being heard.[13]

A consortium called the Digital Opportunity Investment Trust (DO IT) has been formed to encourage this public sidewalk aspect of the Internet, which has been dubbed the **commons** because in it each opinion, idea, and expression is ideally given common weight and attention. DO IT has received many grants from private foundations and has received some appropriations from the federal government, but many argue that the "chance encounters" that DO IT hopes to encourage are already a staple of the Internet experience. The search engine Google.com, for example, gets more traffic than any other site on the Internet, connecting users to an exhaustive listing of Internet content from all corners of the globe. But proponents of the Internet commons, like DO IT, complain that Google.com and other search engines, because they are for-profit businesses, "feature" websites that pay a fee and favor "popular" sites over obscure ones, thus making their results less than the ideal democracy that DO IT proposes.

To some extent, legal culpability concerns and pressure group protests limit democratic hyperlinking "designed to ensure more exposure to substantive questions." Web developers, such as self-described "nonviolent anarchist" and RaiseTheFist.com (Figure 8.3)

Webmaster Sherman Austin, have seen first hand how indiscriminate hyper-linking can lead not just to trouble but also to jail. In 2002, at the age of 18, Austin's Los Angeles home, where he lived with his mother, was raided by approximately 25 heavily armed FBI and Secret Service agents in one of the government's first attempts to exercise the new U.S. Patriot Act. Austin said that he was "interrogated for several hours while they ransacked my room and they seized a network of computers which I used to run my website RaiseTheFist.com. They also seized protest signs, and political literature. Their excuse was a protest guide (which I didn't author) that was posted to my site which a small portion contained information on explosives . . . [This information] doesn't compare to what you can find on many other web-sites such as HowThingsWork.com, Loompanics.com, BombShock.com, Totse.com, Amazon.com, or the many neo-Nazi websites." When Austin is released from jail he will be banned, by court order, from associating with anyone who wants to "change the government in any way."[14]

Controversy over the Collection of Information. With the controversy and pressure about what the Internet delivers to web surfers are concerns about what websites and developers gather from web surfers. As explained in chapter 6, through the use of cookies websites are able to gather, save, and access information about their visitors. Not only do sites use this information for their own purposes, but there is nothing to stop them from selling it to others—and many do.

Web portals, such as Yahoo and Google, instead of buying information about web surfers from third parties, have set up services that allow them to freely collect information from users by scanning their email. These portals offer users of their email services generous storage space on their servers of a gigabyte and more. What many users do not know (and many probably do not care about) is that electronic information, unlike the information contained in U.S. mail or other printed text, does not have the same legal privacy protections. Any information that anyone stores on someone else's computer, or even just passes through someone else's computer on its way to its final destination, is fair game for the owner of that computer to rifle through. In other words, it would be as if, when you hand a bill payment to a postage worker, that postage worker and any other that comes in contact with the letter on its way to its destination could open it up, see what you are paying for, and then use that information to target you for similar products.

Some citizens and legislators have said this is an invasion of privacy. Information about an individual's buying habits, interests, and proclivities, as evidenced by where they go and what they do on the Internet, should not be collected or distributed, they say, because it could be abused. Internet marketers counter that they are only providing a service for consumers and businesses—helping to bring them together. Rather than bombarding and annoying consumers with random advertisements, why not eliminate the guessing game that television and radio are victim to because of their nondynamic, one-size-fits-all medium? Certain television advertisers choose to air their ads on the reality show "The Bachelor" and not on "World News Tonight" for a reason, and some businesses would rather advertise on alternative rock radio stations than talk radio because they assume that the rock audience will be more interested in their products. But these are only assumptions that will not apply to all listeners of the station. Maybe there are alternative rock aficionados who, contrary to marketing stereotypes, are interested in facial care products. Would not the consumer, the radio station, and the advertiser be better served if, in place of a commercial for beer, a commercial for medicated facial scrub with apricot seed extract could be played specifically for the rock consumer concerned about the size and cleanliness of his or her pores?

Though considerable pomp and circumstance goes into complaints about the loss of privacy on the Internet, many, including Michael Lewis, author of the Internet culture-skewering book *Next: The Future Just Happened,* think that consumers are "willing to feign outrage on command, until they see the benefits of relinquishing their privacy." Lewis says that if businesses are able to more efficiently target their advertising, getting more sales out of fewer ads, the savings in marketing costs can be passed on to the consumer in lower prices.[15]

Nonetheless, legislation continues to be proposed to rein in the collection and distribution of information on the Internet. Some have proposed "opt out" legislation, which would allow web surfers the option to disallow collection of data about them, much like the telemarketing "do not call" list enacted by Congress in 2003 bars most telemarketers from making cold calls to those who register their phone numbers with the national registry. Others have proposed more stringent "opt in" legislation, where websites would be barred from collecting information about web surfers unless the surfers specifically request that the website collect information about them.

Contending with Peer-to-Peer Networks. Perhaps one of the most controversial and dynamic developments brought about by the proliferation of the Internet is the facility that the Internet gives to individuals to exchange information and data one on one, or peer to peer. Although the Internet has allowed, in this respect, individuals to share their creations freely and widely to a practically unlimited audience—often, instead of sharing their own creations freely, they have used the Internet to share copyrighted materials created by others without the copyright holder's permission or remuneration.

For many, this rampant phenomenon has called into question the idea of copyright law. These people think that copyright law has far exceeded its original purpose, as outlined in Article 1, Section 8, of the Constitution: "to promote the progress of science and useful arts, by securing for limited times, to authors and inventors, the exclusive right to their respective writings and discoveries." Copyright law has changed throughout the years, but protections were broadly expanded in 1998, to the dismay of many, when Disney fought to keep its copyrights for Mickey Mouse and other central Disney characters. The characters were poised to enter the public domain in 2003 and thus be free game for anyone to profit from or reproduce for no profit—75 years after their debut in 1928. Disney, a $6.3 million contributor to political campaigns in 1997–1998, got a 20-year extension from Congress and President Clinton, and, in the process, gave similar copyright extensions to tens of thousands of other works about to enter the public domain. Some wondered if, in 2023, when the extension is to expire, Disney might decide to make Washington the "Happiest Place on Earth" again with political contributions and get another extension of ownership for its mascots.[16] Copyright law, many argued, is a joke.

But, joke or not, it is the law—a fact driven home when Napster, a peer-to-peer networking program that allowed untold hundreds of thousands of copyrighted songs to exchange hands in the late 1990s, was shut down in 2000. But Napster's demise did not spell the end for a copyright-flouting public whose appetite for getting for free what they used to have to pay for was only whetted by flash-in-the-pan Napster. As high-speed Internet access became more common, with the staple of song swapping, complete first-run movies and television shows started streaming over the web using software and services provided by a host of Napster copycats.

In 2003, the Recording Industry Association of America (RIAA) opened a new salvo in the fight against Internet piracy when it brought lawsuits against individual Internet users who had shared large numbers of copyrighted songs and promised to bring more suits against individuals, which it did in 2004. The RIAA also infamously offered an amnesty program (which many dubbed a "shamnesty") wherein those who had illegally downloaded copyrighted material could admit to it, remove all the ill-begotten files from their possession, and escape prosecution from the RIAA. There were not many takers, however, as legal experts quickly pointed out that although the RIAA could promise it would not bring suit, those who admitted to violating copyrights could still be sued by individual artists and record companies that owned the copyrights to the pilfered works.

Given the limited success of prosecution in copyright cases, many copyright owners have decided to fight fire with fire, putting up fake or corrupted files on peer-to-peer networks that only reveal themselves to be fakes after they have been fully downloaded. The hope is that these hoaxes will discourage would-be pirates when they tie up their computers for hours downloading what they thought would be a full-length motion picture only to find a "gotcha" message.

Giving Them What They Want. Probably the biggest influence on Internet programming, however, is users. More people are turning to the Internet for news, information, commerce, and entertainment. Start-up companies and individuals want to make their mark and claim their space in a medium only bound to grow, even if in fits and starts. Established media companies that want to keep their brands alive see that they must make inroads into the Internet or be left in the dust. The on-demand quality of the Internet holds the promise that anyone could request and receive anything they want whenever they want it, rather than, as with traditional radio and television, having to tune in at a specific time or program a recorder to capture it as it is broadcast. This unique quality of the Internet has drawn in many viewers—and drawn them from other mediums.

The Internet's global reach is also affecting local television and radio programming and producers of Internet content who want to capture a local audience. The lesson is this: If your audience has interests that you are not satisfying, it can and will go elsewhere. At the start of the war in Iraq in March 2003, according to web intelligence company Hitwise, "BBC Online received more U.S. visitors . . . than either of the top U.S. news sites Fox

Figure 8.4
BBC.co.uk received a spike in U.S. visitors at the beginning of the war in Iraq in 2003, outpacing its U.S. competitors. (Image courtesy of www.BBC.co.uk.)

News and *The Washington Post*" (Figure 8.4).

BBC Director-General Greg Dyke, speaking at a journalism symposium later in 2003, attributed the jump in U.S. visitors to BBC's site to U.S. news organizations misjudgment of their audience. "Since 11th September, many U.S. networks wrapped themselves in the flag and swapped impartiality for gung-ho patriotism," he said, suggesting that the mix of journalism and patriotism had turned off U.S. audiences looking for more objective reporting.[17] Perhaps U.S. viewers were not turned off by local coverage but were instead just curious to directly hear what other countries were saying about the events of the day. Either way, viewers turned elsewhere. And for media companies who rely on audiences for revenue or, more benevolently, who want to give audiences what they want, carefully analyzing international web use patterns can, and should, influence the content they offer on local sites and broadcasts.

So far, we have explained where program ideas come from, how they get developed and tested, what the essential ingredients are, and who, besides the program department, influences content. However, all too frequently programmers who have been mindful of all the foregoing destroy their efforts by paying too little attention to where, when, and how the show is scheduled. We move on to this vital process.

EXERCISES

1. Using the definitions of obscenity and indecency earlier in this chapter, examine what you think the local definitions of obscenity and indecency would be for your community. Compare your impression of local definitions with other locales with which you are familiar.

2. Determine several topics that, although not indecent, you think would be on the cusp of raising public protest or advertiser revolt, if discussion of them was broadcast over the radio in your community.

3. Determine if there is more than one station in your local radio market owned by the same company. Compare and contrast the stations to each other, then compare them to stations owned by other companies. Examine any correlations between programming on stations owned by the same company that might be indicative of corporate, rather than local, influence.

4. Listen to a controversial radio talk show host or deejay. Count how many times the host refers to her or his relationship to management of the station. Do you

think the characterization of the relationship between host and management is accurate or just posturing?

5. Do you think that, in the age of the Internet, definitions of obscenity and indecency should continue to be locally derived? If so, how could such standards be enforced? If not, by whom should definitions of obscenity and indecency be determined? Should they be applied only to the Internet or to all media?

6. Do you agree with DO IT, that sites expressing one opinion on a subject should be compelled by law to feature links to opposing opinions? Should these laws be applied to all sites or just to some? If some, to which sites should they be applied?

7. Do you think that websites should be held responsible for objectionable content on sites to which they link?

8. With the Internet's easy ability to link from site to site, how would you define a work "as a whole" on the Internet?

REFERENCES/NOTES

1. Snopes.com. "Radio, Radio," http://www.snopes2.com/rumors/radio.htm. Accessed February 23, 2004.

2. Tom Valentine and Ira Hansen. "Talk-Show Host Learns Tough Lesson About Mainstream Censorship, Free Speech and Israel," http://www.americanfreepress.net/Mideast/Talk-Show_Host_Learns_Tough_Le/talk-show_host_learns_tough_le.html. Accessed January 30, 2004.

3. "Definitions of Pornography, Obscenity, and Indecency," http://www.moralityinmedia.org/index.htm?obscenityEnforcement/obscporn.htm. Accessed February 4, 2004.

4. NewsMax.com. "FCC's Powell Wants Bigger Fines for Indecency," http://www.newsmax.com/archives/articles/2004/1/15/03712.shtml. Accessed February 4, 2004.

5. "FCC Fine Against Clear Channel for 2001 Broadcasts," http://www.radioandrecords.com/Subscribers/TodaysNews/archive/arch012804.htm#FCC%20Fine%20Against%20Clear%20Channel%20For%202001%20Broadcasts. Accessed February 4, 2004 (Subscription-only access).

6. "Radio 'X,'" *Los Angeles Times,* October 17, 1991, p. F-3.

7. Eric Nuzum. "Censorship Incidents," http://ericnuzum.com/banned/incidents/00s.html. Accessed February 24, 2004.

8. Stephen Dinan. "Ads Compare Bush to Hitler," http://www.washtimes.com/national/20040105-114507-1007r.htm. Accessed February 16, 2004.

9. 365Gay.com. "Gay Politician Caught with Pants Down," http://www.365gay.com/newscontent/120103ukPolit.htm. Accessed February 16, 2004.

10. Bill Mears. "Supreme Court Affirms Use of Computer Filters in Public Libraries," http://www.cnn.com/2003/LAW/06/24/scotus.internetporn.library. Accessed February 17, 2004.

11. Sherrie Gossett. "Newssite Shut Down over War Photos," http://www.worldnetdaily.com/news/article.asp?ARTICLE_ID=31709. Accessed February 18, 2004.

12. Jay Lyman. "Investigative Report: Terrorist Web Site Hosted by U.S. Firm," http://www.newsfactor.com/perl/story/17079.html. Accessed February 19, 2004.

13. Clyde Wayne Crews, Jr., and Adam Thierer. "Whatever Happened to Leaving the Internet Unregulated?" http://www.cato.org/cgi-bin/scripts/printtech.cgi/dailys/12-22-02.html. Accessed February 19, 2004.

14. NotInOurName.net. "Support Sherman Austin," http://www.notinourname.net/restrictions/sherman-austin.htm. Accessed February 20, 2004.

15. Crews and Thierer.

16. Chris Sprigman. "The Mouse That Ate the Public Domain," http://writ.news.findlaw.com/commentary/20020305_sprigman.html. Accessed February 19, 2004.

17. Jemima Kiss. "BBC Online Beats US News on Its Own Turf," http://www.journalism.co.uk/news/story637.html. Accessed February 23, 2004.

9 Scheduling Strategies for Television

In this chapter you will learn about the following:

- The importance of scheduling decisions
- The scheduling strategies of commercial and cable networks
- How the urge to compete molds schedules
- How sweeps affect schedules
- How changing a show's time slot on the schedule can improve a show's performance
- How patience or the lack of it can affect a program's success

To construct a successful programming lineup, programmers must do more than just fill the time periods. Many TV shows that, at first blush, seemed to contain all the right ingredients for a long and profitable life have had short and painful demises for reasons apart from their inherent merit. Programs not only have to be developed but also have to be nurtured. Too many productions have simply been tossed on the air with no plan, no promotion, no lead-in, and therefore, no chance.

Once programmers have produced a promising show, they must be equally adept at placing and treating it on the schedule. The time period, the competition, and the receptivity of the audience are all factors to be assessed before the show is committed to the schedule.

TELEVISION SCHEDULING

Many of the strategies used in scheduling commercial television can be found in cable. There are differences, but more similarities exist. Clearly, both share a desire to program to the available audience and a desire to employ scheduling techniques that will work the best for them. Commercial stations, cable systems, and satellite providers all want to protect their programming with the best possible schedules.

It is different with syndication. Syndicators sell to stations and rarely, at least initially, are able to dictate time periods. After a syndicated show has been on the air awhile and has developed a large following, the distributor may be strong enough to demand a specific position on the schedule. One suspects, for example, that when Oprah Winfrey's company, Harpo, launched "Dr. Phil," she was able to require that "Dr. Phil" not compete directly with her and that it be given a good time slot. (In Los Angeles, Oprah airs at 3:00 P.M. on ABC and "Dr. Phil" airs at 4:00 P.M. on NBC.) Certain shows are designed for a particular daypart and cannot be scheduled effectively anywhere else. But the syndicators mostly sell the shows, and the stations place them whenever they wish.

Ideally, programmers seek a large audience with the leadoff show and structure the programs that follow so that the audience will watch continuously throughout the schedule. This is not always possible. Sometimes a competitor's opening program will be an established blockbuster that makes it impossible for others to start effectively. Other times the competitor's strength may be in the middle of the schedule. Then, the only strategy is to ride out the "bad" period and attempt to rebuild when the power block is over and the audience is released.

When putting together a schedule, programmers should consider the elements described in the sections that follow.

Fitting the Show to the Available Audience

As we explained earlier, most programs have a primary appeal to a particular audience. For example, action–adventure appeals principally to men, sitcoms to women, contemporary music to teens, serials to younger women, and talk shows and game shows to older women. Occasionally, a particular show will attract an almost universal audience, as when more than 90% of all the homes in the country watched at least one episode of "Roots" when it was initially aired in 1977. Often something of a current nature, such as the coverage of a war or disaster, will also have wide appeal. But generally the primary appeal of a show is to a specific demographic group.

Therefore, a program must be placed at a time in which its core viewers are available. It makes no sense to schedule a show with a predominant teen appeal on a Saturday night. That audience is not home. They are at movie theaters, basketball games, or anywhere other than in front of the set with mom and dad.

ABC relearned this lesson in the 1990–1991 season. The network bucked the conventional wisdom and scheduled a nightlong lineup for the 18 to 34 year olds: "The Young Riders," "Twin Peaks," and "China Beach" (replaced midseason by "Under Cover"). ABC hoped that if it built the franchise, the young viewers would come. They did not. In the last week of their Saturday telecasts, "Twin Peaks" and "Under Cover" were tied for 85th place among 89 programs rated by Nielsen. But late Saturday night? That is something different. Many young viewers have returned home by then and are eager for entertainment, as "Saturday Night Live" has impressively proved for more than 4 decades.

When buying syndicated shows, station programmers look for series appropriate to the time period. Whenever possible, a network affiliate will try to buy a syndicated show that coordinates with a network lead-in (assuming the lead-in is strong) to continue the audience flow.

Before locking in a program, programmers must study the time period's demographic history. If the target audience is underrepresented, a more favorable position should be sought. No matter how strong the show, if the key viewers are not available, the project will fail.

Dayparting

Closely related to the principle of fitting the show to the available audience is the concept of dayparting. People's needs, activities, and moods change throughout the day, and dayparting takes this into account by changing what is presented and how it is presented.

In the morning, when people first wake up, they often want information to help them plan the day—weather, traffic reports, and important news. Because most people must go to work, they do not have a great deal of time to spend with media. That is why many of the morning shows are divided into short segments. Early morning is also a time when young children watch television, often as their parents are getting ready for work. The children's cable channel, Noggin, for example, offers a pre-school block in the mornings.

As the morning wears on, people who spend time with television are able to do so in a more leisurely fashion. As a result, game shows, soap operas, and talk shows dominate daytime TV.

In the midafternoon, students return home from school. Many television stations change programming fare to appeal to these children. In the afternoon, Noggin offers "Bob the Builder," "Dora the Explorer," and "Oswald." After 6:00 P.M., Noggin appeals to older children, filling out its dayparting schedule for children from the youngest in the mornings to the oldest in the early evening.

As people begin arriving home from work, many TV stations switch from programming oriented toward children and homemakers to news. This allows adults to catch up on the day's events.

The evening is the time for the most leisurely TV viewing of all—the time when all categories of viewers are, in theory at least, able to spend several hours with one or more programs. Comedy, drama, and reality are the primary fare during these hours.

From 11:30 P.M. until 12:30 or 1:00 A.M., the talk/variety form presented in segments has been most popular for two basic reasons: people who are preparing for sleep generally do not want to be overstimulated, and viewers turn in for the night at varying times. Segmented shows permit people to switch off the set after an interview has been completed. In this way, a programmer is able to attract a large number of viewers for at least part of a show. If a 2-hour movie was scheduled, the viewer might be tempted to say, "I can't watch all of it; therefore, I won't watch any of it."

Stations that stay on through the early morning hours, as a service to insomniacs or night workers who do not want to retire as soon as they come home, usually fill the time with inexpensive movies or, on cable, paid programming in the form of infomercials. This is more for economic reasons than daypart strategy. Lately, networks have been supplying news to their affiliates during the wee hours, and a small but devoted audience of news junkies have tuned in.

On the weekend, programming changes dramatically to accommodate the lifestyle of the audience. The daytime lineups are studded with sporting events to reach the male viewers available in abundance. Saturday morning is often devoted to children's programming to accommodate early-rising children and their late-rising parents. Saturday evening schedules are canted toward the older audience in recognition of the absence of teens and young adults. Sunday morning on the networks is wall-to-wall news and public affairs programming. This is partly to take advantage of the availability of adults who have the time to digest the news in deeper more thoughtful quantities, but it is also a way to pay off public service obligations in a commercially insensitive time period. Networks and stations can point with pride to these estimable service shows whenever their community consciousness is called into question without sacrificing large profits in the process.

Eastern Standard Time	Program
6:00 A.M.	"Sesame Street"
7:06 A.M.	"Arthur"
7:43 A.M.	"Clifford the Big Red Dog"
8:20 A.M.	"Dragon Tales"
8:57 A.M.	"Mister Rogers' Neighborhood"
9:34 A.M.	"Barney & Friends"
10:11 A.M.	"Teletubbies"
10:47 A.M.	"Sesame Street"
11:53 A.M.	"Mister Rogers' Neighborhood"
12:30 P.M.	"On Q"
1:00 P.M.	"Hot and Spicy"
2:00 P.M.	"Hot and Spicy"
3:00 P.M.	"Between the Lions"
3:36 P.M.	"Arthur"
4:12 P.M.	"Liberty's Kids"
4:48 P.M.	"Clifford the Big Red Dog"
5:24 P.M.	"Cyberchase"
6:00 P.M.	"The NewsHour with Jim Lehrer"
7:00 P.M.	"Nightly Business Report"
7:30 P.M.	"On Q"
8:00 P.M.	"Dr. Wayne Dyer: The Power of Intention"
Midnight	"On Q"
12:30 A.M.	"Charlie Rose"
1:30 A.M.	"Dr. Wayne Dyer: The Power of Intention"
5:30 A.M.	"America's Home Cooking: Casseroles and Covered Dishes"

Figure 9.1
This schedule for March 8, 2004, for WQED in Pittsburgh is a typical PBS schedule.

Public television stations determine their own dayparting to a much greater degree than the commercial stations affiliated with NBC, CBS, ABC, and Fox. The contract signed between commercial networks and affiliates penalizes a station if it does not run a program when the network wants it to run. Such is not the case with PBS, although in recent years informal pressure has been placed on the major PBS affiliates to run most of the programs at set times. The reason behind this change is that PBS wants to develop national promotional campaigns that tell all viewers exactly when they can expect to see a particular program on their local PBS station. But stations often have minds of their own regarding what time of day certain programs should air in their communities.

Although procedures differ from station to station, most public TV stations daypart, often with shows for children in the mornings and afternoons; programs for women during midday when children are likely to be napping; and news, interviews, and self-help shows throughout the evening into late night (Figure 9.1).

Launching the Show: The First Strategy

For a program to be a success, it must first be sampled. If viewers are unaware of a show, the early ratings will be weak and the series likely will languish quickly. In a soft economic environment, buyers are disinclined to stay with programs that do not instantly indicate promise. Programmers have devised two strategies to hasten the sampling process: introduce the show in a quiet time, and place the premiere when a large audience is virtually guaranteed.

Introducing the Show in a Quiet Time. For many years, the television season was clearly set: it started in the fall and ended in the spring. One reason for this was that business affairs executives insisted that the networks could not afford to air original programs in the summer, ad rates being lower in the summer when viewership is down. To make the shows financially feasible, they argued, it was essential to schedule reruns in the summer.

Competition, the proliferation of viewer options, the marketplace, and the proliferation of reality shows that do not repeat well have helped create a season that runs virtually all year. This has enabled programmers to avoid putting their shows up against heavy competition in the fall or even at the start of the so-called second season in the spring. It is thus a little easier to find a quiet time to introduce a show, avoiding the cluttered "premiere week" of old when only a few shows could survive. There is still a lot of talk and speculation about the shows that will launch a fall season, but this hype belies that a "season" is now essentially year round.

Fox is generally credited with having led the trend toward the expansion to the year-round "season." In the summer of 1991, Peter Chernin, president of Fox Entertainment, declared that his company had fallen into the same "self-destructive" practice of launching all new shows in the fall. He noted that the previous season the four networks had "introduced 34 new series as if it was a massacre. Seventy-five percent failed. No other business debuts its product like that. No longer at Fox. We will roll out new series in every month of the year."[1]

His new plan went into effect in July 1991 with the premiere of "Beverly Hills, 90210." "In the first week," Chernin claimed, "it showed an 84% improvement over its '90–'91 average."[2] By mid-fall it was second in its time period, topped only by the formidable veteran, "Cheers."

Not every show that premieres in an off time becomes a hit, but Fox again showed prodigious off-season results in the summer of 2002 with the reality show "American Idol" and in the summer of 2003 when it introduced its series "The O.C.," about the lives and loves of teenagers in Orange County, California.

USA network, for example, launches its original programming outside of sweeps to get sampling and awareness in a quiet time.

Placing the Show in a Hit Time Period.

A favorite launching strategy is to schedule a newcomer after a monster event, the Super Bowl being the ideal choice. Hardly a year goes by that the network carrying the game does not introduce a new show behind it in the hope that the largest audience of the year will like what it sees and an instant hit will be born. Sometimes it works and sometimes it does not. Although the results vary, the strategy is fundamentally sound. There is no better way to get a program sampled than to place it immediately following a blockbuster event.

A variation of this strategy is to time slot a newcomer in a time period that follows a powerhouse series, such as "Frasier," as NBC did with "Scrubs," or "Everybody Loves Raymond," as CBS did with "Two and a Half Men."

Many industry observers would agree with Alan Wurtzel, NBC's president of research and media development, that 50% of all households that will ever watch a program will get hooked by one of the first two episodes. Obviously, the sooner they sample these shows, the better. This is why broadcasters strive so tirelessly to develop new techniques to bring viewers into the tent from the beginning.

HBO has found an effective way to capitalize on its own version of a hit time period. Because of the success of "Sex and the City" and "The Sopranos," HBO found that by alternating these two shows in the same time period, it could command the Sunday 9:00 P.M. period. HBO may launch most of its

Figure 9.2
"The Sopranos" (a and b) and "Sex and the City" (c) established a stronghold for HBO on Sunday nights at 9:00. (Photo of Edie Falco and James Gandolfini from "The Sopranos" courtesy the Academy of Television Arts & Sciences; photo of "Sex and the City" from Globe Photos, Inc.)

(a)

(b)

(c)

Even though a new show may achieve a higher share of audience in July than in September, the pie is so much smaller that the total audience may still fall short of a conventional launch.

Second, January premieres run into station clearance difficulties. Station managers who commit to programs in the fall are frequently locked into pay-or-play contracts for at least 26 weeks. For purely economic reasons, they may wish to stay with a failing show until the full commitment is satisfied, particularly during a recessionary period. Programs launched in January may have to struggle for months with subpar lineups until additional time periods break open.

To repeat, the first objective of a launch is to get the program sampled. Any technique of timing that enables the program to be introduced when it will confront the least competition is desirable. However, this advantage must be weighed against the less attractive factors of starting in a period of low set usage, being forced to schedule reruns in high HUT months when opponents will be running original episodes, and offering a show for sale when many buyers cannot accommodate it.

original movies Saturday nights, but it has also managed to carve out this Sunday night stronghold (Figure 9.2).

Launching Syndicated Series. There are two major factors militating against any sort of wholesale departure from fall premieres for syndicated shows. First, summer **households using television (HUT)** and **persons using television (PUT)** levels are considerably lower than those in the fall–spring period.

Tentpoling

You have just seen that one of the best ways to gain sampling for a show is to introduce it behind a big hit. The same principle can be applied to programs struggling elsewhere on the schedule. By moving these next to hits, they can often be revived and enjoy healthy, lengthy runs.

Sometimes a powerhouse show is strong enough to hold up programs both before and after it. If a new show is scheduled right before a popular program, people tuning in early in anticipation of the hit will sample the end of the new entry. Hopefully, they will be intrigued and tune in the next week for the entire show. Placing an established show before a hit is not as strong a programming strategy as placing it after, but the method can work.

This concept of scheduling weak or new programs around a strong show is referred to as **tentpoling**—the pole in the middle holds up the two weaker shows, especially the one that follows.

The Fox network made excellent use of tentpoles when it expanded the number of evenings it broadcast. It had developed a strong Sunday lineup that included "The Simpsons," "America's Most Wanted," and "Married . . . With Children." When it expanded to more nights of programming in 1990, it used these popular programs as anchors for the other nights—"The Simpsons" on Thursday, "America's Most Wanted" on Friday, and "Married . . . With Children" on Sunday. Fox has used this strategy several times over the years. For example, after "Malcolm in the Middle" established itself by following "The Simpsons," Fox moved it to Sundays at 9:00 P.M. in the 2002–2003 season, where it became another tentpole for the network.

Tentpoling was far more effective in the precable era, when program choices were fewer and the remote control unit had not yet been invented. The long walk from the couch to the set was more exercise than most viewers cared for, and given a reasonable excuse to stay put, they would. Today they can whiz through 30 channels before the next show's opening credits have rolled, and the pass-along strategy is less assured.

Nevertheless, it continues its usefulness. "A Different World," a comedy spin-off of the "The Cosby Show" was introduced in September 1987 immediately following the parent program, which, at that time, was the No. 1 show on television. The derivative production was an instant success and remained in the Top 10 for 4 years, although the show was often dismissed as simply riding on the "Cosby" coattails. This dismissal was unfair, as revealed by the number of seemingly compatible shows that have failed following "Friends," one of the most successful shows in television history. Four years as a Top 10 show does not just happen as a result of fortuitous placement on a schedule.

Station managers use this same tentpoling strategy with blockbuster syndication series. When "Jeopardy" was launched in its third incarnation in 1984, it was placed behind the triumphant "Wheel of Fortune" in many markets. It quickly became an enormous success and helped form an invulnerable hour of dominance. Although PBS does not carry out scheduling strategies with the same fanaticism as the commercial and cable networks, it also has its tentpole shows, programs such as "American Masters," "Great Performances," "Mystery," and "The NewsHour with Jim Lehrer."

Hammocking

Probably the surest way to generate an audience for a new program is to slot it between two established shows, called the **hammock** principle. With power in front and power behind, the new program benefits from both the pass-along viewing from the preceding show and the anticipated entertainment from the following program. Hammocking is a frequently employed strategy. For example, it is often seen in children's cartoon blocks in which a newcomer is sandwiched between two established series.

Expectations are higher with ham-mocked shows, such as NBC's "Jesse" or "Cursed." Placed between "Friends" and "Will & Grace," these shows were simply unable to take advantage of being in prime television real estate in 1999 and 2000, respectively, and were quickly canceled.

A story (possibly apocryphal) is told about ABC President Leonard Goldenson in the early days of the network, when a running joke was "They ought to put the Vietnam War on ABC—it would be canceled in 13 weeks." Goldenson observed that his competitors were separating two hits and sliding a new show in between. Impressed by this strategy, he supposedly asked his programming chief, "Why don't we do that?" "Because, Leonard," came the response, "we don't have two hits."

Counterprogramming

No program, no matter how popular, can satisfy all viewers. The neglected or dissatisfied audience becomes a good target for competing shows. The tactic of filling a time period with a program whose appeal is dissimilar to an oppo-nent's is called counterprogramming.

The 1991 three-network prime-time lineup Tuesday nights (Fox did not provide programming Tuesday nights in 1991) provides a good example of this device from television history. From

8:00 to 9:00 P.M., ABC scheduled two situation comedies, the second of which, "Home Improvement" was a promising newcomer comfortably placed between the well-established "Full House" and the No. 1-rated series, "Roseanne." CBS countered with "Rescue 911," a fast-paced "actuality" adventure, and NBC introduced "I'll Fly Away," a soft, family-value-focused, dramatic series. In the 9:00 to 10:00 P.M. hour, ABC contin-ued its comedy skein with the afore-mentioned "Roseanne" and "Coach," a show that had blossomed into a hit in its enviable time period. Again, the two competitors had to seek an alternative audience. CBS elected to present feature films, and NBC offered "In the Heat of the Night," a law enforcement adventure series. To close out the night, ABC decided to try a new family drama, "Homefront," in the belief that the lineup's tremendous momentum would pass along a large audience to the new-comer and give it a good chance of success. CBS played the second half of its movie, and NBC followed "In the Heat of the Night" with another crime-and-punishment series, "Law & Order." This nightlong effort on the part of each broadcaster to carve away an audience on which the others are not concen-trating is classic counterprogramming strategy.

Going to Tuesday nights for the 2002 season, six networks were competing against each other instead of three. ABC submitted a comedy block from 8:00 to 10:00 P.M., leading into the steady "NYPD Blue," even though it had no hit show to use as a tentpole and did not have two hits shows to use for a hammock. NBC also went with comedy from 8:00 to 10:00 P.M. Although it had a strong show in "Frasier" to use as a tentpole, "Hidden Hills" proved a failure. NBC went with a news show at 10:00 P.M. to compete with the dramas on CBS and ABC. CBS went with older-skewing dramas for the entire night. Fox countered with a hipper drama, "24," at 9:00 P.M. and used its hit show, "That '70s Show," to jumpstart its night against the competing comedies. "Gilmore Girls" on the WB and "Buffy the Vampire Slayer" on UPN went head to head, targeting the younger demographics at 8:00 P.M., followed at 9:00 P.M. by "Smallville" on the WB and "Haunted" on UPN; "Smallville" won that battle. Six competitors from 8:00 to 10:00 P.M. (and back to three at 10:00 P.M.) makes counterprogramming more complex because the shares of the pie are bound to be a lot smaller, particularly with the influx of cable.

When an opponent has tried to stake a claim on a particular audience but has done so with a relatively weak entry, the best strategy may be to go after that audience with a stronger version of the same genre. If the move is successful, the challenger will capture the viewers and seriously erode the opponent's audience base not only for that time period but possibly for the ensuing ones.

It seems strange that two medical dramas would be scheduled against each other, particularly when schedules are so carefully put together with counterprogramming in mind. This, however, was the case in September 1994 when CBS scheduled "Chicago Hope" at 10:00 P.M. on Thursdays and NBC scheduled "ER" at the same time. It was immediately clear that "ER" had megahit written all over it and that if "Chicago Hope" had any chance of survival, it needed to be moved, quickly. In October 1994, "Chicago Hope" was moved an hour earlier on Thursdays, and in December 1994, it was moved to Monday nights at 10:00 when, under David E. Kelley's masterful hand, it established itself as a solid hit for CBS. Had the network not acted to protect the show, "Chicago Hope" might not have been able to survive the "ER" juggernaut.

This "ER"–"Chicago Hope" scenario raises the question, "What do you do against a monster hit?" Network executives have wrestled with this problem from "I Love Lucy" in the 1950s through the "The Cosby Show" in the 1980s and "ER" in the 1990s to "CSI" starting in 2000. The temptation is to throw up a test pattern, abandon the time period, and hope no one will notice. A pleasant fantasy, but unrealistic. At times programmers have decided to cut their losses and fill the period with the most inexpensive programming available. A strong case can be made for fiscal prudence, but there is a big risk to simply not showing up.

For one thing, stations have to sell commercials around the period, and the spots will be worthless if the program does not register. Also, such a lack of effort says all the wrong things to the company's many constituents (advertisers, investors, etc.). Most executives feel it is best to try something experimental. There is not much to lose, and, who knows, they might just get lucky. Even if it does not work, critics and commentators will applaud the innovative effort and this will help ease the pain of a stricken time period.

Sylvester L. "Pat" Weaver, president of NBC-TV in the early 1950s, recalled, "Whenever the other guys came up with a big winner, I knew it was time to call in my zanies, the guys with the off-the-wall ideas. I knew no conventional show could make it, but maybe something really unusual might click."

ABC scored strongly with this strategy in 1990. CBS's "Murder, She Wrote," preceded by the powerhouse "60 Minutes," had been delivering hammer blows to the opposition since 1984. ABC decided to take a flyer on a program that featured home videotapes shot by ordinary citizens. The novel concept caught on and "America's Funniest Home Videos" became a perennial

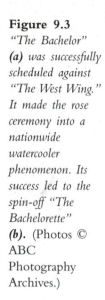

Figure 9.3
"The Bachelor"
(a) was successfully
scheduled against
"The West Wing."
It made the rose
ceremony into a
nationwide
watercooler
phenomenon. Its
success led to the
spin-off "The
Bachelorette"
(b). (Photos ©
ABC
Photography
Archives.)

(a)

(b)

deliver solid, if unspectacular, ratings at an affordable cost to the network.

There are times when it is an excellent strategy to take on a blockbuster hit. The timing must be right, but if it is, the colossus can be toppled. Two conditions are required: the incumbent hit must be in a waning state and the challenger must be a promising show in the early stages of its ascent. These are two critical and delicate judgments for the programmer, and if either is wrong the venture will fail.

When ABC's head scheduler, Jeff Bader, sensed that NBC's prestige drama, "The West Wing," was vulnerable in the fall of 2002, he felt the timing was right to pit an unscripted series, "The Bachelor," against it (Figure 9.3). He was dead on, and the strong, younger demographics that "The Bachelor" and its companion piece, "The Bachelorette," garnered made the victory even sweeter.

Similarly, CBS's Les Moonves was able to take on NBC's seemingly impenetrable Thursday night "Must See

"safety valve" used by ABC as a quick fix when other scheduling was not working. Its ratings never achieved the heights that they did at the start, but the show could always be counted on to

TV" by moving "Survivor" (Figure 9.4) and "CSI" to Thursday nights in 2001, adding "Without a Trace" to the mix to create a powerful assault on NBC's former stronghold.

For independent stations, counter-programming remains simply a way of life. They must always examine the schedules of their network-affiliated opponents and go after the audience left unattended.

Bridging and Supersizing

The less opportunity the audience has to sample your adversary's program, the better chance you have for success. If you have something compelling unfolding when the competition is about to start, you distract the viewer from the temptation to stray.

The most effective use of this strategy is to have a program under way well in advance of the competitor's start time. Networks and stations have often scheduled shows to begin before the start of a powerful opposing show. Viewers who have invested a full hour in a program are unlikely to break away for something else. **Bridging** takes place at different times during the day. For example, the highly rated, long-lasting (it began in 1971) CBS soap, "The Young and the Restless" starts a half hour earlier than the other soaps.

A variation on the bridging strategy is to edit a longform program so that the competitor's start time is spanned by entertainment. Take, for example, a 9:00 to 10:00 P.M. program opposed by 2 half hours. If the producer of the hour-long program schedules a 2-minute commercial from 9:25 to 9:27 P.M., a strong piece of action can be unfolding at 9:30 P.M. when the second of the 2 half hours is about to begin.

Going seamlessly from one show to the next without any commercial inter-

ruptions became popular at the start of the new century as a means of bridging two shows. This continuous action seeks to hook viewers before they have a chance to go elsewhere. And some shows start a few seconds before the hour or half hour, refusing to allow viewers to jump ship.

Supersizing, adding 10 minutes to a half-hour show such as "Friends" or an extra half hour to an hour-long reality phenomenon such as "Fear Factor," also became popular as a bridging strategy in the early 21st century, pioneered by NBC Entertainment President Jeff Zucker. The theory behind supersizing is that viewers enjoying extra time with one of their favorite shows will not turn the dial to another show already in progress. Supersizing is clearly fun and it has been working, although programmers should be wary of overusing it; the novelty can wear off.

As with many other programming strategies, bridging has been affected by the invention of the remote tuner. During commercial breaks, hyperactive TV viewers may zip to five or six channels to find other fare or just to satisfy their curiosity as to what else is playing. If the program they have been watching has been intriguing enough, they will return. But if something else catches

Figure 9.4
"Survivor" host Jeff Probst is flanked by executive producers Mark Burnett and Charlie Parsons as they celebrate the success of their show. (Courtesy the Academy of Television Arts & Sciences.)

Figure 9.5
Legendary programmer Fred Silverman is recognized as the founder of blunting. (Courtesy the Academy of Television Arts & Sciences.)

their fancy, even though it may be almost over, they may become a lost viewer.

Blunting

A cousin to bridging is **blunting.** The goal is the same: minimize the competitor's opportunity to be sampled. Except under the direst emergencies, the premieres of all programs are announced many weeks in advance. The need for notification to advertisers and affiliated stations, plus the time to rev up a promotion campaign, makes last-minute introductions impractical. In a world where competition is king and dominating your opponent often takes precedence over thoughtful programming decisions, the long lead period enables rivals to fashion competitive strategies.

So how do you keep your competitive edge by blunting the opposition? Strong, explosive episodes with marquee guest stars can be used. So can a special program that combines celebrities with other high-appeal elements. A major motion picture featuring a recently announced Academy Award nominee can receive a "world TV premiere" on the competitor's premiere night. Either

the special or movie should bridge the newcomer's start time. If there is sufficient lead time and program inventory permits, a series of extraordinary events and programming can be placed in the time period for weeks leading up to the competition's premiere. The idea is to build a viewing habit so binding that a viewer will not be tempted to seek programming elsewhere.

Blunting requires vigilance and imagination. No programmer should supinely "cave" against the premiere of an opponent's show, especially one that occupies a key position in the schedule. Obviously, no company has the resources to attempt to blunt every competitive move. But if there is a lot riding on the outcome of the new show's launch, every effort should be made to capture the viewer with greater attractions.

The recognized founder of the blunting technique in network television is Fred Silverman (Figure 9.5). When he became program chief of CBS in 1970, he instituted a policy of yearlong vigilance. Large sheets of paper were designed in which space was provided for the programs of the three networks, half hour by half hour, for all seven nights of the week. A sheet was maintained for every week. Each week, key CBS network strategists met to exchange information and update the charts. As soon as one of the other networks made a program announcement, the plotting began. Rarely was an ABC or NBC program launched that was not harassed by CBS diversions and enticements.

The system contributed significantly to CBS's No. 1 status for all 5 years of Silverman's program leadership. He then moved to ABC, where he used the technique to score more winning years. However, by the time he arrived at NBC, both his competitors were schooled in the process and the originator's advantage had vanished. After his stint at NBC ended, Silverman surveyed the programming landscape and was able to carve out an area all to himself with older-skewing shows such as "Matlock," "Diagnosis Murder," and the Perry Mason television movie franchise.

Late-night television is an extremely valuable resource for the networks. As author Ken Auletta observed, in the late 1980s NBC was getting 25% of its profits from late-night programming, making "Here's Johnny" (Carson) a welcome announcement.[3] Over the years, late-night shows have remained a primary source of a network's income. In 1996, HBO produced a television movie, "The Late Shift," based on the book by *New York Times* media analyst Bill Carter, which dramatized how contentious the wars for late-night dominance can be. The failed attempt of ABC's Robert Iger to steal David Letterman from CBS in 2002 further illustrates how tough (and embarrassing) the public late-night blunting wars can be. In 2004, NBC sought to maintain the late-night dominance by securing the services of Jay Leno for five additional years and by naming his successor, Conan O'Brien, thus avoiding another possible contentious battle over the late shift.

Blunting strategies can sometimes end up hurting both parties, as happened during the 2001–2002 season when CBS and NBC tried to blunt each other's reality programming. CBS brought out a special edition of "Big Brother 2" against the launch of NBC's "Lost." NBC countered by using a special edition of "Fear Factor" to hurt the premier of CBS's "The Amazing Race." This showdown ended in a ratings draw, all performing adequately. But, as media analyst Stacey Lynn Korner notes, competitive egos got in the way, hurting the networks and viewers alike.[4]

Gone are the days when the commercial networks could ignore any blunting attempts by cable when making scheduling decisions. In 2004, with cable in more than 60% of homes and HBO, in particular, in 30% of homes, cable can significantly affect commercial television. For example, when HBO powerhouse series "The Sopranos" and "Sex and the City" aired at 9:00 Sunday nights, the commercial networks were clearly affected by the HBO–cable factor. When the final episode of "Sex and the City" aired February 22, 2004, it drew some 10.6 million viewers, making it the second-most-watched show in its time slot, beaten only by ABC, which had 17.5 millions viewers for the premier of the new and improved "Super Millionaire" with Regis Philbin again hosting. Indeed, ABC won the households race, but HBO narrowly beat ABC in the key 18- to 49-year-old demographic. All this with HBO in only 30% of U.S. homes.[5]

Cable and commercial networks frequently clash over blunting. For example, in 2002, NBC scheduled its movie about Matthew Shepard, the gay college student who was beaten and left to die by two young men high on crystal methamphetamine in Laramie, Wyoming, in 1998. The same night, HBO was premiering its movie about Shepard, "The Laramie Project," based on the play by Moises Kaufman. In response, HBO moved up the airing of its movie by a week, with both sides accusing each other of foul play and each proclaiming innocence about the scheduling plans of the other.

Interestingly, when MTV aired its version of the Matthew Shepard story a year before the HBO–NBC showdown, an NBC executive reportedly told his staff that the ratings effect of an MTV cable movie were inconsequential to NBC and could not be considered serious competition. But with commer-

Figure 9.6
Steven Spielberg's Emmy-winning, highly rated limited series, "Taken," starring Dakota Fanning, demonstrated cable's growing stronghold on longform programming. (Courtesy the Academy of Television Arts & Sciences.)

cial television on the decline and cable programming on the rise, it is no longer possible for the commercial networks to ignore the blunting possibilities of the cable channels, particularly when cable airs viewer-friendly **limited series** (Figure 9.6).

CBS 1991 Monday Night Schedule

Time	Program
8:00–8:30 P.M.	"Evening Shade"
8:30–9:00 P.M.	"Major Dad"
9:00–9:30 P.M.	"Murphy Brown"
9:30–10:00 P.M.	"Designing Women"
10:00–11:00 P.M.	"Northern Exposure"

CBS 2003 Monday Night Schedule

Time	Program
8:00–8:30 P.M.	"Yes, Dear"
8:30–9:00 P.M.	"Still Standing"
9:00–9:30 P.M.	"Everybody Loves Raymond"
9:30–10:00 P.M.	"Two and a Half Men"
10:00–11:00 P.M.	"CSI: Miami"

Figure 9.7
The CBS 1991 and 2003 Monday night schedule shows how programs can be stacked.

Stacking

Programmers attempt to develop an audience flow by assembling programs of similar appeal to sweep the viewer from one time period to the next, as PBS does by **stacking** three contiguous cooking shows on Saturday afternoons. A classic example of the stacking strategy was CBS's 1991 Monday night schedule of four sitcoms capped by a humorous, easy-to-take hour. The lineup dominated through the year and on several occasions was victorious in every half hour. In 2003, CBS similarly attempted to stack its programs with four sitcoms and an edgier 10:00 P.M. show, a spin off of its No. 1 hit, "CSI" (Figure 9.7).

Before embarking on such a stacking strategy, a programmer should carefully evaluate two considerations: Is there a powerful show to begin the schedule, and is there a weak link in the chain? Without a strong leadoff program, the lineup will be unable to develop the momentum necessary to start the audience flow. This flow is essential for stacking to work as a scheduling strategy. If a competitor takes a commanding lead at the beginning of the race, it will be difficult for the "stacked" lineup to gain pass-along benefits. Similarly, if there is an especially weak program in the string, viewers will drift to other offerings and the flow will be interrupted. If there is some doubt about the appeal of one of the shows, programmers would be well advised to place it at the end of the lineup.

Stacking to maintain audience flow is a standard procedure in virtually every daypart. In weekly daytime programming, the traditional strategy is to schedule games or other nonserial forms in the morning and serials in the afternoon. For decades, the networks have presented an uninterrupted string of animated shows on Saturday mornings to reach the 1- to

12-year-old audience. Research indicates that the youngest children watch the earliest shows, and, as the morning moves along, the audience tends to get older. In theory, programmers select the order of the cartoons to reflect this development, although how they determine an advancing intellectual content in these programs remains a mystery.

Stunting

Sometimes programs must take extraordinary measures to maintain their audience levels. The competition might be picking up momentum, a series of preemptions might have caused a loss of viewing habit, or a big sweeps week performance might be required to obtain a contract renewal. Whatever the reason, there are occasions when a show needs a major injection of audience appeal. As a short-term solution, programmers frequently resort to **stunting,** the insertion of entertainment elements not normally associated with the series to obtain a ratings spike.

One of the most popular ploys is to construct an episode around a movie personality, athlete, or a celebrity whose recent activities commanded national attention, such as having Elizabeth Taylor visit "General Hospital" in 1981. The appearance of these "names" provides powerful promotional opportunities and allows the program to exploit the public's curiosity about prominent figures.

Another traditional device is the development of a **multiparter** filled with cliffhangers. Story lines usually completed in one showing are extended to two or more episodes because "they're just too big, too important to be told in their usual length." Presumably viewers will be so gripped by the start of the story that they wouldn't dare miss the remaining episodes. Needless to say, the beginning must be strong or

there could be a ratings disaster paving the way to the conclusion, as was the case in 2004 at ABC with Stephen King's multiparter, "Kingdom Hospital," which began with respectable numbers but dropped 45% in its second airing.

In soaps and in prime time, weddings are often the stunt of choice. Conventional programming wisdom maintains a wedding episode can significantly boost the ratings of a show—thus the heavily promoted wedding of Phoebe in the final season of "Friends."

In the closing minutes of the last original episode of "Dallas" during the 1979–1980 season, J.R. Ewing, the power-mad, unscrupulous oil magnate, was shot by an unknown assailant and rushed to the hospital. This shooting was one of the biggest television stunts ever. Throughout the summer and into the first 2 months of the following season, viewers around the world speculated about "Who shot J.R.?" On November 21, 1980, the identity of the mysterious attacker was revealed to an estimated worldwide audience of more than 300 million. In the United States, more people viewed "Dallas" that evening than voted in the presidential election a few weeks earlier. It is still TV's second-most-watched episode, topped only by the 1983 finale of "M★A★S★H."

Reality shows promise twists and surprises (Fox's "Joe Millionaire," for example, was not really a millionaire), but it should be remembered that stunts cannot be overused (the next edition of "Joe Millionaire," the international version, essentially duplicated the original and failed). Stunts cannot make up for weak programming. No audience can be hyped indefinitely, and stunts can be costly. Although programmers often clamor for stunt casting and stunt plot twists to boost ratings during sweeps, it must be remembered that stunting cannot do it all. To be most effective,

(a)

(b)

Figure 9.8
*Crossing "Buffy the Vampire Slayer" **(a)** into "Angel" **(b)** was designed to boost the ratings for "Angel."* (Globe Photos, Inc.)

stunting should be seen as a short-term device.

One downside of stunting should be cited. To accommodate the stunt, producers frequently have to modify the basic idea of the show. A story line that plays up the special appeals of a celebrity guest must necessarily shift the focus from the core ensemble, which is why some producers, such as Dick Wolf, creator of the "Law & Order" franchise, do not engage in stunt casting.

When Pat Mitchell became PBS president and CEO in 2000, she saw the need for PBS to compete more aggressively. This was necessitated partly by the constant pressure PBS faces that its financial base will be severed. Although many individuals, such as Brian Lowry of *Daily Variety* and Chellie Pingree, president of Common Cause, a citizens' organization of more than 250,000 people who support responsible broadcasting, favor keeping PBS healthy and solvent, the financial pressures are real. To stay vibrant, PBS stations create their own stunts, particularly when they are

trying to raise money from viewers during pledge weeks.

Crossprogramming

Crossprogramming is the interconnection of two shows for mutual benefit. In its most sophisticated form, a story is started on one program and is completed on another. It can be highly productive, but it requires an unusual combination of circumstances.

Upon her return to "ER" after her 5-year hiatus from the show, Sherry Stringfield crossed from "ER" to "Third Watch," another John Wells production. Similarly, David E. Kelley introduced a story line in "Ally McBeal" that concluded on "The Practice," with cast members crossing from one Kelley show to the next.

Other examples of crossprogramming occurred when a heart transplant started out on "Homicide" and ended up on "Chicago Hope" and when "Buffy the Vampire Slayer" crossed over to boost the ratings of debuting companion show "Angel" (Figure 9.8).

Elaborate crossovers require substantial advance planning, compatible formats, the good will of all, and, most often, a common production company. Such combinations are rare, which accounts for the infrequent use of elaborate crossprogramming. But when it can be used, it is a powerful programming tool.

Less ambitious versions, which produce more modest results, can also be developed. Appearances by stars on each other's programs and references on one program to events on another are two of the more familiar usages. This harkens back to the early days of radio when Gracie Allen, the comedienne of "Burns and Allen," visited numerous other radio shows looking for her brother.

Crossprogramming works because the avid viewers of the first show can be added to the core audience of the second, thereby producing incremental ratings, primarily for the latter. Obviously, the opening episode should be scheduled on the more popular of the two shows. It is easy to see how this maneuvering can cause resentment among the staff and cast of the higher-rated program. "The production company is just using us to beef up the numbers of the other program," is an opinion a programmer should be braced to hear. It calls for some nimble diplomacy, but the results can make it worthwhile.

Theming

Grouping programs with similar themes is big in syndication, where movies are often combined into theme weeks ("Elvis Week," "Monster Week," or "Romance in the Afternoon Week"), but this scheduling strategy also fre-quently occurs in commercial television and cable.

For example, in 2004, ABC made a concerted effort to have Oscar-related programming before the Oscar telecast on February 29. As Judith Tukich, ABC director of synergy and special projects, observed, "Oscar plotlines are featured in ABC's comedy lineup."[6]

"I'm With Her" had a five-episode story line with Teri Polo, the star of the show, an actress whose boyfriend is a schoolteacher, nominated for an Academy Award. Polo worried about what to wear to the Oscars, how to avoid the wrath of Joan Rivers on the red carpet, and how to deal with her pushy mother, played by Cybil Shepard, who arrived unpredictably, expecting to be given a ticket to the awards ceremony. ABC soaps featured Oscar story lines; "Good Morning America" and "The View" focused on the Oscars.

Cable has clearly embraced the advantages of **theming.** ESPN, part of the Disney family like ABC, discussed the Oscar nominations on its morning show, "Cold Pizza." The Disney Channel also sponsored Oscar-related events, as did A&E and Lifetime.[7]

The Outdoor Channel, which in 2004 programmed to a niche audience of some 26 million outdoor enthusiasts ("real outdoors for real people with nothing too extreme, too expensive or unsafe"), had three theme nights on its schedule: On Monday nights, a 4-hour block of half-hour shows on fishing; on Tuesday nights, a 4-hour block of half-hour shows on hunting; and on Wednesday nights, a 4-hour block of half-hour shows relating to horsepower. According to Wade Sherman, the senior vice president of programming at the Outdoor Channel, this scheduling strategy greatly increased audience flow, enabling the

Figure 9.9
The Outdoor Channel uses theming to build upon its audience base. (Courtesy the Outdoor Channel.)

Figure 9.10
PBS's perennial "Sesame Street" makes up a portion of its children's television programming stack. (Courtesy Children's Television Workshop.)

Outdoor Channel to increase its subscription base (Figure 9.9).

Stripping

Another strategy used by local stations involves **stripping**—placing the same show in the same time period every weekday and sometimes even on Saturday and Sunday. It is done partly for economic prudence and partly because it is a sound audience strategy. For example, PBS uses stripping effectively with children's programs that almost always appear at the same time every day (Figure 9.10). As you saw earlier, stations that buy a syndicated package of off-network shows have a fixed period

within which the agreed-upon number of showings must be run. Usually, the only way to meet this requirement is to schedule the series every day, Monday through Friday.

Placing a show in a predictable time and place enables viewers who are fans of the program to know exactly where and when they can find it. Nothing irritates and frustrates a viewer more that a lengthy search to locate the air time of a favorite series. Even if it were possible for a station to meet its pay-or-play obligations on several series by alternating them night after night, it would not be sensible scheduling. Fans of one show might not like the other, and they could quickly get out of the habit of watching at that time.

Changing a Show's Time Slot

Some shows, such as "Chicago Hope" described previously, *need* a time change, and some shows, such as "Everybody Loves Raymond," can survive being bumped around the dial until they land in the perfect spot. Not all shows, however, benefit from a schedule change.

With so many choices available, the audience does not need to be confused about when a show is airing. There are specials, **preemptions,** and sweeps alterations, and few time slots, apart from "I Love Lucy" or "ER," remain unchanged. But a time slot change can damage a show, taking the wind out of its sails and halting momentum.

When Fox's "King of the Hill" was moved in its second season (1998) to Tuesday nights from its previous Sunday night berth, it struggled mightily until it was brought back to Sunday nights, where it was given a chance to grow and develop a following.

Similarly, Fox's frequent schedule changes and periods of hiatus for the cult favorite "Family Guy" did not help the show get the big ratings, much to the chagrin of loyal fans who subsequently enjoyed the show on record-selling DVDs and on the Cartoon Network's "Adult Swim." The loyalty of these passionate fans paid off as seven new episodes of the show were created in 2004. The cult following kept the show alive, despite the initial on-and-off scheduling.

When ABC decided to switch "The Practice" from its usual Sunday night time slot at 10:00 to Monday nights at 9:00 during the 2002–2003 season, the move failed in several ways. Placed between "Veritas: The Quest" and "Miracles," ostensibly to function as a tent-pole, the Emmy Award-winning "The Practice" fell to fourth in its time slot. In addition, creator David E. Kelley was angered by the time slot switch, accusing ABC of trying to sabotage the show in its seventh season. Kelley was extremely vocal about his displeasure, hurting the all-important ABC/Kelley creative relationship. Ultimately, the show returned to its Sunday time slot, where in the 2003–2004 season it underwent a major change, which we will cover in a subsequent chapter.

Commercial networks are in the habit of making constant scheduling changes. PBS, on the other hand, for many years kept the same schedule for its audience of approximately 100 million people. PBS President Pat Mitchell initiated a pilot program with seven major PBS stations to experiment with different schedules to revitalize the PBS lineup.

Aware that PBS cannot afford to be viewed as stodgy, Mitchell sought to make changes. She moved "Masterpiece Theatre" from Sunday nights, although it was subsequently moved back. Keen on crosspromoting, she sought to establish a closer connection between PBS and NPR by bringing in noted NPR

Figure 9.11
Tavis Smiley, pictured here with Neal Kendall, the executive producer of his show, made a successful transition from NPR to PBS. (Courtesy The Smiley Group.)

commentator Bill Moyers with "Now with Bill Moyers" in 2002. NPR's first African-American talk show host, Tavis Smiley, also became PBS's African-American vanguard in 2004, with his eponymous show (Figure 9.11).

Overexposure

When networks have a hit, the tendency is to capitalize on that show's success by scheduling it too often or by trying to schedule close duplicates too quickly. For example, when ABC had its monster hit, "Who Wants to Be a Millionaire," there was a strong temptation to exploit the show, particularly because it was a relative bargain to produce. ABC scheduled the show a staggering four times a week in 2001, eventually killing the show through overexposure. When ABC brought back a bigger "Super Millionaire" with a top prize of $10 million in February 2004, the network scheduled it five nights in a row but only for one week during the February sweeps and a second week during the May sweeps, seemingly avoiding the overexposure mistakes of the past.

When Fox had its monster hit, "American Idol," it tried to duplicate

Figure 9.12
"I Love Lucy," starring Lucille Ball, pioneered the use of film for weekly television series. The technique enabled the episodes to be rerun with high quality. The programs are still syndicated today, some 50 years after they were first produced.
(Courtesy the Academy of Television Arts & Sciences.)

too expensive for this fledgling medium. Most programs were aired live—mistakes and all. A process called **kinescope recording** was developed so that some programs could be saved or run on the West Coast at the same "clock hours" as their East Coast origination. But these "kines," which were films made off a TV monitor, were of poor quality.

From their beginnings in the early 1950s, Lucille Ball and Desi Arnez filmed "I Love Lucy," and everyone thought they were a little crazy—until the foreign market opened up (Figure 9.12). Then Lucy and Desi began raking in the money from selling their shows to other countries, and a few fellow producers decided to follow suit. It was not long before American broadcasting realized it could play these films, too. Thus was born the rerun.

A basic annual pattern of program scheduling set in. Programs were introduced in the fall, ended their season in mid-spring, went into reruns for the summer, and emerged with new product the following fall. This came about through a combination of reality, surmise, social habits, and economics.

The key reality, as explained previously, was the drop-off in viewing over the summer months. From June through August, daylight remains well into the evening. People stay outside longer, and (according to conventional wisdom) the TV set often stands dark and unattended. Also, during the summer a substantial percentage of viewers are on vacation and are unavailable for, or uninterested in, watching TV. Through the decades a vociferous executive minority has claimed that this assessment is largely an incorrect surmise, grown into a mythic delusion. Defenders of the traditional cycle are quick to point out two important reasons for the summer hiatus—cast and staff demand a rest, and networks need

the success with "American Juniors" in the summer of 2003. Too similar? Too soon? Whatever the reasons, this "Idol" imitation did not achieve the success of its predecessor, losing large chunks of its audience week by week.[8]

Imitations can succeed, for example, NBC's "For Love or Money II" or ABC's "The Bachelorette," modeled after "The Bachelor," but overexposure can take away a show's unique or special quality. Too many repeat showings, called **encores,** can lessen viewer interest. WB calls its repeats of shows during the same week an **easy view** option, and in 2004, NBC presented its hit show "The Apprentice" twice in the same week, but overexposure is a risky business. The public quickly tires when offered too much of a good thing.

Rerunning and Repurposing

In the early days of television, few programs were rerun—for technical reasons. Videotape had not been invented, and film was considered much

the revenue from reruns, as described in the section on introducing a show in a quiet time.

When a repeat of an episode is scheduled, the cost of payments to performers and other guild members ($50,000–$75,000) is the only production expense. Although the value of the commercials is somewhat reduced because of the audience falloff in the summer and the diminished attraction of seeing an episode twice in the same season, the revenue on a reasonably popular program is more than enough to offset costs. Despite complaints of viewers and the frustration of some program and production executives, an annual cycle that incorporates a rerun of virtually every original episode remains a strong possibility. In the summer of 2004 CBS, for example, did very well with reruns of its successful shows.

It is true that a weekly series is physically exhausting for cast and staff. The hours are long, the pressure relentless, and the opportunity to unwind almost nonexistent. A break is necessary so that they do not kill themselves, or each other. Scoffers downplay the fatigue factor and point to the round-the-calendar schedules of daytime serials that have been produced without loss of life or audience over 4 decades. Even NBC's deceased programming genius, Brandon Tartikoff, stated: "If you can make 265 episodes each year of 'Days of Our Lives,' I've got to believe you can make 40 to 45 episodes of "Knots Landing"[9] (Figure 9.13).

As explained in Chapter 2, repurposing, the airing of a show on a different outlet shortly after its initial airing, became a significant scheduling tool, particularly with the proliferation of mergers that created a host of sister companies ready, willing, and able to repurpose. Thus, a show that airs on a Tuesday night on NBC can be repur-

Figure 9.13
For many years, Donna Mills starred in the nighttime soap "Knots Landing," where she delivered the famous line, "Let the second Mrs. Ewing give the third Mrs. Ewing some advice. The first Mrs. Ewing . . . doesn't go away." (Courtesy Donna Mills.)

posed on a Thursday night on Bravo or vice versa. PBS even engages in repurposing with the Latino drama "American Family" by licensing a secondary run to Telemundo.

Repurposing enables companies to get much more bang for their buck from individual episodes. It also enables different audiences to experience the same show. A niche audience here, a mainstream audience there: It all adds up to the benefit of a show's exposure.

Boosting the Audience in Sweep Periods

Although every day in television is important, some are more important than others. Four times a year for 30-day periods (February, May, July, and November), Nielsen conducts special **sweeps** of audience viewing habits in every market in the country. Although many programmers decry sweeps periods as outdated mechanisms, they are unlikely to go away. Sweeps monitoring is vital to the economic health of each station. This statistical data forms the basis of the advertising rates until the results of the next sweep are available. Programmers are under great pressure to build the highest possible ratings for each time period.

For many years, event miniseries delivered heavenly ratings during sweeps. An actor such as Richard Chamberlin was *the* king of sweeps. More recently, pop star Michael Jackson was the crowned king of sweeps programming. *Anything* dealing with Michael Jackson was viewed as surefire ratings gold. Finding a sweeps-worthy event such as the 200th episode of "ER" or the 300th episode of "Law & Order" weighs heavily on the minds of all programming executives. No one wants the affiliates to complain about sweeps programming that did not allow them to command viable advertising rates. Local news shows turn to exposing restaurants where cockroaches abound.

During the February 2004 sweeps, ABC's "Super Millionaire" hit ratings pay dirt on the first night, although it dropped afterward, not giving ABC the much-needed boost for which it had undoubtedly hoped.

It is getting harder to know what will deliver the numbers during sweeps, but the search continues unabashedly. Some turn to specials (awards shows tend to be fairly reliable bullets); others rely on highly rated regular programming, with just a few added weddings, pregnancies, same-sex kisses, and celebrity sightings.

It is proper during sweep periods for stations and networks to employ as many of the audience-building techniques described in this chapter as possible. The battle for viewers (and therefore dollars) is crucial, and spiking devices are a legitimate part of the competitive system.

Patience

Although many of the shows that became part of television history were slow starters that needed time to develop and to nurture a word-of-mouth campaign, patience has been in short supply in recent years. If a show does not connect quickly, programmers find it increasingly difficult to wait it out, hoping to prove that a programmer's instinct was on the money despite a slow start. The competition is too strong and the stakes are too high for top management, concerned with the bottom line, to wait "too long" for a turnaround. With mergers, companies are often run by individuals that are not primarily broadcasters who understand that some shows take time to build; their obligation is to the stockholders, and they do not have the patience or confidence to stay with a show until it finds its audience.

Slow starters such as the original "Dick Van Dyke Show," "Cheers," "Barney Miller," "Hill Street Blues," and "Everybody Loves Raymond" need time. Everyone agrees in theory that patience is needed when it comes to scheduling programming, everyone agrees pressure for the early dismissal of a show should be resisted, and everyone agrees that programmers will obtain a first look at a creator's next project if the current project is given a chance to develop. Still, it is hard for programmers and their bosses to avoid moving quickly if a show performs poorly at the start.

In the 2002–2003 season, Fox canceled its David E. Kelley series, "Girls Club," about women lawyers in San Francisco, after only two airings. In 2003–2004, CBS canceled Kelley's "The Brotherhood of Poland, New Hampshire," about three brothers, after four outings. Also in the 2003–2004 season,

NBC canceled "Coupling," the highly publicized British import seen as a possible replacement for "Friends," after only four airings. That same season, Fox canceled "Skin," Jerry Bruckheimer's look at the world of pornography, after three airings. These were only a few of the many series decapitated that season (Figure 9.14).

If you do not succeed right away in commercial television, chances are that the virtue of patience will not come to your show's rescue.

Cable, on the other hand, tends to be more patient. Having two primary sources of revenue—advertisers and subscribers—enables basic cable to hold off pressing the cancel button. A premium channel such as HBO can allow a show such as "Carnivale," which was not embraced by either critics or viewers, to run its course, which probably would not have been the case on commercial TV. Had "Lucky" been on commercial TV instead of FX, it probably would have been pulled without finishing a full season.

Series	Network Aired	No. Aired Episodes
"Skin"	Fox	3
"Coupling"	NBC	4
"Luis"	Fox	4
"The Brotherhood of Poland, NH"	CBS	5
"The Lyon's Den"	NBC	6
"A Minute with Stan Hooper"	Fox	6
"Karen Cisco"	ABC	7
"Tarzan"	WB	8
"The Mullets"	UPN	10
"Jake 2.0"	UPN	12

In this chapter, we examined the various scheduling strategies for television programming. In Chapter 10, you will learn about specific differences between scheduling for radio and scheduling for the Internet.

Figure 9.14
During the 2003–2004 season, several shows on commercial television were pulled before finishing a full season.

EXERCISES

1. Pick a night and a commercial network and examine that night's schedule. What changes would you make and why?

2. Pick a cable network; identify that network's targeted niche audience. What changes would you make in the schedule to strengthen that network's appeal?

3. What specific show that has been canceled do you think would have eventually found an audience if it had been allowed to grow?

4. What would you do to boost sweeps awareness for a particular show?

5. Describe a crossprogramming idea between two shows that you think would increase the ratings of both shows.

6. What would you do to energize PBS's schedule, both in children's and in prime-time programming?

7. Do you agree or disagree with Alan Wurtzel that 50% of households that will ever watch a program get hooked by one of the first two episodes? Why? Do you have a personal experience that supports or contradicts this position?

REFERENCES/NOTES

1. "Fox: No More Fall Launch Fray," *Broadcasting and Cable,* July 22, 1991, p. 15.

2. Ibid.

3. Ken Auletta. *Three Blind Mice* (New York: Random House, 1991), p. 93.

4. Joe Schlosser. "Reality Slugfest," *Broadcasting and Cable,* September 10, 2001, p. 16.

5. Bill Carter. "Record Ratings for Final Fling with 'Sex,'" *The New York Times,* February 25, 2004, p. B-6.

6. Paige Albiniak. "All Oscar All the Time," *Broadcasting and Cable,* February 16, 2004, p. 26.

7. Ibid.

8. Bill Carter. "Networks Play 'Who Wants to Exhaust a Franchise,'" *The New York Times,* July 7, 2003, p. C-1.

9. "The Sorry State of Network TV," *Los Angeles Times,* May 6, 1991, p. F-1.

10 Scheduling Strategies for Radio and the Internet

In this chapter you will learn about the following:

- The radio scheduling clock or wheel
- Different strategies for scheduling music on music format radio stations
- Approaches to scheduling news, contests, commercials, and deejay spots on radio
- The importance of dayparting in radio
- Strategies for launching new radio stations and formats
- The differences and similarities in scheduling commercial, satellite, and public radio
- The difficulty and lack of necessity for scheduling on the Internet
- Concerns for scheduling live or special content on the Internet
- Using traffic logs to determine Internet scheduling strategies

COMMERCIAL RADIO SCHEDULING

Radio, because it deals primarily with formats rather than individual programs, has an entirely different basis for scheduling than television. Terms such as tentpoling, hammocking, bridging, blunting, stacking, and stripping (all of which refer to the manipulation of individual programs) do not apply to most radio programming. Counterprogramming is inherent within the format; a country music radio station is always counterprogramming an album-oriented rock station.

All-talk formats use some of the television-oriented scheduling strategies because they tend to be composed of individual programs hosted by specific personalities. But even talk shows tend to be long (usually about 3 hours), so there is little need for considering the interrelationships among them.

The Clock

The main scheduling instrument of most commercial radio stations and some of the networks is referred to as a **clock.**

This is a circle that represents an hour broken down into segments. Stations generally program each hour similarly to enable audience members to know what they will hear at a certain time. For example, with an all-news station clock,

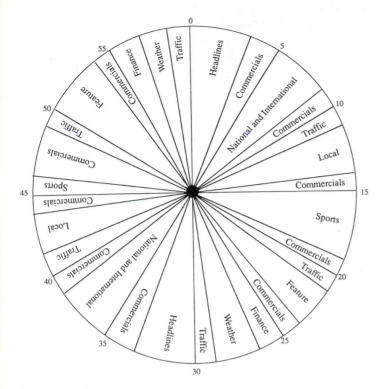

Figure 10.1
A chart of a radio station clock for an all-news station.

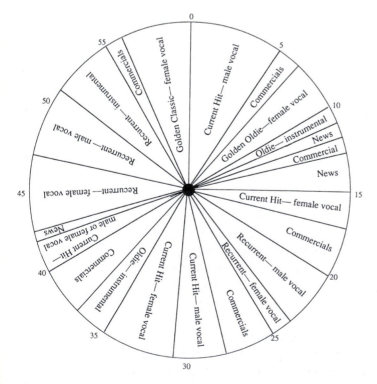

Figure 10.2
A chart of a music station clock.

listeners could depend on hearing traffic every 10 minutes and sports 15 minutes before and 15 minutes after the hour (Figure 10.1).

Music station clocks indicate the placement of news, commercials, and other verbal elements; they also usually indicate the types of music that will be played at various times (Figure 10.2). A great deal of thought and planning goes into the scheduling of music, both the songs to play and the order in which to play them.

Scheduling Music. A station that concentrates on current hits must constantly be on the lookout for music that has the potential to become popular. Program directors and disc jockeys receive copies of new releases from record companies, listen to them, and select for airing the ones they think their audience members will enjoy. Each format and, to some extent each station, has its own sound; as a result, program directors do not all choose the same selections.

To help confirm their decisions, program directors often consult the charts in trade magazines such as *Billboard* and *Radio & Records*. These list the top-selling songs in a variety of categories—country, electronic, pop, Latin, R&B/hip-hop, independent, etc. However, popularity of a record is often a result of its airplay. Airplay leads to sales and listings in the trades; these, in turn, lead to more airplay.

Not all songs played on the radio are current hits. Many are songs from the past that can be roughly characterized as follows:

- **Oldies**—Music from 30 or 40 years ago. If the song was once in the Top 10 and sold about a million copies, it is called a "golden oldie;" if it was No. 1 and sold several million copies, it is "supergold."

- **Classics**—Music from 10 or 20 years ago. These, too, can be golden or supergold.
- **Recurrents**—Music that is no longer current but is not yet considered old.

A note of caution: These terms are not standardized within the industry. Some programmers consider anything more than 3 years old to be an oldie. At some stations, a recurrent is a fading hit; at others, it is music at least 2 years old. Also, the terms differ. For example, supergold may be referred to as "power gold." Mike O'Reilly, program director at WPDC in Elizabethtown, Pennsylvania, divides his music into five groupings—new, familiar, recent, gold, and oldies. Other program directors have their own designations.

A radio station programmer must decide what proportion of current hits, recurrents, classics, and oldies to play. Sometimes the format decides this. An oldies format, for example will consist of only music old enough to qualify. But many formats have a variety of music from different periods.

Some stations use the charts to determine not when they should be playing something but rather when they should not be playing it. Stations trying to break new hits want to air songs before they hit the charts. Some stations stop playing music when it makes the charts and everyone else starts playing it. Other stations want to start playing music as it is falling off the charts. For some segments of the radio audience, familiarity is important.

There is no magic formula for deciding how many songs of different ages and feels to play. The decision is an intuitive one made by the programmer. However, programming consultants, such as Guy Zapoleon of Zapoleon Media Strategies, warn that programming directors, especially in the Top 40

format, should take the long view toward their music mix decisions lest they find themselves in a bind later in the game. Zapoleon wrote the following about the Top 40 format in the early 2000s:

Because Top 40 owners and programmers are steering their stations more and more rhythmic to go where they think music is heading, the national charts, which are already extremely rhythmic, will get more and more rhythmic . . . What we have here is a vicious cycle *that will cause mainstream Top 40 to stop being a variety format.* Rock and pop songs will have a harder and harder time finding a foothold on these increasingly rhythmic radio stations, and so there will be less rock and pop hits. Because of this, and because a lot of the pop rock and pop isn't selling, the labels will put out less rock and pop songs. But this music is so very important to mainstream Top 40 format to hold it together. If this trend toward more and more rhythm continues, then we're back to the doldrums of 1992–94 when we lost 500 Top 40 radio stations.[1]

Other factors go into the makeup of a wheel. Many stations like to alternate male and female vocalists or bands and solo artists. Others take into account the overall intensity of the music, perhaps making sure that each quarter hour contains at least one soft song. Others group songs by the nature of their lyrics.

Thought must also be given to the transition from one piece of music to another. If a fast song immediately follows a slow song, the result can be jarring. Usually a station will program a jingle or some commercials between the two. The same is true when going from soft music to loud music or sometimes from a minor key to a major key.

All of these scheduling strategies are considered by stations programming music and by networks or syndication companies that supply music services. Knowledge of these elements can make music programming more successful, but, as with television, the best strategies usually arise from a competent programmer's instincts.

Scheduling Other Program Elements. Aspects of programming other than music must also be considered in the makeup of a clock. The placement of news, weather, traffic, sports, contests, and even commercials can be important. People tend to be more aware of the time placements of these items than they are of the subtleties of music positioning. They are much more likely to know that they can tune in 5 minutes after the hour to hear the latest sports scores than they are to realize that a station never plays more than two female vocal selections in a row.

All-news stations adhere strictly to their clock because listeners tend to tune in and tune out. If people caught in traffic know that a particular station broadcasts traffic reports 15 minutes, 30 minutes, and 45 minutes after the hour, they are likely to switch to the station at one of those times for the update. Music-oriented stations often have newsbreaks on the hour or half hour, and people become accustomed to tuning in at that time if they want to catch up on the day's events. A station that programs to people whose overriding interest is music can arrange its breaks so that they do not come at the hour or half hour—that way, it can attract listeners who push their radio buttons as soon as the news comes on another station. Other stations vary the clock over the course of the day. They program news in the morning when it seems to matter and do not program news for the rest of the day.

The number of commercials, their frequency, and their position in the clock are all important. Stations that program fewer overall commercials than the competition are likely to attract listeners. However, if they cannot sell their fewer commercials at a higher price, they may not be able to balance the budget. For this reason, the number of commercials often becomes more of a sales and management decision than a programming one. Frequent commercial breaks seem less jarring on stations with talk formats than on those with music formats. Music stations often try to hold their audience members through a commercial break with a "tease"—an announcement of a great new hit or contest coming up right after these announcements.

Radio stations often tout commercial-free periods where they play straight music for 20 or 30 minutes or even an hour. Obviously, in these cases the normal clock changes. Again, such a practice might be good for the audience but not for the bottom line. A programmer who proposes this idea should have in mind a method for recovering the lost revenue.

The placement of commercials within the clock is also important. If your station has a format similar to that of another station in town, it is wise to schedule your commercial breaks at a time different from the competing station. In that way, you catch the button pushers searching for something other than commercials. This means the competing station will be programming music over your commercials and may grab your listeners. Such is the gamesmanship of radio scheduling strategies.

The disc jockey is another element that figures into the clock. If the disc jockey is popular and is the main element attracting listeners to the station, then more time should be allowed within the hour for comments from the deejay. Often this chatter involves contests that are likely to intrigue a substantial portion of the listening audience and that need time for instruction and execution. Many early morning shows have little music and concentrate on the antics of the host. If the deejay is just a facilitator of transitions from one element of programming to another, however, the clock should be more tightly packed.

Variations in Clocks. Nothing is sacred about a clock. It can be fine-tuned as much as necessary to develop the best results. However, refining it too much and too often shows a lack of patience and has the disadvantages already mentioned in regard to patience and television programming. Fiddling with the wheel without giving it a chance to find its audience is not advisable.

Some stations place almost fanatical requirements on adhering to the clock—usually to keep otherwise free-wheeling disc jockeys in line. Some program directors list the specific songs that should be played throughout the entire day, giving the deejay no flexibility. Others, however, use the clock as a guideline that can be ignored for numerous reasons—several current hits are longer than the average musical selections and will absorb more space on the clock; some major news event has occurred and needs to be updated frequently; the winner of a contest is an intriguing personality who should be interviewed at length.

Networks with music formats have clocks, just as stations do. But many networks and almost all syndicators simply supply material for stations to use when they wish. In these cases, the concept of clock does not apply.

Dayparting

One radio scheduling strategy that radio shares with television is that of dayparting. People's activities, moods, rhythms, and uses of radio change greatly over the course of a day. Radio must take people's biological clocks into account to enable programming to progress in a consistent, successful manner.

Early in the morning, people want to know what has been happening (or not happening) overnight. Many listeners wake up to clock radios, so stations that feature primarily music are likely to have more news and information segments in the morning than at other times of day. Early morning disc jockeys are more talkative than their afternoon counterparts. All-news stations have more format competition in the morning than during other periods.

As the day wears on, people engage in other activities (caring for children, driving the car to a sales meeting, etc.), and radio becomes a background to these activities. Music becomes more predominant and talk becomes less predominant on many radio stations. Stations with news, talk, or both formats slide into feature-type material or call-in programs.

In the midafternoon, when students are out of school, teen-oriented radio stations pick up the pace and tempo of the music, often featuring their most popular disc jockeys in the late afternoon.

As people leave work and begin the commute home, radio once again gives them information, but usually in a gentler way than in the morning. People are heading home to relax and do not need the up-to-date facts that they might need before the workday. Some stations will play more soothing music at rush hour than at other times of day to help people relax as they head home.

In the evening, radio is used primarily as background to accompany reading, studying, or other activities. The use of radio is greater by young people than by older audience members, who are more likely to be tuned to television. Some of radio's most exciting and outlandish moments occur late at night when the audience is primarily young adults receptive to innovation. Many recording groups make several versions of their song, some longer than others and some containing more borderline language than others. Late at night, the longer, racier cuts of music are likely to be played.

Some stations change their formats completely at certain times of the day or week, playing music that they would not play at any other time. KBIG 104.3 FM in Los Angeles, for example, features all-disco music Saturday nights and during the lunch hour weekdays. The station's normal format features soft hits from the 1980s and 1990s and select current hits already well worn by Top 40 stations. Other stations take time to focus on a certain segment of their playlist. WXRT in Chicago, for example, plays a "Flashback" show Saturday morning that features songs from a specific year. KROQ, Los Angeles's well-known alternative rock station, has a "Flashback Lunch" hour, featuring songs from a decade or more ago—songs that occasionally get regular airplay as oldies in its lineup.

A radio programmer must take these daypart characteristics into account and merge them, along with format and wheel considerations, into the best possible scheduling strategies.

Launching

Just like when television launches new programming, radio weighs important strategic considerations when it changes format. The new format must be launched so that a new potential audi-ence is made aware of the station. This usually involves using media other than radio to get the message across. Often a station that is changing format will change call letters. It is better to sound like the new guy in town that to have the image of an easy listening format lingering over a contemporary hit format. Besides, the old call letters may not be appropriate. WROC would be negative for a country station. A bus billboard or TV commercial that announces a new station with a new format is often effective.

All-talk stations launch individual hosts or programs and use some of the more traditional TV-type launching techniques. Radio does not deal in seasons; if launches are necessary, they are made when the occasion arises and not necessarily in the fall or any other particular time of year.

SATELLITE RADIO SCHEDULING

Satellite radio, as a nationwide subscription service, has a different set of facts affecting its scheduling decisions. With more than 100 channels offering everything from dozens of format music stations to talk and radio—all on the same service—satellite stations only compete with one another. That competition is relatively meaningless unless users switch from listening to their satellite transmissions to terrestrial radio. Even then, satellite radio companies feel no pain when listeners turn to terrestrial radio for the local touch that their national signals cannot provide—as long as the subscription continues.

Nonetheless, satellite radio tries to make its service as valuable to its subscribers as possible within its inherent limitations. Dayparting, for example, is hard to accomplish with a single signal reaching across several time zones. Even if satellite radio arranged its schedule to favor one time zone, it would not want to broadly advertise this, lest it seem to be leaving other listeners on the sidelines. Nonetheless, XM Radio lists its many special and live broadcasts by Eastern Standard Time, although many extend into the night and morning, making them appeal to earlier time zones in the West (Figure 10.3).

Performer	Eastern Standard Time
Ozomatli	9:00 P.M.
The Mavericks	10:00 P.M.
Patty Griffin	11:00 P.M.
Old 97s	12:00 A.M.
Los Lobos	1:00 A.M.

Figure 10.3 *XM Radio's channel XM 12 (X Country) featured live coverage from the South by Southwest convention March 20, 2004. Times for various performances are listed by XM Radio by Eastern Standard Time and stretch into the morning.*

PUBLIC RADIO SCHEDULING

Programming strategies are not as important within public broadcasting as they are in commercial. As NPR's Bill Buzenberg put it, "Public broadcasting needs to think first about content and less about format and strategies. That's one big way that we differ from commercial broadcasting." But public broadcasting finds some of the typical programming strategies useful.

PRI and NPR affiliates are free to select the network programs they want and intermix them however they wish with locally produced material. Some stations, such as Pasadena, California's KPCC, even choose to broadcast call-in shows, such as NPR's "Talk of the Nation" out of their timeslot—thus not allowing local listeners the opportunity to participate in the program broadcast live hours before.

Despite such strident station autonomy, both NPR and PRI program with dayparting in mind and make suggestions to stations as to when certain programs would play best. NPR's "Morning Edition," for example, would sound ridiculous if it aired at 3:00 P.M. Likewise, most stations that program NPR's evening newscast "All Things Considered" do so in the early evening hours when people are likely to be in their cars commuting home.

NPR presents news differently in the morning than in the evening because people are in a hurry in the morning. "Morning Edition" is more modular than "All Things Considered," and "Day to Day" is less topical and can therefore be scheduled with more flexibility (Figure 10.4). In the morning, no story lasts longer than 8 minutes; in the evening, a single story can occupy as much as 20 minutes—both numbers unheard of by commercial standards.

Both NPR and PRI offer many news-related shows that can be scheduled anytime during the day. These shows attempt to steer away from topics on which significant developments or changes could occur during the day, making the shows seem stale when they air on local stations that have them pro-

Figure 10.4 *NPR's "Day to Day" with Alex Chadwick is recorded in NPR's newest studios in Culver City, California.*

Figure 10.5

PRI suggests times for stations to air Garrison Keillor, but stations can air his program anytime they like without sanction. (Courtesy American Public Radio/Fred Petters.)

aired outside of work hours, sometimes even suggesting the timeslot they would most prefer, such as Saturday nights and Sunday mornings for Garrison Keillor's "Prairie Home Companion," but individual stations are not obliged to conform (Figure 10.5).

Clocks are also important for network public radio programs that may be aired live because stations must know the exact times that they can break in for local news or announcements. Provisions must be made so that stations that do not wish to program local items need not do so. NPR's "All Things Considered" handles this problem by building natural breaks into some stories. For example, it may program a 5-minute story that could conclude at the end of 3 minutes. Those stations wishing to make local announcements can cut off the story after 3 minutes and return to "All Things Considered" 2 minutes later. Other stations let the story run for 5 minutes. NPR also uses short musical interludes called **zippers** that can be played in their entirety by some stations and cut away by others.

Stations are eclectic in their programming philosophies. Some, particularly those that are public-affairs oriented, schedule similar to television in that they air individual programs and pay attention to audience flow from one

grammed in the evening rather than in the daytime, when they were originally produced. PRI's "To the Point," for example, usually focuses on in-depth discussion and analysis of events that occurred a day or two previously. NPR's "Day to Day" tends to provide general background on current events, cover cultural news, and offer commentary.

Public radio is also home to many entertainment programs, some based on current events, others not. PRI and NPR suggest that these programs be

program to another (Figure 10.6). Others, mainly the ones that emphasize music, program more like commercial radio in that they use clocks. However, many of public radio's musical selections, especially classical music, are so long that the clock has few entries on it.

INTERNET SCHEDULING

Is there such a thing as scheduling in the amorphous, interactive, and global environment of the Internet? Many websites with tie-ins to brick-and-mortar entities may vary their content to correspond to current products or broadcasts, although the different time zones and schedules of local brick-and-mortar outlets makes this process complicated. News websites will want to be sure their content is up to date at all times, and web loggers will want to add content to their sites at regular intervals so that the viewers of their sites can develop a habit of coming back.

According to a March 2004 study by the Pew Internet & American Life Project, somewhere between 2 and 7% of Internet users maintain personal blogs. Of those, only 10% update their sites on a daily basis. Most update weekly or even more infrequently. However, visitors to blogs often leave their own comments or responses to the original content. Well-traveled blogs may induce active communication not only between the blogger and the visitors but also among visitors, which can lead to more frequent and dynamic content updating.[2] It may, however, take time and effort to develop a following of regular readers for a blog. Many blogs start and just as quickly end, when bloggers lose patience with their missives heading out into cyberspace to be confronted with a deafening silence. Unable to answer the question of whether a tree

Mountain Standard Time	Program
3:00–7:00 A.M.	Morning Edition
7:00–7:10 A.M.	NPR News/Montana Morning News
7:10–7:33 A.M.	Morning Edition
7:33–7:35 A.M.	Montana Morning News
7:35–8:10 A.M.	Morning Edition/NPR News/Montana Morning News
8:10–10:00 A.M.	Morning Classics
10:00–10:10 A.M.	Stardate/Ask Dr. Science/University and Community Activities
10:10–11:59 A.M.	Morning Freeforms/Writer's Almanac
12:00–12:30 P.M.	BBC World Service
12:30–1:05 P.M.	Chrysti the Wordsmith/Listener's Bookstall/Performing Arts Calendar/University and Community Activities/Alternative Sources
1:05–2:00 P.M.	Dancing with Tradition
2:00–4:00 P.M.	Performance Today
4:00–5:00 P.M.	Pea Green Boat/ Everyday Science
5:00–5:30 P.M.	All Things Considered
5:30–6:00 P.M.	Montana Evening Edition/Native News
6:00–7:30 P.M.	All Things Considered/Earth and Sky
7:30–8:30 P.M.	This American Life
8:30–9:30 P.M.	Selected Shorts
9:30–10:00 P.M.	Making Contact
10:00–11:00 P.M.	In Other Words
11:00–2:00 P.M.	Night Train
2:00–3:00 P.M.	BBC World Service

that falls in the forest makes a sound if no one is there to hear, they put down their axes. So, on a more personal level, as with television and radio, patience—or a lack thereof—can become an issue.

Some websites feature live chats with celebrities, politicians, or experts in which these people answer questions posed by a live Internet audience. These chats must be scheduled to optimize

Figure 10.6
Montana Public Radio's Wednesday Schedule. (http://www.mtpr.net/programs/. Accessed March 7, 2004.)

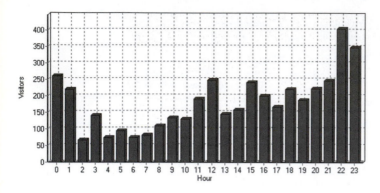

Figure 10.7
This traffic chart for a university club's website shows that the high traffic periods are late at night. If the club wanted to sponsor a special web event, it would probably want to schedule it during the peak hours.

access for the interested audience. But transcripts are usually posted of the chats, allowing interested parties to access them any time after the chat even if it does not allow them to participate and ask questions. These chats are not usually a free-for-all anyway but are moderated by a screener who selects questions from the Internet audience to pose to the personality. Often the personality is not even at a computer. Instead, questions may be relayed over the phone by the moderator; the responses are then transcribed and posted in the chat by a typist.

Looking at the statistics of visitors to websites, most webmasters can see that their sites have general patterns of high and low traffic periods. These statistics may help to determine times when special or live content would be best to incorporate into the site. Operators of

Internet radio stations might also be able to analyze this usage information to strengthen content or to beef up programming in lower traffic periods to build audiences (Figure 10.7).

The "scheduling" of Internet content mostly is determined by users of the Internet searching for the content they wish to consume whenever they are hungry for it. If the content involves other users, however, as in a chat room, there may be peak and lull times. A night owl in the United States who wants to engage in a little Internet chat may have to browse to a chat room in the Philippines, for example, to find numerous available chatters.

One Internet characteristic that may be tangentially related to the concept of scheduling is the choices that Internet content developers make about which content they feature in "prime" spots on their sites' home pages and which they bury several clicks from the home page in "nonprime" locations.

After all the development, testing, strategizing, and scheduling is completed, there remains the question—did it work? This brings us to the scorekeepers: Who are they? How do they get their numbers? How accurate are these? Chapter 11 deals with program evaluation.

EXERCISES

1. Chart an hour of content on a local popular music radio station, characterizing the types of songs, commercial breaks, promotional spots, and deejay breaks that occur. Chart another hour and compare the results between the two hours. If there are significant deviations, do these seem to occur for some reason—such as to play up a popular deejay or artist?

2. Chart an hour of content on a local radio station whose format most closely resembles the first station you charted. Do there appear to be competitive programming strategies between the two stations? How could these strategies be improved?

3. Sample several radio stations for a half hour each, four times throughout the day, noting differences in content during the morning rush hour, midday, evening rush hour, and night. How could these approaches be improved to attract more listeners or keep listeners listening longer?

4. Visit a blog indexing site, such as Blogger.com or Weblogs.com, to set up and view your own or others' blogs. After a month of visiting and posting to your own blog, analyze the experience and your reaction to it. Were you able to work blogging into your personal schedule? Were the schedules of the blogs of others able to keep your interest? What did you find frustrating and interesting in the experience?

REFERENCES/NOTES

1. Guy Zapoleon "Hit Radio—One Size Doesn't Fit All," http://www.zapoleon.com/zms/kbase.asp?article_id=54. Accessed March 5, 2004.

2. Anick Jesdanun. "Study: Blogging Still Infrequent," http://www.pcmag.com/article2/0,1759,1541128,00.asp. Accessed March 7, 2004.

11   Program Evaluation

In this chapter you will learn about the following:

- The purpose and uses of programming evaluation
- The history of metering technologies and strategies
- The two main players in the ratings game: Nielsen and Arbitron
- Current practices in metering audiences
- Ways data is parsed out to represent different audience behaviors
- Special measures taken to capture underrepresented populations
- How the sweeps rating periods are used—and abused
- New metering technologies in development and deployment
- How programmers use and are affected by ratings
- Longstanding concerns about and investigations into ratings accuracy

Theoretically, media programming could be evaluated any number of ways—the number of fan letters received, the artistic merit of the programs as rated by critics, the social good accomplished by airing the material, etc. Sometimes one or more of these methods is used, depending on the goal of the program (see Chapter 6). But the most prevalent form of evaluation is body count: how many and who. The procedure involved in counting the number of people or households watching, listening to, or interacting with a particular program is called **audience measurement.** The common term used to refer to the numbers obtained through audience measurement is "ratings."

Advertising fees, which provide revenue for TV, radio, and the Internet, are based on these audience measurements and ratings statistics. Over the years, buyers and sellers have agreed upon certain scorekeepers whom they believe are able to estimate audience sizes and demographics with reasonable accuracy. The most prominent of these systems are described in this chapter.

Because a programmer's job is to attract audiences that will produce a profit for the company, he or she should know who is doing the counting and how the numbers are calculated. Sometimes programming executives feel uncomfortable with the mathematical orientation of research. But if they do not understand the underpinnings of ratings, they may find that people in the research department will be making decisions that should be the domain of programming.

The purpose of this chapter is to give a basic overview of audience measurement so that you understand how it can (and should) be used. The chapter avoids the complex mathematics involved with the statistical computations. It offers guidelines that allow you to understand the basic strengths and weaknesses of the ratings process and enable you to communicate effectively with researchers.

TELEVISION

Nielsen is the primary service used to compile ratings information for

Figure 11.1
This 1949 audimeter is one of the first that could be operated without a technician's assistance. People in the survey could remove a tape and mail it to Nielsen. (Courtesy Nielsen Media Research.)

commercial and cable television. Until 1993, Arbitron also compiled television ratings (primarily for stations), but it now only reports on radio; Arbitron is nevertheless working with Nielsen to perfect a portable and improved **people meter** for television. In addition to Nielsen and Arbitron, many other specialized audience research firms conduct in-depth research or use methodology different from that of Nielsen or Arbitron. These firms include Magna Global, Griffin Publishing, Paragon Research, or Strategy Research. Strategy Research, for example, specializes in conducting face-to-face interviews to provide data concerning TV viewing in families where only Spanish is spoken.

Nielsen

The leader in audience research, Nielsen, which boasts divisions and

subdivisions that have countless ways to gauge audience size, dates back to 1923, long before the days of television audience research. A.C. Nielsen, Sr.'s main customer during the early days of his company was the drugstore industry. He asked several drugstores to save their invoices; then his company analyzed the invoices and sold the information to drug manufacturers so that they could predict future sales.

Meter History and Development. In 1936, Nielsen bought a crude machine called an **audimeter** from two MIT professors. This device consisted of a moving roll of punched paper tape that could be attached to a radio so that it would record when the radio was turned on and to which station it was tuned. Nielsen perfected this device and, in 1942, started using it to measure radio program audiences. The equipment was so complicated that specially trained technicians had to visit each of the the 1000 homes where Nielsen had placed the audimeter at least once a month to take off the old tape and put on a new one. But Nielsen was able to analyze this information and sell it to stations, advertisers, and others interested in knowing how many people were listening to particular radio programs (Figure 11.1).

Both Nielsen and the audimeter have changed greatly over the years. The company started measuring TV in 1950 and then in 1964 dropped radio because the audimeter was not suitable to handle the programming changes, mobility, and audience fragmentation that radio was undergoing. Nielsen now handles only television.

The audimeter went through many modifications to make it more user friendly, allowing ordinary mortals, rather than only trained technicians, to change the tape. Eventually the device was connected directly through phone lines to the computers in Nielsen's Florida office. The revised device recorded when the TV set was turned on or off and what channels it was tuned to or switched to while it was on.

With the improvements, the audimeter underwent several name changes, for example, the "instantaneous audimeter," the "storage instantaneous audimeter," and eventually the "recordimeter." Today, it is generally called the "set-tuning meter." It measures local markets during data-collection sweeps and is used with written **diaries** that participants in the rating process are asked to fill out by hand, which augment and are compared with automatically collected data. These diaries indicate which members of the family are watching which programs. They also provide demographic information, such as age and sex, for the viewers of various programs.

In the late 1980s, Nielsen introduced a device called a people meter (Figure 11.2). In 1987, it replaced all its audimeters measuring national prime-time programming with people meters, and it has gradually introduced people meters for calculations in large cities. For example, Boston converted to people meters in 2002. But because of the expense involved in changing meters, most local markets are still measured by set-tuning meters and diaries.

For a people meter, each person in the family has a special button on a remote control device that he or she must push periodically while watching TV. (Buttons are also available for visitors.) When the set is turned on, all people watching should push their remote buttons. Anyone new entering the room to watch should push the appropriate button. When a person stops watching, he or she should turn off the button. In this way, information is gathered not only about when the TV is on and what channel it is tuned to but also

about who is watching. In other words, the people meter gathers the information previously collected by both the audimeter and the diary. In the middle of the night, the data recorded by the people meter is automatically sent over phone lines to Nielsen's main computer.

There is a great deal of controversy involving the switch to people meters from the combination of diaries and settuning meters. Under pressure, in the spring of 2004, Nielsen postponed its plan to replace diaries for sweeps reporting with people meters in New York, the largest market in the country, because of concerns that people meters contain flaws that would make the gathering of data for African-Americans and Latinos increasingly vulnerable. Although Nielsen argued that the people meters would produce better data for these minorities, concerned citizens and the Fox network feared that the use of people meters in large local markets might undercount as much as 25% of young and minority viewers, particularly if the meters did not come with detailed instructions. Test usage of the people meters produced marked drops in ratings for some programs traditionally highly rated in the minority

Figure 11.2
An early Nielsen people meter. (Courtesy Nielsen Media Research.)

population under the old audimeter. UPN's prime-time show "One On One," for example, saw its numbers drop 62%, and ABC's "My Wife and Kids" fell 27%. These dramatic shifts and the ensuing outcry from the affected networks prompted postponement of the transition to the people meter, although Nielsen pointed out that minorities did not simply disappear from ratings "universe"; there were ratings increases for some minorities on some cable networks.[1]

Sampling Size: National, Local, and Syndication. How are people selected to participate in the Nielsen surveys? Although soliciting volunteers would probably produce participants who would be motivated to be thorough in their usage of the ratings technology and diaries, Nielsen does not accept volunteers, fearing that volunteers might not accurately represent typical television viewers. Instead, it chooses households through random sampling. Theoretically, almost anyone who can receive a particular TV program or service has a chance to be selected. Understandably, people who work in the TV industry, such as station and network programmers, are not allowed to participate.

National ratings numbers provide information about the country as a whole, and local numbers refer to viewership in a specific market. Both measurements are important. Networks and national advertisers care about the national numbers, and individual markets and local advertisers need to know how they are performing in relation to the country as a whole and in relation to other local markets.

For measurement of national program sources, such as commercial broadcast networks, cable networks, Spanish-language networks, and national syndicators, the sample might include almost

any place with a TV set. For years, only residential homes were included, but objections arose in the late 1980s concerning viewers who did not have a chance to be in the sample because they were in college dorms, bars, hotels, hospitals, and the like. As a result, Nielsen began to extend its sample base beyond homes.

For local measurement, the sample potentially includes all places with TV sets in the particular market of the TV station. Nielsen divides the country into 210 **designated market areas (DMAs)** to find samples for particular geographic areas. DMAs are nonoverlapping areas where people generally have access to the same stations. Generally they are cities, such as Boston, Cincinnati, and Salt Lake City, but sometimes they are several cities close together, such as Albany-Schenectady-Troy, New York.

In each local market, 400 to 500 households are given set-tuning meters, which are attached to television sets; these meters are different from the people meters used in the national samples, and one household or location cannot be included both in the local sample and the national sample. During sweeps, in addition to the set boxes, participants in the 210 local markets are given diaries to detail their television-watching habits.

Where the sample universe for national programming includes people across the nation, and the sample for local programming consists of only local participants, the sample universe for a syndicated show, naturally, is limited to all places with TV sets in markets where the syndicated program is airing.

For its national sample, Nielsen selects 5100 households (averaging about 13,000 individuals total) out of a total population of 108.4 million television dwellings, which makes someone's chances of becoming part of a Nielsen household extremely remote (about 1 in 21,255).

But Nielsen tries to make these 5100 dwellings in the national sample as representative of the total United States public as it can. The goal is to have the sample mirror the interests and demographic characteristics of the total population. To do this, Nielsen attempts to locate every housing unit in the country. It mostly uses readily available government census data to find households, but surveyors employed by Nielsen have found living quarters in railway cars, beer trucks, trees, and caves, all equipped with TV sets.

Once all the nation's housing units are uncovered, they are symbolically placed in a large hat from which 5100 are chosen. Actually, a computer program randomly selects the sample group so that each location has an equal chance of being selected. The computer program ensures that no more than one housing unit per block is chosen. To do so would introduce bias; television usage in two homes in one block would be similar because of factors such as TV reception and the presence of cable TV.

Once a sample member has agreed to participate, Nielsen sends a field representative to the home (or apartment, dorm room, or other domicile) for training.

People participating as part of the Nielsen sample receive a small token payment. Nielsen found that paying people makes them feel obligated and that they therefore perform their duties (pushing their buttons and filling out their diaries) more faithfully.

Calculations. Once the Nielsen computer has gathered all of the data from all of the people meters, set-tuning meters, and diaries, it undertakes the calculations that result in audience measurement data. A human looks over the computer's "shoulder" as the data comes in to check for obvious accuracy problems. If, for example, a people meter reported that someone watched TV for 26 hours in 1 day, something is awry. Such data is unusable, and a field representative is dispatched to the home to check the health of the people meter.

The national count consists of tabulating viewership in 31-second intervals. A viewer is counted as watching a show if he or she watches for 31 seconds at a time. Thus, someone watching 31 seconds of a show on NBC will give NBC credit for 1 minute because 31 seconds is the greater part of 1 minute. If the viewer then switches to CBS and watches for at least 31 seconds, CBS will get credit for 1 minute. The minutes are then tallied to provide the total count.

The local count operates on a 15-minute cycle instead of a 1-minute cycle; a viewer must thus watch more than half of the 15 minutes to be counted as a viewer.

During sweeps, a combination of results from set boxes and diaries is used to determine ratings numbers.

Ratings, Shares, and Cumes. The statistics most important to television programming executives are ratings, **shares,** and, increasingly, **cumes.**

A rating is simply the percentage of households tuned to a particular program out of all the TV households in that universe. The universe for all network shows is all households in the United States. For mathematical simplicity, assume there are 10,000 households in the United States. If 2000 of them are watching a show on NBC, the rating for that show is 20 (2000/10,000 = 2/10 = 0.2, or 20%). If 1500 are

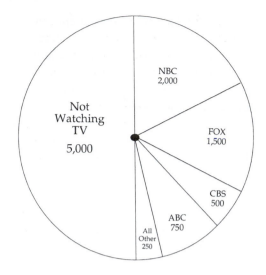

Figure 11.3

A pie chart showing ratings based on 10,000 homes.

watch different programs on different TVs and people watch more TV outside of their homes. With the people meter, Nielsen can easily break down the data for individuals rather than households. That is the current trend because individual viewing is considered more important to advertisers and networks than household viewing.

With the rating there is the share. A share is the percentage of households viewing a particular show measured against all households that have their sets on at that time. So if, out of 10,000 homes owning TVs, only 5000 of them have sets turned on, then 2000 of those watching a particular program would give that program a share of 40 (a share most programmers would be thrilled to have in a time of declining ratings and shares).

If out of the 5100 Nielsen sample homes only 2550 of them are watching TV, then 2550 is used as the base for determining the share. For a program to have a share of 50, 1275 of the homes would have to be watching that program (1275/2550 = 0.50, or 50%). That same program would have a rating of 25 (1275/5100 = 0.25, or 25%) (Figure 11.4).

Shares, like ratings, are starting to be reported in terms of people rather than households. When shares are reported for households, they sometimes add up to more than 100% because of homes that have more than one TV set.

Programmers sometimes also use HUT or PUT levels. This is simply the percentage of homes that turn the TV set on to anything or the percentage of people who watch TV. When HUT and PUT levels go down, everyone in the business experiences the jitters because most shares and ratings (and hence dollars of income) go down, too.

Another of the many statistics used in audience measurement is the cume. This term is short for "cumulative" and refers to the total audience impressions. For

watching a show on Fox, that rating is 15 (Figure 11.3).

As you know, there are not 10,000 households in the United States; there are 108.4 million, and almost 100% of them have TVs. If the NBC show has a rating of 20, that means 21.68 million households are watching. One rating point is worth 1.084 million homes (1% of 108.4 million homes), thus 20 × 1,084,000 equals 21,680,000.

Historically, ratings have been tied to households. Today, when ratings are reported, they usually refer to the number of households with a TV set tuned to the program. But TV viewing is becoming more of an individual activity as people within the same household

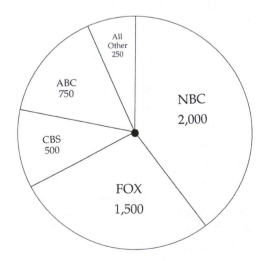

Figure 11.4

A theoretical distribution of shares using the same numbers as in Figure 11.3.

example, some syndicated shows run once during the week and once on the weekend. The production company combines the numbers from the two showings and sells a cume audience to the advertisers.

As the viewership for television continues to fragment, emphasis on cume totals has intensified. This is especially true for cable television. Cable's niche programming ratings and shares are typically smaller than the ratings and shares for commercial television's general audience fare, so cable stations have to find ways to quantify strengths (and weaknesses) for advertisers.

Because a cume measures the number of different people who watch a channel or program over time, a cume can show differentiation between two channels, both of which have only a 2 rating at a specific time. Advertisers are particularly interested in cumes because they often place their ads on cable channels several times during one day. For example, a perfume manufacturer might have an ad run at 7:00 P.M., 7:35 P.M., 8:10 P.M., and 8:40 P.M. and want to know how many different people were exposed to that commercial. Channels likely to have short-term viewing, such as CNN and The Weather Channel, particularly like to refer to their cumes, showing that although the number of their viewers may not be impressive at one time, over any period large numbers of viewers drop in and become available for advertisers' messages.

The numbers most important to most programming executives are the demographics. High ratings, shares, and cumes are good, but these numbers mean little if the people watching the programs, no matter how many, are not the people advertisers want to target. A young demographic is desired. The emphasis placed on demographics cannot be overstated. Media observer Jonathan Dee reported that "People over the age of 50 account for half of all the discretionary spending in the United States" but they account for less than 10% of the advertising money spent. Advertisers surmise (and back up with solid research—and common sense) that as young people grow into older people they usually carry the spending habits and brand loyalties from youth into their more affluent adult lives, where they are less likely to be "taught new tricks" or swayed from their beaten path by new advertising. Advertisers, therefore, want to strike while the iron is still hot.[2]

Reports. From the data collected and calculated by the computer, Nielsen publishes rating reports. So-called fast nationals, which provide next-day data about the top 56 markets, are available around 10:30 A.M. Eastern Standard Time. These fast nationals give a good indication of what the full national ratings will be when they are released several hours later, although they can sometimes be misleading. Some research analysts select a representative city from the 56 cities to predict what the rest of the country will do, as opposed to embracing the fast national numbers as a whole, but the fast nationals come out first and are usually the numbers executives seize upon.

Cable ratings, which Nielsen began tracking as far back as 1972, used to take longer to be tabulated. Today, they are available daily, although in 2004 no fast nationals were available for cable. As cable increases its dominance, it becomes essential for commercial television executives to be able to compare and contrast cable ratings with broadcast television ratings quickly and easily. Some executives long for the day that both sets of ratings will be reported together rather than separately.

The reports dealing with national TV are referred to as the **Nielsen Television Index** (**NTI,** Figure 11.5). The

NIELSEN HOMEVIDEO INDEX
CABLE NETWORKS WEEKLY PROGRAM RANKINGS FOR WEEK OF: 04/26/2004-05/02/2004
MONDAY-SATURDAY 6:00AM-6:00A, SUNDAY 6AM-3AM
RANKED BY HOUSEHOLD AUDIENCE

(NOTE:When comparing a cable network's ratings to another cable network or to a broadcast
   network, use the "Total U.S. Rating.")

BASIC CABLE

RANK	PROGRAM NAME	NET	DAY / TIME	DUR	HOUSEHOLD AA(000)	HOUSEHOLD US AA 3/6	HOUSEHOLD CVG AA 3/6	PERSONS 2+ AA(000)
1	WWE ENTERTAINMENT (WWE RAW ZONE)	SPIKE	MON 10:00 PM	67	3584	3.3	4.1	5109
2	WWE ENTERTAINMENT (WWE RAW)	SPIKE	MON 9:00 PM	60	3468	3.2	4.0	5053
3	SPONGEBOB	NICK	SAT 9:30 AM	30	3431	3.2	3.9	4634
4	FAIRLY ODD PARENTS	NICK	SAT 10:00 AM	30	3254	3.0	3.7	4383
5	NBA PLAYOFFS (ROCKETS/LAKERS)	TNT	WED 10:20 PM	163	3153	2.9	3.6	3963
6	SPONGEBOB	NICK	SUN 9:30 AM	30	3002	2.8	3.4	3907
7	REAL WORLD XIV	MTV	TUE 10:00 PM	30	2970	2.7	3.4	3720
8	FAIRLY ODD PARENTS	NICK	SUN 10:00 AM	30	2619	2.6	3.2	3617
9	NBA PLAYOFFS (KINGS/MAVERICKS)	TNT	MON 9:40 PM	171	2609	2.6	3.2	3481
10	SPONGEBOB	NICK	SUN 9:00 AM	30	2796	2.6	3.2	3355
11	FAIRLY ODD PARENTS	NICK	SAT 10:30 AM	30	2789	2.6	3.2	4088
12	PUNK'D	MTV	SUN 10:00 PM	30	2725	2.5	3.1	3599
13	FAIRLY ODD PARENTS	NICK	SUN 10:30 AM	30	2722	2.5	3.1	3530
14	SPONGEBOB	NICK	SAT 9:00 AM	30	2719	2.5	3.1	3618
15	JIMMY NEUTRON	NICK	SUN 11:00 AM	30	2717	2.5	3.1	3613

PAY CABLE

RANK	PROGRAM NAME	NET	DAY / TIME	DUR	HOUSEHOLD AA(000)	HOUSEHOLD US AA 3/6	HOUSEHOLD CVG AA 3/6	PERSONS 2+ AA(000)
1	SOPRANOS, THE	HBOM	SUN 9:01 PM	59	5970	5.4	16.6	5959
2	DEADWOOD	HBOM	SUN 10:02 PM	49	2917	2.7	9.2	4291
3	MATRIX RELOADED, THE	HBOM	SAT 8:01 PM	138	1827	1.7	5.8	2680
4	REAL SEX XTRA : SIZE MATTERS	HBOM	THU 11:01 PM	56	1102	1.0	3.5	1362
5	SIX FEET UNDER	HBOM	SUN 8:01 PM	53	931	0.9	2.9	1393

*Coverage area ratings are within each cable network's universe.
*Total U.S. ratings and household projections are based on 108.4 million TV homes.
*For inclusion in the rankings, telecasts must be promoted as distinct programs and
  must be of 5 minutes minimum duration. Telecasts indicated as breakouts are excluded from this report.

~This report includes only those cable networks who supply program names to the industry.
  Any network that does not supply program names is not included in this report.

Program estimates for HBO, Cinemax, Showtime and The Movie Channel reflect only tuning to the
primary plex or channel of these networks.

(a)

Nielsen Television Index Ranking Report
NETWORK PRIME HOUSEHOLDS AND PERSONS
Current Week
05/03/04-05/09/04

RANK	PROGRAMS	IND	ORIG	HOUSEHOLDS AA%	HOUSEHOLDS SHR	HOUSEHOLDS AA(000)	PERSONS 2+ RANK	PERSONS 2+ AA%	PERSONS 2+ AA(000)	SPTC	DAY(S)	S TIME	T DUR	EPISODE TITLE
1	FRIENDS		NBC	29.8	43	32303	1	19.0	52458	CS	...T...	9:00 PM	66	
2	FRIENDS CLIPSHOW SPCL(S)	S	NBC	22.0	35	23860	2	13.4	36893	CS	...T...	8:00 PM	60	
3	E.R.		NBC	18.1	29	19581	3	10.3	28367	GD	...T...	10:06 PM	61	
4	AMERICAN IDOL-TUESDAY		FOX	13.6	22	14744	6	8.3	22817	GV	.T...	8:00 PM	60	
5	SURVIVOR ALL-STARS REUNION(S)	S	CBS	13.1	22	14175	5	8.7	23919	GV	......S	10:13 PM	50	
6	SURVIVOR ALL-STARS FINALE(S)	S	CBS	13.0	21	14096	4	9.0	24758	GV	......S	8:00 PM	133	
7	CSI		CBS	12.8	18	13901	8	7.4	20393	GD	...T...	9:00 PM	61	
8	AMERICAN IDOL-WEDNESDAY		FOX	12.3	20	13327	7	7.7	21176	GV	.W...	8:30 PM	30	
9	NBC MOVIE OF THE WEEK-MON(S)	S	NBC	12.2	19	13189	9	7.2	19872	FF	M...	9:00 PM	120	10.5 PART II
10	CSI: MIAMI		CBS	11.6	18	12575	11	6.4	17617	GD	M...	10:00 PM	60	
11	SURVIVOR: ALL-STARS		CBS	11.0	17	11950	10	7.0	19214	GV	...T...	8:00 PM	60	
12	EVERYBODY LOVES RAYMOND		CBS	10.9	16	11620	12	6.3	17266	CS	M...	9:00 PM	31	
13	TWO AND A HALF MEN		CBS	10.5	15	11398	13	5.9	16200	CS	M...	9:31 PM	29	
13	WITHOUT A TRACE		CBS	10.5	16	11340	14	5.8	16037	GD	...T...	10:01 PM	59	
15	DATELINE NBC SPECIAL 5/5(S)	S	NBC	10.3	16	11132	15	5.3	14712	DN	.W...	9:00 PM	120	
16	FRASIER		NBC	9.4	14	10138	16	5.2	14326	CS	...T...	9:00 PM	32	
17	CSI-SPCL(S)	SR	CBS	9.3	15	10077	17	4.8	13331	GD	.W...	10:00 PM	60	
18	JUDGING AMY		CBS	9.0	15	9726	20	4.4	12214	GD	...T...	10:00 PM	60	
19	LAW AND ORDER:SVU		NBC	8.9	14	9685	18	4.7	13038	GD	...T...	10:01 PM	59	
20	CROSSING JORDAN		NBC	8.1	13	8753	21	4.3	11862	GD	M...	10:00 PM	60	
21	60 MINUTES		CBS	7.7	16	8358	23	4.2	11460	DN	......S	7:00 PM	60	
22	AMERICAN IDOL: FINAL FIVE(S)	S	FOX	7.6	12	8225	21	4.3	11731	GV	M...	8:00 PM	60	
23	LAW AND ORDER:CRIM INTENT		NBC	7.5	12	8168	23	4.2	11643	GD	......S	9:00 PM	60	
24	FEAR FACTOR		NBC	7.4	12	8002	19	4.5	12321	PV	M...	8:00 PM	60	
25	SCRUBS		NBC	7.3	11	7916	25	4.0	11105	CS	.T...	9:32 PM	29	
26	BACHELOR, THE		ABC	7.1	11	7727	30	3.7	10325	PV	.W...	9:00 PM	62	
26	STILL STANDING		CBS	7.1	11	7732	25	4.0	10952	CS	M...	8:30 PM	30	
26	24		FOX	7.0	11	7640	25	4.0	11086	GD	.T...	9:00 PM	60	
28	EXTREME MAKEOVER-WED		ABC	7.0	11	7553	30	3.7	10081	PV	.W...	10:02 PM	58	
28	NAVY NCIS		CBS	7.0	12	7592	30	3.7	10134	GD	.T...	8:00 PM	60	
31	GUARDIAN, THE		CBS	6.9	11	7496	36	3.5	9645	GD	.T...	9:00 PM	60	
32	SWAN, THE		FOX	6.8	10	7402	30	3.7	10128	PV	M...	9:00 PM	60	
33	JAG		CBS	6.7	12	7227	30	3.7	10158	GD	....F..	9:00 PM	60	
33	O.C.		FOX	6.7	10	7234	29	3.9	10716	GD	.W...	9:00 PM	60	
35	60 MINUTES II		CBS	6.6	11	7191	38	3.4	9279	DN	.W...	8:00 PM	60	
35	ABC SP PRESENTATION-5/9(S)	R	ABC	6.6	11	7104	25	4.0	11143	FF	......S	7:00 PM	240	H.POTTER AND SORCERER'S STONE
35	LAW & ORDER:SVU-SAT-RPT		NBC	6.6	12	7112	35	3.6	9653	GD	...S..	10:00 PM	60	
35	THIRD WATCH		NBC	6.6	12	7179	38	3.4	9395	GD	....F..	10:00 PM	60	
39	EVERYBODY LOVES RAYMOND SPL(S)	SR	CBS	6.5	10	7039	40	3.3	9158	CS	.W...	9:30 PM	30	
39	FRIENDS 5/5 8:30P(S)	SR	NBC	6.5	11	7064	40	3.3	9221	CS	.W...	8:31 PM	29	
39	NYPD BLUE		ABC	6.5	11	7076	36	3.5	9568	OP	.T...	10:00 PM	60	
42	KING OF QUEENS		CBS	6.4	10	6909	40	3.3	9185	CS	.W...	9:00 PM	30	
43	COLD CASE-SPCL(S)	SR	CBS	6.3	12	6823	40	3.3	9112	GD	M...	10:00 PM	60	
44	YES, DEAR		CBS	6.1	10	6595	45	3.2	8913	CS	M...	8:00 PM	30	
45	DATELINE FRI		NBC	5.9	11	6427	49	2.9	8089	DN	....F..	8:00 PM	120	
45	THAT '70S SHOW		FOX	5.9	11	6428	40	3.3	9044	CS	.W...	8:00 PM	30	
47	FRIENDS 5/5 8P(S)	SR	NBC	5.9	11	6320	49	2.9	8110	CS	.W...	8:00 PM	31	
48	JOAN OF ARCADIA		CBS	5.7	11	6130	47	3.0	8169	GD	....F..	8:00 PM	60	

As of September 1, 2003, there are an estimated 108.4 million television households in the USA. A single national household ratings pooint represents 1 1/4 or 1,084,000 households.
Copyright 2004 Nielsen Media Research

(b)

Figure 11.5
A sample NTI report that shows cable rankings (a), and a sample page from a weekly NTI report that shows prime-time rankings (b). (Courtesy Nielsen Media Research.)

NTI is published twice a year in booklet form and once a week in an abbreviated form. The NTI booklet includes all the necessary data, including a summary of households using television, reports on daytime network programs, cume audiences, and reports that show 3-year trends. There is also a Nielsen Hispanic Index (NHI); the NTI and NHI are expected to merge. Nielsen also publishes a special report called Nielsen Home Video that covers not only cable TV but also VCRs and home satellite dishes. Special statistics are often reported such as the percentage of home dish or VCR penetration in each market, the types of programs people are most likely to record with their VCRs, or the average number of channels on cable systems in each market.

Nielsen publishes a supplementary report on public television. Although public television places less emphasis on ratings than the commercial networks, ratings are becoming increasingly important. Solid ratings are necessary to keep underwriters sponsoring programs. Public television is also interested in knowing whether its programs are serving the public for which they were designed.

As former PBS President Bruce Christensen said, "While looking at an overall audience, we also want to know the makeup of that audience. Are children's shows being watched by kids and their families? Are programs we're producing for various age levels and categories of people being viewed by those people?"[3]

In his keynote speech at the Broadcast Educators Association convention in 2004, Christensen, who ran PBS when Ken Burns's highly rated, groundbreaking "The Civil War" premiered (Figure 11.6), stressed that PBS must continue its mission to serve the public rather than be concerned with the market-

place. Overemphasis on the marketplace would only lead to, in his words, "the worst kind of programming."

More important to PBS than ratings is an annual evaluation of programming undertaken by a subcommittee of the PBS board. This subcommittee sends surveys to stations and gathers input from producers, minority advocacy groups, underwriters, the press, and other people who have a stake in the national program service. Armed with the results of this survey, PBS programmers make decisions. They usually consider three major questions: What is the value of the program to the overall schedule? Is the program valuable to the overall goals of public broadcasting? Is the program meeting its own objectives? These are goals Christensen would

Figure 11.6
*"The Civil War,"
which featured
stories about people
such as these
Confederate
volunteers of the
First Virginia
Militia, received
much-acclaimed
ratings as high as
9, but in general,
public broadcasting
does not place as
high a value on
ratings as do the
commercial
networks.*
(Courtesy
Florentine Films.)

clearly have embraced in his quest to keep public broadcasting serving the public's needs.

Sweeps. Generally, station ratings are undertaken four times a year in November, February, May, and July—the sweeps periods. The weeks of the sweeps are important to local stations because the numbers produced determine advertising rates for the following 3 months. The report containing station data is called the Nielsen Station Index, and it, like the NTI, breaks the information into various forms, including demographics. Nielsen also publishes reports for syndicated programming and for public television.

The various (and numerous) Nielsen reports are purchased by networks, stations, advertisers, and any other companies that need to know audience statistics. They are available in hard copy, on diskette, or online. There is also a website specifically for clients. The cost is generally kept quiet, but is estimated to be in the neighborhood of $6 million a year for networks and somewhat less for advertisers, stations, and others.

Special Considerations Associated with Cable and Audience Measurement. The advent and growth of cable has caused numerous problems for the rating companies. For one thing, it has fractionalized the viewing audiences, making it harder to analyze everything. During the 1950s, 1960s, and 1970s, three networks dominated the airwaves and most cities had only four or five stations. Ratings for each network were generally in the 20s and shares were in the 30s. Now, not only have network ratings decreased into the low teens, but ratings as low as 1 or 2 have become common for TV stations and cable services. The probability of error in rating estimates on numbers this small is high.

Another problem with cable TV ratings revolves around ascertaining the program lineup on every channel on each cable system. When only networks and stations existed, Nielsen and Arbitron could keep track of channel numbers in each market and know, through published schedules, what was playing on each station. In addition, if there were doubts, company personnel could call local stations to verify programs and time periods. But when cable came along, people in one part of town might have WXXX on channel 6, those down the street had it on channel 12, and those across town watched it on channel 37.

The cumbersomeness of dealing with these inconsistencies led Nielsen to develop **automated measurement of lineups (AMOL),** which it introduced in 1982. Each network and syndicated program is coded invisibly in a manner similar to grocery store bar codes. Then, as the program plays, Nielsen equipment tracks this code and can determine what program is shown on which channel at what time. This has been particularly helpful for calculating ratings for individual syndicated programs that may be playing on innumerable stations and cable systems throughout the country.

VCRs, even more than cable, have presented difficulties for the rating companies. Generally, programs are counted as being watched if they are recorded. But many recorded programs are never watched, and some are watched several times. In addition, people playing back a tape often zip through commercials, destroying the purpose of ratings.

Because ratings are so important and because viewing patterns are constantly changing, audience measurement must constantly be revised or updated. For example, in the summer of 2005, Nielsen will start to record viewership of shows on digital video recorders using active/passive meters to rate time-shifted programming (i.e., programming watched at the time other than when it originally aired). To be counted, a show must be played within 7 days.[4]

Ratings Massage. Ratings drive advertising rates, which is why so much importance is attached to them. In the same way that politicians strive to redistrict voting districts to gain an advantage, heads of networks seek ways to improve their chances in the war for ratings.

For example, Nickelodeon gained a temporary ratings edge when it split its ratings for Nickelodeon and Nick at Nite after the first quarter of 2004. Before the split, both had been considered a single network. With the change, the two were rated individually. Nielsen approved this change because Nickelodeon and Nick at Nite sell their programs to advertisers separately.

In the first quarter of 2004, Nickelodeon was the most-watched cable network, according to analyst Scott Collins. TNT was second. Had the split of Nickelodeon and Nick at Nite been in effect for this quarter, Nickelodeon would have remained No. 1 but Nick at Nite would have been No. 2, bumping TNT to No. 3. Similarly, Lifetime, which held the No. 1 spot in the key demographic of women 18 to 49 years old, would have yielded that honor to Nick at Nite.[5] The separation irked the other networks, causing Nielsen to end the 3-month split between Nickelodeon and Nick at Nite.

Despite the situation engendered by the Nickelodeon and Nick at Nite, cable systems generally place less emphasis on ratings than do commercial systems because cable has two sources of income: advertisements and subscribers. Therefore, cable systems and networks often factor in subscriber statistics to evaluate their success, or lack thereof.

One of the important subscriber concepts for cable systems is **penetration.** This refers to the number of homes in the cable system's territory that connect to cable. If the number of households served by cable is 10,000 and the number of households that have asked to have cable hooked to their TV sets is 6,000, cable penetration is 60%. A penetration of about 80% is considered viable.

Cable also likes to keep its **churn** rate low. Churn refers to the number of people dropping the service even though they may later reconnect. For obvious financial reasons, pay cable networks like their subscribers to stay with them, not to drop out for several months and then resubscribe. Cable networks are reluctant to release data on their churn rates, leading some to consider churn to be cable's "dirty little secret."

Indeed, some analysts estimated cable churn rates to be as high as 5 to 6% per month in 2003–2004. Interestingly, digital cable churn rates were particularly high in 2003 because many people who only watched 15 to 18 channels felt they did not need the additional channels that digital cable offers. Thus, many canceled their digital subscriptions in favor of cheaper services that gave them access to the smaller number of channels they regularly watched.[6]

Cable systems are averse to losing and regaining large numbers of customers. They lose money when people disconnect even if they sign up again later. Worse than churn is the permanent disconnect—the subscriber who tries cable, does not like it, asks to have the service removed, and never comes back.

COMMERCIAL RADIO

As mentioned earlier, Nielsen dropped radio ratings in 1964, but Arbitron

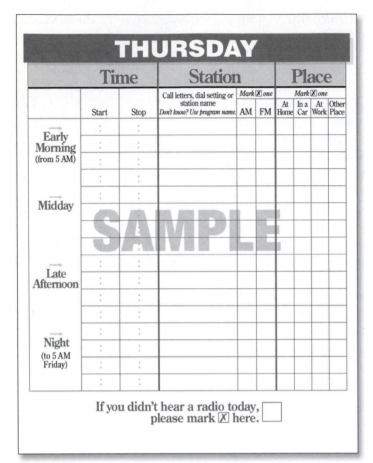

Figure 11.7
Sample of Arbitron diary card. (Courtesy Arbitron.)

measures radio station audiences and is generally considered the primary radio ratings company. Other companies have entered (and left) the business. Because of the mobility and fragmentation of radio listening, collecting ratings data is expensive—which led to the demise of entrepreneuring companies. In addition, radio's tendency to play fast and loose with the concept of national networks and syndicators makes it much more complicated to quantify and vet ratings for national network programming often aired, with the same national commercials intact, on thousands of stations across the nation at different times and in different contexts. An industry-supported organization, radio all-dimension audience research (RADAR), therefore has been developed to measure radio network audiences.

Arbitron

Arbitron's radio ratings are determined entirely by diaries (not meters) and are based on people (not households). So much of the radio audience consists of one person listening to one radio outside of the home that meters placed on household radio sets, as is done with television sets, would be inadequate for gathering meaningful measurements.

Samples are drawn on a household basis in a random manner similar to how households are selected for TV ratings. However, with radio, each person in the household over 12 years is asked to keep a diary for 1 week and then mail it to Arbitron (Figure 11.7). No one is asked to keep a diary for longer than 7 days. If the survey lasts longer than 1 week, different people are used for each week.

Radio ratings cover two areas for local stations—**metros** and **total service areas (TSAs).** Metros correspond to the government's metropolitan statistical areas and are primarily individual cities. Usually a station's metro is the city to which it is licensed—an area in which it can be heard clearly. TSAs are larger than metros and often include part of some other metro. The weaker stations of a metro area often cannot be heard clearly throughout the TSA. This difference in carrying power led Arbitron to break down ratings for the two areas. If ratings were reported only for the TSA, the lower-powered radio stations would be unjustly penalized (Figure 11.8).

Once the diaries are mailed back to Arbitron (the return rate is about 50%), they are edited, taking a variety of points into account. If someone has listed a dial setting, program name, or personality rather than the call letters, an Arbitron employee finds and enters the correct call letters. Diaries postmarked before the survey period ended are eliminated, as are identical diaries from the same household or diaries that indicate someone listened to the radio 24 hours a day for the whole week. As with TV, diaries from a particular demographic group may be weighted if that group, as a whole, returns a low percentage of diaries.[7] Indeed, **ethnic weighing,** as the practice is called, can significantly skew data.

The valid edited information is processed through a computer that calculates audience measurement statistics. Rating and share are important to radio, just as they are to TV, but the usual method for calculating these revolves around the **average quarter hour (AQH).** AQH ratings and shares are developed by adding the number of people who listen to a station for at least 5 minutes during a 15-minute period and then dividing that by the number of quarter hours in a particular daypart. Figure 11.8 shows an example in which 100 KXXX listeners are keeping diaries; if 40 of these people listen to KXXX for at least 5 minutes between 7:00 and 9:00 A.M., the station's AQH rating would be 5.

AQHs are used because radio is not as structured as TV. A great deal of button pushing occurs in radio listening, especially for all-news stations that people tend to dip into briefly. Measuring in small blocks helps find the audience.

The cume is also important to radio. As with cable, advertisers are often interested in knowing how many different people their ads reach if the ads are placed at various times.

Arbitron surveys all of its radio markets at least once a year. The large markets are surveyed more intensively than the smaller markets; some very large markets are measured almost year round.

One of the interesting uses made of Arbitron data relates to the network–affiliate relationship. Radio networks look at ratings to decide what stations they wish to affiliate with. As Leon Cleveland of National Black Network

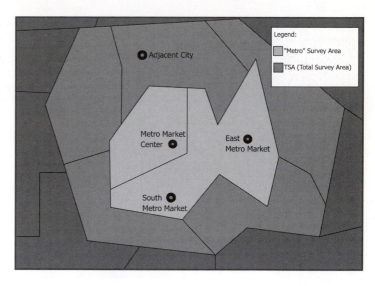

Figure 11.8
Map of a Metro and TSA.

pointed out, "We want to affiliate with stations that have high ratings. So we look at the ratings and then try to sell our service to stations that target our type of audience and have high ratings."

RADAR

Theoretically, radio network material can be extrapolated from Arbitron statistics. Local stations air network programming included in various quarter hours, so if a network knows when its material is being aired, it can find its ratings. However, the inconsistency with which network material is programmed makes such a process complicated.

As a result, a group of about 20 networks (which has grown to more than 80 in 2004) joined to support RADAR. These companies initially paid a company named Statistical Research to track their programming by telephone recall methodology. Trained interviewers randomly phoned selected potential sample households and asked one person in each household to recall what radio programs he or she listened to yesterday and the day before yesterday. If the interviewee could not remember specific programming, the interviewer asked for slogans, dial position, or

Quarter Hours	No. People
7:00–7:15 A.M.	3
7:15–7:30 A.M.	5
7:30–7:45 A.M.	7
7:45–8:00 A.M.	10
8:00–8:15 A.M.	3
8:15–8:30 A.M.	5
8:30–8:45 A.M.	4
8:45–9:00 A.M.	3
= 8 quarter hours	= 40 people
40/8 = 5	

Figure 11.9
If 40 of 100 people keeping diaries listen to KXXX for at least 5 minutes between 7:00 and 9:00 A.M., the station's AQH rating would be 5.

anything else that might help define the material. The interviewer also assisted the respondents with probes such as "Did you wake up to a clock radio?" or "Did you listen to the car radio while driving home from work?"

This type of phone research had a 63% response rate; in other words, 63% of people agreed to be interviewed. This was about 13% higher than diary returns, probably because people could answer the questions instantaneously and need not remember to write or mail anything. The drawback, however, was that it relies on recall, which is often incomplete or inaccurate. More importantly, the RADAR process was expensive and, in many ways, redundant with Arbitron's work. So, with a few tweaks, the RADAR ratings were folded into Arbitron, which now conducts this research using its weekly diary reports, selecting representative samples from the different metro areas for a sample that reflects the national audience.

When networks sell their programming to local stations, the local station agrees on a time that it will air the material in its lineup. Arbitron uses these "clear" times, in conjunction with diary entries, to determine how many audience members listened to the network

material. Local stations, however, have missed the mark occasionally (or frequently) when it comes to airing network programming in the cleared time period. If the network content is not aired at the reported time, then the ratings for that material will not be accurate. Therefore, to give confidence to advertisers and network executives, Arbitron conducts random monitoring: Arbitron records samples of radio broadcasts and compares the material with the clearance information it receives from the local stations and networks. Ratings are adjusted accordingly, and reports of discrepancies found in the monitoring process are given to the involved parties for follow-up.

THE INTERNET

Radio and television, broadcasting continuously whether there is an audience or not, must rely on companies such as Arbitron and Nielsen to estimate the number of people experiencing their product. The Internet, on the other hand, waits until a request is made by an audience member to broadcast its content. These requests can and are automatically tabulated in site activity logs, giving website owners a ready-made set of statistics related to site activity and audience traffic.

These statistics, however, can be deceptive. Although they keep track of how many times files on the site were accessed, the amount of accurate information they can provide about who accessed the site, for what purpose, in what context, and for how long is limited. Take this scenario: An avid collector of TY Beanie Babies, on word that he or she must move to another country, decides to sell the entire collection of plush toys in online auctions. The seller wants to provide pictures of each item but does not want the trouble of taking the pictures. Instead, a website, perhaps the official TY site, is found that already contains pictures of the items. The seller copies the addresses of the pictures from the TY website and uses the pictures directly in the auctions. Thus, every time an auction is viewed, there is a hit on the TY website because the files are stored on that site and simply linked to in the seller's auctions—but none of these hits represents someone visiting the TY website. So, if number of "hits" was the criteria by which advertisers determined how many viewers would be exposed to their ads, they could be sorely mistaken.

Likewise, many times sites are visited but advertisers would be loathe to count these visits toward the number of consumers that have seen their ads. Search engines, a crowded field including Google.com and Yahoo, are constantly scouring the Internet, indexing the content of sites. Automated programs, called spiders, visit hundreds of thousands of web pages per day, checking for new sites, new content, and dead ends that should be removed from the system. In the competitive world of search engines, a company loses face, and customers, if its search results are not complete and up to date. Advertisers, however, do not benefit from counting spiders as consumers.

In addition to traffic from automated spiders, webmasters and other employees of companies that maintain websites may visit a site numerous times a day to make sure that changes they have made are operating correctly. One way that websites can remove these visits from their log is by placing identifying cookies on the computers of visitors to specifically identify visitors on subsequent visits.

Thus, a simple log of the number of hits or visitors must be viewed with a grain of salt by advertisers who want to get the biggest bang for their buck. Nielsen, Arbitron, and emerging companies, therefore, have thrown their hats in the ring to provide Internet audience measurements.

Combining hit data with traditional metering strategies, Nielsen has developed the NetRatings service, which measures Internet audience numbers and behaviors and keeps detailed track of advertising trends on the Internet. Meanwhile, Arbitron is developing a new system capable of tracking radio, television, and some Internet content (See sidebar on following page).

Another form of Internet ratings is a site's positioning on popular search engines. Although the methodology for ranking sites for display in the coveted Top 10 position is made intentionally obscure and mercurial by search engine companies to avoid having systems duped, many factors clearly go into these rankings. First, and most easily understood, is relevance to the keywords entered by the search engine user. But if the user puts in a broad search phrase or word, such as "happiness," millions of sites will contain that word. Therefore, factors other than relevance are taken into account in ranking. Most search engines nowadays take into account how many other sites have links on them to a specific site; if other webmasters have found the content of a specific site so compelling that they put a link to it on their own site, then the site must have value. Knowing that propagating links to their sites will give them a better ranking on search engines, webmasters have taken to exchanging links (e.g., "If you put a link to my site on your site, I'll put a link to your site on mine"). No system is going to be perfect, but even in link exchanges, at least it can be assumed that the webmaster who would go to the trouble of exchanging links broadly across the Internet would also go to the trouble of creating interesting and valuable content.

Figure 11.10
Arbitron's portable people meter features a pager-sized metering device and a nighttime docking station that serves as both a battery charger and a communications hub, sending collected data to Arbitron every night. (Courtesy Arbitron.)

Amazon.com, in 2004, launched a new search engine, A9.com, that not only ranks sites in the traditional ways but also allows users to review sites. So, if you visit a site and you like it, you can give it a 5-star ranking and leave some comments, just as you might review a book listed for sale on Amazon.com.

Internet programmers will want to work to get their sites ranked high in search engines; it will usually mean not only more traffic will come to the site but also more advertisers will be attracted to paying to have their messages viewed by those visitors.

THE PORTABLE PEOPLE METER

When Nielsen introduced AMOL in 1982, it hit on a technology and concept that is now being expanded. AMOL puts a code into television broadcasts that helps audience measurement set boxes determine which programs are playing on any channel at anytime. Arbitron has been working since 1992, in an on-again–off-again relationship with Nielsen, on a portable, crossmedia audience measurement system that also works through encoded programming.

The portable people meter (PPM) is a pager-sized device that survey participants carry with them throughout the day (Figure 11.10). The device has a built-in microphone that monitors all audio occurring in the vicinity of the device wearer. Radio and television broadcasts, as well as Internet audio broadcasts, can be encoded with an audio signal undetectable by the human ear but recognizable by the device. Each radio station, television channel, and web stream can be given a different code, and the PPM can keep track of when and how long participants are exposed to each discrete signal throughout the day. With this system there is no need for diaries, for interviews, or for participants to push buttons, turn knobs, or interact except

to wear the device wherever they go. This method also helps to easily account for media exposure outside of the home—anywhere the participant may go.

The PPM augers many other potential uses as well. Retail outlets, for example, can broadcast an undetectable code in their stores, keeping track of which stores participants visit and how long they stay. Potentially combining this information with checkout receipts, stores could determine how much the participants spend and the exact products they purchase. Aggregating this information with the knowledge of the participants' exposure to radio, television, and Internet media and advertising, a correlation could potentially be drawn between exposure to advertisements and purchases. All of this could add up to unprecedented amounts of detailed information about media consumption and its effects on consumers. But as of 2004, although test runs of the PPM had been successful on many accounts, there were still many details to work out, both in terms of the technology and in terms of the methodology of administering the surveys and interpreting the data.

DO RATINGS WORK AND DO SAMPLES SAMPLE?

The main issue that a programmer has to deal with concerning ratings is determining how much weight to place upon them in relation to all the other factors involved in program decision making. Should a commercial TV network programmer cancel a series if it ranks in the bottom half of the ratings? Should a cable TV network be removed from a cable TV system if it never achieves a rating higher than a 2? Should a radio disc jockey be fired if the ratings for his daypart fall from 5 to 4? Should "Sesame Street" be moved to a different timeslot if most people watching it at 2:00 P.M. are men in their 30s? One of the factors involved in determining how much weight to place on ratings revolves around whether the ratings are accurate or, perhaps more appropriately, accurate enough.

Variables That Affect Rating Accuracy

Even the rating services do not claim that their numbers are totally accurate. Nielsen, in its booklet *What TV Ratings Really Mean,* writes, "Note that when we described the rating, we used the words 'statistical estimate.' That's because a rating is subject to a margin of statistical error."[8] But beyond statistical error, there are problems that can affect rating accuracy.

Sampling. Sample size is one aspect of ratings frequently questioned when it comes to determining rating accuracy. How can a company possibly report on what people are watching when only 5100 out of 108.4 million homes are sampled? No two people are alike, and even households with the same number of children and same income do not watch exactly the same television. Nielsen's answer to this is as follows:

Try this interesting experiment (hypothetically—unless you happen to have 100,000 beads handy). Imagine 100,000 beads in a washtub: 30,000 red and 70,000 white. Mix thoroughly, then scoop out a sample of 4000. Even before counting, you'll know that not all beads in your sample are red. Nor would you expect your sample to divide exactly at 1200 red and 2800 white.

As a matter of fact, the mathematical odds are about 20 to 1 that the count of red beads will be plus or minus 60 beads—or a range of 28.5 to 31.5 of the sample.

So, in short, you have now produced a "rating" of 30, plus or minus 1.5, with a 20 to 1 assurance of statistical reliability.

These basic sampling laws wouldn't change even if you drew your sample of 4000 from 90 million beads instead of 100,000—assuming that the 90 million beads had the same ratio of red and white.

This is a simple demonstration of why a small sample is just as adequate for a nation of 90 million households as for a city of 100,000.

Yes, but people aren't beads. Of course not, but, then, neither do we attempt to measure people in all their complexities. In some ways, measuring a television audience is as simple in principle as counting beads. We're asking questions such as: "Is the set on?" and "If on, is it tuned to channel A, B, C, or D?" These questions are just as simple as asking if the bead is red or white. The answer in each case is a simple yes or no.[9]

Statisticians generally agree with Nielsen and other audience measurement companies that sampling works. The sarcastic retort given to those who do not believe in the accuracy of sampling is, "The next time you go to the doctor to get blood taken out, tell him to take it all because you don't believe that the small amount placed into the vial will give accurate results."

Statisticians have found that, in general, the larger the sample, the smaller the sampling error. Unfortunately, doubling the sample size does not cut the sampling error in half; the sample size has to be quadrupled to do this. This type of increase is costly. Nevertheless, as the population of the country increases, Nielsen is planning to double its sample size to 10,000 by 2006.

Where Did the Men Go? In 2003–2004, programming executives and viewers alike began a new round of serious questions about the accuracy of the Nielsen rating system. Was it antiquated? Did it try to do too much, for example, in 2004 by measuring how many times television viewers see sponsorship signs at sports stadiums? Or, again in 2004, by tracking video game playing?

In particular, the 11 to 12% drop in television viewing by young men at the start of the 2003–2004 season alarmed broadcasters who thought that a rise in video game playing and Internet usage could not be responsible for the sudden precipitous drop in the number of young male viewers. Nielsen responded that its system was sound and that broadcasters were simply unwilling to accept the new reality of decreased viewing by young men.

MTV's "Sunday Stew" lineup, including reality shows such as "Viva La Bam," with intentionally juvenile stunts; "Punk'd," with its staged tricks on celebrities; and the car makeover show, "Pimp My Ride," managed to capture the coveted young male demographic that the major networks found missing in 2003–2004. What the majors saw was that a significant number of males 18 to 34 years old stopped watching.

Where did some 750,000 young men suddenly go? Or was there a flaw in the Nielsen system? With NBC leading the charge, the majors, trying to keep advertising rates high, accused Nielsen of shoddy sampling and reporting practices. Nielsen asserted that the numbers were as accurate as ever, responding that if the networks wanted an answer to the drop in ratings, they should look at their own programming strategies, strategies that offered little to interest young men. In other words, if MTV's "Sunday Stew" can't get men, it was not Nielsen's fault. This controversy exploded in the fall of 2003 with Nielsen and the networks exchanging blame, although subsequent ratings data showed the number of male viewers edging up again.

Are Minorities Adequately Represented? Nielsen also received significant questioning over the years for its gathering of minority data, specifically information about Latino and African-American viewership. Many think that Nielsen's sampling does not include a fair proportion of minority viewers, although some industry analysts say that the sampling of minorities is more than adequate and is representative of the country as a whole. Because Nielsen has shown signs of moving from diary reporting and toward more automated statistical gathering, there has been significant outcry, especially when the data has differed markedly regarding minority viewing. For example, when Nielsen distributed its people meter for sweeps in various markets in 2004, many Fox network shows reportedly showed a drop in minority viewership, fueling the controversy. Nielsen, however, has maintained that as the local ratings picture becomes more accurate, with better sampling techniques, many established stations and programs could experience ratings declines and other cable and satellite channels could register gains.

Rating Techniques

Beyond sampling, there are many other problems that can creep in to the ratings process. People who know their viewing or listening habits are being monitored may act differently than they ordinarily do, watching higher-end programs than they might normally.

Households with people meters suffer from button-pushing fatigue, thereby artificially lowering ratings. Some groups of people are more likely to push buttons than others. When the people meter was first introduced, sports-viewing ratings soared and children's program ratings decreased significantly. One theory was that men, who were watching the sports intently, were reliable about pushing the button, perhaps some even out of fear that the TV would shut off if they did not keep pushing that button. Children, on the other hand, were confused or apathetic about the button, therefore underrating children's programming.

Contrary to the controversy that raged in 2004 in favor of keeping diaries instead of converting to people meters during sweeps, diaries have innumerable documented problems. The return rate is low, and many diaries that are returned have missing data, data that is then "filled in" statistically by computer. To some ratings customers, this practice of filling in missing data in a statistical sample with statistical numbers gleaned from other samples (also called **Monte Carlo audience ascription**) is indefensible.

Also, many people do not fill out the diaries as they watch TV or listen to the radio. They wait until the last minute and try to remember everything they have watched or listened to, perhaps aided by a copy of *TV Guide* or a radio schedule. Some people are not honest about what they watch. Perhaps they do not want to admit to watching game shows, to listening to radio sex and psychology shows, or to forgetting what they watched. They may simply put down a well-known show, ignoring the "little" cable show that does not figure as readily in their memory.

With telephone interviews, people can be influenced by the tone or attitude of the interviewee or, again, they can be less than truthful about what they watched or listened to out of embarrassment or in an attempt to project themselves in a respectable light. People are also hesitant to give information over the phone because they fear the person calling is a salesperson.

Studies and Investigations

Because of the possibility for all these sampling and methodology errors, ratings have been subjected to numerous tests and investigations. In 1963, the House of Representatives became so skeptical of ratings methodology that it held hearings. Most of the skepticism arose because of a cease and desist order from the Federal Trade Commission (FTC) telling several audience measurement companies to stop misrepresenting the accuracy and reliability of their reports. The FTC charged the rating companies with relying on hearsay information, making false claims about the nature of their sample populations, improperly combining and reporting data, failing to account for nonresponding sample members, and making arbitrary changes in the rating figures, all pretty heavy accusations.

The main outgrowth of the House hearings was that broadcasters established the Electronic Media Rating Council (EMRC) to accredit rating companies. This group periodically checks rating companies to ensure their sample design and implementation meet preset standards that broadcasters have agreed upon, to determine whether interviewers are properly trained, to oversee the procedures for handling diaries, and to ensure in other ways that the ratings companies are compiling their reports as accurately as possible. Today, all the major rating companies have EMRC accreditation.

Also, as a result of the 1963 hearings, broadcasters undertook several basic studies to determine the accuracy of ratings. They tested sample size and found, as mentioned previously, that the larger the sample, the smaller the sampling error. They also found that people who cooperated with rating services watched more TV, had larger families, and were younger and better educated than those who would not cooperate. And they found that the telephone technique gets a 13% higher cooperation rate than diaries.[10]

Programming Aberrations

As if life were not tough enough for the ratings companies, programmers often try for end runs around the ratings system. TV stations program their most sensational material during sweeps ratings periods: "Reverse circumcision. See how it is done. Tonight on channel 8." The strategy of using sensational stunt techniques to increase ratings is called **hypoing.** TV networks preempt their series and show star-loaded specials so that their affiliates will fare well in ratings and, therefore, can increase their advertising rates. Cable networks show new programs rather than reruns. Radio stations run unique and financially rewarding contests that require listeners to "keep listening for further clues."

All of this negates ratings' real purpose: determining the largest regular audience. It simply indicates which network can manipulate the sweeps game better than the competition.

What is at stake is advertising fees that can translate into millions of dollars. It is easy to understand why programmers under intense pressure from their managements to perform well during sweeps are tempted to do almost anything to maximize the numbers. The better program directors will stay within reason. The people who should remain vigilant are the advertisers and their agencies. They are the losers if they pay rates based on a stunt that artificially stimulated the ratings and bears no resemblance to the programs in which the sponsor is investing.

How Programmers Should Use Ratings

Ratings are not foolproof, nor are they the only measurement of program success or failure. There are many other indications of a show's vitality and its potential for a productive run. Even Nielsen cautions, "Rarely . . . should a programming decision be made on just one ratings report; *repeated* measurements substantially reduce the range of statistical error that applies, as well as provide broadcasters with a vital sense of direction as to whether an audience is building or dropping off."[11]

Furthermore, the greater the fractionalization of the audience, the less precise the measurement. Nielsen admits it is dealing with numbers that 95% of the time are plus or minus 1 or 2 points from the real rating. The other 5% of the time, the rating is even less accurate.

It is true that in commercial broadcasting ratings are the way the score is kept. But the savvy programmer will use them as an aid, not a crutch. It would be foolish for a programmer to make a judgment on a show based on 1 or 2 rating points (to say nothing of a judgment made on 0.1 or 0.2 points). Also left out of the mix is the intensity with which viewers watch certain shows. An audience of 10 million devoted fans may be more valuable to a broadcaster and an advertiser than 12 million viewers involved with two or three other activities while sitting in front of the set.

When looking at ratings, programmers should be more concerned about trends and tendencies than a single raw number. Even if a current rating is low, if it is part of a gradual increase it could have positive significance, as in 2004 with the WB's "One Tree Hill" (Figure 11.11). Conversely, a higher number that is part of a flat pattern may indicate a problem down the road.

The ratings-as-a-crutch approach to programming has a certain appeal. A number is easily understood, it permits facile comparisons, it has the look of science about it, and it offers a more compelling argument than such vague statements as "I have faith in the show," "My gut tells me it will work," or the familiar laugh getter, "Trust me." But good programmers are made of sterner stuff. They factor in the other considerations (trends, demos, fan letters, the "feel" of the show, etc.) and, if there is enough there to rebut a number, they

Figure 11.11
The cast of "One Tree Hill," which started slowly on the WB but built into a hit, justifying the WB's faith in keeping the show on the air. (Globe Photos, Inc.)

take a stand, as NBC's Jeff Zucker did with the low-rated, quality show, "American Dreams" by renewing it for a third season in 2004.

But sometimes the numbers are bad not by tenths of a point but by many points. Something has to be done. How programmers go about making the necessary changes is your next field of study.

EXERCISES

1. Conduct a sample in your class. Ask each person in your class to keep, for 1 day, a diary of television viewing, radio listening, Internet surfing, or a combination of these. Tally all of the results from the class, then put the diaries in a hat and draw 10% of them. Do the results from the 10% sample reflect the results of the group as a whole?

2. After you have conducted Exercise 1, describe whether you and your class think your viewing, listening, and surfing habits were altered by the use of the diary.

3. Find a low-rated show on a ratings report. View or listen to the show and advertising on the show, taking into account its competitors in the timeslot. What factors do you think have kept the show on the air, despite its poor ratings?

4. Examine a ratings report. How could ratings information be presented to make the ratings appear more or less favorable for specific shows than they appear in the presented format?

REFERENCES/NOTES

1. Steve McClellan. "Fuzzy Math," *Broadcasting & Cable,* March 8, 2004, p. 11.

2. Jonathan Dee. "The Myth of 18–34," *New York Times Magazine,* October 13, 2002, p. 60.

3. "PBS's National–Local Balancing Act," *Broadcasting,* July 18, 1990, pp. 37–38.

4. John Higgins. "Nielsen To Rate Time-Shifted Programming," http://www .broadcastingcable.com/article/CA401075 .html. Accessed March 3, 2004.

5. Scott Collins. "Nickelodeon Squeezes 2 Ratings Out of 1 Very Diverse Network," *Los Angeles Times,* March 25, 2004, p. C-1 through C-4.

6. Peter Grant. "Millions Rejecting Digital Cable," http://www.delawareonline .com. Accessed April 12, 2004.

7. Arbitron's main book describing its radio methodology is *Arbitron Radio: Description of Methodology* (New York: Arbitron, 1996). Its website at http://www .arbitron.com also contains a great deal of methodological information.

8. *What TV Ratings Really Mean* (New York: Nielsen Media Research, 1989), p. 8.

9. Ibid., pp. 13–14.

10. Ibid., p. 12.

11. Details of these studies can be found in *ARMS—What It Shows, How It Has Changed Radio Measurement* (Washington, DC: National Association of Broadcasters, 1966); *CRAM—Cumulative Radio Audience Method* (New York: National Broadcasting Company, 1966); and *Television Ratings Revisited: A Further Look at Television Audiences* (New York: Television Information Office, 1971).

12 Changing and Canceling Programs

In this chapter you will learn about the following:

- When programs require changes to avoid cancellation
- What changes can be made to keep a program viable
- How a time change can make or break a program
- Why programs are canceled
- The best way for executives to handle giving a cancellation notice
- The types of and reasons for changes and cancellations in radio
- Potential controversies that could spring from show cancellations
- Why websites stay active or go to the cyber graveyard

Sometimes a program will be painstakingly researched, carefully developed, launched with carefully crafted marketing and promotion—and fail. In previous chapters, you observed that experienced programmers know the general elements of successful showmaking; they can, however, be defeated by taking some wrong turns along the programming highway. When this happens, changing and canceling programs becomes necessary.

TELEVISION

There are several reasons for changing a television program, not all of which call for a cancellation. Programmers should remember that salvaged shows can represent enormous economic savings—specifically, not running finished episodes after a show has been banished is not cheap and the lure of syndication dollars can keep a program on the air. Efforts should be made to keep shows viable. But there are times when cancellation seems the best, or only, alternative. Cancellations are usually caused by one of the items described in the sections that follow.

Unsatisfactory Ratings

Most commercial television shows are canceled because they fail to achieve satisfactory ratings. The cause may lie elsewhere, but low audience levels are the reason for the cancellation. In some cases, these low-rated shows did not belong on the schedule. Not all shows that succeed are quality shows (look at the successes of many inane reality shows), but many canceled shows simply are poorly conceived, executed, or both and should not have been scheduled. They landed on the air because of contractual commitments, an absence of alternatives, or bad judgment by a decision maker, and the disappointing ratings should not come as a surprise.

It can be perplexing to note that some shows with weak ratings remain on the schedule but others with similar or better ratings are canceled. For example,

Figure 12.1
"Alias" has developed a cult following among college students despite mediocre ratings. (Photo © ABC Photography Archives.)

Figure 12.2
The Outdoor Channel, being on cable and able to attract targeted advertisers, can thrive with ratings that would be anemic to another network. (Photo courtesy Tom Kelsey, The Outdoor Channel.)

days, a timeslot considered valuable real estate for CBS, and the ratings that "The Guardian" received were deemed inadequate. When "Century City" aired in that timeslot, it garnered worse numbers than "The Guardian." "Century City" was also canceled.

It is interesting to note that in 1970, CBS dropped three highly rated shows, "The Red Skelton Show," "Jackie Gleason Show," and "Petticoat Junction," to rejuvenate CBS.[1] This was a controversial move at the time, but one CBS profited from. It suggests that there are several ways to interpret ratings. CBS found that, in terms of its long-range program planning, it had to replace these highly rated shows to attract a broader audience.

in May 2004, CBS canceled "The Guardian" after three seasons. The show consistently received adequate, if not spectacular, household numbers, often winning part or all of its timeslot. For the 2003–2004 season, it clocked out at No. 42 of 161 series, ahead of renewed shows such as Fox's "24" and CBS's "Joan of Arcadia." It aired at 9:00 P.M. Tues-

Rob Lowe's series following "The West Wing," "The Lyon's Den," was also part of the 2003–2004 season. It came in at No. 57 for the season, ahead of renewed shows such as ABC's "Alias" (No. 71, Figure 12.1), the WB's "Everwood" (No. 125), "Charmed" (No. 126), or "Gilmore Girls" (No. 128). Again, the cancellation of "The Lyon's Den" has to do with ratings expectations in a timeslot (10:00 P.M. Tuesdays) too valuable for ratings leader NBC to allow to underperform. What a struggling network like ABC accepted as satisfactory ratings for a show like "Alias," ratings leaders and fierce competitors NBC and CBS refused to accept, forcing the cancellations of "The Lyon's Den" and "The Guardian." Similarly, tiny ratings for a cable niche network such as the Outdoor Channel (Figure 12.2) will prove satisfactory, but equivalent numbers will mean disaster for the major networks.

Exhaustion

Unfortunately, all shows are mortal. Eventually, they just run out of gas. No more variations can be tried; no more aunts, uncles, cousins, and babies can be added to the cast without destroying the show's integrity. As gifted as the writers and producers of "The Cosby Show" were, there were no more arrows left in their creative quiver. Similarly, after Ed got married on "Ed" in 2004, there was nowhere to take the show (Figure 12.3). "Sex and the City" had many fans, but the producers wisely chose to go out on top in 2004 rather than try to mine more gold from a formula beginning to tire.

The reality show "Joe Millionaire" was the hit of the 2002–2003 season, but when programmers got greedy and tried to repackage the same program as "Joe Millionaire 2" during the 2003–2004 season, the concept was already exhausted. It had worn out its welcome. The traditional wisdom about reality is that it does not repeat well, and the visible failure of "Joe Millionaire 2" proved that even a successful format cannot go on indefinitely. Programmers must bow to the inevitability of fatigue and reluctantly say farewell to friends who can no longer deliver.

A Lack of Focus

New programs, such as David E. Kelley's "Girls' Club" for the 2002–2003 season, can lack focus, thus diminishing their chances for success. Established programs can slowly (or quickly) lose their focus. Producers on established shows get wrapped up in new projects and forget to maintain the old ones; stars become "difficult," convinced they are indispensable; writers go off course; and suddenly a successful series bores or insults its audience because it has lost its way. "Moonlighting," once a sophisticated comedy–adventure on ABC featuring witty, acerbic banter between Bruce Willis and Cybill Shepherd, lost

Figure 12.3
"Ed" finished its run on NBC in 2004 after Ed got married. The show had completed its primary story line with the wedding. (Globe Photos, Inc.)

its charm when internal friction and bizarre scripts diminished the chemistry between the leads. Similarly, "Dawson's Creek" took too many detours, resulting in convoluted story lines that diminished the show's appeal. The last season of "Roseanne" in 1997 also lost its focus when Dan and Roseanne won $108 million in the Illinois lottery, abandoning the show's working class roots.

When John Ritter died during the run of ABC's "8 Simple Rules," the show lost its focus. Gone was the parental figure who defined the show's essence. Attempts to "save" the show by introducing James Garner and David Spade into the cast in 2004 did not fill Ritter's shoes. For many viewers, the show has lost its focus even though hit-starved ABC needed to keep the show on the air.

In some instances, a candid, air-clearing discussion among the principals can put a show that has drifted off course back on track. Often, too much has transpired and the program, sadly, is

Figure 12.4
"The Brady Bunch" reflected the times in which it was made. Although it still has fans, the show would not mesh with the social climate of today. (Globe Photos, Inc.)

irretrievable. Cancellation then becomes the only viable solution.

Social Changes

"The Brady Bunch" was a harmless sitcom salute to traditional family values. Launched by ABC in 1969, it brought together a widower with three sons and a widow with three daughters (Figure 12.4). Their featherweight adventures were scheduled on Friday evening during the family hour, and the show achieved reasonably strong ratings for three seasons.

However, by 1972 CBS was presenting such gritty hits as "All in the Family," "Maude," and "M★A★S★H" and such sophisticated and well-turned series as "The Mary Tyler Moore Show" and

the "The Bob Newhart Show." As the audience members responded to these adult themes, their appetite for the marshmallow episodes of "The Brady Bunch" diminished, and the show was off the air by August 1974. Changing tastes and the social climate had rendered it obsolete.

Interestingly, shows that portray a simpler time are finding receptive audiences on TV Land or Nick at Nite. Somehow, young people who were not alive in the 1950s and 1960s are drawn to the television fare of those periods, enabling television to provide a kind of history lesson about cultural values.

The influx of programming about gays is one social change that revolutionized television starting around 2000. The number of shows that contain one or more gay characters has increased by leaps and bounds. Shows such as "Will & Grace," "Queer As Folk," "Queer Eye for the Straight Guy," or "Boy Meets Boy" would not have been accepted by a public watching "The Brady Bunch." Nor would that audience have accepted Ellen DeGeneres' declaration over an airport loudspeaker, "I'm gay."

As Robert Greenblatt, Showtime's president of entertainment, said, "In terms of how TV is developed, I think network executives and advertisers are much more open to gay characters than they have ever been before."[2]

There may still be complaints by groups objecting to the proliferation of gays on television, but it is clear that the social climate has enabled writers and producers to explore gay story lines in a way that would not have been possible a few years back.

Aging Demographics

Programming executives are attuned to aging demographics because they are frequently taken as a sign that a show is "on the bubble"—that is, in trouble. Aging demographics are often the first sign that a show is at risk. The usual pattern with programs is that the longer they are on, the older their demographics become. Young viewers tend to be restless; they are the first to seek new and different programs, and the first to leave them. Older viewers come later but then become fiercely loyal and are often willing to stay tuned for years. The departure of the young audience makes the program unappealing to advertisers, dictating a change. Sometimes the addition of new, youth-oriented elements in the program can slow the departure rate. It is always worth a try if the alternative is cancellation.

The Wrong Time Period

Programs have to be scheduled *sometime*. A programmer cannot leave gaping holes in the schedule. This is true for both commercial television and cable. Test patterns do not attract viewers, although some cynics might claim that test patterns are more entertaining than some of the shows that make it to air. Not all spots in the schedule are desirable. Some, however, are less desirable than others. Lower expectations for a show in a particularly difficult timeslot can allow a show a little breathing room, but a truly incompatible timeslot can quickly destroy a program's chances.

There are many examples of a badly scheduled show, but many would agree that the way Fox mishandled Seth MacFarlane's "Family Guy" is a textbook example of what not to do. Not content with the strong ratings that the show received when it followed "The Simpsons," in 1999 Fox scheduled the show against "Friends," where it garnered abysmal ratings. Fox then put the show on hiatus, eventually scheduling it

Tuesday nights where it stagnated with its companion piece, "Greg the Bunny," before putting the show on another hiatus.[3] Only the loyalty of fans and stellar DVD sales allowed the show to come back for the 2004–2005 season. Few shows have been moved around as much as "Family Guy," and few shows have been placed in as many poor timeslots.

During the 2003–2004 season, two shows in particular were placed in the wrong time periods: NBC's "Miss Match" and Fox's "Wonderfalls." "Miss Match" starred Alicia Silverstone as a lawyer with a knack for matchmaking, and "Wonderfalls," a quirky show about a girl who conversed with inanimate objects, starred Caroline Dhavernas. Both shows were scheduled Friday nights when the intended young audience is traditionally not at home watching television.

Excessive Relocation

"Hill Street Blues" is a classic case of a good program maneuvered into near extinction. In its first 4 months on the air, NBC shunted it around three time periods, much to the mounting fury of Grant A. Tinker, then the president of the producing company, MTM. Tinker recalled: "I watched them bounce the show around from pillar to post. [The NBC management] was crazed trying to find an audience. They were in a manic state even when they had something as good as they had with 'Hill Street.' So they put it on Thursday at 10:00, then Saturday at 10:00, then Tuesday at 9:00. Then they said, 'Make me two and we'll play it as 2 hours.' It was just no way to run a railroad." Fortunately, the program survived the changes, finally settled in at 10:00 P.M. Thursdays, and for 5 years was one of television's most popular series.

Not all shows can survive changes, particularly when there are so many choices a viewer can select. For example, NBC's "Just Shoot Me," once a strong ratings provider, was unable to overcome time and night changes. It performed well for 5 years on Thursday nights but was then moved to Tuesdays where it plummeted, causing the show's eventual cancellation in 2003.

Relocating "Buffy the Vampire Slayer" from the WB to UPN in 2001 split "Buffy" and its companion piece on the WB, "Angel," hurting both shows.

A Lack of Awareness

With so many choices available, it becomes a serious problem for programmers to ensure viewers know a show is on the air. Competition is fierce; many shows come and go making little or no noise. Even the most ardent television fanatics often do not know what is available. Wanda Sykes complained bitterly that nobody knew that her 2003–2004 show, "Wanda at Large" was on the Fox schedule before it was inevitably canceled. Similarly, who knew that the WB had a show called "The Help" or that UPN had "The Mullets" on the air during the same season?

Bringing on the Understudy

When patience is in short order, the show that was not placed on the schedule can start to look good, particularly if the chosen program is starting to stutter. Backup shows held in inventory are like backup quarterbacks. Every football fan knows that the most popular person in the stadium when things are going badly is the quarterback on the bench. He is always perceived to be the savior: fresh, exciting, gifted, and unflappable—until he gets in the game. Then, more often than not, he proves why he is No. 2.

Generally, the show in inventory was available when the schedule was set. It did not get on because it was judged weaker than other available choices. In effect, many replacements are rejects given a second chance. Programmers would do well to remember this before pulling a lineup apart too quickly.

The Desire for Something New

When new managers arrive, significant changes generally follow. They have been brought in to make things happen, and standing pat will not get it done. New officers also bring their pet projects, attitudes, and personnel with them; all of these usually find a place on the schedule, a strategy that does not always improve ratings. Often, the new ownership makes a dramatic across-the-board realignment of programming. A sure way for newcomers to make their presence felt is to get rid of the development of their predecessors. Cynics might add that it is easier to throw out the projects accumulated by the prior team than to review them. If change is called for, why not change everything?

For example, when Disney took over channel 9 (KHJ) in Los Angeles in the late 1980s, it changed not only the call letters to KCAL but also the programming philosophy. The station abandoned all entertainment shows in the evening and presented nothing but news. This was an extreme form of a new broom sweeping clean.

Mindy Herman changed everything about E! when she first got the position as head of the channel. Like most managers who take over a programming function, she wanted to leave her mark by making E! edgier than it had been. She stirred things up (before she was fired in 2004) with her hard-hitting celebrity exposes and by giving model

Anna Nicole Smith her own show. New hires want to break with the past. They want to try something new. It is how the television entertainment business operates.

When major concept changes occur, the networks often adopt different names—following the advice that it is better to start with a clean slate than have the remnants of the old failure hanging overhead. Christian Broadcast Network was originally religious programming. When it decided to change to wholesome family-oriented material, it became The Family Channel; now that it is owned by Disney, it is ABC Family. Likewise, when Daytime and Cable Health Network merged, they changed the name to Lifetime. Viacom's HA! and Time Warner's Comedy Channel merged to form Comedy Central. New names suggest a new direction, a new beginning, and hopefully a new larger audience.

Programming Options

When a show is not clicking or is stumbling, one of three changes may be necessary: placing the show in a new time period, adjusting program elements, or canceling the show.

Placing a Show in a New Time Period.
If a program is compatible with its time period, programmers are well advised to leave the program where it is. Remember, once the program is moved, the recruitment of viewers must start over. As we explained in the section on excessive relocation, unnecessary jockeying can be counterproductive.

There are two valid reasons for relocation: the program is underviewed and may prosper in a new period, or the show has developed independent strength and is ready to occupy a more important timeslot.

Programs placed in inhospitable periods have little chance of success. They may be against solidly entrenched opponents and not have a fair opportunity to be sampled. The time period may not offer the best demographics for the show's primary appeal. Or both. In these instances, if the programmer still has faith in the show, a move should be tried.

Even a show as mighty as "M★A★S★H" could not succeed everywhere it was placed. It premiered on Sundays at 8:00 P.M., a dismal spot for a dark comedy about the madness of war, and was almost canceled after its first season. The following year, CBS hammocked it Saturday nights at 8:30 between the phenomenally strong "All in the Family" and the equally powerful "The Mary Tyler Moore Show." It zoomed to fourth in the season's ratings. Once it had established its following, CBS management confidently moved it to Tuesdays at 8:30 P.M. behind the popular "Good Times," where it continued to perform well. But 1 year later, CBS inexplicably shuttled it to 8:30 P.M. Fridays to blunt the ratings of the then red-hot "Chico and the Man." The strategy backfired; "M★A★S★H" was shifted to 9:00 P.M. Tuesdays for 1 year and then spent 5 smash years at the same hour on Mondays.

The movement of a show to take on a more important role in an overall schedule can be an effective strategy. If the timing and judgment are correct, the relocation can attract a "bonus" audience for the entire night. As you have just seen, "M★A★S★H" was nurtured in a hammock position, developed its own large and loyal audience, and then "graduated" to a key time period to anchor a night's schedule.

The key element in relocation is timing. It must be done early in the show's life, as was done in 1994 when

Figure 12.5
Emmy Award-winning producer David E. Kelley vehemently objected to the relocation of his show, "The Practice." (Photo © ABC Photography Archives.)

restored to its original position, but it never recaptured its previous popularity. A costly maneuver indeed.

On the other hand, "The Simpsons" challenge of the "The Cosby Show" in 1990 paid off because the timing was right. In its second season on the air, when Simpson mania was at its zenith, the animated show moved against the perennial ratings champ then beginning its seventh year. It not only held its own, it knocked "Cosby" out of the Top 10. The following year, the season–long rating for "The Simpsons" was less than 2 points behind "Cosby" and toward the end of the run was topping it on occasion.

Sometimes a time change can cause significant friction. For example, in 2003, when ABC moved "The Practice" from its established timeslot on Sunday to Monday, überproducer David E. Kelley (Figure 12.5) complained vociferously about the change, which he interpreted as ABC's attempt to kill the show or to negotiate a lower license fee because of the lower ratings that the show would be getting as a result of the move. He was also widely quoted as saying that trying to understand ABC's thinking about scheduling was impossible because there was nothing in the minds of ABC schedulers.

CBS moved "Chicago Hope" so that it would not be up against "ER." The relationship between an audience and a time period is fragile. When the habit is disconnected, it is difficult to reconstruct. Only when a show is in its ascendancy is it prudent to risk a change.

An example from television history illustrates this point. In 1979, ABC took "Laverne and Shirley" out of the Tuesday 8:30 P.M. timeslot, where for 3 years it had been a successful extension of "Happy Days," and moved it to Thursdays at 8:00 P.M. The show's rating plummeted. At midseason, it was

There are risks as well as advantages to placing a show in a new time period. If a changed timeslot does not seem the best option, perhaps an adjustment in the program can solve the problem.

CHANGING CHANNEL NUMBERS ON CABLE

Cable systems frequently make changes in their channel lineup. Often, however, the only thing that is changed is the channel number. MTV may be switched from channel 12 to channel 26. The reasons for this are many.

Sometimes the system rebuilds to add channels and is then able to add more services. But rather than lumping all the new ones at the end, the system may want to give some rhyme or reason to channel numbers. For example, it may want to group all music services (MTV, VH1, Country Music Television, etc.). If the only music service it had been carrying previously was MTV, grouping these services may involve moving MTV. Sometimes channel moves are made to bring a whole region into conformance. Systems in a particular geographic area may decide that they should all place MTV on channel 26 so that MTV's programming can be promoted regionally without confusing the viewer.

Other times, cable systems remove certain services and replace them with other networks. Sometimes this is done from altruism—the desire to add a service that will serve the subscribers needs more effectively. More often, however, the decision is economic. One network's cost to the cable system will be less than another's cost. Or the system may feel it can make more from a pay-per-view service than from a basic network. To confront the cost issue, some favor an **à la carte** system. With à la carte programming, viewers only pay for the channels they watch. For example, if a household does not watch ESPN, one of the more expensive channels system operators pay for, then that household's channel options will not include ESPN at a savings to the household. Because most people do not watch all channels available to them, the à la carte option has many advocates.

Rarely will a system replace one pay service with another, such as eliminating Showtime and adding Cinemax. Reeducating all of Showtime's subscribers so that they switch to Cinemax is costly—and generally ineffective. The main result is loss of subscriber income for the system owner.

One of the chronic criticisms of cable systems is their inability (or lack of desire) to communicate channel changes to their subscribers. To subscribers, the alterations look wanton. One day they turn on the TV and the channels are flipped around—mass frustration. Systems are often wary of communicating exact details if the change involves eliminating some service. There are always people who will kick and fuss when something is taken away. What cable systems often do is send subscribers an innocent-looking channel card with their monthly bill. This lists the new lineup without indicating what has been eliminated.

Adjusting Program Elements. Many long-running shows, such as "ER" or "NYPD Blue," manage to stay fresh and engaging by introducing interesting story lines and captivating characters. They avoid exhaustion and readily adapt to changing social customs, adjusting program elements over time. Sometimes, however, elements need to be altered without the benefit of time.

During the pilot process, for example, casting adjustments need to be made quickly for the show to have a chance. During the 2004–2005 pilot season, many roles were recast once shows were picked up. Once a show is officially on the air, there is a risk that a casting change will disorient viewers. Sometimes, however, a program requires a change of personnel. Performers can become arrogant or sloppy in their work and begin to alienate viewers. On rare occasions, backstage demands by one cast member may stir up such hostile feelings among other principals that cast changes ensue. For example, the Hollywood rumor mill maintains that David Caruso was so difficult in the early years of "NYPD Blue" that both Amy Brenneman and Sherry Stringfield left the show.

When a show opens well but quickly begins to lose audience, it is a sign that viewers liked the idea but found something wanting. A change seems indicated. Too often producers are content to make cosmetic modifications: redesign the set, create a new theme song, or develop new graphics. These are not meaningful; even though they may be improvements, they do not influence a viewer's decision to watch.

The fundamental problem, whatever it is, must be addressed. To discover it, programmers are advised to commission the most definitive research possible in the shortest span of time. Setting up a series of focus groups in a variety of markets throughout the country is a useful approach.

As soon as the problem is defined, programmers should move immediately to make the adjustment. Speed is essential. The longer the show appears with its damaging flaw, the greater the number of core viewers who will be alienated. The hardest job in television is to recapture viewers who have sampled a program and rejected it. They tried it, have not liked it, and have gone on to other things, as was the case in 2003–2004 with Stephen King's "Kingdom Hospital," a show that began with positive ratings and quickly went downhill.

To remain viable and to continue to be funded, PBS has made interesting adjustments. In addition to programming more American shows and importing fewer from England, PBS, under the leadership of Pat Mitchell, has adjusted its programming philosophy to include programs that reflect a more conservative point of view.

Rightly or wrongly, PBS has been perceived to have a markedly liberal agenda, with Bill Moyers as the key liberal spokesman. To correct the impression that PBS espoused liberalism at the expense of other voices, Mitchell, who became the head of PBS in 2000, recruited significant conservative voices to public television, such as Tucker Carlson, the co-host of CNN's "Crossfire," and Paul Gigot, the editorial-page editor of *The Wall Street Journal*.

PBS must have funding from the government; Congress provides approximately 15% of PBS's annual budget, approximately $2 billion in 2004.[4] Mitchell's programming adjustment silenced complaints about PBS's liberal bias and enabled it to continue to receive needed financial support.

Cable is more tolerant than commercial television. Quick cancellations are more common on commercial television than on cable. As cable matures and builds more advertiser support, it may find it necessary to succumb to some of the quick cancellation policies of the networks. At present, cable services are unlikely to remove it once they have produced it.

Cancellations. Since the early to mid-1980s, the rate of program cancellations has accelerated. Patience is hard to come by, and in an environment increasingly controlled by conglomerates, parent companies are reluctant to take a wait-and-see approach to programming. The introduction of **overnight** or fast national ratings to virtually every major market and the expansion of the number of cable channels have accelerated the cancellation rate. These factors have intensified competition, thinned the audience size for most shows, and supplied buyers with immediate rating information. In such a superheated environment, buyers are disinclined to wait to see whether a program can find an audience. In the area of network prime-time programming, the rate of cancellation for new shows approaches 80%. The syndication story is much the same.

Public broadcasting, on the other hand, has been the most traditionally benign of all forms when it comes to cancellation. Programs such as "Masterpiece Theatre," "The MacNeil–Lehrer NewsHour" ("The NewsHour with Jim Lehrer" since the death of Robert

MacNeil), and "Sesame Street" (Figure 12.6) have been on for decades, virtually unchanged. The problems within public television have not revolved around coping with change but rather around initiating any, but this too may be changing.

Giving a Cancellation Notice

The joy of the business is issuing pickups. Everyone is happy, hands are pumped, and optimism abounds. Buyers enjoy this function; it makes them heroes and reasserts their power. Unfortunately, there is a reverse side to the ceremony, the dreaded cancellation announcement. All shows come to an end—some after a few episodes, some after a decade. Whenever it happens, a member of the buying side must inform the people on the production side. Although always an uncomfortable, sometimes painful process, there are certain procedures that, if properly observed, can ease the discomfort and form the basis for renewed relationships.

The first thing representatives on both sides must remember is that the industry is small and time moves swiftly. Buyers need sellers and sellers need buyers. It is imperative that both parties separate in a manner that permits, even encourages, future associations. The cancellation conversation is no time for vindictiveness, vituperation, or settling old scores. The brief pleasure such an outburst might afford can have disastrous consequences. Buyers who satisfy themselves by letting loose a diatribe against the producer may be cutting themselves off from future hits; sellers who unleash a blast are simply reducing by one the potential buyers for their next project.

Even in a competitive town where everyone claims to be making the "tough decisions," executives do not want to be the bearers of bad news. One

Figure 12.6
"Sesame Street" which began in 1969, has had great longevity on public television and is one of the reasons funding for public broadcasting survives. Whenever funding is threatened, the prestige and love for the show is invoked. "Sesame Street" draws guest stars, such as Whoopi Goldberg. (Courtesy Children's Television Workshop.)

experienced producer, for example, maintains that executives who promise to get back to you with an answer in a few days simply will not initiate the call that delivers bad news. If a producer wants a clear answer, he or she will have to keep calling to force a reluctant executive to speak up. Otherwise, 3 to 4 weeks (or months) without a response is assumed to be a "no."

The guidelines for cancellation are few but important:

1. The head person should do it
   a. Too many program leaders try to duck the assignment. It is awkward and difficult, and they would rather not. That is a mistake. Production company executives admire the head buyer who has the courage to say the tough words, and it is somehow less painful to hear it from the summit.
   b. When the cancellation notice is delegated to a lower level staff member, as when NBC's Jeff Zucker had subordinates call Julia

Louis-Dreyfus to inform her that her show, "Watching Ellie," was canceled,[5] the production people are left with a second-class feeling that, when added to their already depressed condition, can result in a deeply resentful attitude.

c. Sending an email announcing a cancellation, reportedly done to staff members of Fox's "Cedric the Entertainer Presents,"[6] is similarly not the way to handle the situation.

2. The producers must be the first to know

a. This is not always easy in a visible business with a highly refined rumor mill. However, the quality buyer will always take every precaution against the premature leak of a cancellation decision. It is grossly unfair for a producer to read about his or her show's demise in a trade article or through some other unauthorized source. Nothing will guarantee a quicker and longer-lasting rupture between the buyer and the seller than a clumsily handled cancellation that embarrasses the producer and the staff.

3. Tell the right person

a. This can vary from show to show. The prevailing rule is to notify the person with whom the original deal was made. For the major production companies, the appropriate party is usually the head of television production at the studio. Chances are this was the person with whom the agreement was first reached, and it is fitting that the circle be completed with the same principals. Sometimes, because of personal relationships or other unusual dynamics, the right contact is the executive producer or producer.

b. With smaller production entities, the key person is often the agent representing the project. The agent might have put the package together, negotiated the deal, served as an intermediary in disputes, and generally been acknowledged as the pivotal business element in the enterprise. For these programs, it is appropriate to notify the agent first.

4. Make additional calls

a. After the chief person on the production side has been contacted and has had a reasonable opportunity to inform the talent and staff, it is wise and humane for the programmer to follow up with calls to cast members and key staff personnel. The personal touch will be appreciated, and the conversations (brief is best) give the programmer an opportunity to express gratitude and establish a warm basis for future associations.

b. The cancellation dialogue is as much about the next show as it is about the defunct show. What is gone is gone. Both parties should conduct themselves a manner that makes another program possible.

RADIO

Changes and cancellations in radio can vary: slowly phasing a song out of play rotation, pulling the plug on a host or disc jockey no longer perceived to connect with the desired demographic, or even erasing a station's format and supplanting it with new hosts, songs, call letters, and all other content. As with commercial TV, the driving force behind change is nearly always ratings.

Adjusting Program Elements

If a station does reasonably well overall in the ratings but one daypart is low, then it is time to look to the elements that make up that segment of time. Sometimes the problem is inherent in the clock—there may be too much news, advertising, or chatter. Those problems are easy to correct. But more often the problem lies with the on-air personality—the disc jockey, talk show host, or anchor newscaster.

Focus groups and TVQ-type tests can confirm this possibility. A disc jockey on a contemporary-oriented station may simply grow older and no longer relate to the teenage audience. Such was the case when comedic staple deejay Rick Dees was bumped off youth-oriented Top 40 station KIIS-FM in 2004, replaced by the younger, up-and-coming deejay and "American Idol" host Ryan Seacrest. Weekly shows, such as "American Top 40," have seen a procession of hosts. Casey Kasem began the show in 1970 to be followed, in 1988, by a 10-year stint with host Shadoe Stevens. In 1998, Kasem returned to host the show until he was supplanted in 2004 by Seacrest. Seacrest saw his demographic appeal change over time—although in an atypical direction, from adult to youth markets. Before he started dodging potshots about his "metrosexual" preening from notorious "American Idol" judge Simon Cowell, Seacrest was host of an afternoon drive radio show on the more adult-oriented Los Angeles station STAR 98.7 (Figure 12.7).

The career of another STAR 98.7 disc jockey, Richard Blade, shows a more common career trajectory in terms of demographic appeal. Born in England, where he cut his teeth on the BBC, in the early 1980s Blade saw a Clint Eastwood movie and asked himself the question, "Do you feel lucky, punk?" His answer was yes, and he packed his headphones and headed for California, where he quickly became the No. 1

Figure 12.7
Ryan Seacrest's cache with youth after hosting "American Idol" primed him to take over coveted radio positions with KIIS-FM and American Top 40. (Globe Photos, Inc.)

Arbitron-rated radio personality during the heyday of Los Angeles's alternative rock station, KROQ. With his radio duties, he took on various television hosting positions (much as Seacrest is doing in the new millennium). The 1990s saw a slow waning of Blade's cache in the youth-oriented radio market, and in 2000 he moved to the Caribbean to teach scuba and write scripts, returning in 2002. Soon he began to host VH1's "Bands Reunited" show, taking advantage of his contacts and memories of VH1's older demographics and starting his deejay stint with STAR, playing "Flashback" songs from his 1980s heyday at KROQ.[7]

When a personality must be fired, the executives should exercise the same care described regarding commercial TV show cancellations—the news should come from the top, and the person involved should be the first to know. Every on-air person has some supporters, and a messy firing can lead to negative press for the radio station.

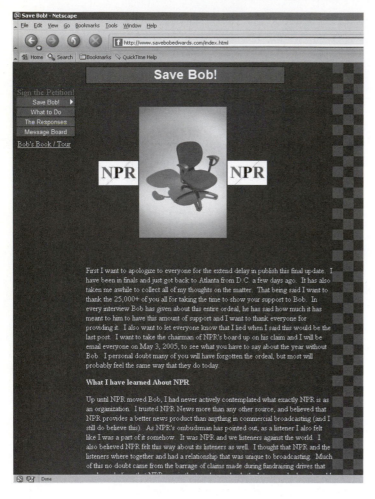

First I want to apologize to everyone for the extend delay in publish this final update. I have been in finals and just got back to Atlanta from D.C. a few days ago. It has also taken me awhile to collect all of my thoughts on the matter. That being said I want to thank the 25,000+ of you all for taking the time to show your support to Bob. In every interview Bob has given about this entire ordeal, he has said how much it has meant to him to have this amount of support and I want to thank everyone for providing it. I also want to let everyone know that I lied when I said this would be the last post. I want to take the chairman of NPR's board up on his claim and I will be email everyone on May 3, 2005, to see what you have to say about the year without Bob. I personal doubt many of you will have forgotten the ordeal, but most will probably feel the same way that they do today.

What I have learned About NPR

Up until NPR moved Bob, I had never actively contemplated what exactly NPR is as an organization. I trusted NPR News more than any other source, and believed that NPR provides a better news product than anything in commercial broadcasting (and I still do believe this). As NPR's ombudsman has pointed out, as a listener I also felt like I was a part of it somehow. It was NPR and we listeners against the world. I also believed NPR felt this way about its listeners as well. I thought that NPR and the listeners where together and had a relationship that was unique to broadcasting. Much of this no doubt came from the barrage of claims made during fundraising drives that

Figure 12.8
When NPR decided to remove Bob Edwards from its flagship morning program, "Morning Edition," there was great outcry, including the launch of a website, Savebobedwards.com. This occurred despite the advance notice the network provided to try to dull any controversy.

NPR hoped to dull this kind of negative reaction in listeners when, in 2004, it decided to replace the 3-decade anchor of its "Morning Edition" news program, Bob Edwards. It announced the decision some time before Edwards's last day hosting the show. Despite the early notice, the outcry from listeners and even from some member stations and other on-air talent was far from muted. One listener started a website, SaveBobEdwards.com (Figure 12.8), to give other disgruntled listeners a place to combine their efforts to contest the decision and even discuss whether they would stop contributing to NPR. Many listeners worried that, in dropping Edwards from the show (despite keeping him on as a senior correspondent for the

network), NPR was kowtowing to demographics and ratings just as commercial radio does. Everyone at NPR, including Edwards, danced around the reasons for the change. NPR's senior vice president for programming, Jay Kernis, said, in a cryptic response to a petition from SaveBobEdwards.com, "this is about our broad commitment to delivering the kind of high-quality in-depth coverage that makes our reporting remarkable," noting, in a seeming contradiction, that "we know that [Edwards] will continue to make an extraordinary contribution in his new role."[8]

Another element that leads to program adjustment is **burnout.** The popularity of current songs does not last. Programmers must know when to remove a hit from airplay so that listeners do not turn to another station simply because they are tired of hearing the song. Watching the charts in the trade journals can give some indication of burnout, as can the telephone research described in the evaluation chapter.

Programmers can make rough predictions about when burnout will occur by considering the complexity of the music. Complicated music takes longer to burn out than simpler music. Songs with irregular rhythm and more verses last longer than songs with regular rhythm and repetitive choruses. Also, the more often the song is played on the radio, the faster it is likely to burnout. Songs on their way to burnout should be played less often than songs at their peak.

Network Changes

Some radio networks produce programs subject to cancellation, but few are given the ax. Once a program has gained an audience, it often continues in perpetuity unless it is closely related or eponymous with its host and that host departs or dies. NPR, for example, did not need to cancel its flagship "Morning Edition" program just because its originating host, Bob Edwards, was replaced. Similarly, "American Top 40" has survived the departure of Casey Kasem—twice. When, in 2003, Rush Limbaugh left the airwaves temporarily to seek drug treatment, the show was able to survive on a string of guest hosts, but had Limbaugh's absence been protracted, the show would not have been able to continue, at least not under its Rush Limbaugh moniker.

When a network alters its programs, the change is usually not traumatic. As Ed Salamon, president of programming for Unistar, said, "All our programming is produced in-house. When something is canceled, people can move from one project to another within the company. Our main problems are with the advertisers. If an advertiser is on a show that is not doing well and we need to cancel it, we have to decide what to do with the ads. Usually we can transfer them to another program. Also, if a station was dependent on the program we are canceling, we try to help them find something else."

Canceling and changing are not major issues for radio. When ratings (and hence dollars) are low, alterations are called for. But because some stations do not even use ratings as part of their sales pitch, a well-thought-out programming philosophy can keep advertisers and audience happy for long periods.

Dealing with Unwanted Changes

Dan Jensen of PRI noted, "We received a lot of complaints when we stopped the extensive Gulf War coverage [in 1991]—even though the war was over." Even worse for PRI was the cancellation of Garrison Keillor's "Prairie Home Companion." Keillor left because he wanted to explore new vistas unrelated to radio. "The audience really complained," said Jensen. "We tried airing reruns of his programs, but that didn't work very well. When Garrison finally decided to return to public radio several years later, his following came back almost instantly."

In 2004, Clear Channel yanked "The Howard Stern Show" off all the network's stations that had been airing it (only six—although one in the major market of San Diego) after a caller to the program used a racially charged word and was hung up on by Stern. Nonetheless, the show continued to air on more than 40 stations owned by Clear Channel competitor Infinity Broadcasting. Stern argued that the same racially charged word had been used countless times on his show in the past. What, he asked, made this instance any different? He asked his listeners to scour what other radio programs were airing and alert his show to any "offensive" content that others were getting away with without the kind of sanctions he had suffered both from the FCC and from Clear Channel. His listeners found no dearth of such instances, giving Stern justification for claiming that the crackdown on his show was not motivated by the words or situations it contained but by some other reason— political or religious agendas, he surmised. "As soon as I came out against [President George W.] Bush, that's when my rights to free speech were taken away. It had nothing to do with

Figure 12.9
Although primarily apolitical or antipolitical in the past, Howard Stern took to criticizing President George W. Bush and even supported his Democratic rival in the 2004 election, Senator John Kerry. Stern was soon removed from Clear Channel's lineup and saw his troubles with the FCC mount, which he says proves that the censorship against him was politically motivated. (Globe Photos, Inc.)

THE INTERNET

Content on the Internet comes and goes as regularly as a high-fiber diet. Because web developers do not have to worry about finding room in a temporal schedule for their material, decisions are not either/or, as they are on radio and television. If some content is deemed worthy of putting resources into developing, another project does not have to be sidelined to make room for it; however, more production money must be spent to develop two projects rather than one. Once developed, content can stay online as long as it is desired. For many reasons, however, the desired time may not be long.

Is It Worth the Trouble?

As explained in previous chapters, one of the cardinal rules in web development is to keep content fresh—if you want audience members to have the incentive to return after their first visit to the site. When in an early episode of NBC's "Will & Grace" the character Jack mentioned he was starting a Just-Jack.com website, NBC had the site running in time to rope in all the show's diehard fans who would undoubtedly log on to see whether the site existed. It did, although it was composed of only of a few pages, rarely updated and soon gone, replaced by a page that simply redirected visitors to the main "Will & Grace" website. Obviously, executives at NBC did not find a way for the Just-Jack.com site to help the bottom line of the show enough to justify the expense of keeping it up to date.

On the other hand, public television's "American Family" series started off with a companion website relating to one of the characters, Cisco, and "Cisco's Journal" on the web has continued to expand as new episodes to the show are aired.

indecency," Stern said March 19, 2004[9] (Figure 12.9).

Obviously, this kind of sniping by a nationally syndicated personality, such as Stern, could turn off some listeners from Clear Channel stations as a matter of principle. But with Clear Channel's dominance of the radio market after deregulation, many argue that a listener who wants to boycott Clear Channel as a result of this issue would practically have to throw his or her tuner in the trash.

Granted, with a more continuous story line than the episodic "Will & Grace," perhaps "American Family" is a better fit for a web journal, but it is doubtful that it would survive to the extent that it has were the show on commercial television and subject to the financial exigencies of the commercial market.

If the resources or time are not available to keep a site up to date, there is little reason to embark on the project. The only way that a blog, for example, attains a consistent and growing audience is if there is constant activity on it. If a web surfer visits a site once and likes what she or he finds there but on several successive visits finds nothing new, chances are that interest will drop, no matter how strong the initial attraction was. A blogger whose posts are infrequent will soon find he or she might as well keep a journal unlocked on his or her coffee table—it will probably attract more viewers that way.

TMI: Too Much Information

Some bloggers or persons that maintain personal sites sometimes take down sites for reasons other than not having the time to keep them up to date or thinking that what they put up might be going into the great abyss of anonymity. With carefully honed search engines, some may worry about what others will find out about them if, for example, they are looking for a job. Maybe a

potential employer will "google" them and find some crass comment they made in response to a post on a bawdy blog somewhere in the Internet ether. Webmasters of sites that invite public posts are often approached with requests that posts be expunged.

Facelifts and Add-ons

But unless they are failing financially (in which case they simply drop off of the map), most websites—like television shows and, to a lesser extent, radio—simply go in for occasional facelifts. This keeps them fresh and lets them incorporate new technologies and ideas. A television show running out of story lines might have a crotchety, recently widowed in-law move in so that it can continue and move into the lucrative syndication market; a website might want to get more out of its audience by adding content or new branches to the well-traveled trunk of its offerings.

As this chapter and most of the others have pointed out, the programming process involves many hard decisions in the spheres of both interpersonal relationships and global concepts. Programmers are faced with many alternatives and temptations as they attempt to meet the goals of their organizations and their own needs. How these decisions can be handled is the subject of our final chapter—programming ethics.

EXERCISES

1. Pick a current radio or television program that in your opinion might be at risk of cancellation. Suggest specific changes that might help keep the program on the air.

2. Select a current program you would cancel. What specific reasons would you provide to back up your decision?

3. When listening to the radio, note when you change the station. What, if any-thing, could the station change, in its programming, to keep you tuned in?

4. You are the executive in charge of giving a cancellation notice for a scheduled program. Prepare what you would say. How would you ensure you could work with the production team in the future?

5. Identify some specific social changes that have influenced program adjustments or cancellations.

REFERENCES/NOTES

1. Les Brown. *Television: The Business Behind the Box* (New York: Harcourt Brace Jovanovich, 1971), pp. 55–56.

2. Paula Hendrickson. "In His Own Words: Robert Greenblatt," *Emmy,* Issue No. 3, 2004, pp. 72–74.

3. Jon Ganahl. "Family Guy," an unpublished paper, May 8, 2003, pp. 1–5.

4. Ken Auletta. "Big Bird Flies Right," *The New Yorker,* June 7, 2004, p. 42.

5. Elizabeth Jensen. "The TV Stars, the Ads and All That Jazz," *Los Angeles Times,* May 12, 2003, p. E-12.

6. Greg Braxton. "'Cedric' Gone but Not Quite," *Los Angeles Times,* June 20, 2003, p. E-32.

7. "Richard Blade: The DJ that Helped Shape the New Wave Music Scene is Back and Exclusively on STAR 98.7," http://www.star987.com/richardblade.html. Accessed June 11, 2004.

8. Jay Kernis. "NPR's April Response," http://www.savebobedwards.com/npr_s_april_response.html. Accessed June 11, 2004.

9. Maureen Farrell. "The Clear Channel Controversy, One Year On (Why Howard Stern's Woes Are Your Woes, Too)," http://www.buzzflash.com/farrell/04/03/far04009.html. Accessed June 13, 2004.

13 Programming Ethics

In this chapter you will learn about the following:

- Ethical dilemmas regularly faced by television, radio, and Internet programmers
- The thin line that separates a legal matter from an ethical one
- How the blending of news with entertainment has made ethical debates increasingly complicated
- Some "real life" case studies that reflect the complexities associated with programming ethics
- Guidelines instituted to address programming ethics
- Student interest in a required course in ethics as preparation for future entertainment careers

The way the story goes, the devil appeared to a network executive one day and said, "I'm going to offer you a deal. For the upcoming season, I will arrange it so that you can have on your schedule, *and no one else's,* Ray Romano, the reunited cast of 'Friends,' 'The Simpsons,' and *all* of the shows created by Jerry Bruckheimer. In exchange, you must turn over your soul to me for all eternity." The executive thought for a moment and said, "What's the catch?"

Many a joke has been leveled at the industry's cynical ethical behavior, partly because it is true, partly because it is a highly visible business, and partly because its participants have a gift for self-mockery. The famed radio comedian, Fred Allen, once commented, "You can take all the sincerity in Hollywood, stuff it into a gnat's navel, and still have room for six caraway seeds and the heart of an agent."

As an industry, entertainment is probably no worse than any other, which is not much of a compliment. However, television, radio, and the Internet are the most far-reaching and persuasive communication tools ever developed; therefore, those involved in these media bear a greater ethical burden than most companies. Unfortunately, cynical realism often prevails: Get the deal first, sort out the ethics later. Do not worry about the people who got screwed; they will be back. With mergers, megacompanies become the only game in town, and those who want employment have few alternatives, no matter how they are treated.

The hope is that the next generation of broadcasters will aim higher and do better. Toward that end, this chapter includes some guidelines for ethical behavior. We encourage you to keep these in mind when analyzing the case histories that are the focal point of this, the final chapter of the text.

THE MEANING OF ETHICS

Ethics is a code of moral principles. It is the value system relating to human conduct by which actions are deemed right or wrong. To be sure, there is a sizable gray area in the evaluation of most ethical behavior, but broadcasters should strive to recognize ethical right and wrong, even under difficult circumstances. It is often said that the key to being successful in programming is the ability to think quickly on your feet. This includes being able to quickly decide what is the ethical thing to do and what is not.

Students have found that ethics and values are increasingly important in the workplace but that most disciplines do not do enough to prepare them for the real world.[1] In this chapter, we approach programming ethics from several perspectives to enable you to make informed, ethical decisions.

Ethics and Illegality

It is important to make a distinction between what is legal and what is ethical. The two are not synonymous. Payola is against the law: A record company cannot bribe a disc jockey by giving him or her money to play a song. However, a record company can "present" a song as an advertisement and pay the station for airing the ad—and song. In 2004, when this newest pay-for-play strategy came to light, it was not illegal, but is it ethical?

As explained in a previous chapter, performers touted pharmaceuticals without disclosing that they were paid spokesmen for the makers of the drugs. Illegal? No. Ethical? A story line on ABC's "According to Jim" has the characters from the show doing a commercial for the Disney Cruise Line; ABC is a part of Disney. Illegal? No. Ethical?

Video news releases from companies and even the government are frequently offered to beleaguered news programs strapped for money. Some of these "news segments" have phony news anchors, but they are not illegal. Are they ethical? For example, the use of video news releases came under scrutiny in 2004 when they were used by the Bush administration to introduce a newly passed Medicare plan (and, doubters suggest, to gain political points for the Republican-controlled White House and Congress). Produced by the Department of Health and Human Services using tax dollars, these releases appeared to be stories reported by legitimate news anchors, but the on-camera anchors (actors, not newscasters) read scripts prepared by the government. The videos have drawn criticism from some news media ethicists, who consider them at odds with journalism's mission to verify independently the claims of corporations and governments.[2]

"RED CHANNELS": A TEST THAT TELEVISION FLUNKED

With the disintegration of the Soviet Union well behind us, it is difficult for Americans today to realize how frightened people were in the 1950s of the perceived imminent spread of communism. This national fear provided the television industry with an early test of its integrity, and it failed.

At the conclusion of World War II, hysteria gripped the United States. Nazism had been defeated, but a new and potentially more destructive opponent had surfaced—communism. When the Soviets exploded an atomic device in 1948, thereby ending America's exclusive hold on nuclear armament, the country was terrified over the prospect of an Armageddon-like showdown with the "Red Menace."

Fueling these fears was Senator Joseph McCarthy, who claimed to have knowledge of communists, "pinkos," red sympathizers, and dupes in the United States Cabinet, Army, State Department, and all levels of national and state government. Citizens desperately attempted to establish their own patriotic purity and expose the traitorous intent of others.

This paranoid environment had a devastating effect on the entertainment industry. Because radio, television, and motion pictures were capable of reaching millions with their messages, the superpatriots resolved to prevent any possibility of sinister influence by denying employment to anyone even remotely tainted with communist sympathies. Thus was born the pernicious policy of "blacklisting."

In 1947, some former FBI employees formed a newsletter titled "Counterattack," a publication designed to battle communist infiltration in the United States. Shortly thereafter, they published the first edition of "Red Channels," a booklet containing the names of those in the entertainment media considered politically unacceptable.

A person could be listed for a variety of reasons: membership in an organization deemed subversive, a relationship with someone with communistic links, attendance at a leftist function, signing a telegram congratulating the Moscow Art Theater on its 50th anniversary, etc. Much was based on hearsay and unsupported evidence, but once a name made the list, it was virtually impossible to have it removed.

The booklet was distributed to networks, stations, advertisers, and their agencies. The implications were clear: any broadcaster or sponsor who hired someone on the list was knowingly aiding the cause of communism in the United States.

Other organizations supplemented "Red Channels" in the search for offenders. The American Legion's Commission on Americanism developed "Firing Line," a publication that identified dupes and red-fronters, and a supermarket operator in Syracuse, NY, Laurence A. Johnson, founded the Syracuse Crusade. Whenever a manufacturer advertised on a program that employed a "listed" person, Johnson threatened to hang a sign on the shelves where the offender's products were displayed stating that the company supported subversives.

These "patriotic" efforts were dismayingly effective. The networks and the agencies instructed producers that no performer, writer, or director was to be hired without undergoing a clearance procedure. If the person's name appeared in "Red Channels" or any of the other lists, he or she would be rejected. However, the existence of a blacklist was never to be acknowledged. Producers were told to use such phrases as "you're not right for the part" or "we've found someone a little more qualified." This led some talented people to despair, financial ruin, and even suicide.

In some instances, the malevolence of the practice reached ludicrous levels. On one occasion, Mark Goodson, television's foremost producer of game shows, was stunned to learn that a panelist on one of his shows had been declared unacceptable by the sponsoring advertising agency and was to be dropped immediately. She was an English actress named Anna Lee, and she had no known political affiliations and a seemingly innocent history. Goodson dug into the matter and discovered that she had been confused with another Anna Lee who wrote occasional articles for the *Daily Worker,* a leftist newspaper. When he confronted the agency with this information, the executives said, "Yes, we know that, but she still has to go. We're already receiving letters." Goodson exploded and stormed out of the meeting. He was later told that as soon as the door closed someone asked, "Is he a pinko?" Lee stayed on. So did the show. And so did blacklisting, at least until the late 1950s.

continued

Ironically, one of the main contributing forces to the end of the practice was television. The famed TV journalist Edward R. Murrow (Figure 13.1) presented a program that exposed McCarthy and his methods. This program is generally cited as the beginning of the senator's declining influence. In 1954, network TV covered congressional hearings in which McCarthy accused U.S. Army personnel of having red sympathies. He and his aids bullied witnesses to such an extent that the public became outraged and the Senate voted to censure McCarthy.

Will censorship and character assassination of this magnitude ever again plague the television industry? Vigilance, ethics, and courage by the next generation of programmers will help prevent a reoccurrence.

The surge in reality programs has resulted in a series of complex legal and ethical questions. What does getting a release from a reality show contestant mean? Can an 18-page release form entitle a programmer to do whatever the show's creative team demands? If a contestant has signed a full release, is nothing private? For example, can the camera follow you everywhere, including the bathroom? Is nothing off limits when competition for "eyeballs" gets fiercer every year? A programmer may be covered legally if the phalanx of lawyers has done its job, but will he or she be covered ethically?

Had the Kentucky-based Center for Rural Strategies not pressured CBS to abandon its reality show, "The Real Beverly Hillbillies," could the show have made fun of the transplanted Southern rural families every time they were baffled by the sophistication of glamorous Beverly Hills? (One CBS executive made the mistake of talking about the hilarity that would ensue when the hillbillies went about interviewing maids.[3]) Might ethics have been slighted at the expense of rural America, even if the releases covered all the legal bases? CBS dropped the search for the right families (some called it "a hick hunt"), seeking to save face by claiming it simply could not find the right participants for the show, which, by that time, had become a public relations nightmare.

Ethics in Programming Decisions and Business Practices

For those in the media, ethical conduct involves two constituencies: the audience and the people in the industry. The audience develops a feel for the character of a broadcaster by the messages put on the screen. Overly hyped and misleading promos, excessive violence in newscasts and entertainment programs, disregard for important but perhaps low-rated local events, wanton commercialism, shabby productions, and sweeps specials drenched in sensationalism are clues to the viewer about the broadcaster's ethical standards.

Within the industry, producers, executives, and others build or harm their

Figure 13.1
Newsman Edward R. Murrow did a show that exposed Senator Joseph McCarthy's tactics during the era of blacklisting in the late 1940s and 1950s. (Globe Photos, Inc.)

Figure 13.2
Producer Steve White, shown here on the set of one of his Halloween Disney Channel movies, has found that writing up the key points discussed at meetings helps avoid confusion and misunderstandings. (Photo courtesy Steve White.)

reputations if they do not treat suppliers, advertisers, and fellow employees honorably. If the word gets out that whatever a particular executive says means nothing, that executive is going to have a hard time getting people to deal with him or her. Nobody wants to do repeat business with someone whose word is meaningless.

Ethics and Lying

In broadcasting, lying is probably the most common form of unethical behavior. The euphemist might prefer to call it "fudging the truth," but no matter how you perfume it, it is an intentional untruthful declaration to another person. German philosopher Immanuel Kant held that any lie, no matter how virtuous the intent, is unacceptable because "it vitiates the source of law."[4]

Broadcasting is fast paced. Much of the dealmaking is done over the phone or at meetings in which the recording of agreements is either impossible or impractical. It is essential that both parties honor their commitments even if there are no other witnesses and no documents. Trust has to be the foundation of the contract. If one of the parties is lying, or later denies commitments, all future contact between the parties will be contaminated.

Experienced producer and executive Steve White has a simple solution to the confusion that often follows a meeting involving a lot of people covering a lot of ground. After a meeting, he writes down what was said and sends his notes to the executive at the network for confirmation that he got the details right (Figure 13.2). For him, this solves many problems of interpretation.

Some fine distinctions about ethics and lying need to be made about the buying and selling process. A certain tolerance is allowed for the hyperbole and enthusiasm of a seller. When a salesperson says, "This is the hottest show since

'Friends,'" the buyer knows that this is **puffery;** it is not to be taken literally.

Puffery is one thing, but an outright lie is something else. For a producer eager to make a sale to say that "Adam Sandler and Julia Roberts are scheduled to guest star in a series' first week," when both have flatly refused to appear, is a breach. Many executives avoid telling lies not simply for ethical reasons but also because it becomes too hard to remember what lie was told to what person. It is too easy to trip up.

The buyer–seller exchange is akin to the evasive moves of the ball carrier in a football game, the head fakes by the basketball star, or the luring traps of the chessmaster. They are all designed to mislead, and are "lies" in a sense, but within an environment where such actions are accepted. The behavior this chapter addresses relates to words and actions presented as truth and intended to be accepted as truth. Anyone who exploits that belief to misdirect and deceive is guilty of unethical conduct.

Then there is the Internet. Relative anonymity makes it a fertile breeding ground for lies and awkward or rude behavior among individuals who may not otherwise mix and may never meet in person. Etiquette on the Internet (or Netiquette) has special ethical concerns. Step into any public chat room on AOL or Yahoo and, despite the strident terms-of-use guidelines that forbid it and promise banishment, the room will doubtless, at some point, be flooded with expletives, hateful or rude comments, or just a stream of unfathomable nonsequitors. Perhaps you will initiate a chat with someone who will intrigue you with weird responses to your first few questions then send you a web link to a site, and you will realize you have been trying to talk with an impersonal program, or "bot," designed to increase traffic to the site.

More disturbing still is the "flaming," or insult throwing, that happens in online discussion groups, forums, or just email. With the anonymity of the Internet, and the numerous communication cues lacking in much of the text-based interaction online, it is easy to be misunderstood or to jump to conclusions and respond without thinking first. Many an aggressive or demeaning word is typed online, even if the person doing the typing would not dare respond so offensively anywhere other than in cyberspace. When people allow themselves to act so out of their normal character, is that, in some ways, a lie? Many people, doubtless, go online simply to cause trouble, which can be disturbing to those who want earnest business interactions or social contact. For some, flaming has become an art—coming up with the perfect quip to squash unsuspecting web surfers. Often one quip leads to an equally acerbic response and a flame war might start, throwing whatever civilized discussion might have been occurring off of its tracks.

For these reasons and more, many people have suggested Netiquette, some common principals of which are as follows:

- Act in your Internet interaction as you would in your real life.
- Remember that you are (usually) dealing with another human being, not just a disembodied string of words.
- Respect other people's time. If you are in a playful or not-serious mood, are looking to blow off steam, or simply want to waste time online, try to make this clear to anyone with whom you may be engaging and make sure that person is on the same page.
- Respect other people's privacy. It is easy to go blabbing about other

people online, in discussion groups, in mass emails, or on a blog. If you are not sure that someone would appreciate having personal facts advertised, change the name or details to make the person unrecognizable or just share details about yourself.

- Do not add fuel to the fire of a flame war. When others are engaged in an annoying string of insults, although it may be tempting to tell them how infantile, moronic, and tiresome they are being, doing so will likely only invite a string of new insults toward you. It is better to leave or simply ignore what is happening and hope cooler heads will eventually prevail.
- Contribute your expertise. Everyone is good at something or has some useful knowledge or experience to share with others. If you know a way to easily remove melted wax from plush carpeting, by all means post it on the Internet. You will save someone's day.

ETHICAL GUIDELINES

Most of the great philosophers—Hume, Mill, Kant, Augustine—have written extensively on the subject of ethics. Their works are available in libraries, and we encourage you to consult them. It is not this book's intent to endorse any particular ethical system. It is simply our hope that a heightened awareness of ethical considerations will help you make sound judgments and improve the moral environment of the industry.

Several ethical codes have been drawn up by professional media organizations to help guide people in the industry. These codes often contain vague language and none of them are enforceable, but they serve as guidelines to ethical behavior. For example the Radio–Television News Directors Association has drawn up the following standards,

and its members have pledged to follow them:

1. Strive to present the source or nature of broadcast news material in a way that is balanced, accurate, and fair.
   a. Evaluate information solely on its merits as news, rejecting sensationalism or misleading emphasis in any form.
   b. Guard against using audio or video material in a way that deceives the audience.
   c. Do not mislead the public by presenting as spontaneous news any material that is staged or rehearsed.
   d. Identify people by race, creed, nationality, or prior status only when it is relevant.
   e. Clearly label opinion and commentary.
   f. Promptly acknowledge and correct errors.
2. Strive to conduct yourself in a manner that protects from conflicts of interest, real or perceived. Decline gifts or favors that would influence or appear to influence judgments.
3. Have respect for the dignity, privacy, and well-being of people with whom you deal.
4. Recognize the need to protect confidential sources. Promise confidentiality only with the intention of keeping that promise.
5. Respect everyone's right to a fair trial.
6. Broadcast the private transmissions of other broadcasters only with permission.
7. Actively encourage observance of this code by all journalists, whether members of the Radio–Television News Directors Association or not.[5]

The National Association of Broadcasters also provides guidelines:

The challenge to the broadcaster often is to determine how suitably to present the com-

Figure 13.3
ABC's "Good Morning America" was once classified as an entertainment program, but it is now classified as news. (Photo © ABC Photography Archives.)

plexities of human behavior without compromising or reducing the range of subject matter, artistic expression, or dramatic presentation desired by the broadcaster and its audience. For television and for radio, this requires exceptional awareness of considerations peculiar to each medium and of the composition and preferences of particular communities and audiences.

Each broadcaster should exercise responsible and careful judgment in the selection of material for broadcast. At the same time, each broadcast licensee must be vigilant in exercising and defending its rights to program according to its own judgments and to the programming choices of its audiences. This often may include the presentation of sensitive or controversial material.

In selecting program subjects and themes of particular sensitivity, great care should be paid to treatment and presentation, so as to avoid presentations purely for the purpose of sensationalism or to appeal to prurient interest or morbid curiosity.

In scheduling programs of particular sensitivity, broadcasters should take account of the composition and the listening or viewing habits of their specific audiences. Scheduling generally should consider audience expectations and composition in various time periods.[6]

CONSIDERING ETHICS

Probably the most effective guidelines are those people of conscience develop for themselves. One veteran executive has a simple rule of behavior: "I picture myself describing a situation to my family at the dinner table. If I can tell them what I plan to do and I am comfortable while I say it, I go ahead and do it. If I get itchy, I go back and rethink it."

When it comes to programming targeted at children, there are concerns other than whether an idea makes you "itchy" to consider. Programs designed primarily for children should take into account the range of interests and needs of children—from educational material to a variety of entertainment material. Children's programs should attempt to contribute to the sound, balanced development of children and to help them achieve a sense of the world at large.

CASE HISTORIES: ACTUAL INCIDENTS

The following sections describe several incidents that involve some key ethical decisions. In this text, the primary emphasis has been on entertainment programming. In this chapter, however, we also focus on news. This is because the distinction between entertainment and news has been blurred, and this blurring has raised several ethical questions. When respected newsperson Diane Sawyer hosts a reality special about wild or wacky weddings; when the morning networks' shows "Good Morning America" (Figure 13.3), "Today," and "The Early Show" are classified as news and not entertainment; when, for political candidate equal-time provisions, the FCC classifies "The Howard Stern Show" as news; and when the celebrity interviews Barbara Walters conducts after the Oscars are also considered news, it is time to reevaluate the preexisting separation of entertainment and news and to examine the frequent overlaps.

We encourage you to think about how you would act if confronted with situations similar to those described here, remembering that the individuals involved in the following actions have to justify, or at least accept, their decisions. Can you live with yourself if money or survival is the sole justification, with no regard for ethical behavior? As you review these case histories, assume that you have just left the boss's office where you have been told in direct language that ratings must improve or heads will roll.

Checkbook Journalism

During 1991, when the William Kennedy Smith rape trial was big news, the syndicated show "A Current Affair" paid $40,000 to one of the key witnesses to appear on the show and discuss the case. This payment was questioned by media watchers, but a spokesperson for "A Current Affair" said, "Sometimes we compensate for stories of interest to the public and in so doing, we are no different from any other network or syndicated show of this type."

Av Westin, executive producer of a similar program, "Inside Edition," agreed that fees are often paid to people, sometimes for exclusive rights to their story and sometimes as reimbursement for travel expenses or lost workdays. "We would have no problem offering [an interviewee] money," he said. David Bartlett, president of the Radio–Television News Directors Association, said compensation has become a sticky issue. "Is there a substantive difference between paying $150 for a limo drive or $40,000 for an interview? Yes, about

$39,850. But does that constitute an ethical difference? I'm not sure I'm prepared to make that call."[7]

In 2003–2004, CBS News was involved in several negotiations that seriously threatened CBS's preeminence in television news reporting. Sought after interviews, known as "gets," resulted in package offers that seemingly undermined journalistic ethics. For example, CBS laid a compensatory carrot of temptation in front of Aron Ralston, who severed his arm to free himself from a boulder, and Private Jessica Lynch, after her rescue from an Iraqi prison, offering them multiple opportunities within the Viacom family—CBS News, CBS Entertainment, MTV, MTV2, Simon & Schuster publishing, Country Music Television—all ready to service the get.

As Jim Rutenberg observed in *The New York Times,* "CBS's dangling of movie, television, and book deals in front of potential interview subjects has troubled some media critics who worry that in an age of media conglomerates, where news operations coexist with their entertainment counterparts, journalistic independence can suffer in the race for **synergy.**"[8]

CBS's complicated package deal with singer Michael Jackson, which resulted in Jackson's appearance on "60 Minutes," further tarnished the reputation of CBS News. As part of the package, Jackson was originally scheduled to do an entertainment special, but when his legal troubles surfaced, the entertainment special was canceled. Instead, Jackson was left only with a "60 Minutes" appearance. Still, $1 million was paid to Jackson, bringing into question the stated policy that CBS News does not pay for interviews. CBS defended itself by saying that the entertainment division paid for Jackson's "60 Minutes" appearance, but the ethical question remains: a paid interview is a paid interview, no matter who or what division pays for it.

Reflecting the growing concern about the trend of checkbook journalism, the Edinburgh International Television Festival scheduled forums to examine the practice and to discuss the effect of televised trials on the justice system.

Make the Deal, but Don't Close It

The CEO at a small production company wanted to be perceived as a real player. He instructed his development staff to go out into the community and to generate deals. He sought action from his crew, and at the weekly staff meetings demanded to know what projects had been sold. Meanwhile, as the company's financial difficulties increased, the CEO secretly instructed his head of business affairs not to close any of the deals that the development executives presented to him. Thus the CEO could see himself as a player without putting up any money.

An On-Air Murder Confession

In June 1990, two deejays at the KROQ radio station in Burbank, California, staged an event that triggered a nationwide police search for a nonexistent killer. On their morning show, the two personalities, Gene Baxter and Kevin Ryder, developed a comedy element titled "Confess Your Crime" in which listeners were encouraged to call in and reveal their transgressions on the air. To punch up the feature, they conspired with an Arizona radio performer, Doug Roberts, to fabricate a homicide. On June 13, Roberts phoned the show and "confessed" that he had badly beaten his girlfriend. When one of the deejays asked, "Is there a chance that you killed

her?" the caller responded quietly, "Yeah, I know I did."

Over the next few days the station was inundated with calls and faxes from people trying to help solve the crime. The network TV series "Unsolved Mysteries" twice broadcast a tape of the conversation and was deluged with responses. Burbank police coordinated their efforts with police agencies around the country to investigate the hundreds of leads generated. The most persistent callers were a mother and father in North Carolina desperate to unravel the mystery surrounding the death of their daughter. In April 1991, the deejays admitted it was a hoax undertaken to increase the ratings.

Under the rules then in effect, the FCC had limited options for punishing hoaxers. It could either admonish a station or revoke its license. Revocation could be enforced only if there was proof of management participation or perjury. In the KROQ case, the executives of Infinity Broadcasting, owner of the station, said the deejays did it on their own and nobody else knew about it. Their testimony held up under the FCC's scrutiny, and the station's only penalty was a 4-page letter of admonishment for "deliberate distortion of programming." The commission also stated that the letter would be entered in the station's file and could be taken into account when its license comes up for renewal.

The deejays were suspended for a week without pay and were forced to reimburse the police investigative costs, approximately $12,000. Within a year, the FCC crafted and adopted a rule that allowed it to fine stations up to $250,000 if they broadcast "false information concerning either a crime or a catastrophe if it is foreseeable that broadcast of such information will cause substantial public harm, and broadcast of the information does in fact directly cause such harm."[9]

Sex in Public Places

When radio shock jocks Opie and Anthony (Greg Hughes and Anthony Cumia, Figure 13.4) instigated their sex in public places competition, which resulted in a couple having sex in St. Patrick's Cathedral in New York, they got more than a week's suspension; they were fired by Infinity-owned station WNEW-FM in 2002. Some felt that the laxity the FCC had demonstrated over the years was party responsible for Opie and Anthony's infraction, but most felt that the sex in public places stunt was simply going too far.

Sharing the Wealth

An executive at a production company and a producer sold a project to a network. When the production company went bankrupt, the executive wanted to remain with the project as an executive producer, sharing the producer's fee. The executive said he had earned this because the project originated with the executive and the producer. The producer disagreed, saying that because the production company was no longer going to be involved as a deficit financier, the executive had no claim on the project.

Who Is to Blame?

An executive at a network was seriously reprimanded by her boss for letting a hot project get away. The executive defended herself by saying her assistant had not told her that the call from the producer controlling the project was an important call that should be returned immediately. The secretary simply wrote down the name of the producer who had called on the call sheet without

Figure 13.4
Radio personalities Opie and Anthony created a stunt that encouraged callers to engage in sex in public places.
(Globe Photos, Inc.)

noting what the call was about or that it was an important call. The secretary said that she did her job; she wrote the call down and gave the call sheet to her boss. She added that the executive was purposely "rolling her calls" to avoid this particular call so that the project would end up with another producer, someone she preferred. What was the result? The secretary was chastised for not writing more detailed messages on the call sheet and she was moved to another desk.

Anonymous Complaints at E!

In 2004, Mindy Herman was fired from her job as president and CEO at E! based on complaints sent in anonymous letters. The complaints included abusive behavior, using company funds to host baby showers for herself, employees' fears that if they did not produce suitable (meaning expensive) baby gifts they would be fired, and commandeering gifts sent to others in the company. Herman is credited with making E!

more vibrant and edgy, but the anonymous complaints were enough to get her fired. Are Herman's faults more egregious than those of other top executives? What is interesting here is the credibility granted the anonymous complaints. Given the state of the business, with the threat of lawsuits ever present, can an employer elect to disregard anonymous complaints?

According to an employment attorney at a major entertainment company, there is more emphasis on complaints today than there was 10 to 15 years ago, partly because the laws have changed and partly because some companies have their own detailed policies. Every anonymous complaint will be read, but not all will be investigated. Whether someone investigates becomes a judgment call based on what the law requires, what company policies require, and whether sufficient specific information has been provided for the investigation. In terms of evaluating a complaint, the attorney is more wary of complaints that surface after an employee has been disciplined by the department supervisor. He or she also pays a great deal of attention to the number of complaints filed against an individual or department and evaluates the seriousness of an anonymous complaint. There are existing laws in place that focus on retaliation against employees; however, an anonymous complaint by, for example, an intern or show extra will be considered thoroughly because these categories of employees would necessarily be more likely to submit an anonymous complaint for fear of not being employed regularly. Thus, the anonymous complaint is clearly no longer dismissed.

A Suicide on TV

In January 1987, Pennsylvania State Treasurer R. Budd Dwyer, who was being investigated for fraud, called a news conference. After making a brief statement, he pulled out a gun and shot himself—while TV cameras taped him. Because the footage was available, stations and networks had to decide whether to air it.

CNN, ABC, NBC, and CBS chose not to show the suicide, but they broadcast Dwyer talking at the press conference before he shot himself. Several Pennsylvania TV stations showed the entire event—suicide and all.[10]

Images of the Iraqi War

Should graphic images of war be shown on television? Should body parts be visible on television sets anytime day or night? Should the funerals of soldiers killed in Iraq be shown? What about the bodies of dead "enemy combatants" or civilian, so-called collateral, casualties? In 2004, controversy erupted over showing the on-air decapitation of American captive Nicholas Berg by Iraqi insurgents. The decapitation was widely available on the Internet even if the network news organizations did not show it. Several teachers who showed their students the decapitation were reprimanded because parents and school administrators objected to its graphic nature.

It is interesting to note the role that the Internet has played in making previously guarded or classified materials readily available to large numbers of people. Because of the Internet, it is harder to close the book on secret or sensitive topics. Websites based in other countries—not under the jurisdiction of U.S. law, reflecting ethical standards or viewpoints different from those prevalent in the United States, or both—can easily broadcast whatever text, images, audio, or video they want over the Internet. Anyone in the United States who can find it can view it—often without the benefit of context provided by reporters. Many hold that this is no different from the Cold War-era U.S. policy of broadcasting "Radio Free Europe" around the world to provide those in countries oppressed by totalitarian governments news and information they could not get in their own countries. With media conglomeration in the United States, some say the full story has become unavailable within the U.S. broadcasting system. Several U.S. individuals now broadcast radio programs over the Internet and shortwave radio that they have dubbed "Radio Free America," providing information not covered by traditional media.

The Right to Privacy

Arthur Ashe was one of the finest tennis players ever produced in America. For a decade, he generally ranked within the Top 10 and in 1975 won the men's singles championship at Wimbledon. In 1984, Ashe underwent surgery for a heart condition that involved some blood transfusions. The blood was contaminated and he contracted human immunodeficiency virus. Although his condition required constant monitoring, all those connected with his medical treatment respected his request to keep the condition from becoming public knowledge. Ashe and his wife were raising a young daughter, and they felt her childhood would be far happier if her father's condition remained unpublicized.

In 1992, a reporter at the newspaper *USA Today* learned of Ashe's infection and asked him for a confirmation. Fearing the imminent publication of the information, Ashe called a news conference and emotionally announced that he was HIV positive.

The newspaper vigorously defended its actions on the basis of the public's right to know. Others disagreed. Ashe was no longer an active athlete and therefore not a legitimate news figure, he was not an officer of a publicly traded company whose health might affect stockholders' investments, and he did not hold public office where his illness might prevent him from representing his constituency effectively. Why, many asked, did the public have to know about his personal situation? Where, they further inquired, should print and electronic reporters draw the line when their pursuit of a story conflicts with an individual's right to privacy?[11]

The First Amendment vs. the Sixth Amendment

The First Amendment deals with freedom of expression, and the Sixth Amendment deals with the right to a fair trial. In many instances, the two collide, resulting in difficult ethical decisions for all concerned.

In 1987, NBC aired a highly rated miniseries, "The Billionaire Boys Club," about a group of prep school friends whose get-rich-quick plans involved murder. It was based on a publicized, ongoing case, providing tabloid-like revelations about the rich and rich wannabes and their sordid lives. Two of the defendants in the case, Joe Hunt and Jim Pittman, were portrayed in the film committing crimes for which they had not been convicted. Their lawyers filed an injunction against the airing of the miniseries, which was denied. NBC's on-air promos teased viewers, branding the film as "the movie Joe Hunt tried to keep you from seeing." This promotion was quickly attacked as being in poor taste and was subsequently pulled off the air. But the questions remain about a dramatized portrayal of a true story *before* the trials have been

Figure 13.5
Brian Lowry of
Daily Variety *and*
Broadcasting &
Cable *frequently*
writes about ethical
dilemmas peculiar
to the
entertainment
industry. (Photo
courtesy Brian
Lowry/*Daily*
Variety.)

strong ratings. If ratings are most important, should First and Sixth Amendment
concerns go by the wayside?

Entertainment Programming Ethics

Brian Lowry (Figure 13.5), a keen
observer of the entertainment industry
writing for both *Daily Variety* and *Broadcasting & Cable,* notes that in Hollywood
it is assumed everyone is for sale. In a
town where nepotism is rampant and
power is the currency of choice, Lowry
finds that entertainment journalists are
often seen as wanting to "hop the
fence," leaving lowly paid journalism
jobs for the glamour and high-voltage
pay of production. A producer who
wants positive press from a journalist
might say, "You're such a good writer,
I'm sure you've got some ideas that
would make terrific stories."

For Lowry, it is ethically unacceptable
for a journalist to transition from a possibly adversarial relationship, asking
tough questions of an interviewee, to a
collaborative one developing projects
together. If a journalist financially
depends on someone, such as a producer, the journalist has crossed an
ethical line. For example, if a journalist
is encouraged to give a script to a producer or if the journalist requests that
the producer being interviewed read his
or her script, ethical behavior has been
compromised.

Everyone craves good press; in a town
where perception matters more than
reality, everyone wants to spin the best
version of events. It is thus tempting for
an interviewee to dangle a creative
carrot in front of a journalist who has
the power to write a positive or negative piece.

For Lowry, an entertainment journalist constantly has to be on guard regarding ethics. Are you allowing personal

concluded. What is better: protecting
a fair trial or protecting the right of
freedom of expression?

Can a fair trial be possible if there has
been a television portrayal of the events
that have not been resolved in a court
of law? Is an individual who has been
convicted of similar crimes in the past
"libel proof" even if he or she has not
been convicted of the crimes shown in
a TV dramatization?

"The Billionaire Boys Club" is not
the only telefilm to air before the conclusion of the legal process. For
example, in 2004, USA aired another
highly rated film about Scott Peterson,
accused of killing his pregnant wife. It,
too, was a highly publicized case, cap-
turing many tabloid headlines. The film
was called "The Perfect Husband," and
it starred former television Superman,
Dean Cain. Except for the last shot of
the film, a close up of an orange-suited
Peterson in jail, the film was objective,
avoiding taking sides about Peterson's
guilt or innocence, but it remains that
the film aired before a resolution.

Both "The Billionaire Boys Club"
and "The Perfect Husband" achieved

feelings about an actor, producer, or director to color your opinions? Can corporate ownership sway your coverage of a division within the corporation that pays your salary?

As an aside, Lowry draws an interesting ethical line between product placement and product integration. He sees no inherent ethical conflict with product placement in a show where a can of Coke or some other marketable item is used as a prop. He feels that product placement is recognized by the viewing public for what it is, namely, product placement that viewers accept as "being sold." However, he finds that the growing trend of product integration, where a story line is constructed around a particular product, is misleading to a viewer. For him, product integration results in program-length commercials that violate essential boundaries between advertisement and programming content.

Lowry also questions the ethics behind the kind of controlled interview pioneered by the powerful PMK public relations firm. The controlled interview works like this: For an interview to be granted with a top star such as Tom Cruise, certain questions are off limits. If the journalist does not agree to the stipulations dictated for the interview to be granted, the interview simply does not take place. Is this all right? Is this ethical? The more handlers guard access to their clients and the more journalists agree to the handlers' demands, the more biased reporting becomes the norm.

Lowry notes that programming positions at the networks do not last forever. Three- or four-year tours of duty seem to be the average. Thus, executives have to plan their next jobs while they are in the present positions. If an executive does favors for a particular production company, does that increase his or her chances of being hired when the

network gig ends? Lowry finds that it is maybe too tempting for executives to keep their futures in mind when they are dealing with producers. Are ethics ignored when programming executives looking to feather their nests make choices that can pave the way for future job offers? Lowry calls it "the rule of two." In other words, if high-level executives do favors for the right people, they not only can count on getting a new position after their current one expires but also can be confident of a job after that. That gives them assurances of employment for many years, so it is tempting for programming executives to think twice about projects they are advocating or passing on and production company heads they are helping or "hosing down."

A SERIES OF ETHICAL DILEMMAS

Instead of exercises at the end of this chapter, we included additional ethical situations for you to contemplate. What would you do and why? How would you explain your action to others and, possibly more importantly, to yourself? Keep the realities of the business fully in mind when you answer.

1. Should you go through the trash of a competitor to get documents or information you can use to bolster your position?

2. Should you, as a radio station programmer, pay people to call a competing station and request unpopular songs in hopes that the listeners will switch to your station for a better selection of music?

3. Should you release the name of a rape victim on the Internet or on a radio or television program?

4. Should you pitch a story you do not have the rights to see whether there

is any interest in the story before you go to the expense of acquiring an option?

5. Should you reenact news footage because the footage you had of the event was of poor broadcast quality?

6. Should you show graphic depictions of crimes that can be duplicated (copycat crimes) by people in the viewing audience (think of "The Sopranos," for example)?

7. Should you pay students to moonlight at research companies and report on competitor's projects?

8. Should you, as a programmer, allow that swimming pool you have always wanted to be built in your backyard for free because it will serve as a set for one scene in a miniseries you have just commissioned?

9. If you get a tip that a candidate running for office is going to spend the weekend at a motel with a starlet, should you send a cameraperson to hide in a nearby tree to capture "appropriate photographic material?"

10. If you have agreed verbally to hire one actor as the lead in a miniseries, should you withdraw your verbal agreement because a better, more marketable actor becomes available hours before you are scheduled to sign the written contract for the first actor?

11. Should you hire the editor of a magazine that covers the entertainment industry as a consultant on one of your projects to make sure that the magazine gives your project favorable coverage?

12. Your telefilm has tanked in the ratings. Should you tell the production community that the network was happy with the ratings because, for example, the competition was fierce, even if the network said otherwise?

13. To make a true story more acceptable to an audience, should you alter facts that do not coincide with the story you would like to tell?

14. The on-air spots for your program are misleading. Do you keep quiet, assuming the experts know how to promote a show, or do you suggest ways in which the spots could be made more accurate?

15. You do not agree with the politics of the news anchor your boss has just hired and you think your audience will turn away. What should you do?

16. Your boss has requested on your first week on the job that you do something you cannot agree to in good conscience. What you are asked to do is not illegal, but it feels unethical to you. What should you do?

Ethical considerations in the electronic media too frequently receive short shrift. The urgency to complete the deal and make the profit tends to overwhelm the moral considerations. When this attitude pervades the entire industry, the reliability of all within it suffers. Every handshake leaves a doubt, every commitment becomes suspect. Only if broadcasters make "right" decisions a priority, only if they create a climate of honor, can the industry become a workplace of trust. Admittedly, the ground rules are vague and many of the calls are borderline. Sometimes the only guideline is that pesky inner voice that does not want to go away. Listen to it. How else are you going to make it better?

REFERENCES/NOTES

1. Lynnley Browning. "Ethics Lacking in Business School Curriculum," *The New York Times,* May 20, 2003, p. C-3.

2. Robert Pear. "U.S. Videos, for TV News, Come Under Scrutiny," *The New York Times,* March 15, 2004, pp. A-1, A-16.

3. Meg James. "Beverly Hillbillies? CBS Has Struck Crude, Appalachia Says," *Los Angeles Times,* February 11, 2003, p. A-1.

4. Sissela Bok. *Lying: Moral Choice in Public and Private Life* (New York: Vintage Books, 1979), p. 40.

5. *Code of Broadcast News Ethics* (Washington, DC: Radio–Television News Directors Association, n.d.).

6. Board of Directors, National Association of Broadcasters. "Statement of Principles," http://www.nab.org/newsroom/Issues/NAB%20Statement%20of%20Principles.html. Accessed June 26, 2003.

7. David Bartlett. "Checkbook Journalism Bounces Back," *Broadcasting,* December 9, 1991, p. 5.

8. Jim Rutenberg. "To Interview Former P.O.W., CBS Offers Stardom," *The New York Times,* June 6, 2003, pp. A-1, A-12.

9. Claudia Puig. "Will KROQ Get Away With Murder?" *Los Angeles Times,* April 22, 1991, p. F-1; "FCC Panel Clears Infinity, KROQ Management in Hoax," *Daily Variety,* November 26, 1991, p. 3; and "FCC Adopts $25,000 Fine for Hoaxes," *Broadcasting,* May 18, 1992, p. 5.

10. David E. Tucker. "Teaching Broadcast Ethics," *Feedback,* Spring 1989, p. 18.

11. Victor F. Zonana. "Ashe Case Raises Fame vs. Privacy Debate," *Los Angeles Times,* April 10, 1992, p. A-26.

Glossary

Advertising agency: A company that places its clients' commercial messages on radio, television, the Internet, or in print media.

Affiliated station: A radio or TV station aligned with a network.

À la carte system: Cable subscribers pay for the channels they want rather than for a package of channels, some of which they may not be interested in.

Ambush: Getting talk show guests to confront one another on air. An ambush often occurs when one guest reveals a secret about another, setting up an ambush.

Ascertainment: A process that required stations, as part of their license renewal process, to interview community leaders to learn what they believed were the main problems in the community.

Audience flow: Schedulers strive to group compatible shows so that the audience will stay tuned from one show to the next.

Audience measurement: Methods that endeavor to determine the number and kind of viewers watching a program, listening to a station, or viewing a website.

Audimeter: Nielsen's metering device that was attached to TV sets to measure minute-by-minute viewing of sample households.

Auditorium testing: A research technique in which numerous people are brought into one place to record their reactions to TV or radio programming material.

Automated measurement of lineups (AMOL): Nielsen's method of picking up special codes from programs so that it can determine which programs are on which channels in each market.

Average quarter hour (AQH): An audience measurement calculation based on the average number of people listening to a particular station for at least 5 minutes during a 15-minute period.

Bandwidth: The capacity for data transfer of a communications system; more complex files, such as graphics, audio, and video, consume more bandwidth than text does.

Banner: An advertisement on a web page that, when clicked, will bring the user to the product's web page.

Barter: The sales practice in which a station forfeits a certain amount of commercial time to a supplier in exchange for the right to broadcast a program.

Basic cable: Programming services that cable systems offer subscribers for a monthly fee, as opposed to **premium cable,** which requires additional payment. Basic cable programming usually contains advertisements; premium cable usually does not.

Bible: A detailed report that describes a program's essential elements, such as the premise, story line, main characters, locations, and future story growth.

Blogger: An Internet user who writes personal and opinion journals or diary entries displayed on websites.

Blowback: When a publicity campaign backfires, creating the opposite effect of what was intended.

Blunting: A competitive strategy that attempts to minimize the effectiveness of the early episodes of an opponent's programs.

Bouncing the needle: A trick used by producers to have their shows test well by including things in shows that test audiences will like. Producers usually try to bounce the needle at the beginning with a dramatic or sexy sequence so that test audiences will be likely to view the rest of the program in a positive light.

Branding: Giving a channel, network, or Internet site a clear identity.

Brick-and-mortar store: A traditional, physical retail store, as opposed to an Internet store. Some stores have both Internet and brick-and-mortar stores.

Bridging: A programming strategy in which the start time of a competitor's show is arched by an ongoing program.

Broadcast standards and practices: A department at a network that rules on the acceptability of program content.

Burnout: When songs played on a radio station start to lose their appeal to the station's listeners.

Cable-based study: A testing process in which the program to be examined is transmitted on a cable channel to a preselected universe of homes.

Callout: A telephone survey conducted by a radio station, most commonly used to find out which musical selections should be taken off a radio station and which should be added. Sometimes it is used for other elements, such as determining the popularity of a new disc jockey.

Call screeners: In talk radio, station personnel who interview callers to a program before letting them on the air.

Churn: The rate of turnover in cable subscribers as a result of disconnects and new customers.

Classics: Music from 10 to 20 years ago.

Clock: A radio station's program schedule in which each hour is divided into carefully timed units.

Commons: An idealized use of the Internet in which each opinion, idea, and expression is given common weight and attention.

Compression: A technology that allows more audio, video, or both types of information to be carried through the airwaves, over the Internet, or on a cable TV system.

Concept: The main idea of a program.

Concept testing: Testing that evaluates the main idea of a show.

Concert promotion: Revenue in the music industry comes from record sales, airplay, and live shows—or concert promotion. As companies that own radio stations have entered the business of live shows, or concert promotion, there has been some fear that airplay will be driven by a desire to gain concert sales rather than to play music of interest to the public.

Cookie: A small file that websites create and store on a web user's computer. The file can contain personal information such as a user identification code, customized preferences, or records of pages visited. The file can be read by the web server on subsequent visits, allowing the website to customize itself to the individual user.

Coproduction: An agreement between two or more companies to combine the underwriting, development, and production responsibilities of a program.

Copyright: The individual or company that controls the copyright has sole ownership of a given property.

Cosponsorship: Two or more organizations that share the costs of producing a program.

Counterprogramming: The strategy of scheduling a program that appeals to an audience not being reached by rival shows.

Cross-ownership: Newspapers, cable channels, television stations, or a combination of these owned by the same company.

Crossprogramming: The tactic of having performers in one series make guest appearances on another program.

Cume: Cumulative audience, or the total nonduplicated audience for one program or commercial message or for a series of programs or messages.

Dayparting: The practice of dividing the broadcast day into segments according to the size and composition of the available audience.

Deficit financing: The difference between the license fee and the cost of production. This amount is covered by a production company that hopes to recoup the deficit amount through foreign sales, syndication, etc.

Demographics: The classification of audiences based on social and economic conditions such as sex, age, income, education, ethnic origin, and occupation.

Deregulation: Any action by Congress or the FCC to reduce or remove restrictions governing any portion of the industry over which it has regulatory authority.

Designated market area (DMA): A term used by Nielsen to define a geographic area in which the local stations receive the largest audience share.

Development: The process by which a program is nurtured from initial concept to pilot; in public broadcasting, the process of trying to obtain funding for a program or series.

Development ratio: The number of programs put into development in relation to the number of programs made. Producers are fond of low development ratios because it means that if a project gets into development, it stands a good chance of getting made.

Diary: A questionnaire on which respondents are asked to record their listening or viewing activities for a specified period.

Drive time: Considered peak hours by many radio stations, this is the time that listeners are driving to or from work.

Dropping in: Several shows or well-known movies contain scenes viewers are eager to see every time the material is aired, even if viewers do not watch the entire show. This is called "dropping in" for a particular sequence.

Easy view: A euphemism for a repeat episode.

Email marketing: A campaign of product or service solicitations delivered through email.

Encore: A euphemism for a repeat episode.

Equal time: A provision in Section 315 of the 1934 Communications Act that states that if a broadcast licensee permits use of its facilities by a political candidate, it must offer an equal opportunity to all other legally qualified candidates for the same office.

Ethnic weighing: The policy of some audience measurement organizations of counting diaries returned by members of certain ethnic groups more heavily than diaries returned by members of other ethnic groups because the percentage of diaries returned by one group is much lower than the return rate by the other group.

Fairness doctrine: A series of FCC rulings and court cases that required a broadcaster to afford a reasonable opportunity for a discussion of conflicting views on issues of public importance. The fairness doctrine is no longer in effect.

Family hour: No longer in effect, this was a voluntary effort by broadcasters to present programs from 7:00 to 9:00 P.M. that would be suitable for all members of the family.

Financial interest and domestic syndication (fin-syn): An FCC ruling that prohibited the three major networks from owning or controlling the rebroadcast rights of the shows they presented on their airwaves. This rule is no longer in effect.

First-run show: A program that makes its initial appearance in domestic syndication.

Focus group: A collection of sample listeners or viewers, usually no more than 10 to 12, who offer their opinions about programs or performers under the guidance of a moderator.

Format: The dominant type of programming an electronic media operator (particularly a radio station) selects, such as all news, country music, or children's programming.

Format-dominant program: A show structured around a specific concept or premise.

Franchise: An agreement between state, local, or both types of government and a cable television service that awards the right to install a coaxial or fiber-optic cable in a community to deliver cable TV programming.

Golden age of radio: During the 1930s and 1940s, radio produced programs that listeners embraced for their originality and daring.

Golden age of television: During the 1950s, television aired high-quality programs that enriched the medium. Many programs during this golden age aired live.

Hammocking: A scheduling strategy that places a new program between two established shows.

High-concept show: A project whose premise is accessible and quickly grasped.

Hold: A period during which a project is contractually committed and cannot be shopped elsewhere.

Households using television (HUT): The percentage of homes in a survey area with one or more sets in use during a specific period.

Hyperlink: A clickable electronic object link providing direct access from one distinct URL or place in a document to another.

Hypertext: A clickable electronic text link providing direct access from one distinct URL or place in a document to another.

Hypoing: Using as many stunts and publicity tricks as possible to boost ratings.

Indecency: An offense against recognized standards of propriety and good taste in a particular community.

Independent station: A station that has no network affiliations. Stations allied with Fox are still called independents because that was their status before the new network originated.

Indie: Another name for an independent station; also a small production company that supplies programs to networks.

Infomercial: A commercial message in the form of a full program, usually 30 minutes but sometimes longer.

Invasion of privacy: An illegal or insensitive intrusion into the life of another person.

Kinescope recording: A record of a television show made by filming it off a television monitor.

Libel: A statement about a person, broadcast or printed, that is unfavorable and false.

License: Formal permission from the FCC for a broadcaster to operate a station.

License fee: The amount of money a network or distributor pays to a production company to make a program, or the amount of money a station or cable operator pays to a distributor for the right to broadcast a syndicated program.

Lifestyle research: Research that focuses on how people live to determine whether a particular show will appeal to people's lifestyles.

Limited series: A program that has a set number of episodes, usually between four and eight.

Link: See **Hyperlink.**

Link sharing: A process in which web developers put hyperlinks to other websites on their own sites in exchange for a reciprocal link. This drives more visitors to sites and improves placement or ranking on search engines.

Log line: A one- or two-sentence description of a project that captures the essence or theme of a project.

Longform: Television programs more than an hour in duration.

Lottery: The involvement of chance, prize, and consideration (money) for a game or contest—barred from broadcasting by Section 1304 of the United States Criminal Code.

Magazine concept: A sales policy in which advertisers buy commercials within a show purely on the basis of its audience size and with no involvement in its content.

Metro: An area, usually an individual city and its environs, used to determine radio station ratings.

Minipilot: A film or tape that presents a few key scenes of a sample show rather than a completed episode.

Miniseries: Television movies more than 2 hours long, usually airing over two or more nights.

Minitheater test: The testing of a program before an audience in a small auditorium of 35 to 40 seats.

Monte Carlo audience ascription: The practice of some audience measurement companies of filling in missing diary data by making educated assumptions about what would have been filled in had the diary keeper completed the diary correctly.

Movie package syndication: Several movies grouped and sold as a unit into syndication.

Multiparter: A story line that carries over several episodes to capture the viewer's attention.

Multiple system owner (MSO): A company that owns more than one cable system.

Music callout: Research, usually by phone, conducted to determine which songs should be taken off a station and which should be added.

Music mix: A strategy for combining different types of musical selections to appeal to the broadest audience possible within a format.

Music within format: Songs that adhere to a defined genre.

Must-carry rule: An FCC ruling that compels cable operators to present the programming of the television stations broadcasting in the system's local area.

Narrowcasting: Directing programs toward specific demographic audiences or limited interest groups.

Nielsen Television Index (NTI): A Nielsen service that provides audience estimates for all sponsored network television programs in the United States.

Obscenity: Action or language that depicts sexual acts in an offensive manner, appeals to prurient interests of the average person, and lacks serious artistic, literary, political, or scientific value.

Off net: Programs that first appeared on a network and are then available for rebroadcast on other outlets.

Oldies: A format that features music from 30 or 40 years ago.

On-demand media: Media delivered when, how, and where the consumer wants it, typically audio or video streamed over the Internet.

Overnights: Nielsen household ratings and shares provided to clients the morning following the telecast.

Owned and operated station: A station owned and managed by a network or by one of the large station groups, such as Group W or Tribune Company.

P1 listener: The name radio stations use to describe core audience members, a person for whom the station is preference number 1.

P2 listener: The name radio stations use to describe secondary audience members, a person who listens to the station occasionally but not as a first preference.

Package commission: A fee exacted by an agent or agency based on the cost of an entire production as opposed to a commission on just the person in the production whom the agent or agency represents.

Pay-per-view system: A user fee system in which subscribers pay per program rather than with a monthly subscription.

Payola: The practice by radio management or personalities of taking cash or other payments in exchange for playing specified records.

Peer-to-peer network: A set of protocols that allow two computers to directly communicate with each other through a network, allowing file swapping.

Penetration: The proportion of television or cable households to total households in an area.

People meter: A mechanical device developed by Nielsen that contains a button for each individual in a household to engage when watching television.

Perceptual callout: A phone call made to a radio listener to ask questions about elements of radio other than music, such as the likeability of a talk show hostess or the recognizability of a station logo.

Persons using television (PUT): The percentage of all people or of people within a given demographic category in the survey area viewing television during a specific period.

Pilot: A sample episode of a projected series.

Pitch: A presentation by program creators to prospective buyers, the goal of which is to obtain a commitment for further development.

Playlist: The musical selections played by a radio station.

Plugola: Paying cash or bestowing some other favor on producers, performers, disc jockeys, or others connected with a program in exchange for a visual or verbal promotion of a product or service.

Pod deal: A contractual arrangement between a studio and a full-fledged production company—not with individual writers, producers, or directors, as in an **umbrella deal.**

Preemption: The substitution of a special production for a normally scheduled program. Local sports coverage often preempts scheduled programming.

Premium cable: Cable channels that offer specialty fare without advertisements. Premium channels charge payment beyond the charge for basic cable.

Prior censorship: When an official agency, such as a court or the FCC, punishes a station or tells it not to air something before it actually airs it; such a practice is outlawed by the Communications Act of 1934.

Product integration: A product becomes a major part of a story line, as opposed to being simply featured in a show, as with **product placement.**

Product placement: Many programs gain additional revenue by featuring products in programs. With product placement, an advertiser avoids being zapped during commercials.

Promise vs. performance: A procedure whereby a station promised what it would do during a license period and then was judged on the fulfillment of its promises when its license came up for renewal. It is no longer in effect.

Public access: Programming planned and produced by members of the public for local cable TV channels.

Puffery: Extreme boasting about the virtues of a given project.

Qualitative research: Research that goes beyond ratings statistics to gather information about the factors that influence audience viewing patterns.

Quiz show scandals: When the public discovered that the popular quiz shows of the late 1950s and early 1960s were rigged, audiences felt betrayed by the medium.

Quota: A limitation on the amount of TV programming produced in a foreign country that can be shown on a national TV system.

Rating: The estimate of the size of a television, radio, or Internet audience relative to the total group sampled, expressed as a percentage; for example, the rating of a national television show is the percentage of 108.4 million households tuned to the program.

Reach: The area in which a radio station's transmission can be received.

Recurrent: Music that is no longer current but is not yet considered old.

Repurposing: When a program is broadcast on a different outlet shortly after its original airing—for example, a show that airs one night on NBC is repurposed on Bravo a few nights later.

Rerun: The airing of a program beyond its initial play. This differs from repurposing in that the program is aired on the same outlet.

Safe harbor: The hours between 10:00 P.M. and 6:00 A.M. when indecency is allowed (when it is assumed children might not be members of the audience).

Sampling: The selection of one or more elements (individuals or households) from a universe to represent the universe.

Satellite: A space vehicle that receives radio and television signals and then transmits them back to earth.

Scarcity theory: The belief that broadcasters should be rather heavily regulated because there are not enough station frequencies available for everyone to have one and that the people who own them should, therefore, act in the public interest.

Search engine: On the Internet, a program that searches for keywords in files and documents found on the World Wide Web. Some search engines are used for a single Internet site, such as a dedicated search engine for a website. Others search many sites, using automated programs, such as **spiders,** to gather lists of available files and documents and store these lists in databases that users can search by keyword.

Share: The percentage of the households or people using a radio or television tuned to a specific program or station in a specified area at a specified time.

Showrunner: The individual responsible for the day-to-day operation of a show.

Simulcasting: A process of broadcasting the same material in two mediums, most commonly broadcasting the signal from a terrestrial radio station over the Internet.

SLAPS test: For a work to be defined as obscene, it must lack Serious, Literary, Artistic, Political, or Scientific value.

Spider: A software program that "crawls" the web, searching and indexing web pages to create a database that can be easily searched by a search engine.

Spin: Information presented in such a way that a negative is turned into a positive.

Spin-off: A new series developed out of an existing one, usually by lifting secondary characters and making them leads.

Spot: A commercial message placed within or between programs in such a way that the company is not directly associated with the program.

Stacking: A scheduling strategy in which several programs of similar appeal and demographics are placed consecutively for all, or the bulk, of a daypart.

Star-dominant program: A show created around the personality of a particular performer.

Station compensation: The money paid by a network to its affiliated stations for carrying its programs.

Sticky: Web content designed to keep a web surfer on a website.

Streaming media: A technique for transferring data so that it can be downloaded and experienced simultaneously. The alternative would wait for the data to be completely downloaded before viewing or hearing it. Also refers to live transmissions over the Internet.

Stripping: The strategy of scheduling a series in the same period throughout the week.

Stunting: The use of imaginative scheduling or programming devices to produce immediate ratings increases.

Supersizing: A bridging strategy that adds extra minutes to a program to encourage viewers to not switch channels.

Superstation: A station whose signal is available through a satellite to cable systems around the country.

Sweeps: A period, usually 4 weeks, during which all local TV markets are simultaneously measured and reported by a rating service.

Syndicated exclusivity: An FCC ruling stating that if a cable system imports a program on a distant channel that is already being broadcast in a market, the cable system must black out the show and substitute other programming.

Syndication: A program delivery system through which shows are provided directly to stations or cable networks by the production company or its distributor.

Synergy: When different departments or divisions join forces and pool resources for a common goal.

Telephone research: Obtaining information in question-and-answer sessions over the telephone.

Tentpoling: Placing a well-established show at a pivotal time to provide strength to the programs around it.

Theming: Grouping programs of similar content or tone into a schedule.

Tier deal: A syndication buying practice among TV stations in which prices and other sales arrangements are established for a range of times.

Toll station: The early radio technique of charging a fee to anyone who wished to use a station's facilities to present a message.

Top 40: A radio format that plays a rotation of the most popular songs of the day.

Topless radio: The presentations of salacious material by radio personalities or by listeners who called in to talk shows.

Total service area (TSA): Arbitron's division for radio station ratings of large geographic areas that may not receive all stations clearly.

Treatment: A synopsis of a program's story line that may also include other pertinent data such as descriptions of principal characters and key locations.

TVQ: A research technique that attempts to determine the intrinsic popularity and recognizability of performers and programs as opposed to their ratings.

Umbrella deal: A contractual arrangement between a creative person (producer, director, or writer) and a production company in which the company supplies money and services to the creator in exchange for the exclusive right to his or her output.

Underwriter: A company that pays for the production or distribution of public broadcasting programming.

Uniform resource locator (URL): A specific address for a page on the World Wide Web.

Unique selling proposition: Something about a project that distinguishes it from all others.

Unit of good: A public broadcasting term used to designate the inherent, uplifting worth of a program.

User interface: A set of commands or menus through which a user communicates with or navigates through a computer program or website.

Vertical integration: When a company controls the production and the distribution of a product.

Viewer awareness: A way to gauge how familiar audiences are with a particular program, the assumption being that if people are aware of a show that show has a better chance at success.

Voice tracking: A method of recording radio program content that can be compiled and broadcast in several markets or at a different time, creating the impression that the broadcast originated locally, is live, or both.

Web ring: Related websites that are interlinked so that you can visit each site one after the other, eventually returning to the first website.

Window: The period between when a movie is shown in the theater and when it is made available to various television media forms.

Zipper: A short musical interlude in public radio programming that allows stations to cut away and program something else.

Index

Nickelodeon, 45, 52, 109–110, 126, 261
Nielsen, 17, 64, 101, 106, 108, 216, 235, 251–261, 264–268, 270
Nielsen Station Index, 260
Nielsen Television Index (NTI), 257–260
Nixon, Agnes, 137
Nixon, Richard, 174
Nolan, Kathleen, 108
"Northern Exposure," 228
Nostalgia Television, 125–126
"Nova," 41
NPR. See National Public Radio
NTI. See Nielsen Television Index

O
Obscenity, 183, 189, 199–201, 206
Oldies, 112, 240–241, 244
O&O. See Owned and operated station
"Oprah Winfrey Show," 40, 42, 78, 131
O'Reilly, Bill, 39, 60, 91, 154
Outdoor Channel, The, 144, 231–232, 274
Overnight, 282
Owned and operated station (O&O), 40

P
Pacifica Radio, 53
Package commission, 72
Paley, William, 6
Paramount, 16, 30, 52, 61
Parkin, Judd, 134
Pay cable, 22, 31, 261
Pay-per-view, 31, 126, 281
Payola, 57–59, 201, 292
PBS. See Public Broadcasting Service
Pennycamp, Peter, 114
People meter, 252–256, 266, 268
Pepsi Cola, 166
Persons using television (PUT), 220, 256
Petrie, Dan, 7–9
Philbin, Regis, 137
Phillips, Irna, 137
"Phyllis," 33
Pierce, Fred, 130

Pilot, 24, 31, 79, 81–84, 96, 100–104, 117, 139, 178, 233, 281
Pitch, 72–77, 82, 89, 91, 142, 144, 146
Playboy, 62
Plugola, 201
Poltrack, David, 108
"P.O.V.," 176–177
Pressure groups, 162, 165–167, 193, 207
Product integration, 21, 23, 43, 305
Product placement, 21, 43, 305
Public access, 29, 46
Public Broadcasting Act of 1967, 12
Public Broadcasting Service (PBS), 12–13, 20, 37–38, 41, 78, 94, 109, 126–127, 148, 163–164, 176, 218, 221, 228–235, 259, 282
PUT. See Persons using television

Q
"Queer as Folk," 147
"Queer Eye for the Straight Guy," 139, 143
Quiz show scandals, 9–11

R
RADAR. See Radio All-Dimension Audience Research
Radio All-Dimension Audience Research (RADAR), 262–264
Raisethefist.com, 208–209
Rakolta, Terry, 167
Ratings, 11, 48, 86–87, 94, 106, 108–113, 124, 135, 144, 152, 169, 193, 218, 227, 229, 236, 251–271, 273
Ratings Massage, 261
Reagan, Ronald, 169, 175
Realism, 134
Recurrents, 241
"Red Channels," 292–294
Red Water, 8
Reiner, Carl, 136
Remote control, 156, 221, 253
Rerunning, 39, 234–235
Reruns, 14, 39, 93, 163, 219–220, 234–235, 270, 287
"Rescue 911," 222
Resing, George, 146